IRELAND'S HIGH PLACES

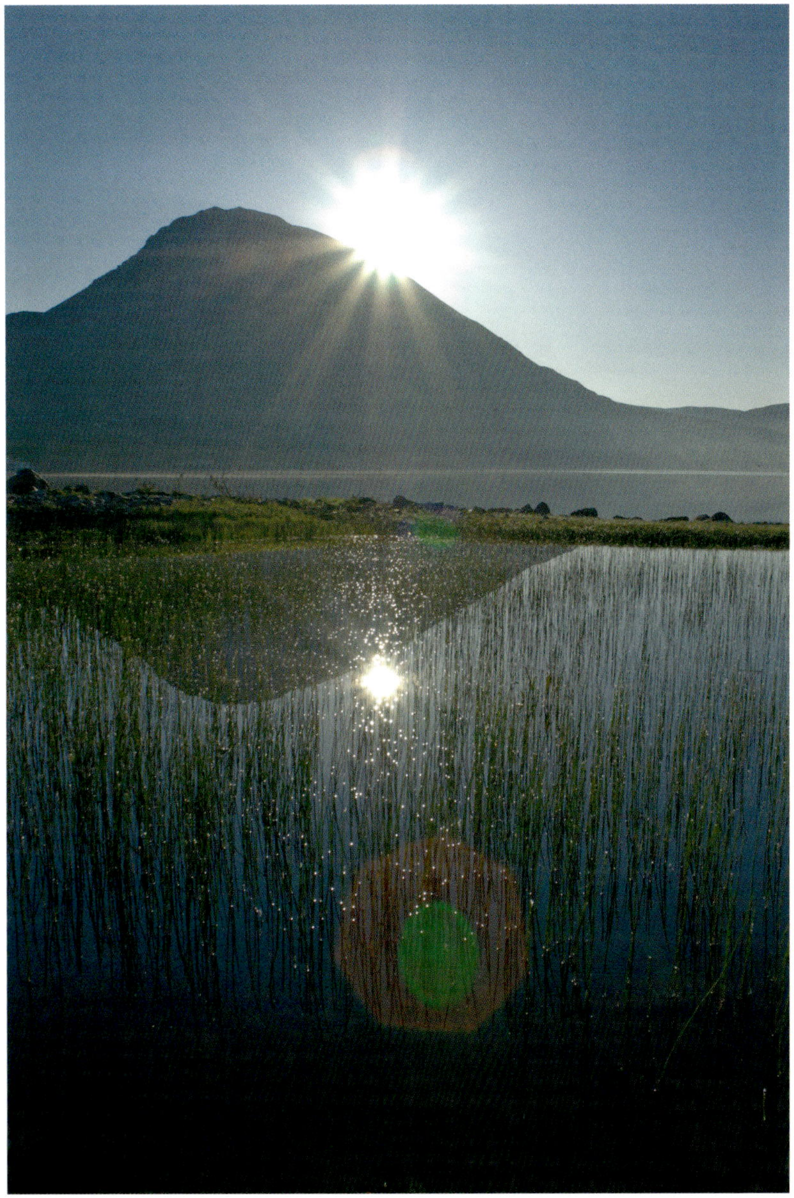

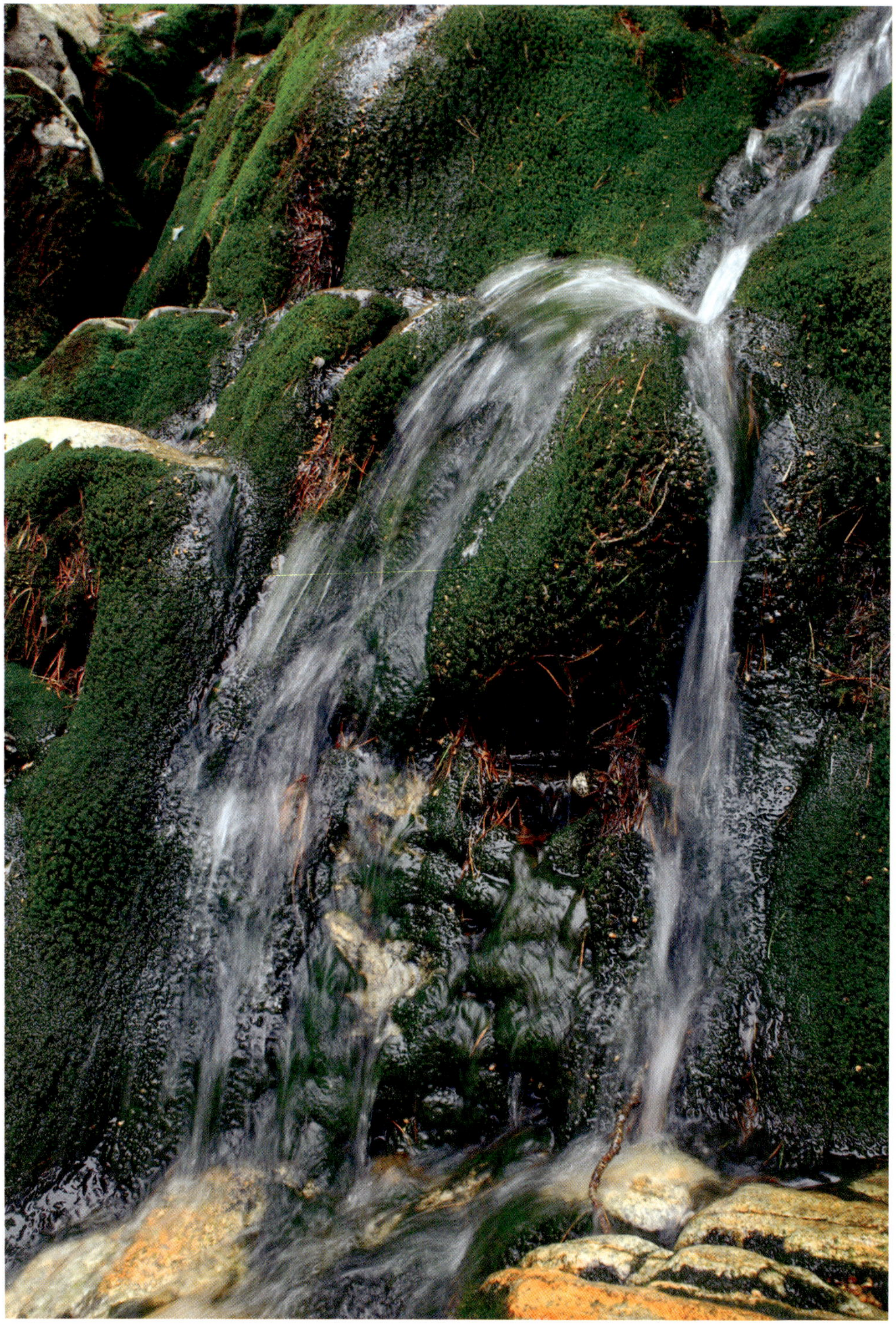

IRELAND'S HIGH PLACES

FROM THE MOUNTAINS TO THE SEA

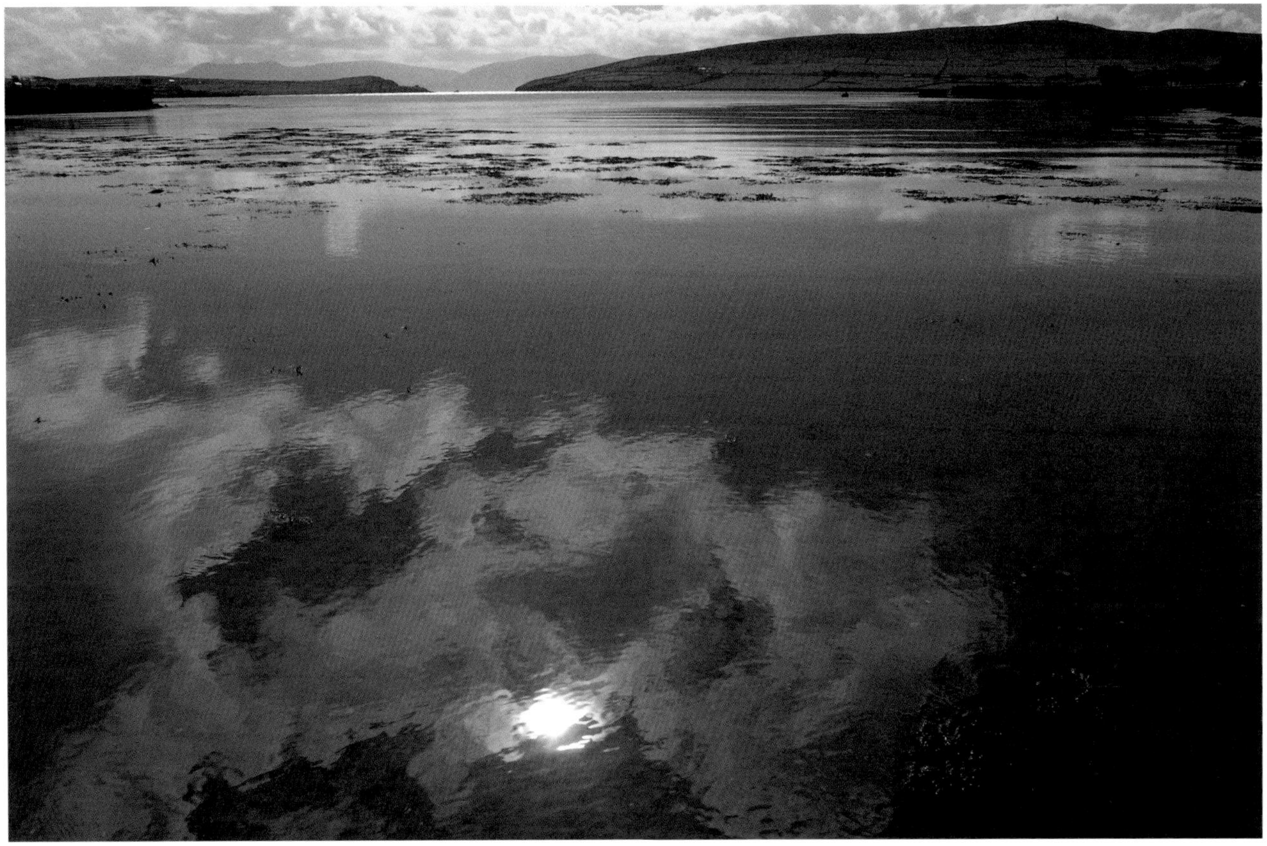

ROB BEIGHTON

The Collins Press

To fellow travellers on the great journey

Published in 2008 by
The Collins Press
West Link Park
Doughcloyne
Wilton
Cork
Ireland

A CIP record for this book is available from the British Library

ISBN 978 1 90517 245 0

Design and typesetting by Rob Beighton

Typeset in Californian FB, Charlemagne Std and Cataneo BT
Printed in China by Everbest Printing

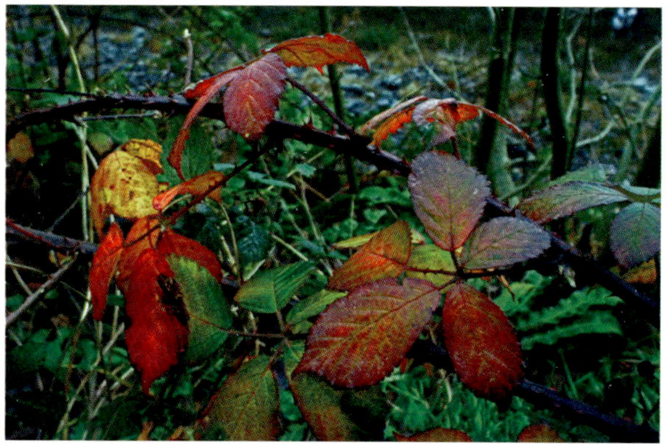

CONTENTS

DREAMS OVER THE HORIZON

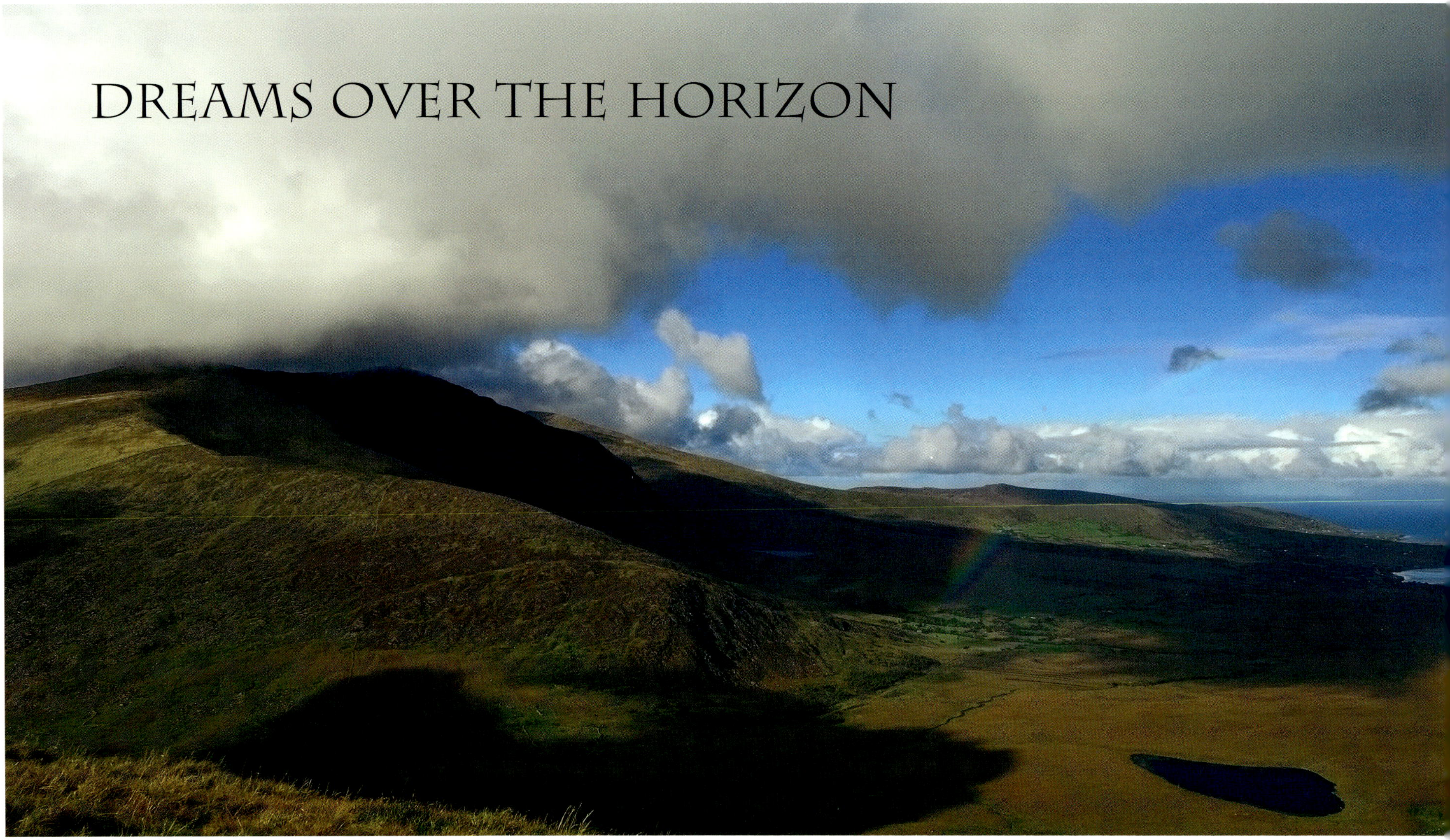

In the good fortune of my country childhood, in a place of few cars, I was king of a huge realm of natural wonders, which I explored on foot and mapped in my visual mind from my early years. In this fabulous place, my father, a passionate lover of nature, introduced me to the magic of the natural world. We walked countless hours together there, and in the land which lay beyond the edge of my kingdom. These hills rose, over the course of seven or eight kilometres, from the Cheshire plain of north-west England to the wild moorland on the edge of the Pennines which themselves ran uninterrupted northwards to Scotland. An ancient herd of red deer roamed here, grazing the sedge tussocks, roaring their rut in autumn. As we strode, we talked about and explored whatever we saw, whether landscape or plant or animal; our discourses delved into the nature of life.

Looking towards Brandon Bay across the slopes of Mount Brandon from Conor Pass.

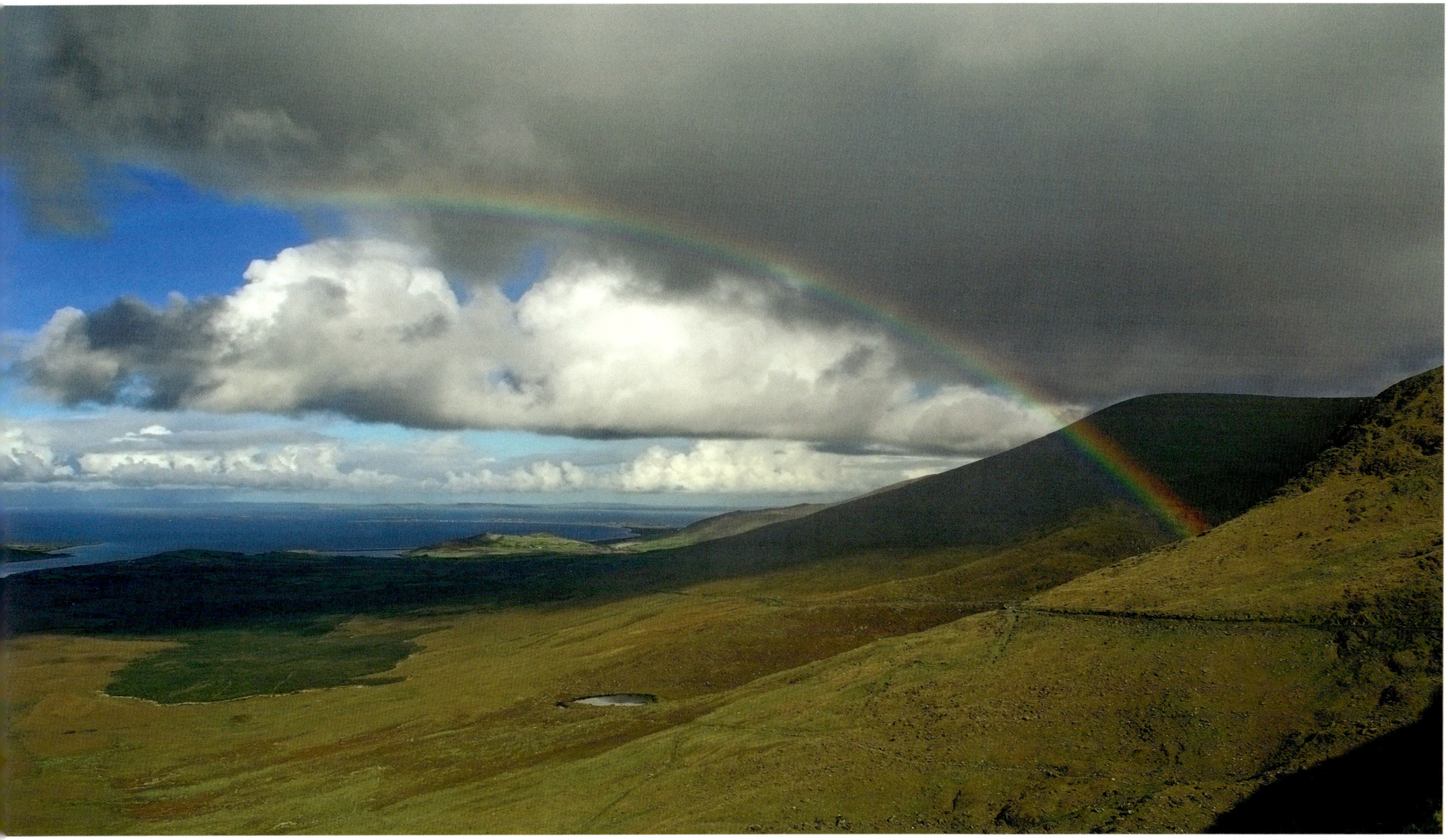

Eventually, I walked these ways on my own, before and after school, and grew ever more curious about the country that lay beyond our hills. Spreading far and brownly eastwards was the almost mystical land of the Peak District of Derbyshire, beckoning to be explored. In my later teen years a tidal wave of thirst for adventure broke over me, taking me on foot, on a bicycle, or on rock into every crevice of this wonderful and subtle landscape of moors and dales. This quest expanded into exploration of mountain regions throughout Europe, America, and the Himalayas, where I ventured onto precipices of rock and snow in search of challenge, beauty, spiritual uplift, and fascination with the wonder of nature in all its forms. In the following pages I will outline the scope of this journey, before moving into the particular theme of this book, the Mountains of Ireland.

A mountain, for me, is a symbol of many things...

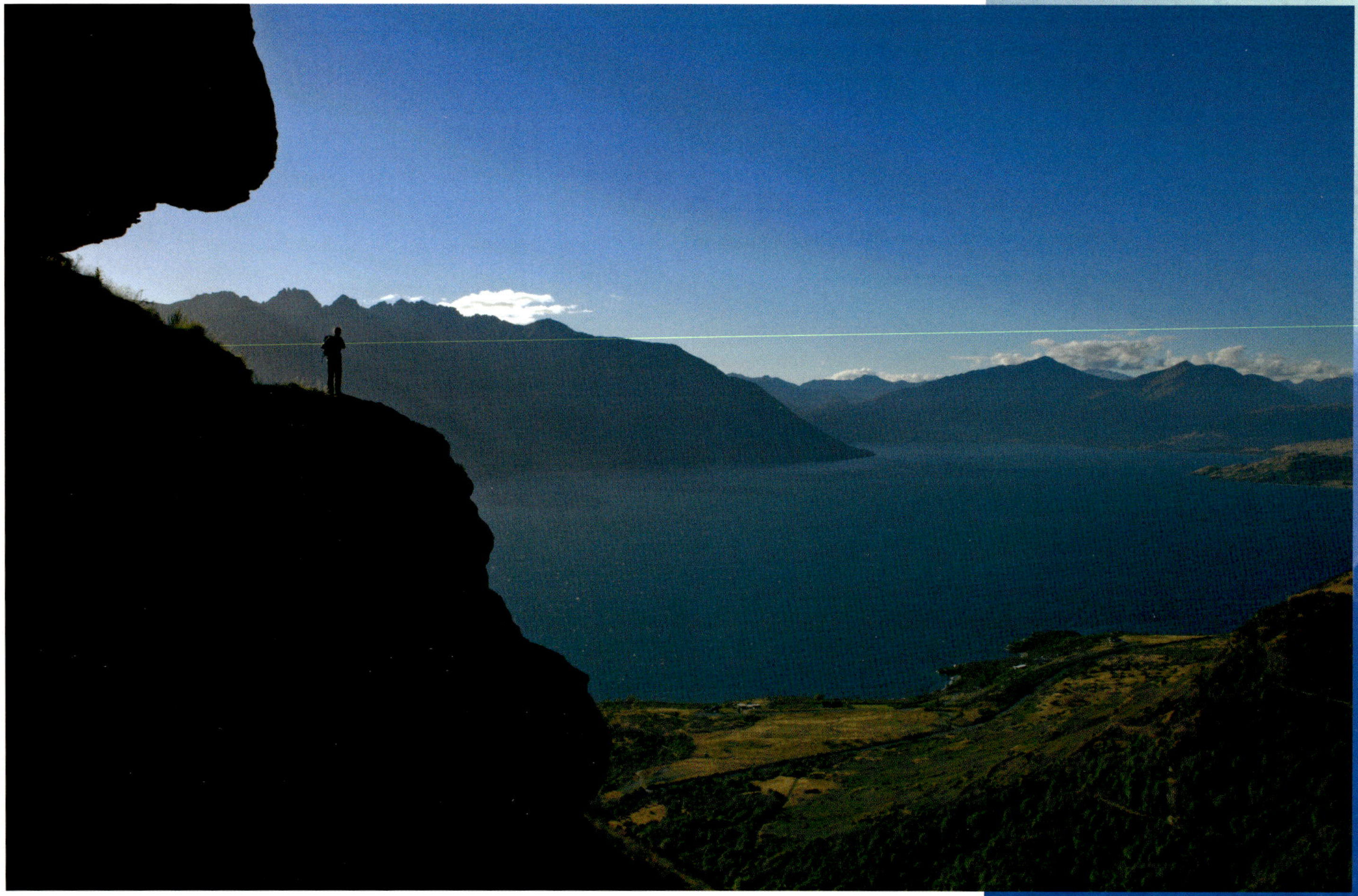

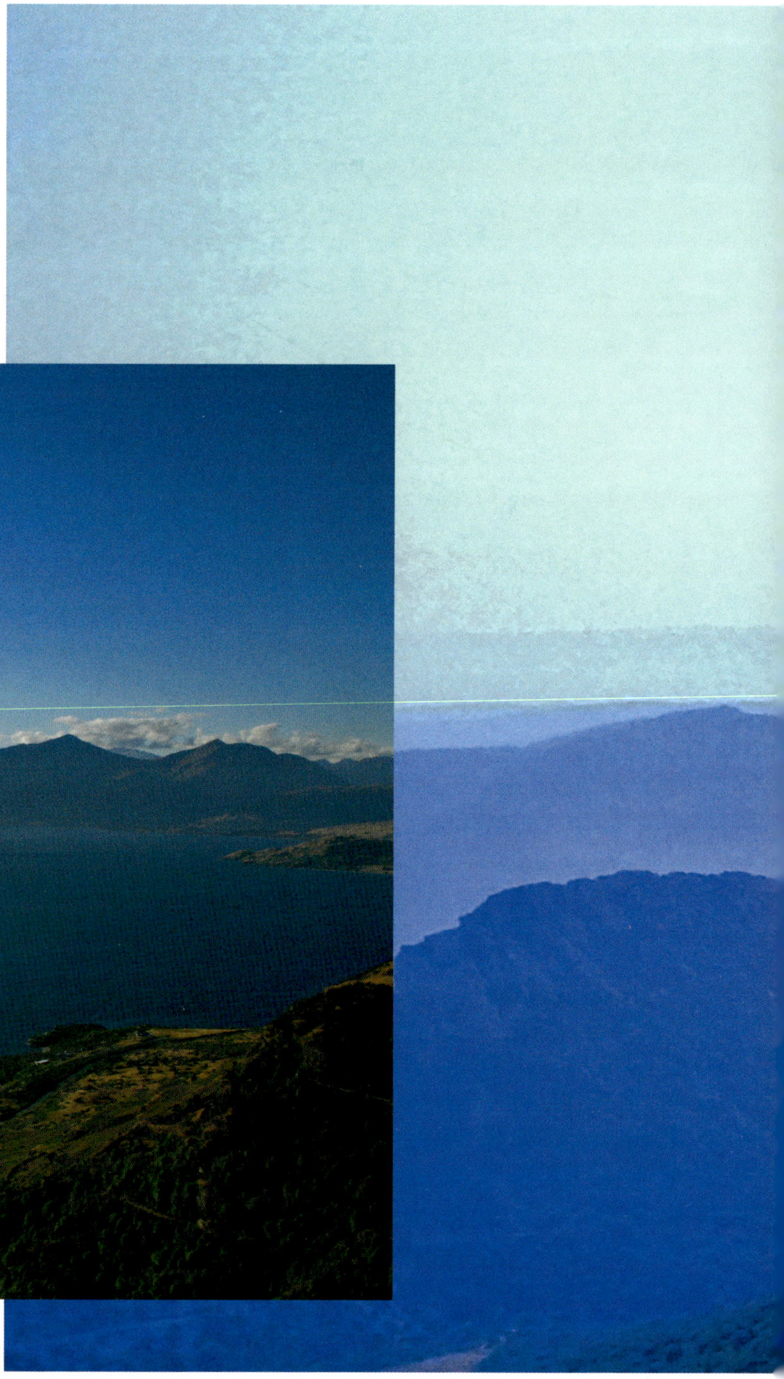

ABOVE At Wye Creek, Queenstown, New Zealand.

OPPOSITE On the Dentelles de Montmirail, Provence, France.

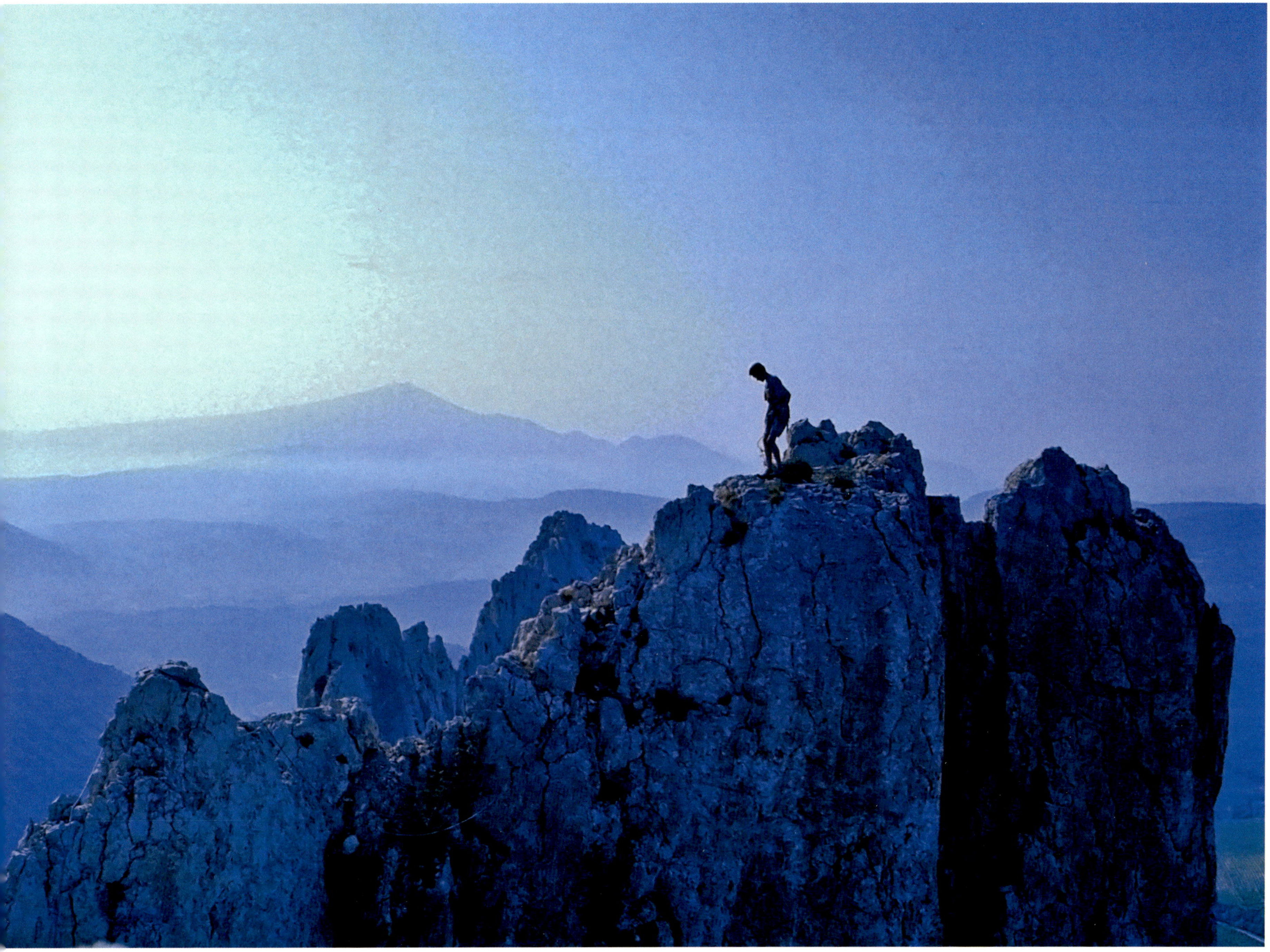

...of adventure, to be in a place of uncertainty where life is at the edge,

...of physical tests and personal challenge in high and inspiring places,

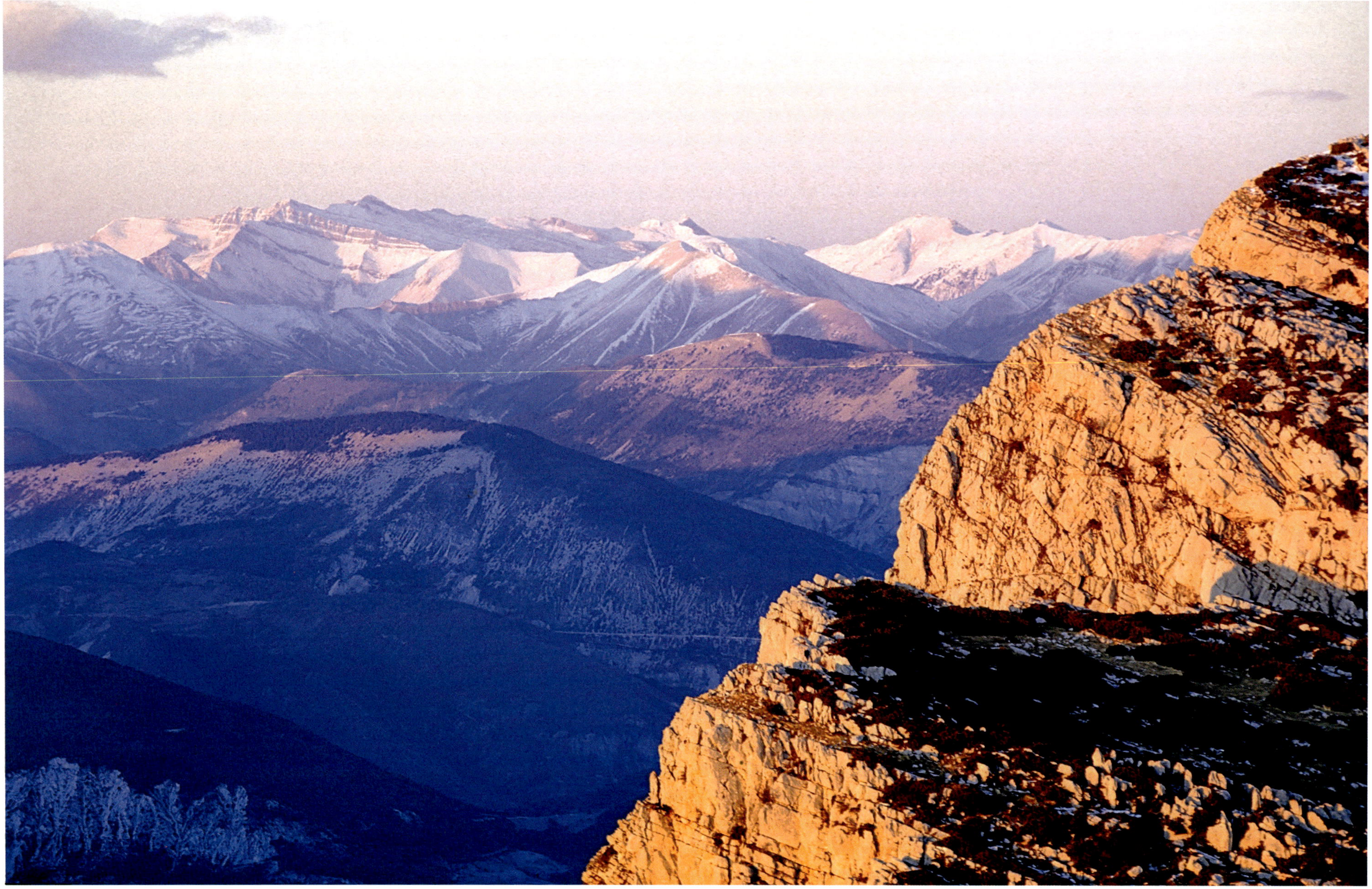

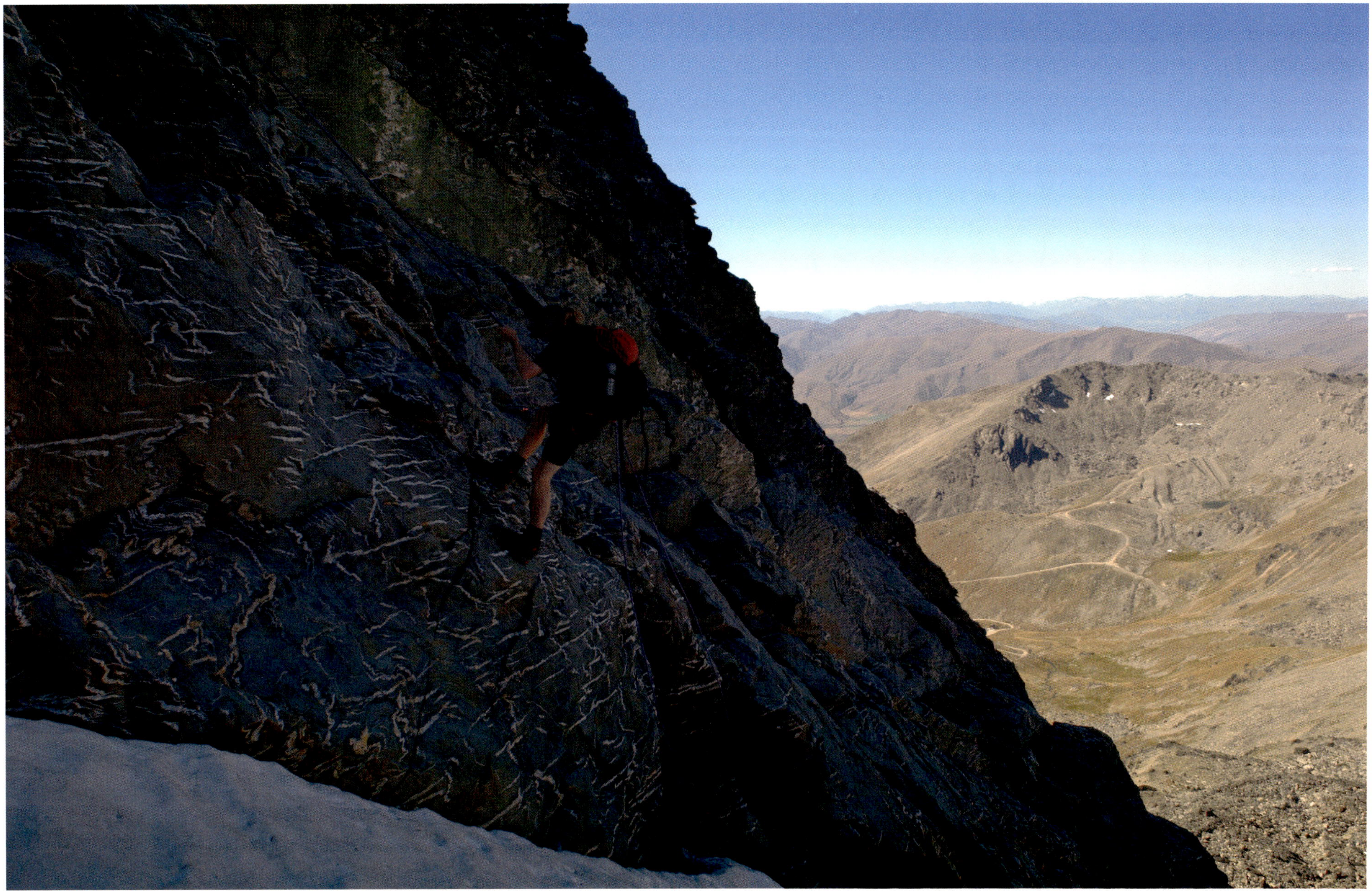

where the outcome of each moment rests in your own hands.

ABOVE Descending Single Cone on The Remarkables, Queenstown, New Zealand.

OPPOSITE Haute Provence, France, looking towards Cheval Blanc.

...of spiritual uplift

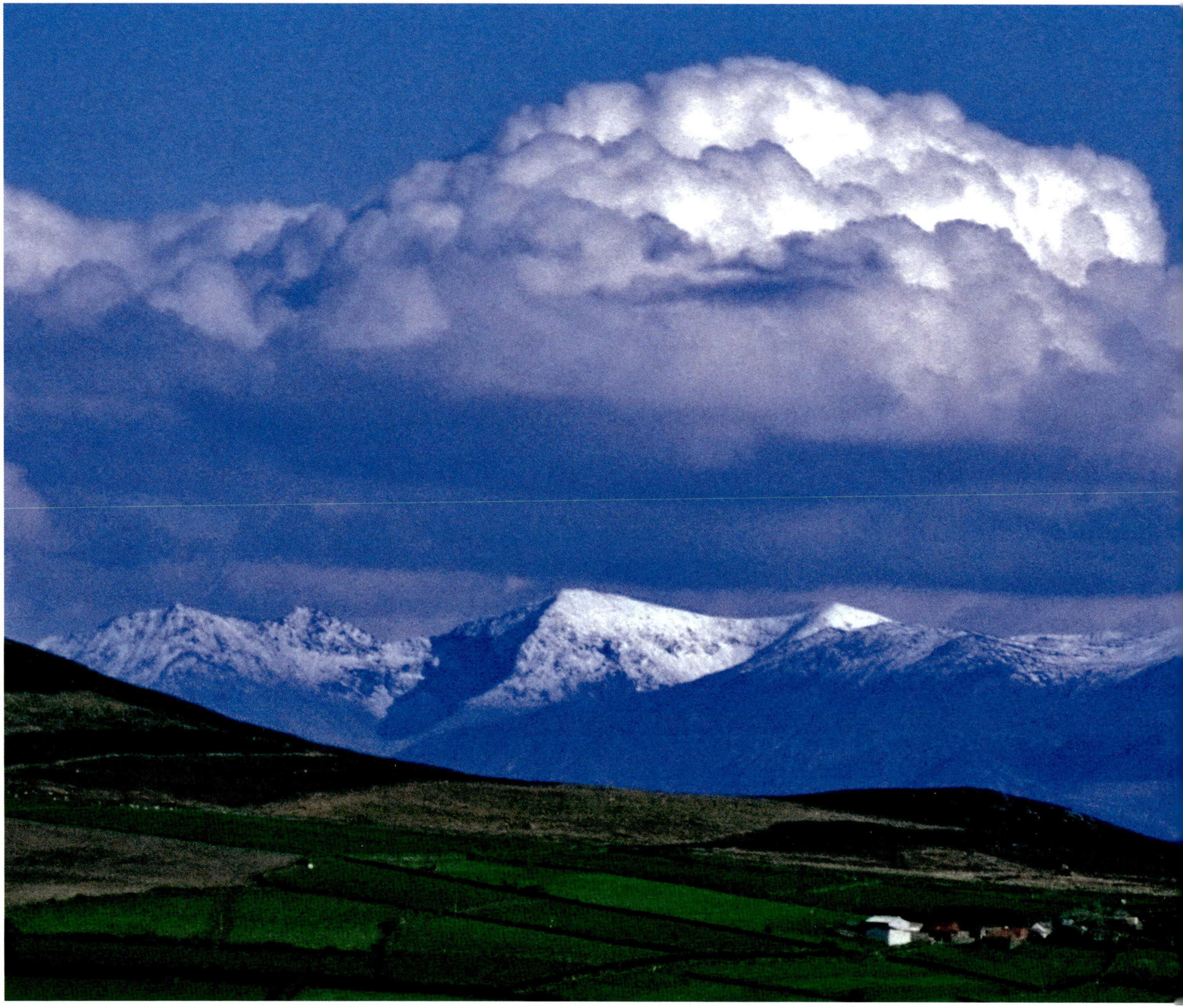

The beautiful sweep of the Macgillycuddy's Reeks in winter, seen from Coom Dubh on the Dingle Peninsula. It is rare for snow to remain for more than a few days in the warm south-western corner of Ireland. When this does happen, though, hills are transformed into mountains.

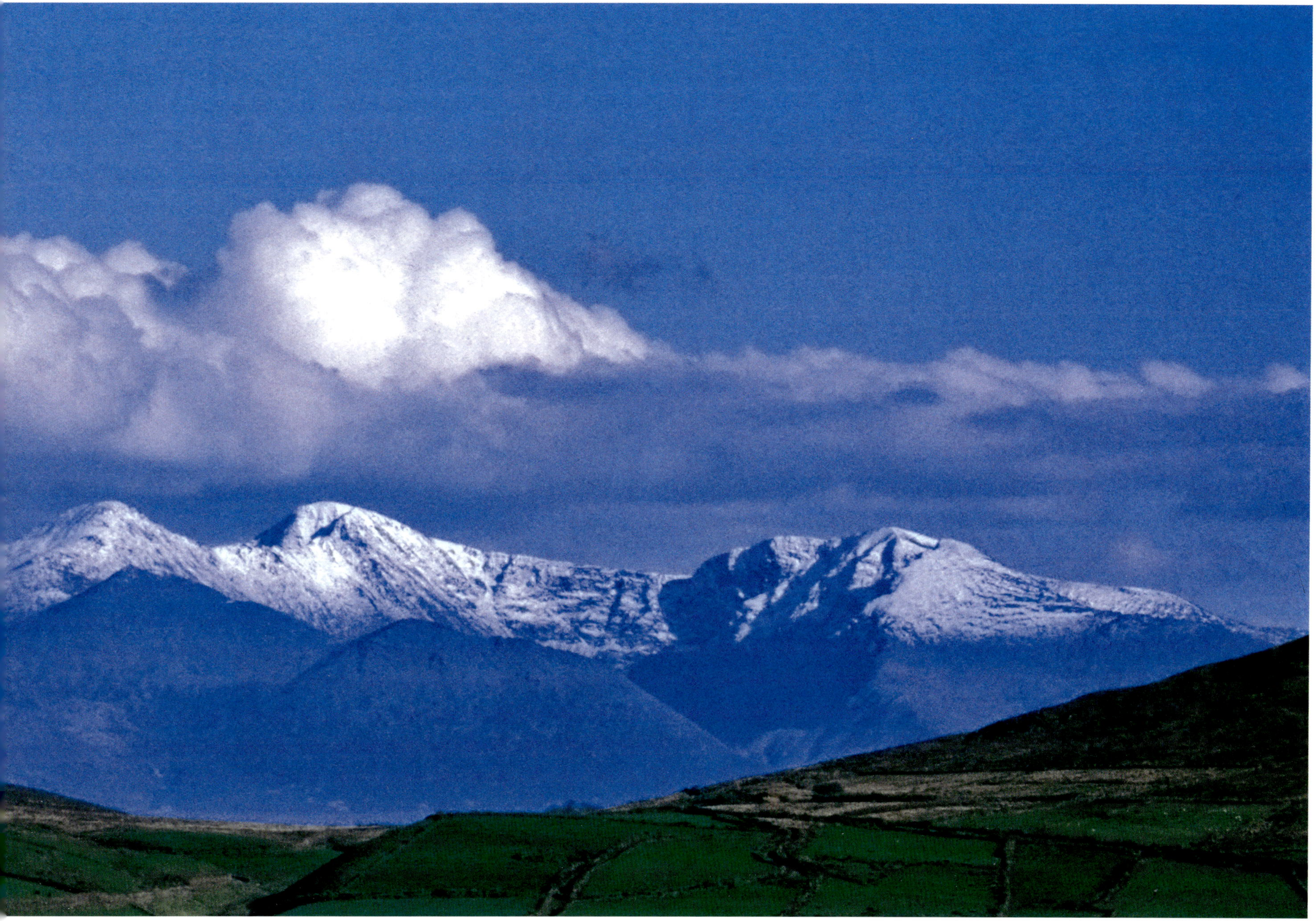

...of aesthetic beauty

OPPOSITE A subtle dawn creeps over the waters of Lough Inagh, to the south of the Twelve Bens in Connemara.

BELOW Mountain avens, one of the rare alpine species to be found in the sheltered crevices on the limestone pavements of the Burren.

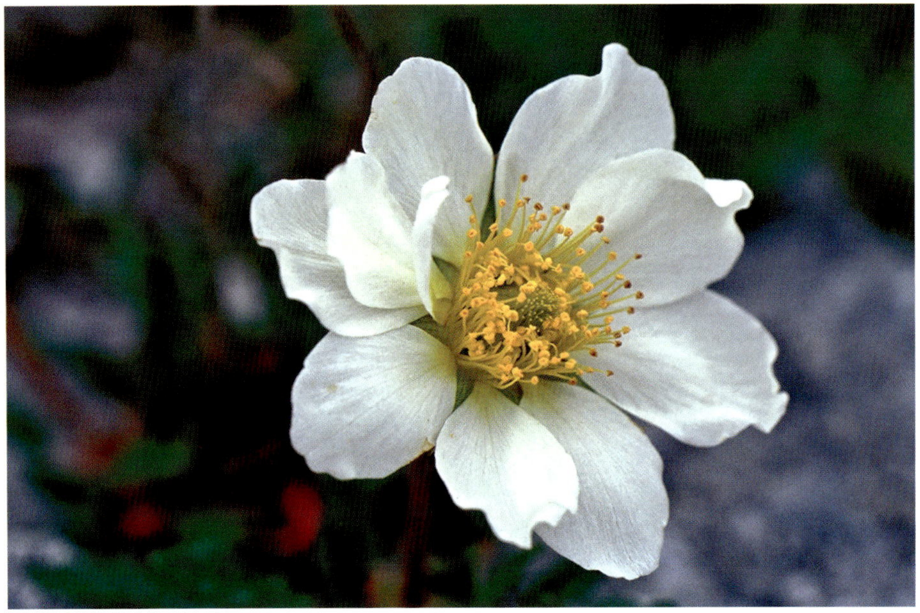

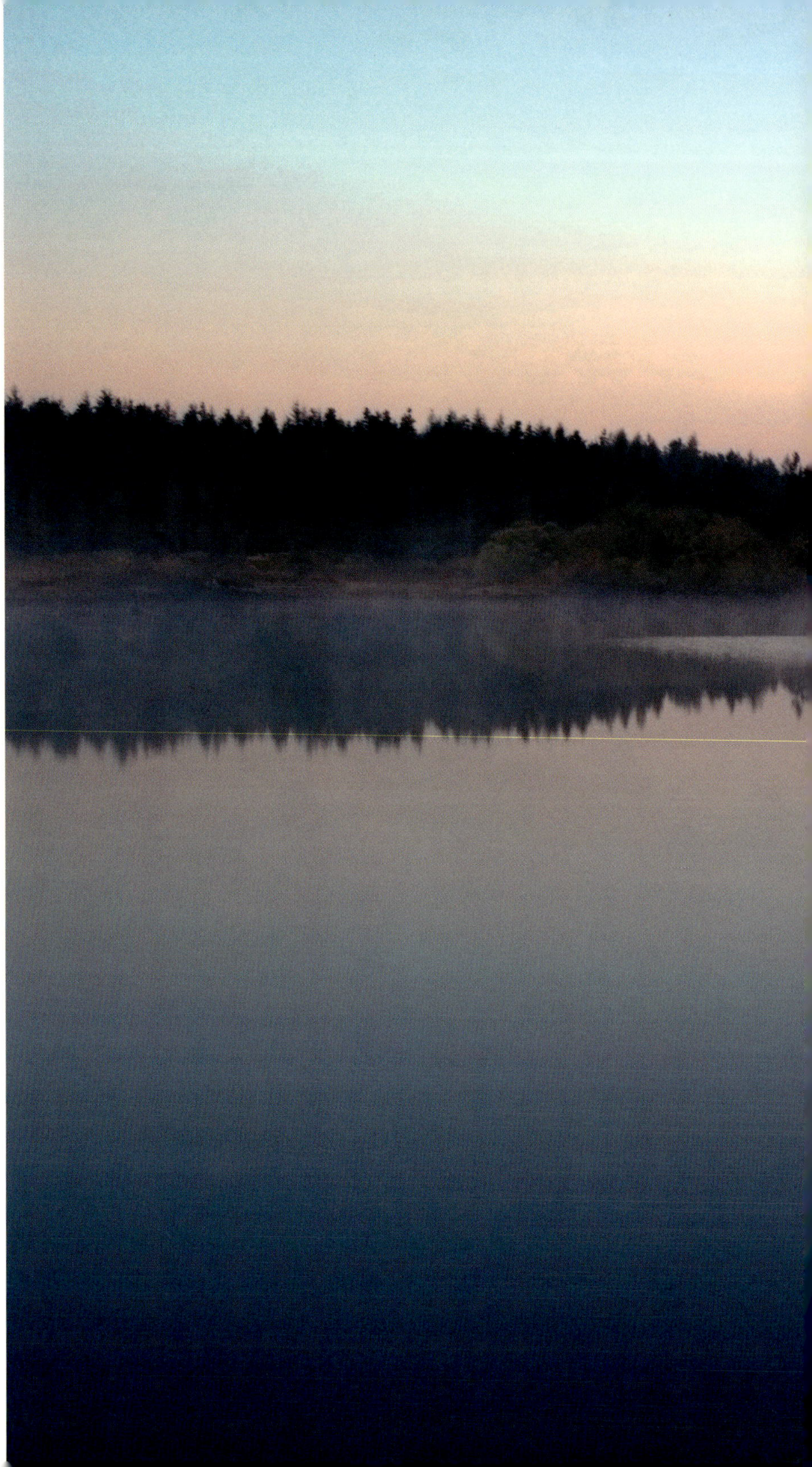

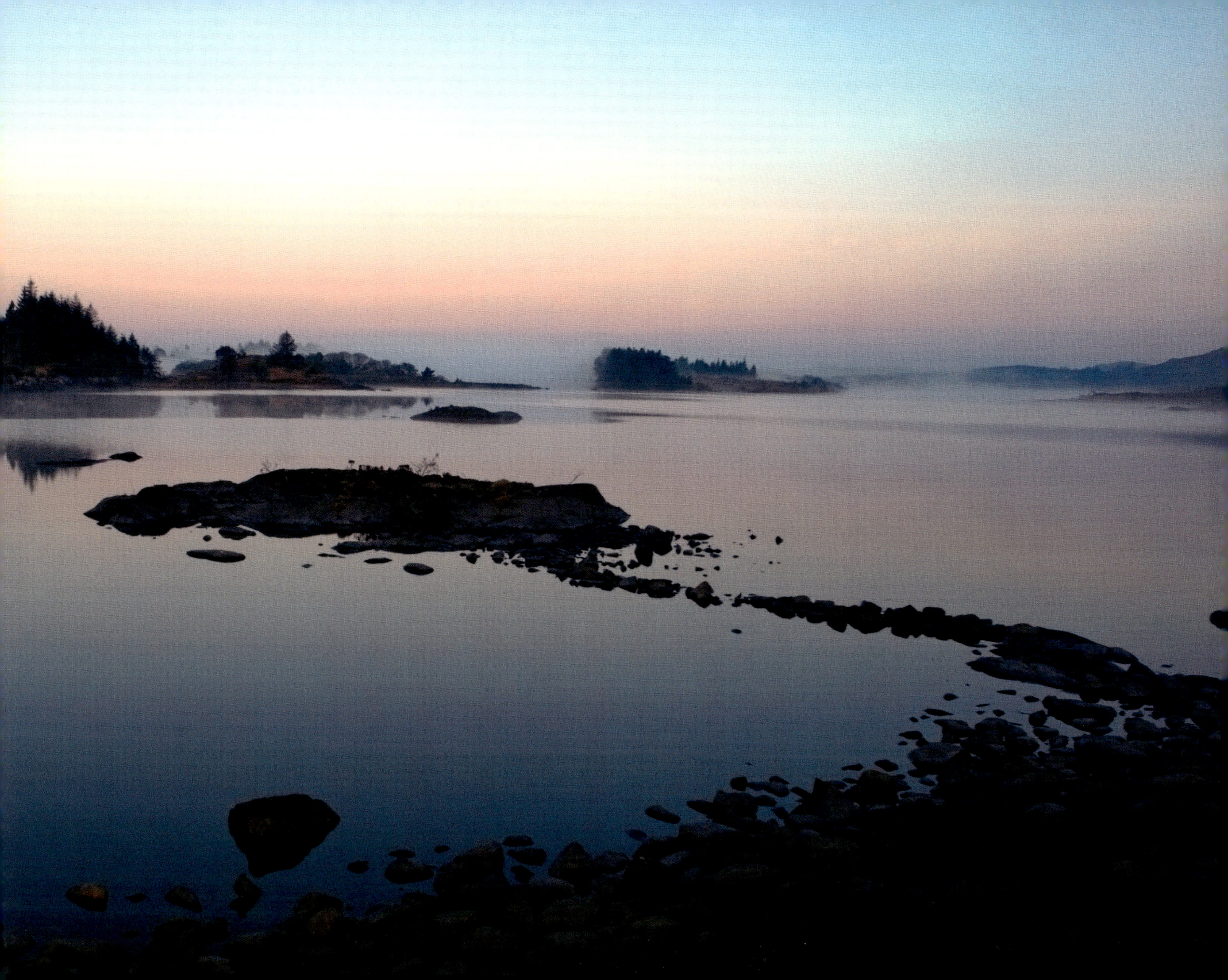

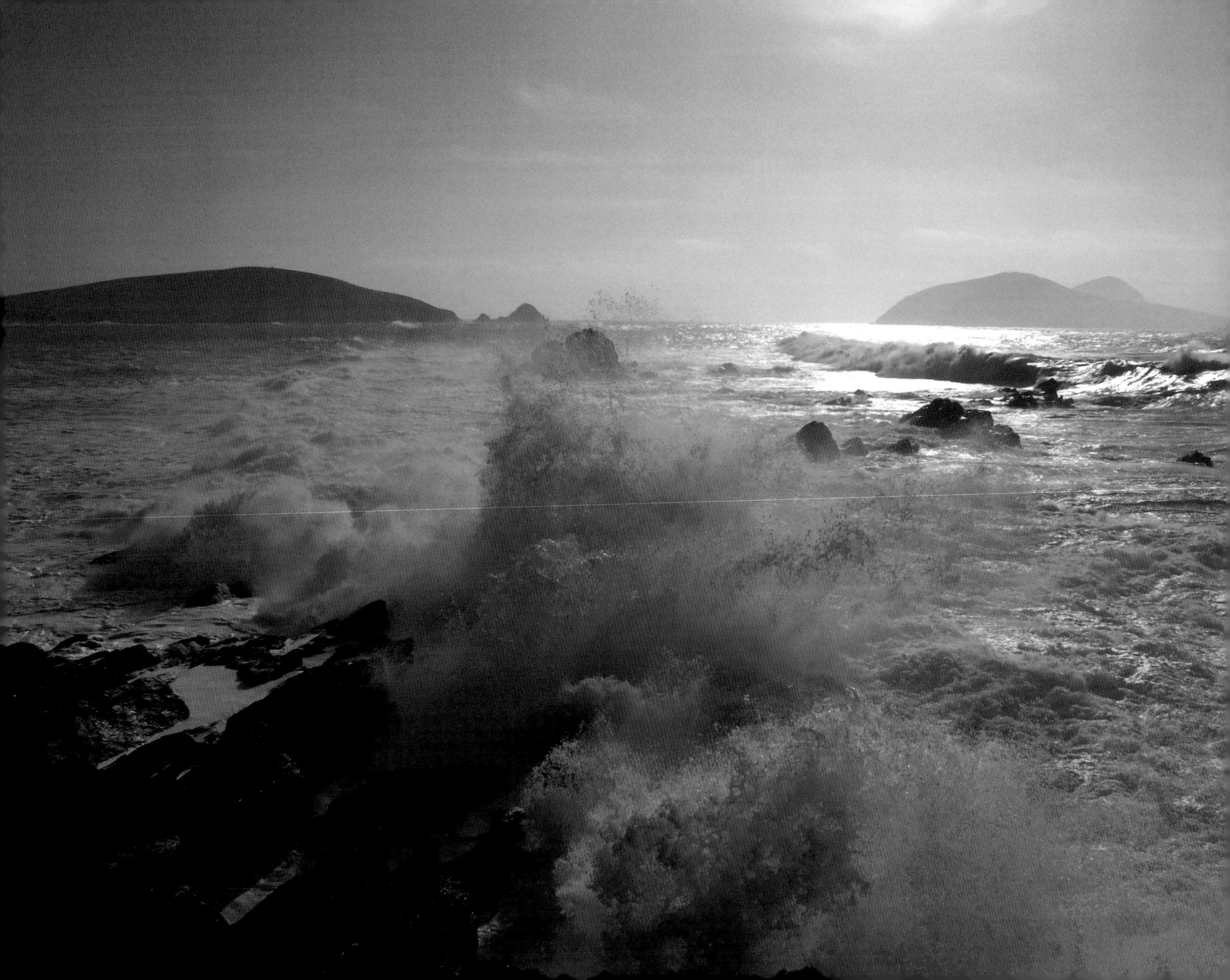

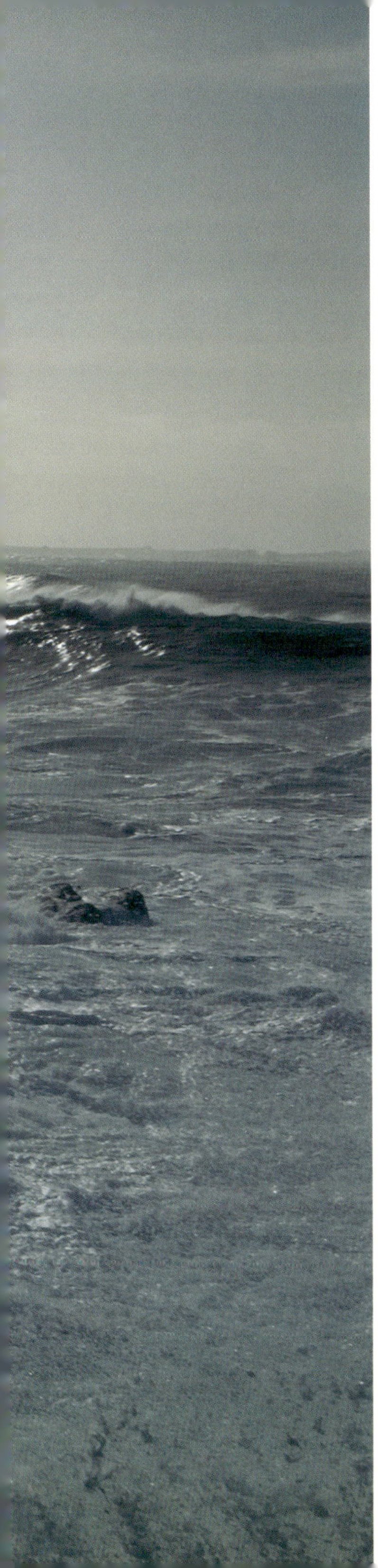

...of the raw energy of the elements

OPPOSITE Vicious and prolonged storms hurl themselves at the Blasket Islands, the most westerly point in Europe.

BELOW Strands of seaweed torn from the ocean bed by one of the frequent storms of winter.

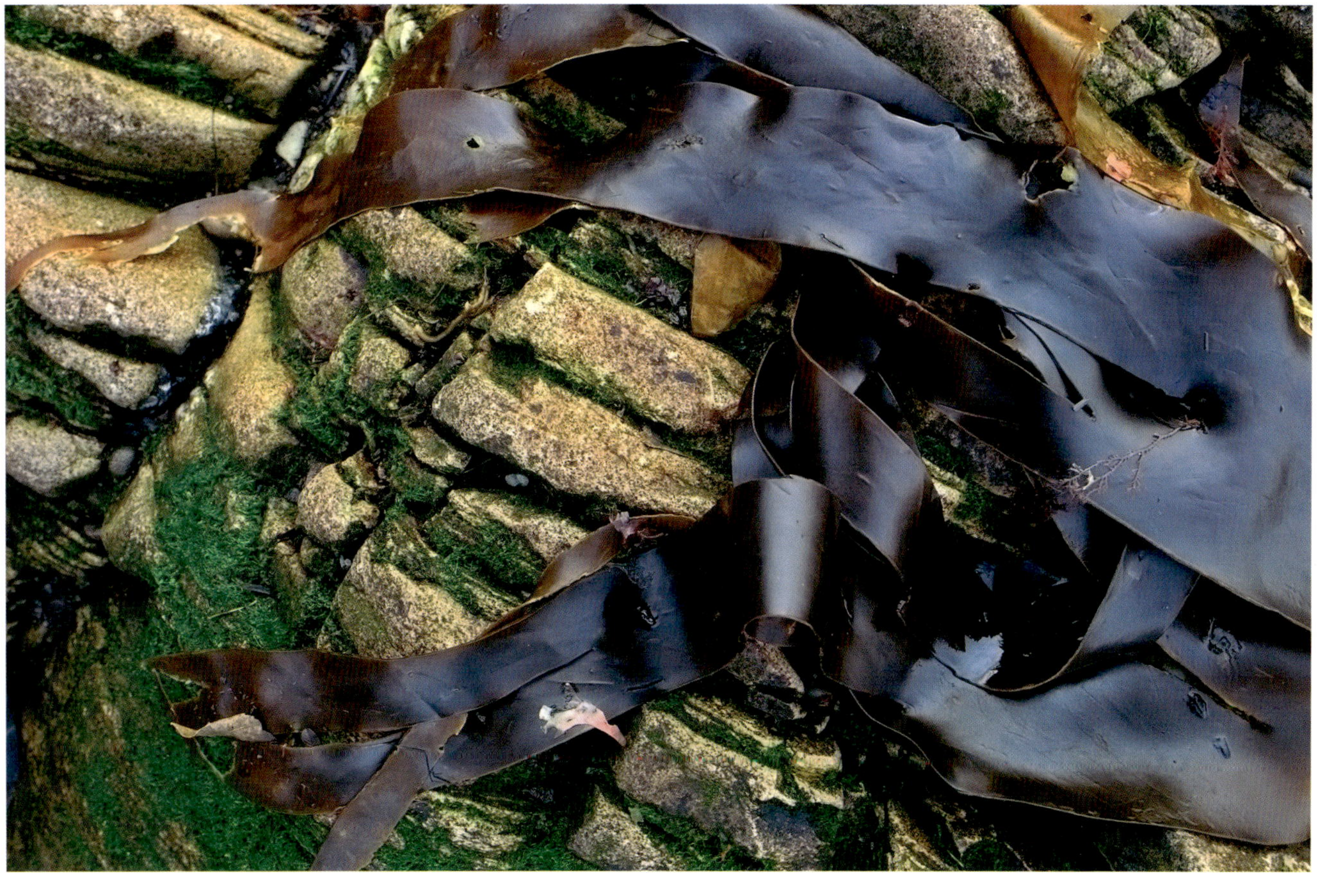

...of the wonder of nature.

OPPOSITE *The wonderful mountain landscape of the Twelve Bens in Connemara, with a huge outcrop of quartz.*

BELOW *Chill winter winds have left blades of ice on the stems of rushes.*

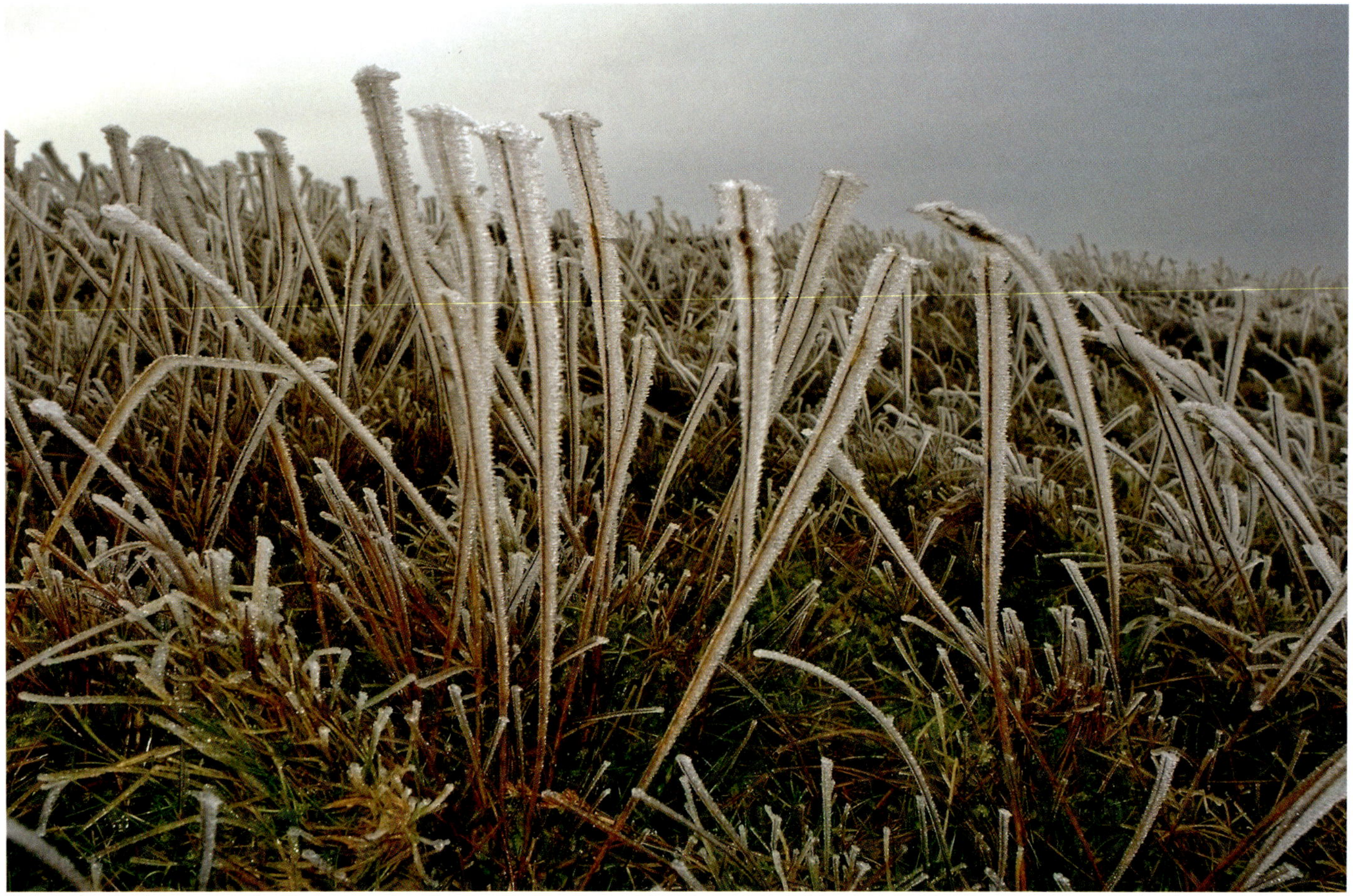

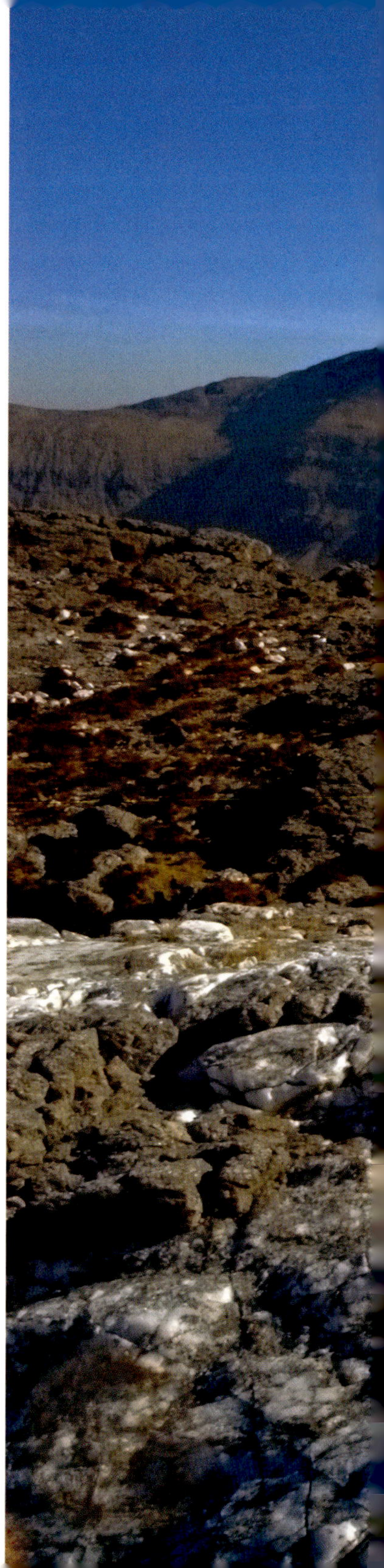

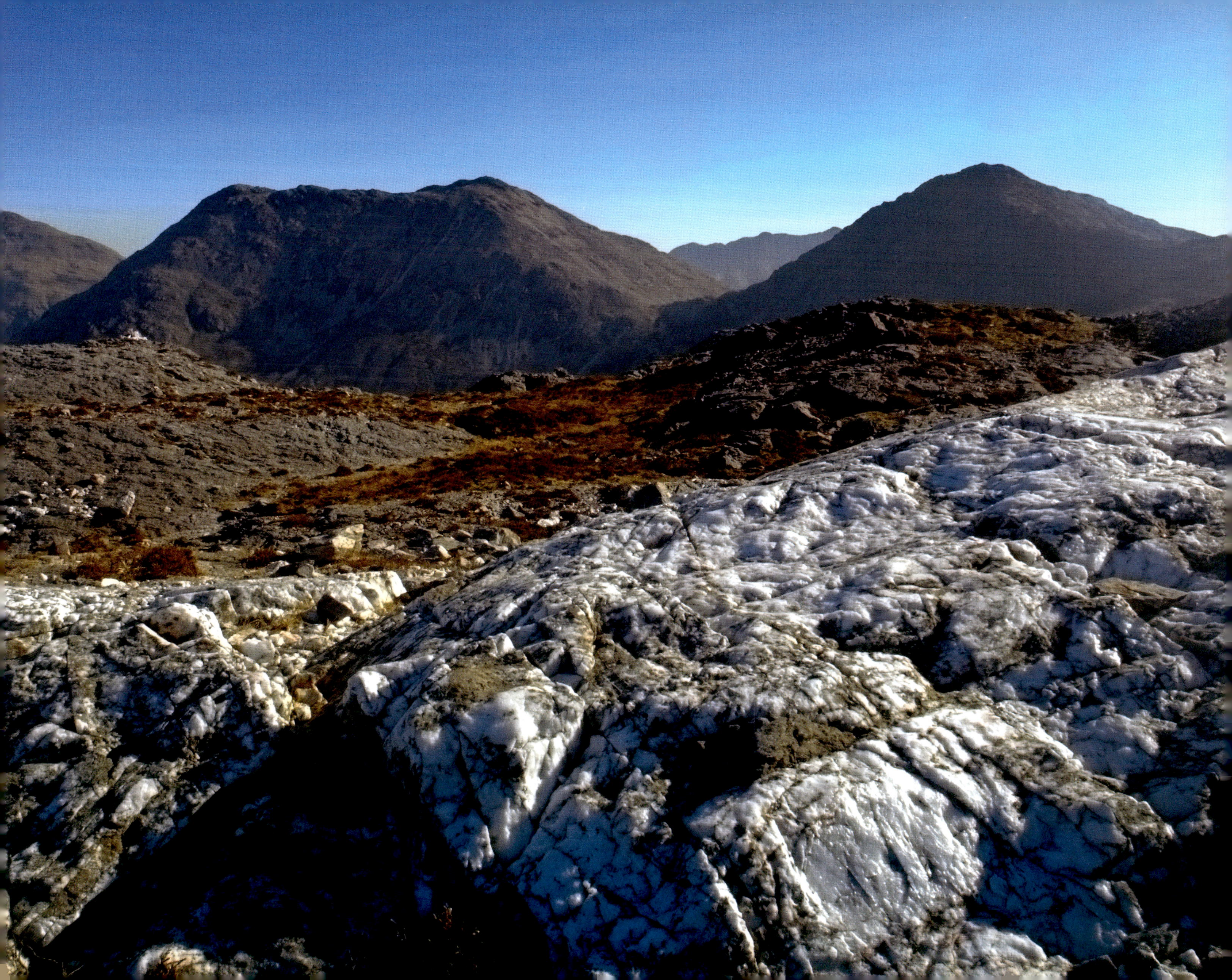

THE IMAGES

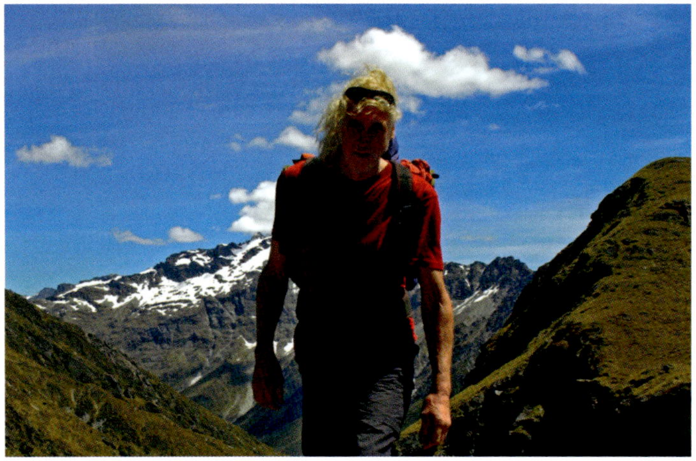

OPPOSITE The awesome cliffs of Slieve League, falling 595 metres to the sea. This place is one of the many wonders of Donegal.

LEFT Your eccentric guide to this erratic journey, seen in his natural habitat.

Photography is a means to express the passion I feel for nature, a feeling that has been with me since early childhood. My alignment in life is with the mysterious, rather than with the rational; things tend to happen when you allow yourself to respond to subtle, scarcely noticeable voices inside yourself. You find yourself in the right place at the right time in a way that no planning could bring to you. Somewhere, at some moment, the perfect image is waiting to express itself. Photographs are not taken, they are received; as such, an image is beyond the self, an imprint of something universal. The medium of photography is fundamentally technical; however, the place from which the images spring is of greater importance. Simple mastery of technique is no guarantee of finding powerful images, ones that will affect people at the level of the heart.

The camera which I use is a digital SLR; with this I use two lenses which reflect the way in which I see, the greater scene contrasted with the detail. I use a wide-angle lens, a 27 mm, to express the big picture, and a telephoto lens, a 150 mm macro, to abstract elements of this vista. Single-focal length lenses have a greater capacity to represent fine detail than zoom lenses, those with a variable focal length. The limitation of choice that this imposes refines the way I select and compose the image, which is apparent in the image itself. An aspect of beauty which we perceive at an unconscious level is that of quality. All the parts of the process, from the selection of the equipment, to the refinement of the composition, and to the way the light is used, contribute to the ultimate quality, and thus to the power of the image when it is viewed.

In this book, I will take you on a journey into the wonders of one of the most beautiful environments on earth. We will explore aspects of our own inner nature, and have a glimpse of the possibility of living life magically.

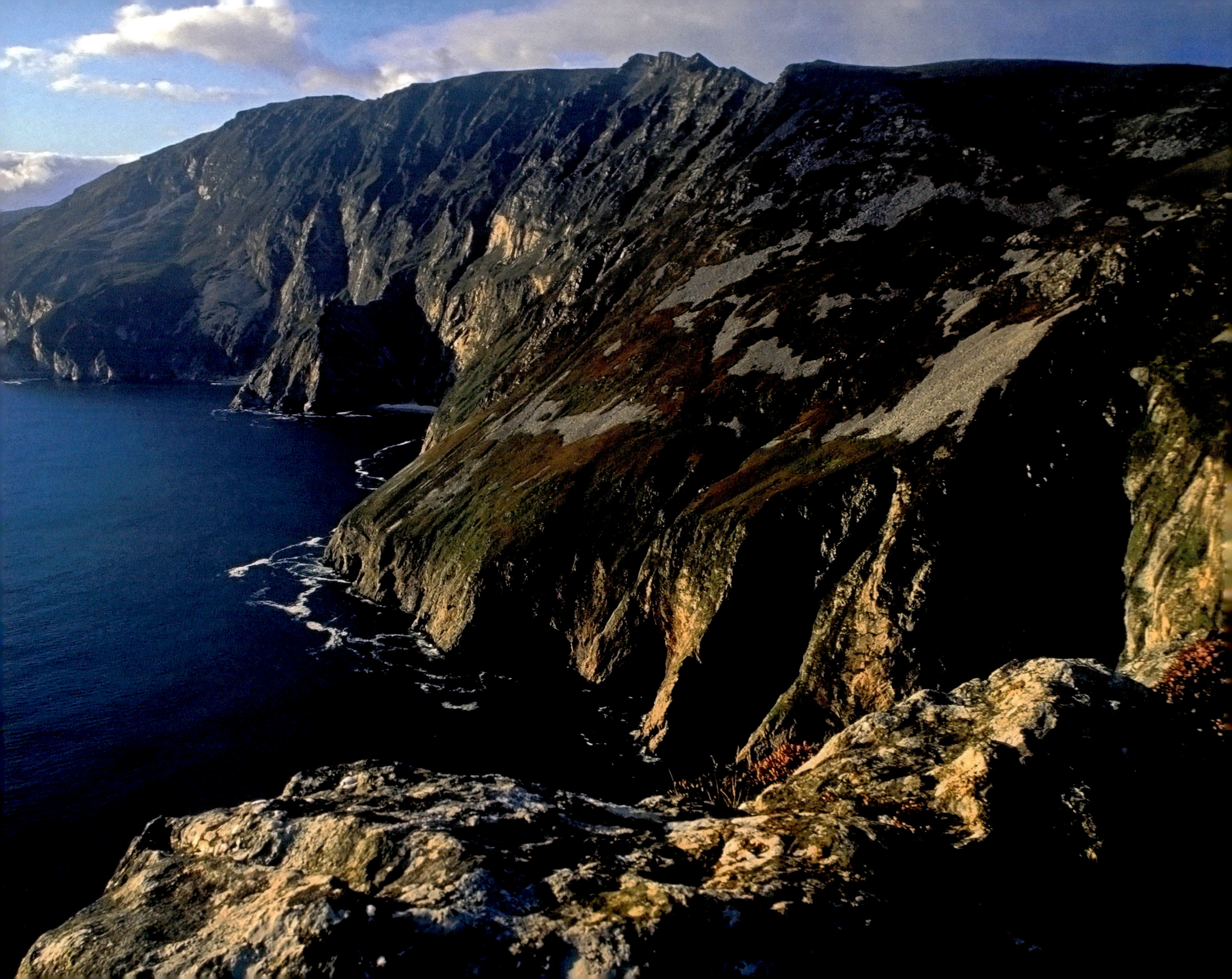

A JOURNEY OF DISCOVERY

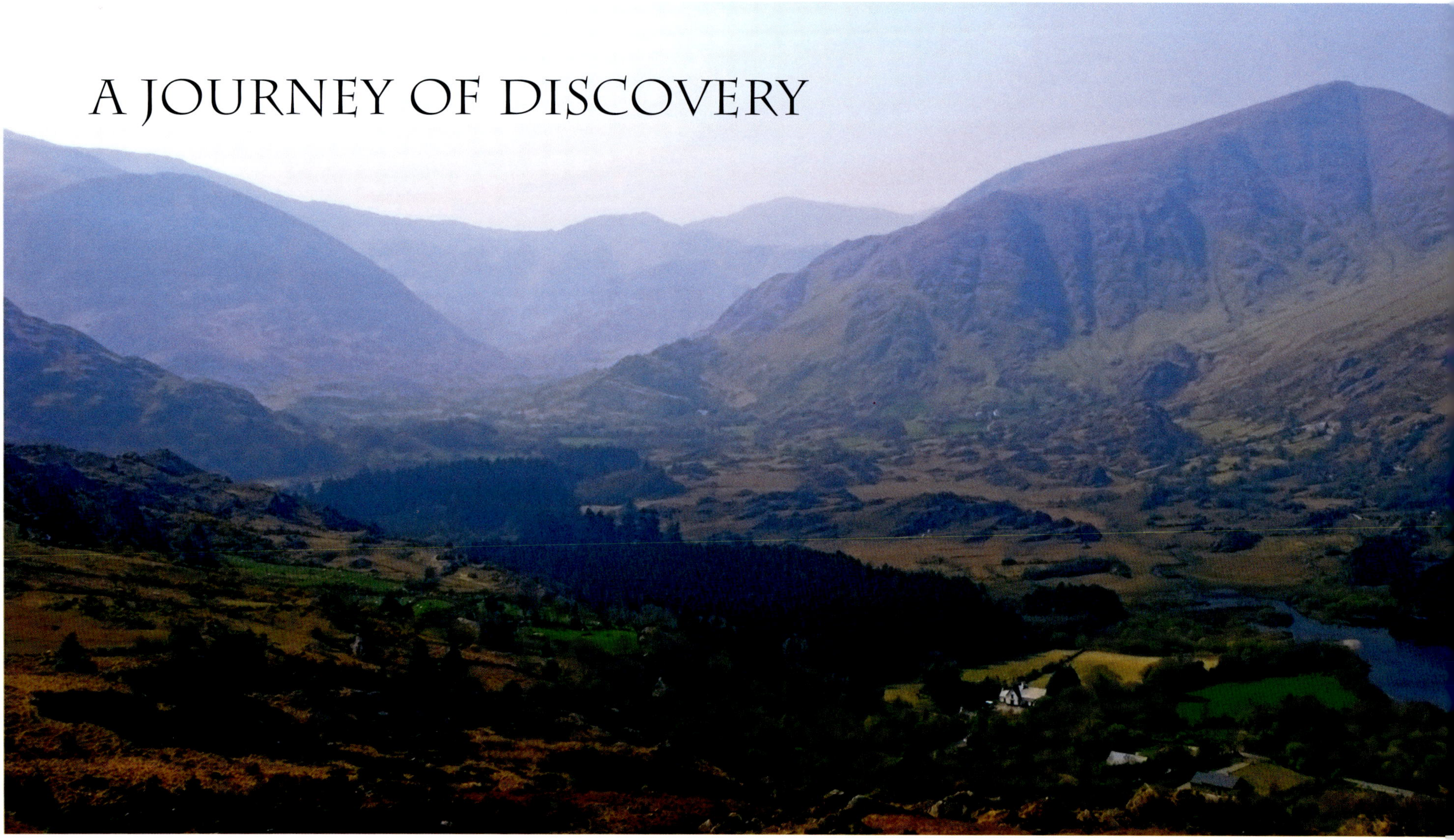

A mountain is also a symbol of attainment, of reaching the heights, whether in a physical sense of simply height above sea level, or in a more metaphysical sense of a goal, the end-point of a journey. In this chapter we will explore the more tangible reality of a mountain. A common perception of a mountain is of an inaccessible place, requiring much effort to reach, and beset with danger, often unexpected. Such aspects as rock and ice, bottomless precipices, fierce weather, complicated terrain, remoteness, great height, would feature in the description. Such places are common in the Himalayas, rising to over 8,000 metres in the mountain regions of Asia. Few would begrudge these remote uplands the name 'mountain'. Similarly, the Alpine regions of America and Europe, although in the region of 4,000 metres in height, are indisputably mountains in the terms we have laid out. But the mountains of Ireland! Surely those endless brown hills couldn't qualify for the term 'Mountain'?

The Caha Mountains on the Beara Peninsula, seen across Glanmore lake.

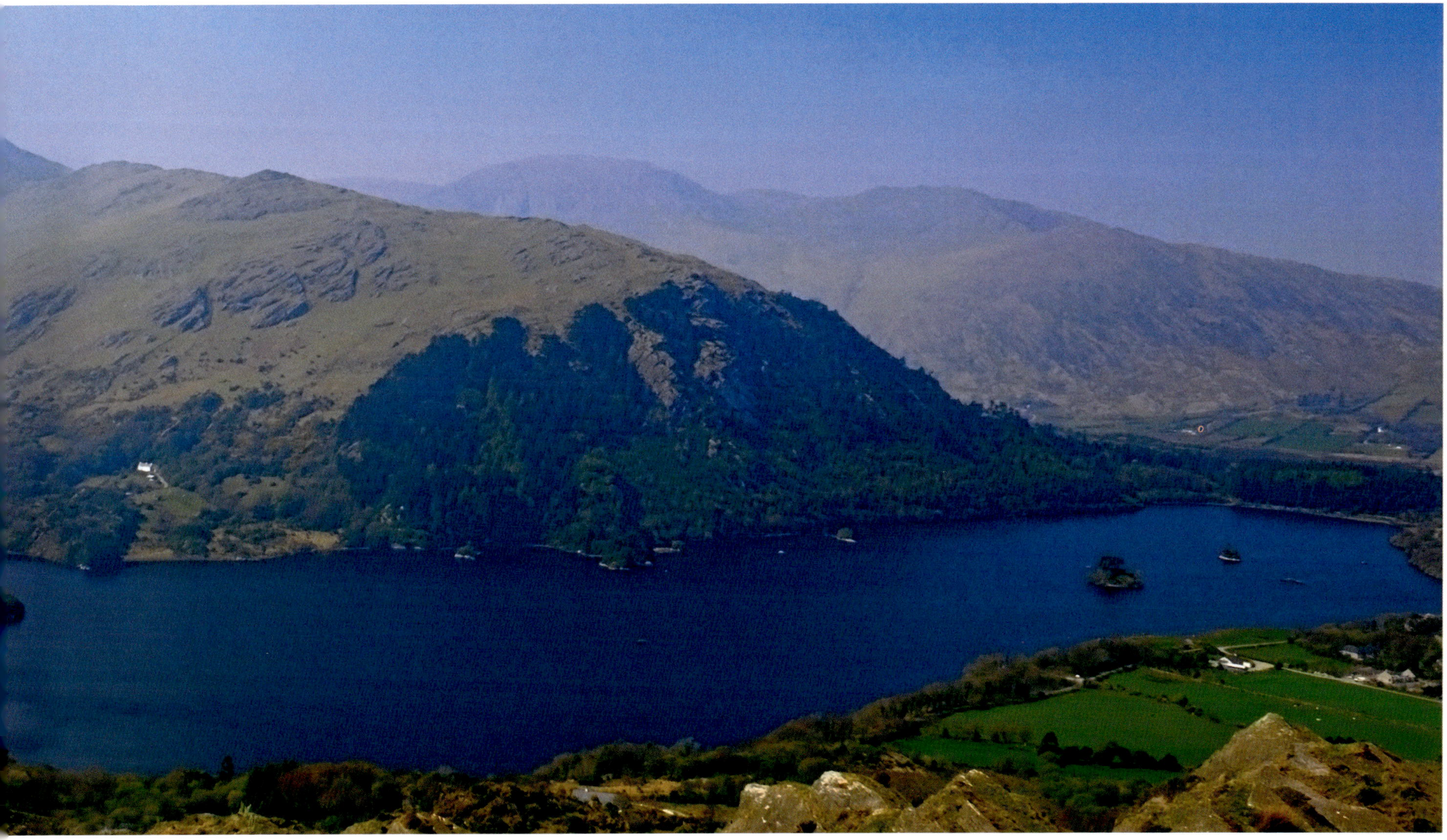

And yet they do have qualities which set them in that place. These hills, before the Age of Play decscended upon us, were the backdrop to lives lived hard; to an adversity in ordinary days beyond imagining in our soft lives. Few would have ventured onto the heights before the arrival of domestic sheep, but they were always present, remote, inaccessible, dangerous, and often beset with rain, mist, or snow, and harsh winds, and perhaps the abode of mysterious and frightening beings. The still largely trackless nature of these little hills, the highest scarcely over 1,000 metres, barely ever with snow, often without rock, and the unpredictability of the weather, sets them apart in a realm other than the ordinary. The idea of playing in the outdoors has arrived late in Ireland so, aside from a very few places, a day in the mountains will be passed in solitude between you and the sky. In the following pages we will explore, from Kerry northwards, the wonderful variety of landscape in this fabled land.

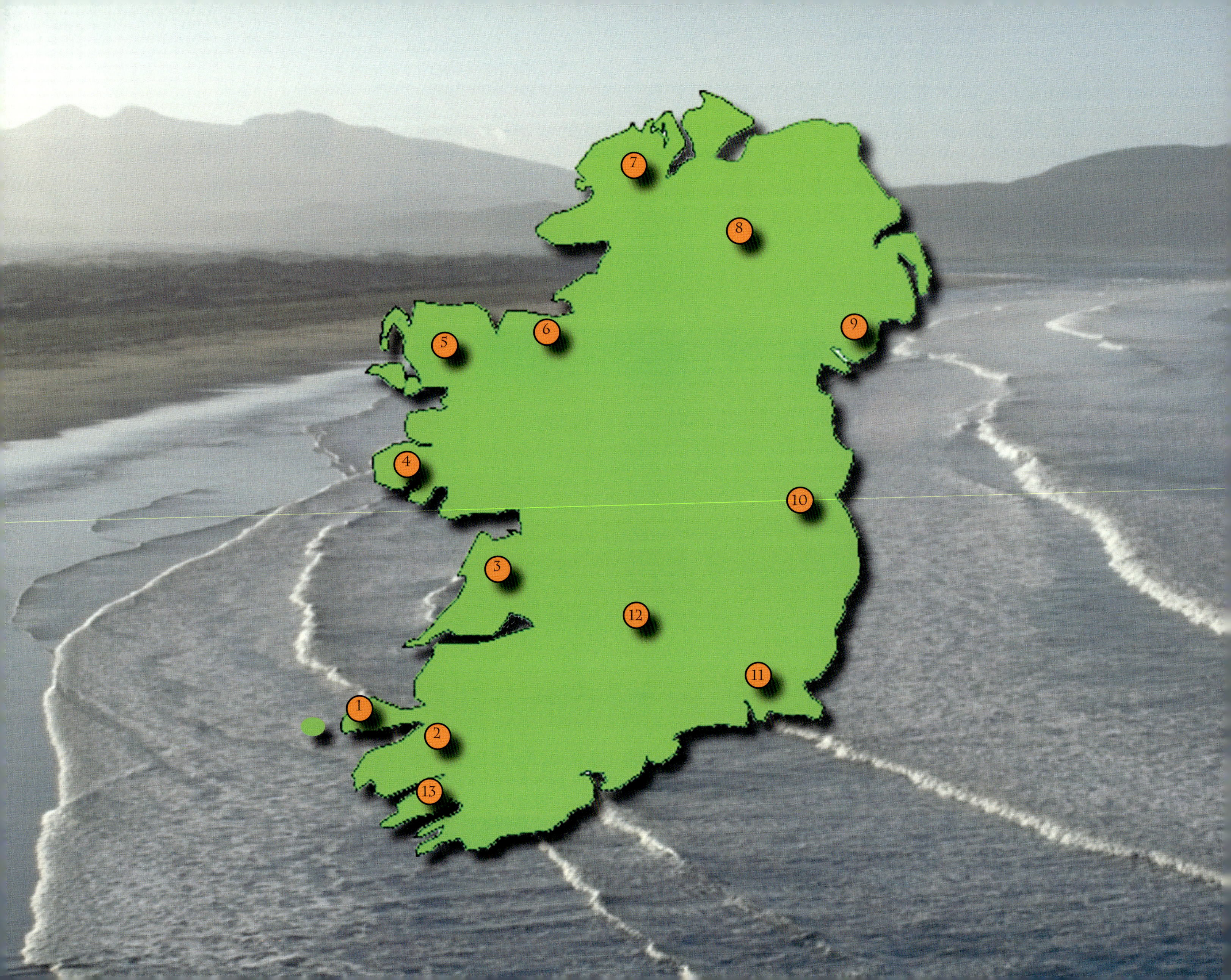
7
8
5
6
9
4
10
3
12
11
1
2
13

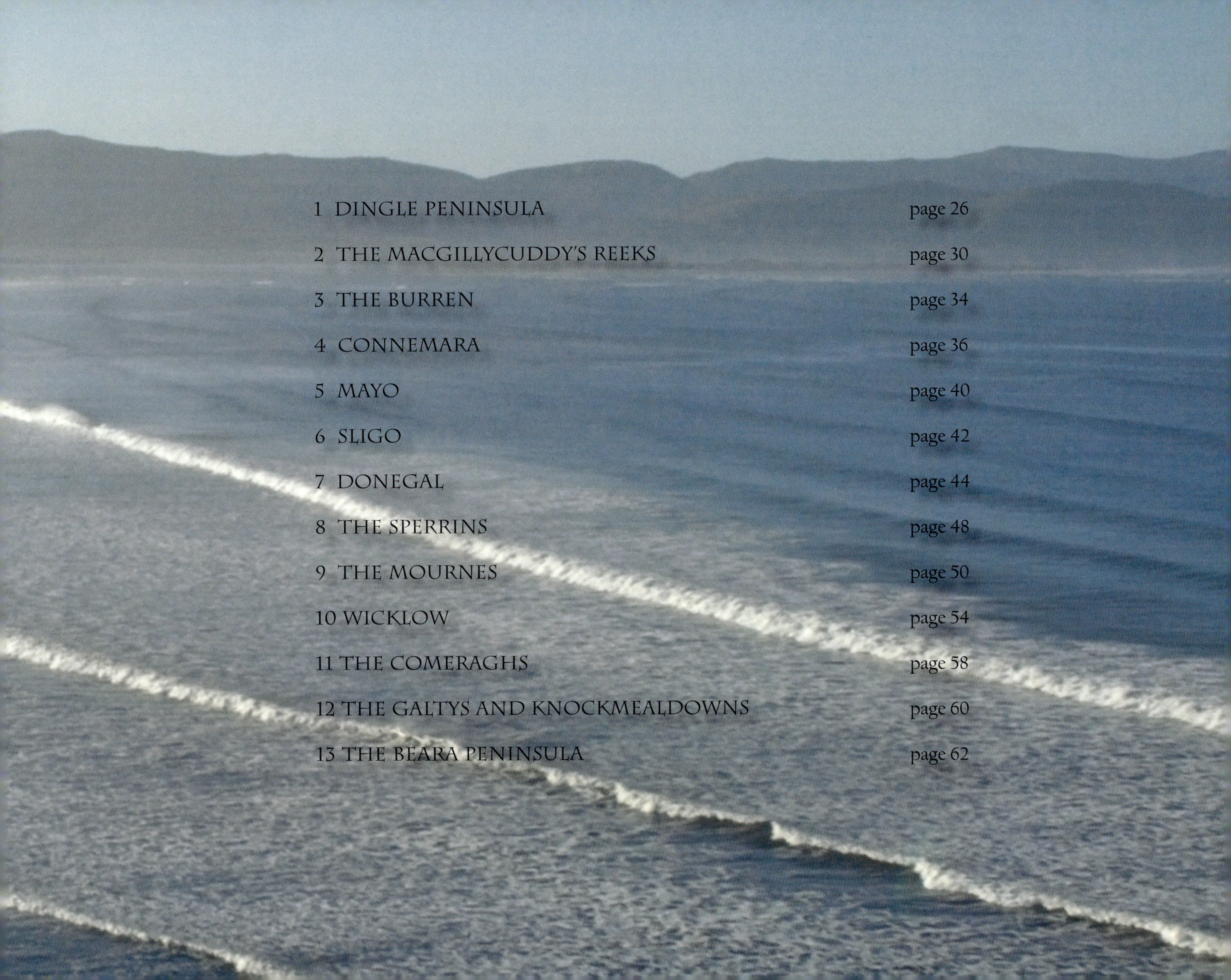

THE DINGLE PENINSULA

The Dingle Peninsula is the most westerly point of Ireland. Although relatively small, perhaps 35 kilometres long by 7 kilometres across, it contains some of the most aesthetically beautiful, and most satisfying mountains in Ireland, with unrivalled views to the ocean. The highest of these hills, and the second highest point in Ireland – Mount Brandon – rises in a continuous sweep from sea level in the space of a kilometre to 950 metres. Days spent on its wonderful paths and ridges are in the company of the sea in a way that is unique in the country. The waymarked trail of the Saints' Path leads easily from the west side to the summit oratory of St Brendan. Below, to the north, lies Brandon creek, where St Brendan set off in a leather boat for America.

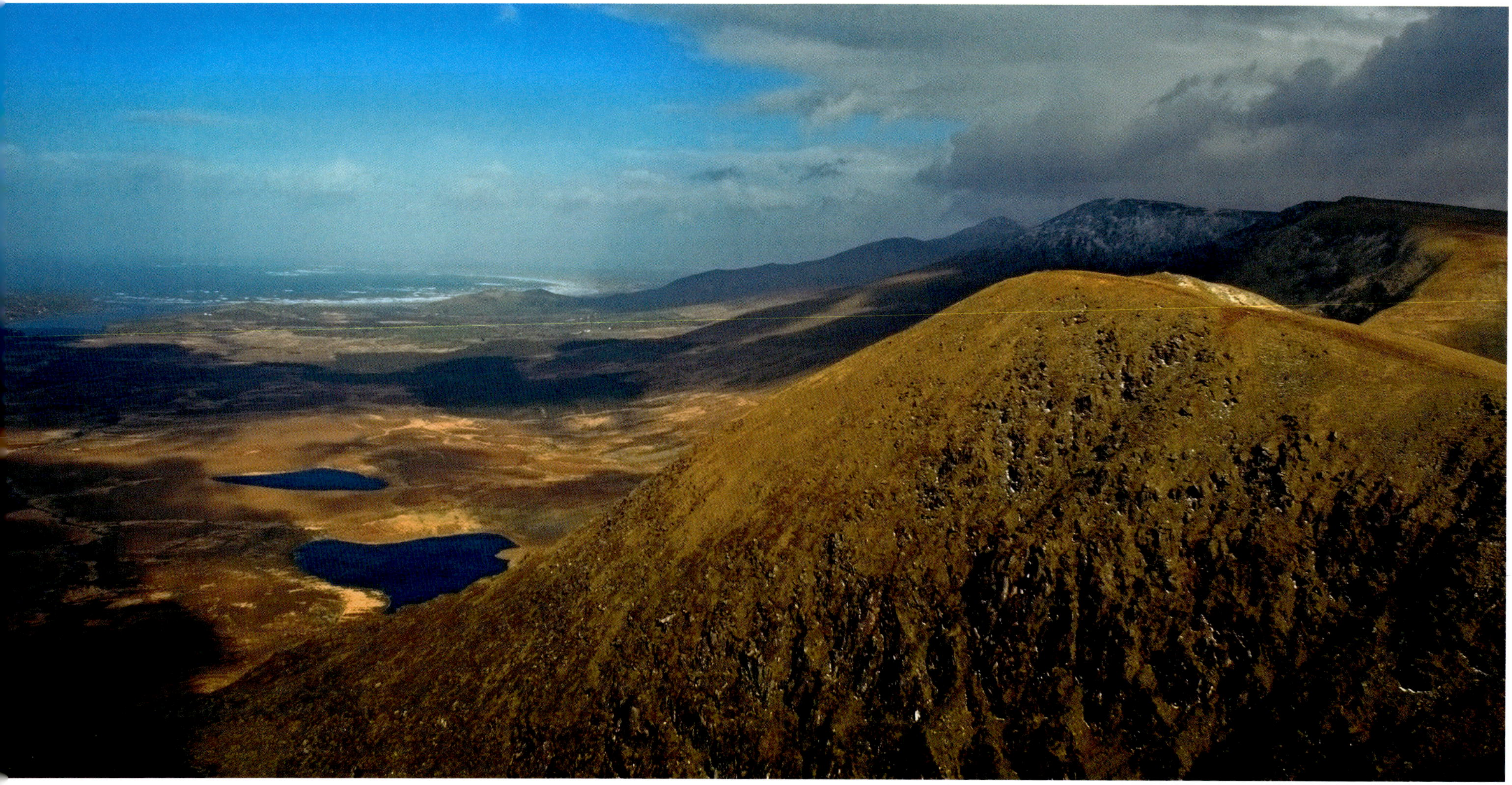

Looking towards Stradbally Mountain from Conor Pass, with Brandon Bay beyond.

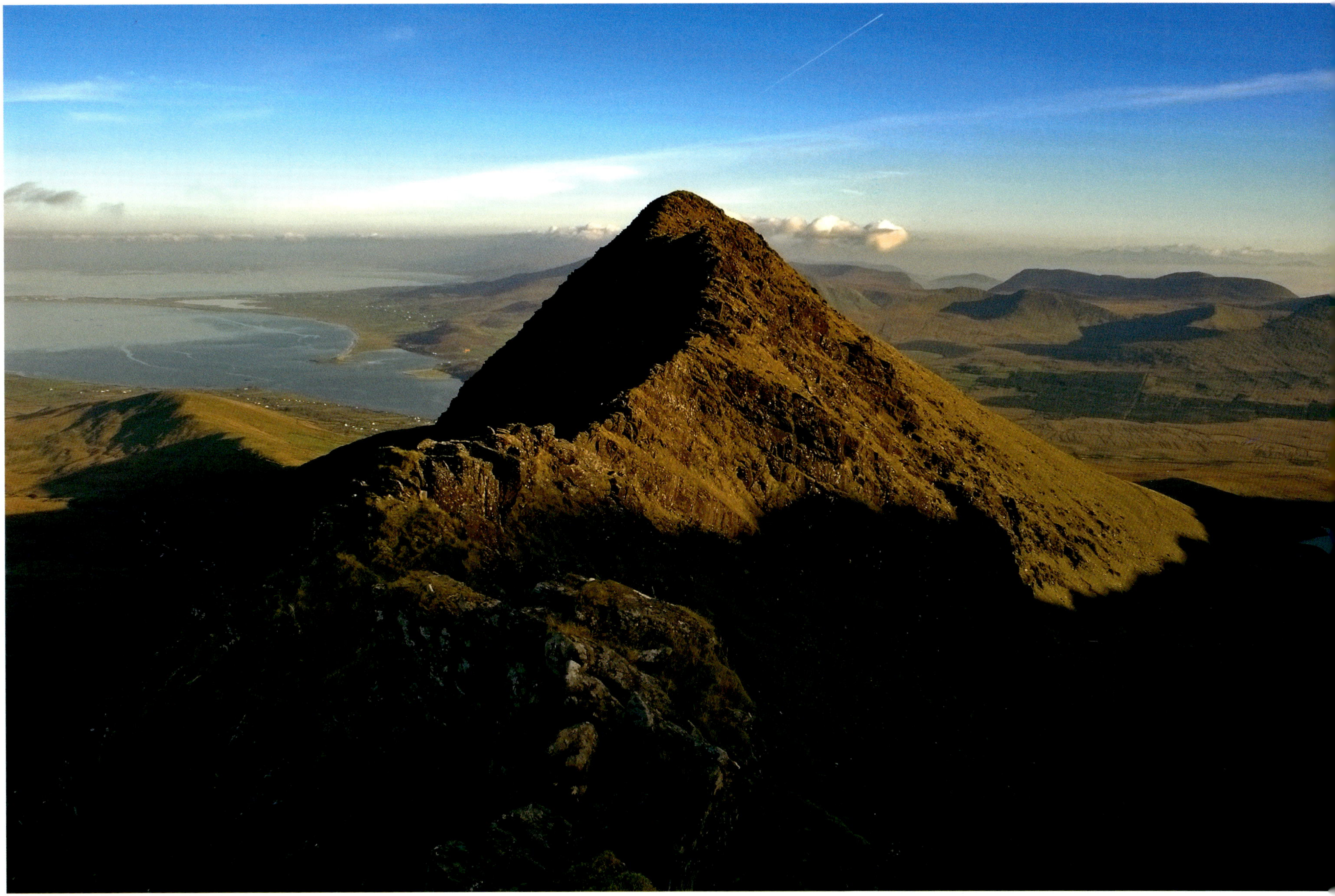

The Faha Ridge on Mount Brandon, looking towards the Maharees.

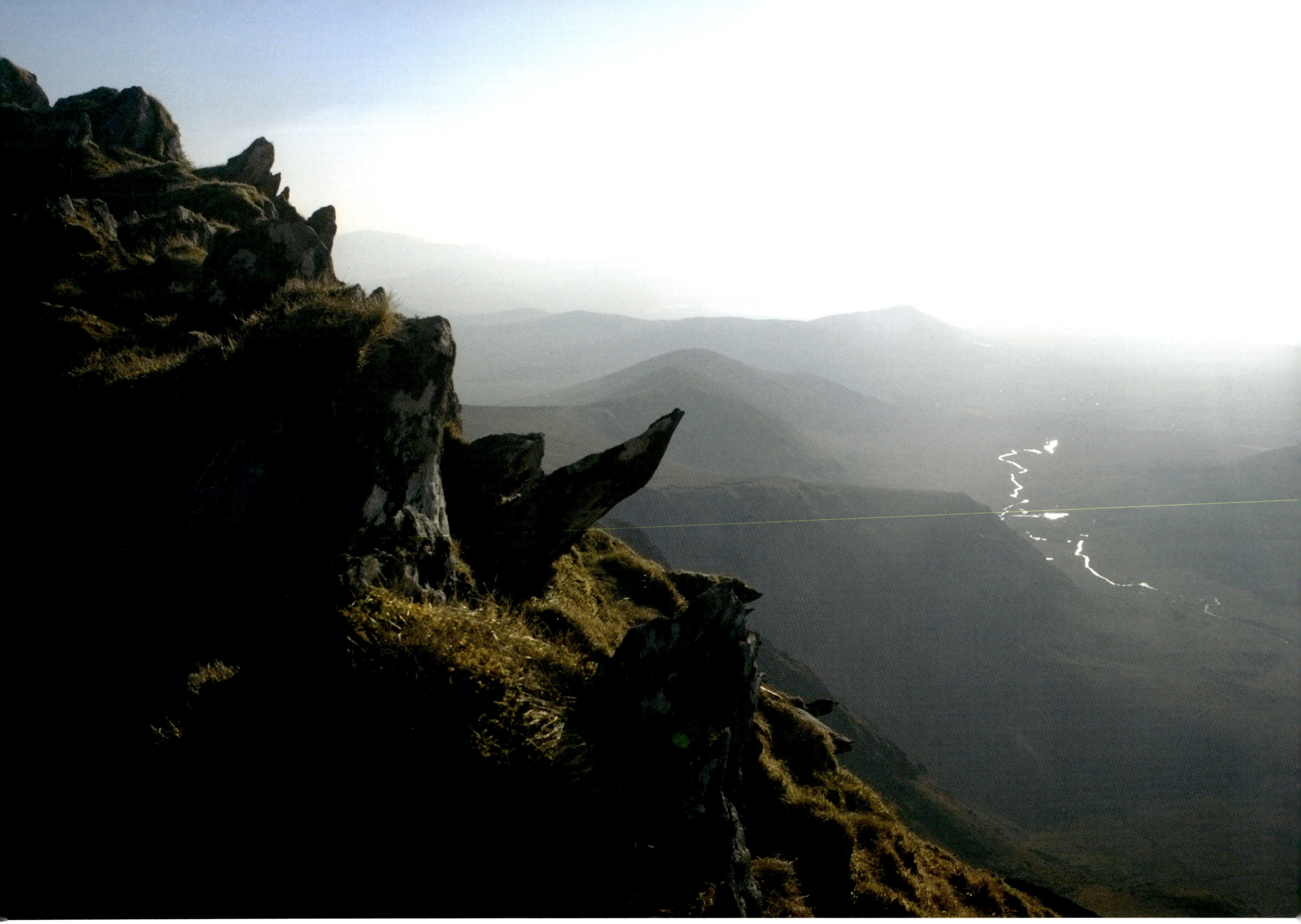

The spectacular road crossing at the Conor Pass separates Brandon from the next group, the hills around Stradbally Mountain. This area is rough underfoot and remote, with small jewelled lochans under the escarpments, and few tracks. A fine pass on foot crosses from Annascaul Lake, past spectacular waterfalls in the rugged Coom Dubh, to the north coast. To the east lie the Slieve Mish Mountains, seldom visited, and rising past the ancient fort of Caher Con Rí to the summit of Baurtregaun at 851 metres, with amazing views to the 5-kilometre sweep of Inch Strand, and across the bay to the Macgillycuddy's Reeks.

OPPOSITE Looking along Baile an Lochaig towards the Blasket Islands, from the south-west ridge of Brandon.

BELOW The wonderful flash of bog asphodel lights the hills in June.

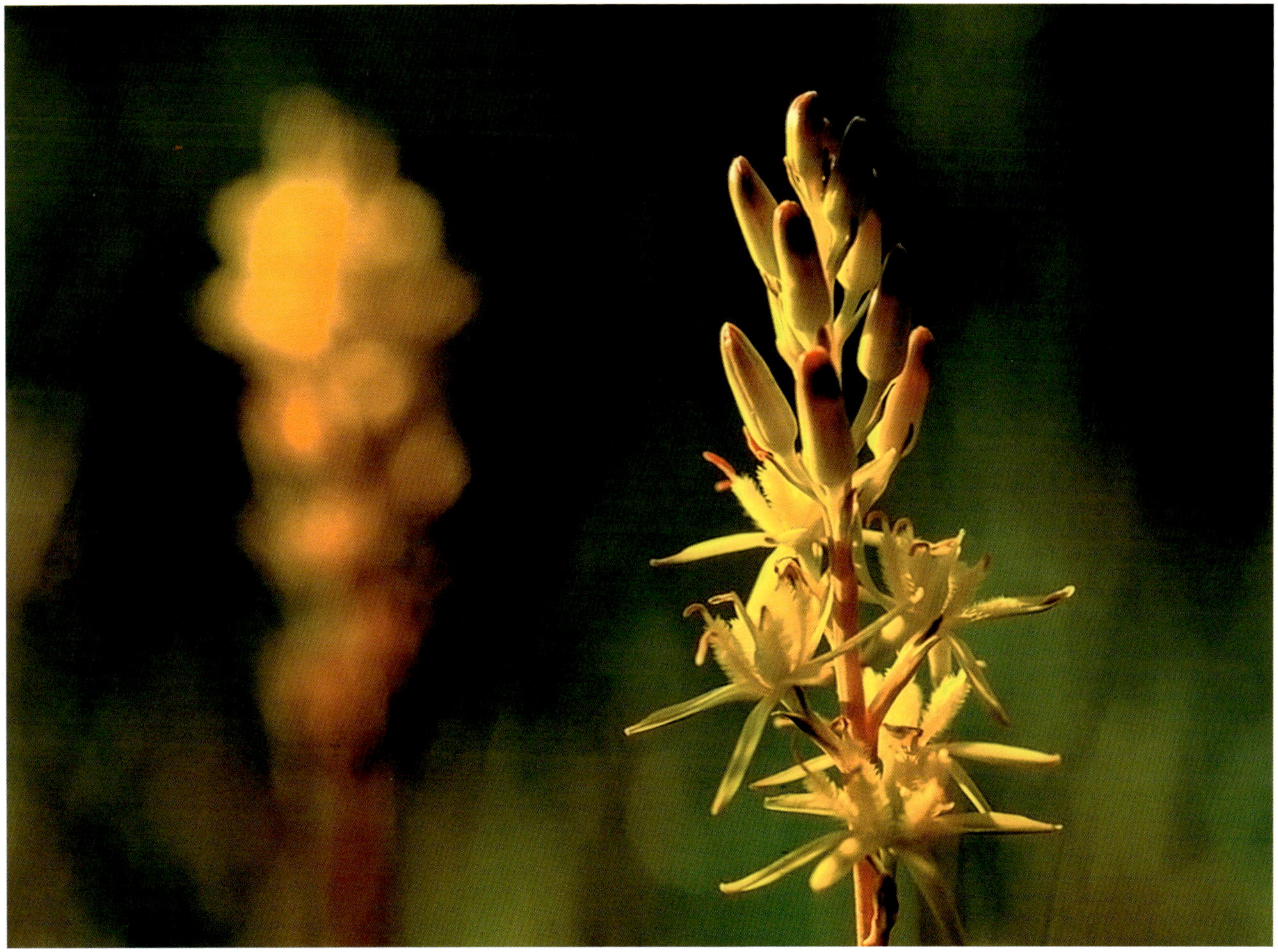

THE MACGILLYCUDDY'S REEKS

The Macgillycuddy's Reeks lie to the south of Killarney. They extend westwards from the edge of the Killarney National Park, which is centred mainly around the lakes of Lough Leane and the former Muckross Estate, to Glencar. From there a string of remote and rugged hills stretches along the length of the Iveragh Peninsula. Eastwards, the hills of Mangerton and the Paps run towards County Cork. The Reeks are serious hills, difficult to escape from in bad weather, and include the highest point in Ireland, Carrauntouhil at 1,039 metres. The easiest, and most popular approach to climbing Carrauntouhil is from the Hag's Glen. The more straightforward route takes the gully at the head of the glen, known as the Devil's Ladder, now badly eroded, but the most convenient way to descend. A more interesting route strikes up to the right to climb either left up through the Heavenly Gates, or right up O'Shea's Gully to join the ridge from Beenkeeragh. Another very beautiful route takes the ridge of Caher to reach the summit from the west. The traverse of the main ridge of the Reeks is a long and exciting outing. Much rock climbing exists in the Gap of Dunloe, and in rare winters of prolonged low temperatures and snow, there is good ice-climbing on the northerly cliffs of Carrauntouhil.

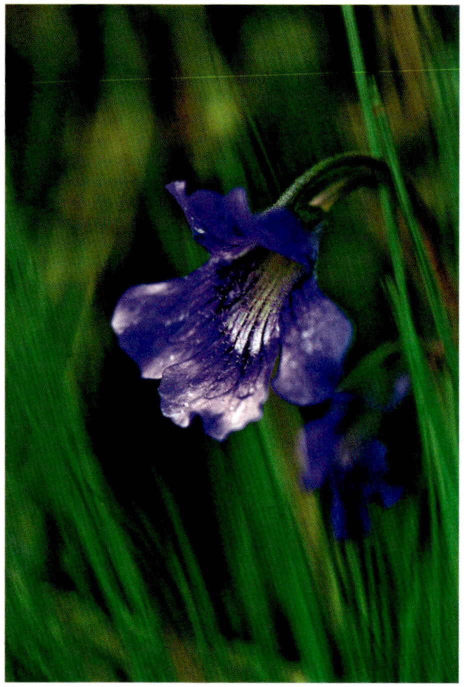

RIGHT 'Kerry' butterwort, a large-flowered variety of the common butterwort found only in this area.

FAR RIGHT Sunrise on Carrauntouhil from the Hag's Glen.

OPPOSITE Looking across to the Reeks from Torc Mountain, late on a summer evening.

OVERLEAF Evening light on the magnificent spread of the western end of the Macgillycuddy's Reeks. The peaks extend from Beenkeragh (left) to Caher, Broaghnabinnia and the Bridia Valley.

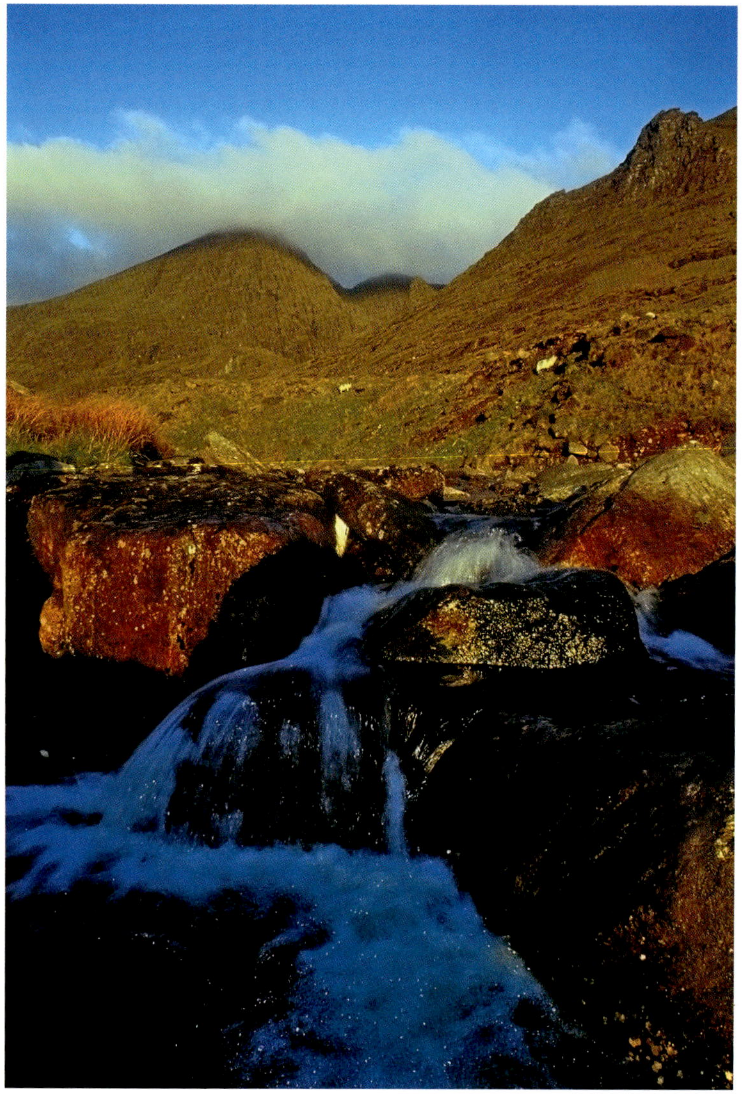

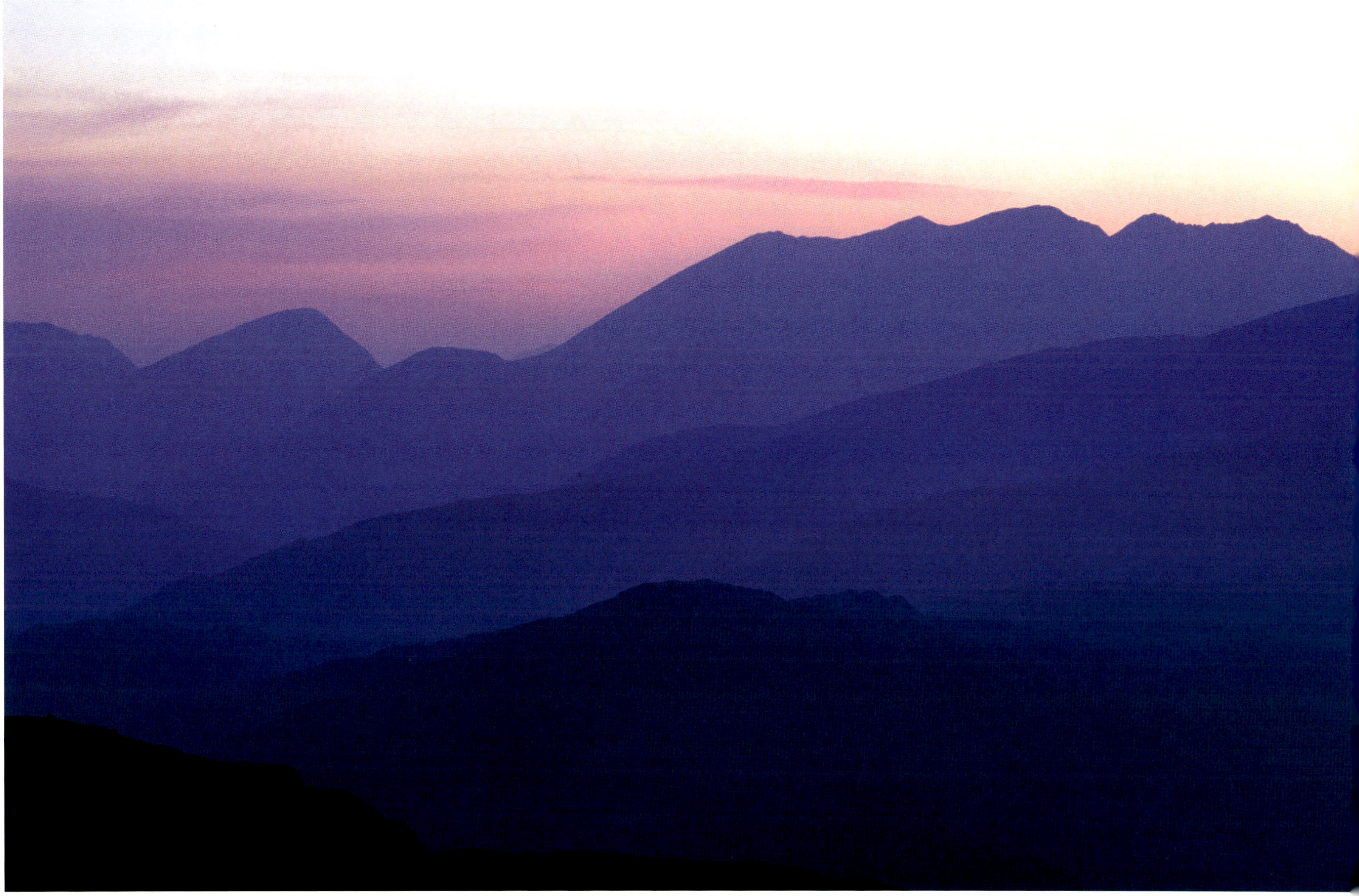

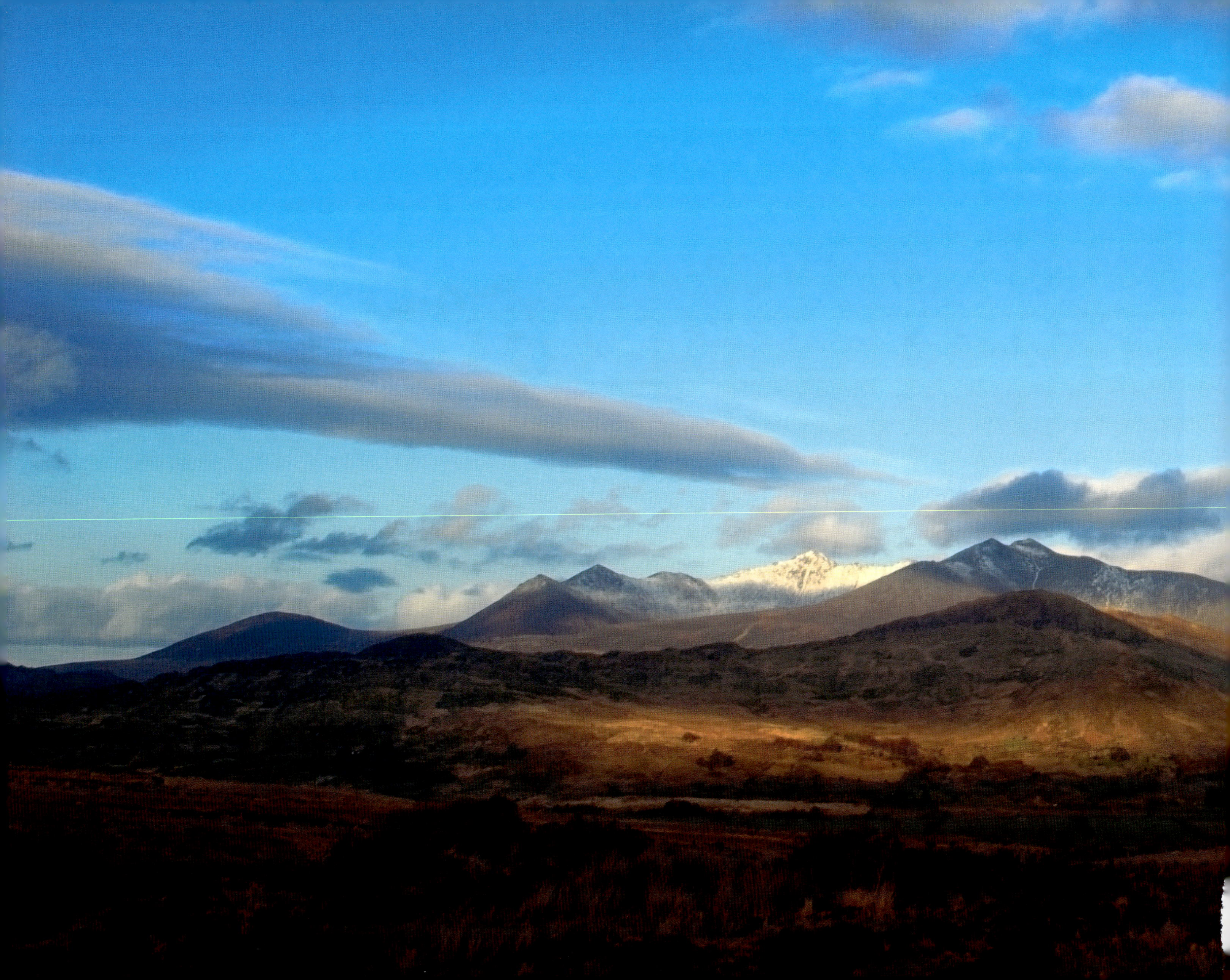

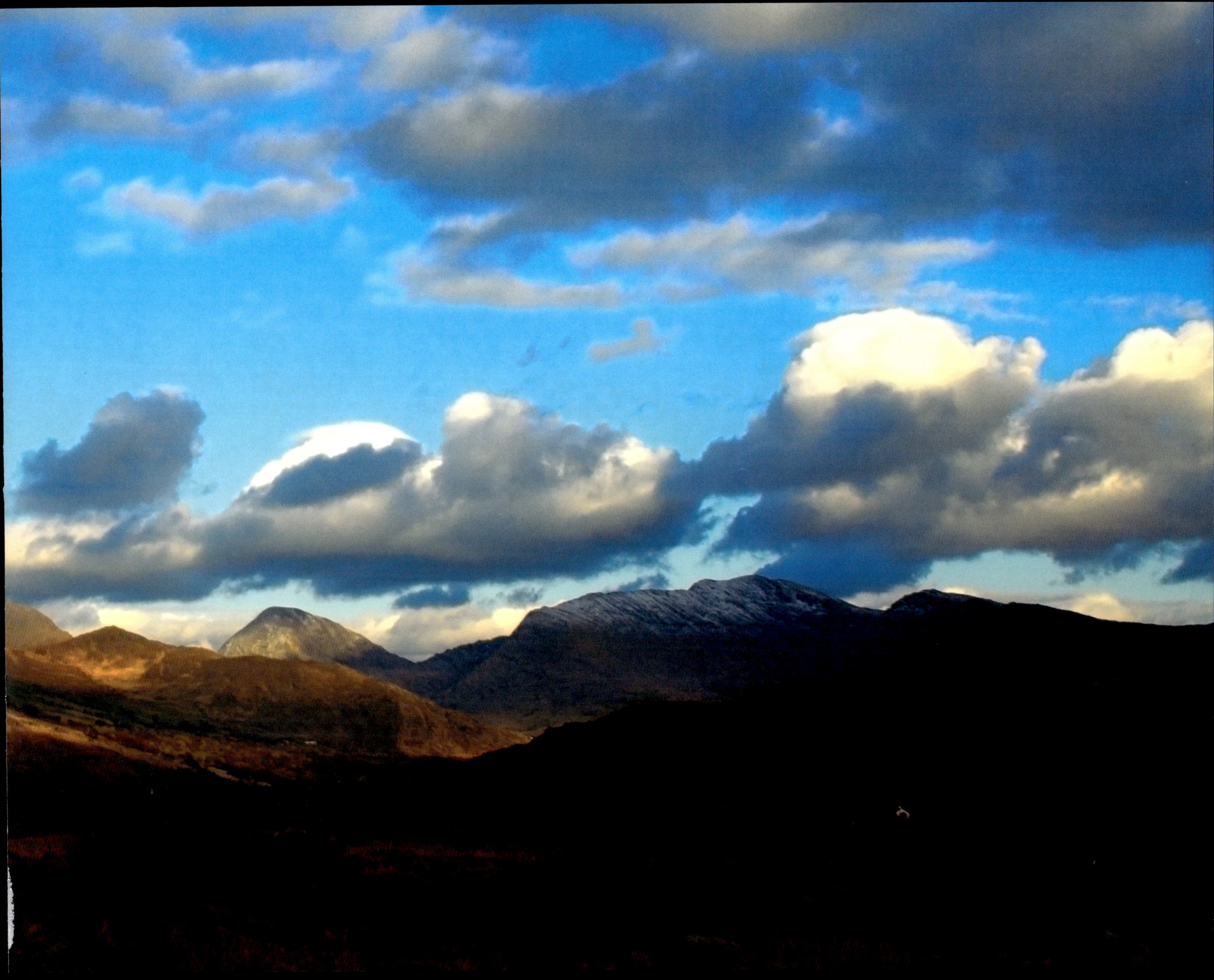

THE BURREN

In the northwest of County Clare, the sheet of limestone that underlies the predominantly sandstone rock of south-west Ireland, emerges as the fantastic seamed wonderland of stone that is the Burren. The water-eroded crevices of these waves of bare hills offer shelter to plants found only in this place in Ireland, and in Europe only in the Alpine regions of France and Italy. These hills rise to a mere 343 metres on Slieve Elva, but have every bit the feeling of mountains; the rocky, fissured terrain can be difficult to negotiate. April and May see the emergence of the flowers, reaching a blazing peak in late June. Days spent here at that time, under a wide clear sky with the skylark singing overhead, feel like a preview of heaven.

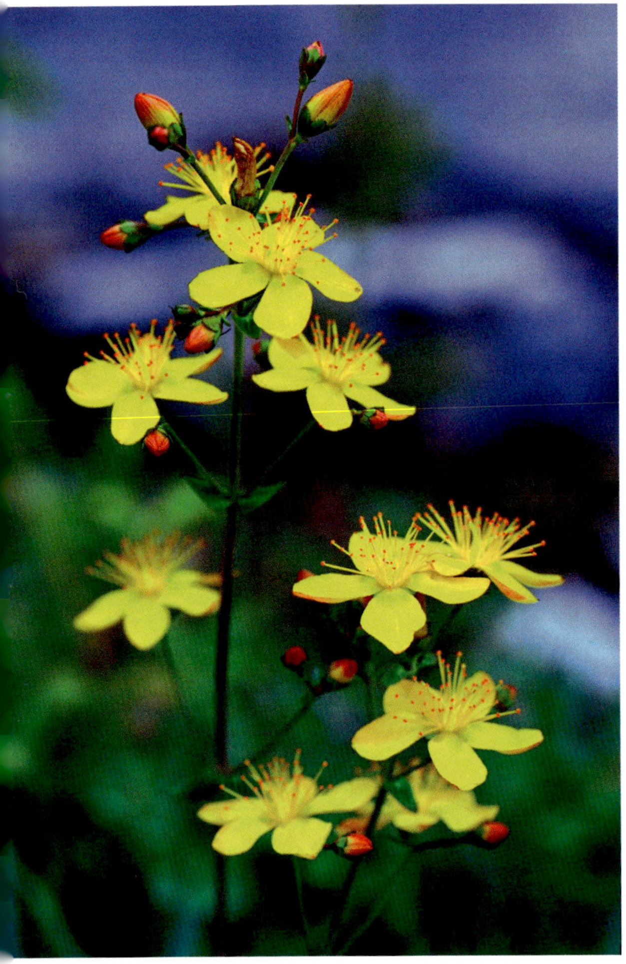

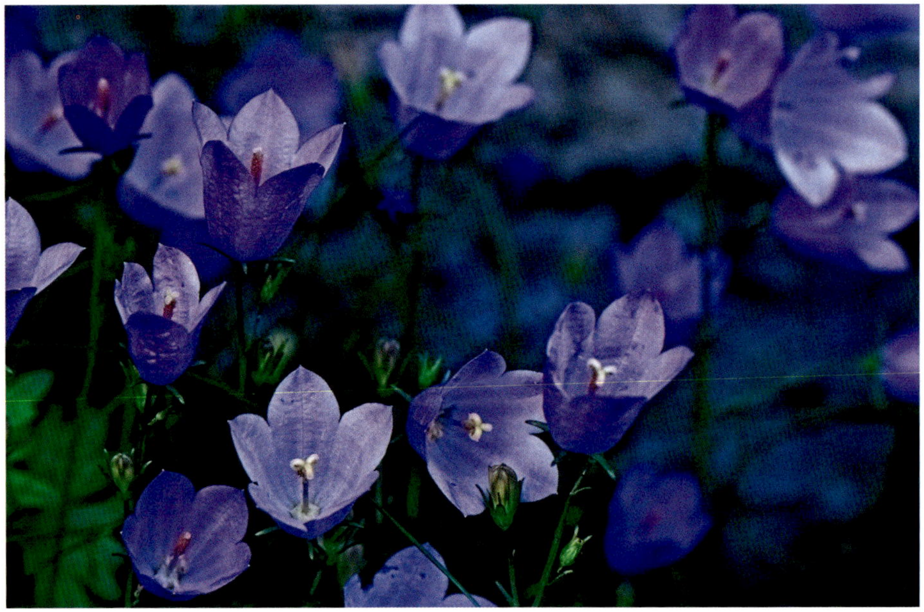

LEFT St John's Wort, one of the many unusual plants which thrive in the shelter of the crevices of the Burren's seamed limestone landscape.

ABOVE Harebell, a lover of limestone soil, flourishes here in summer.

OPPOSITE The striking stratified pavements of limestone above Fanore in the northwest of County Clare, the heart of the Burren.

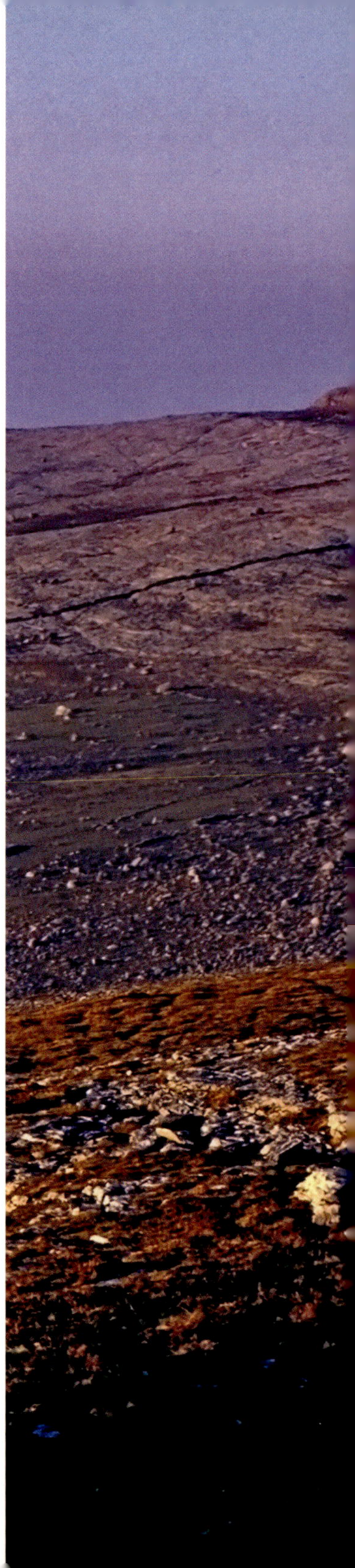

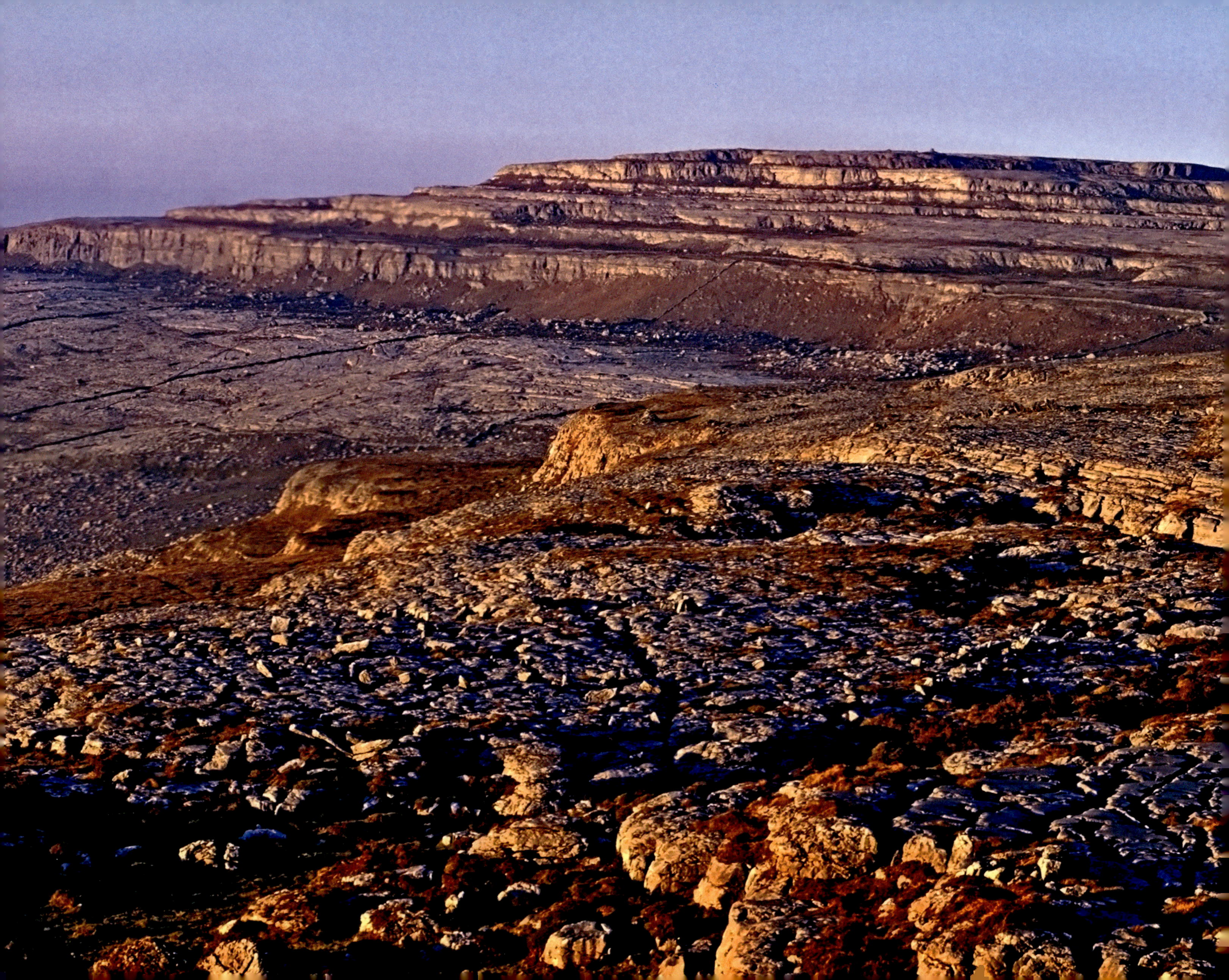

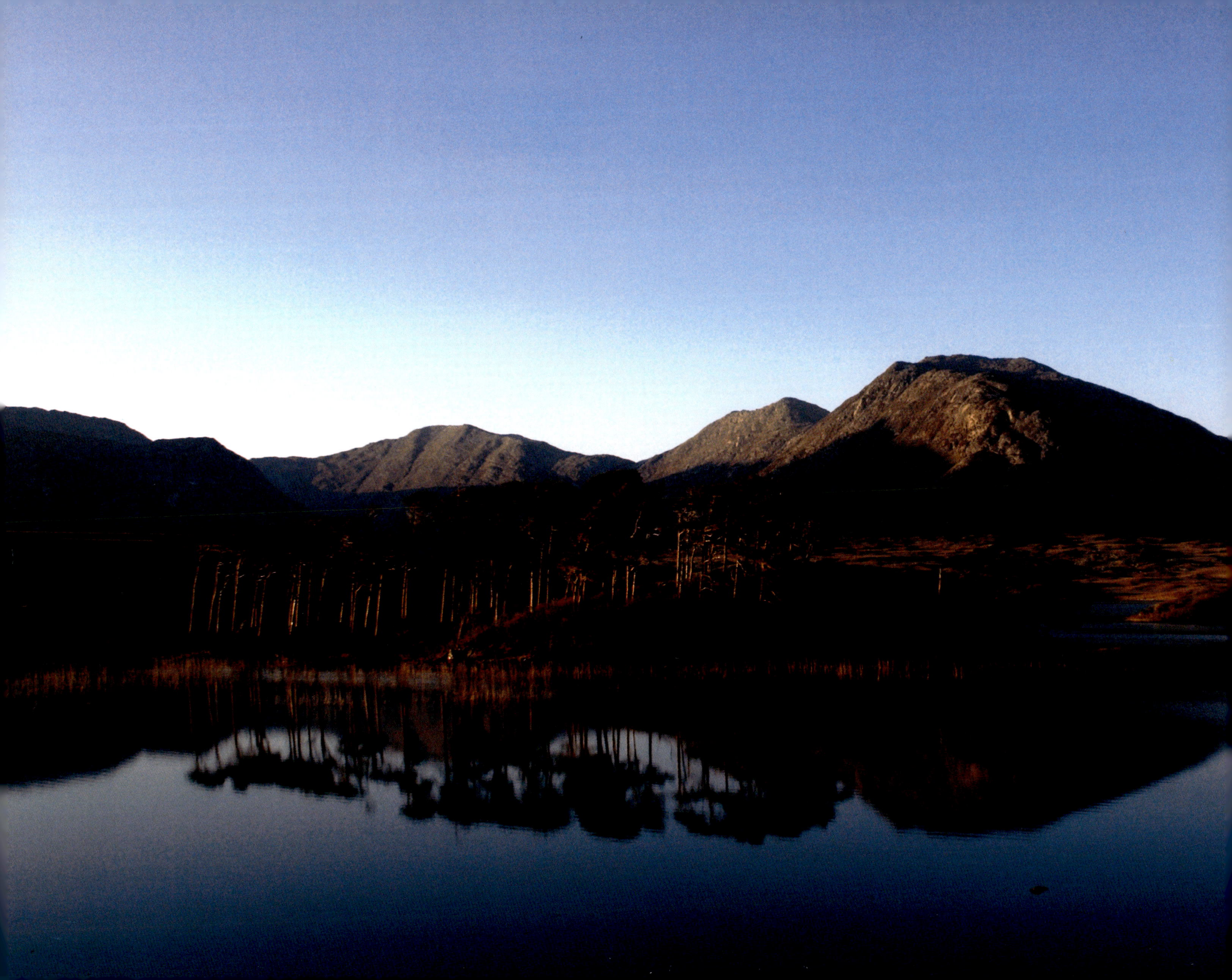

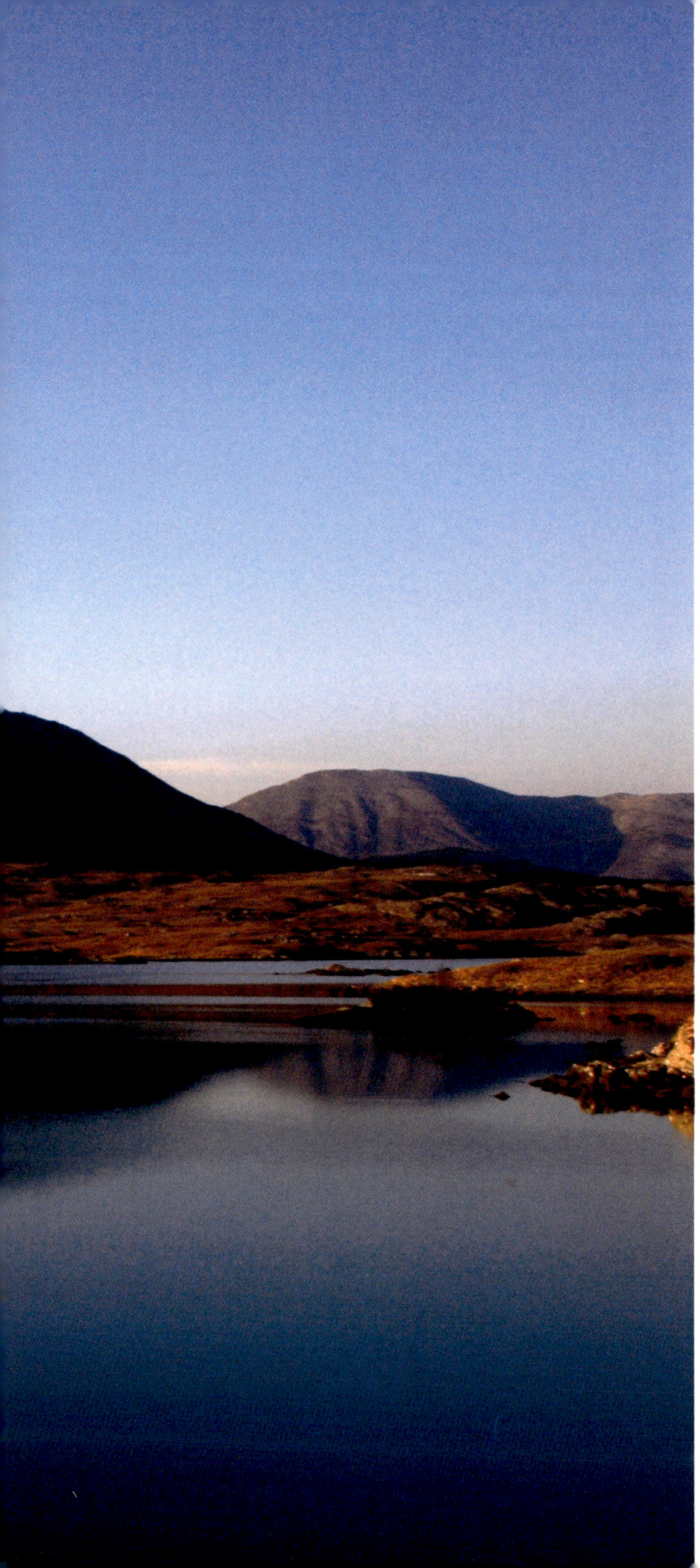

CONNEMARA

Connemara is wild, variations on a theme of water and stone. The Twelve Bens, twelve summits in a rough horseshoe around the headwaters of the Owenglin River above Clifden, reaching a height of 727 metres on Benbaun, stand in isolation amidst bogs strewn with many hundreds of lakes. The northernmost peaks are included in the Connemara National Park. Aross the Inagh Valley to the east lie the Maumturk Mountains, less rocky and more rounded, but equally wild. The proximity of the Bens to the sea leaves the hills exposed to a maritime climate of successions of storm and sun; here is weather in variety. The approach to the hills is wet and generally intricate, with few paths, but the reward of reaching the heights is magnificent. Quartzite rock, with huge outcroppings of pure white quartz, lies at the surface of the succession of ridges, giving wonderful, dry walking of a kind which is rare in Ireland.

OPPOSITE The south-eastern end of the Twelve Bens from Lough Derryclare, with the Maumturks on the distant right.

BELOW Bell heather thrives on the boggy slopes of the Bens.

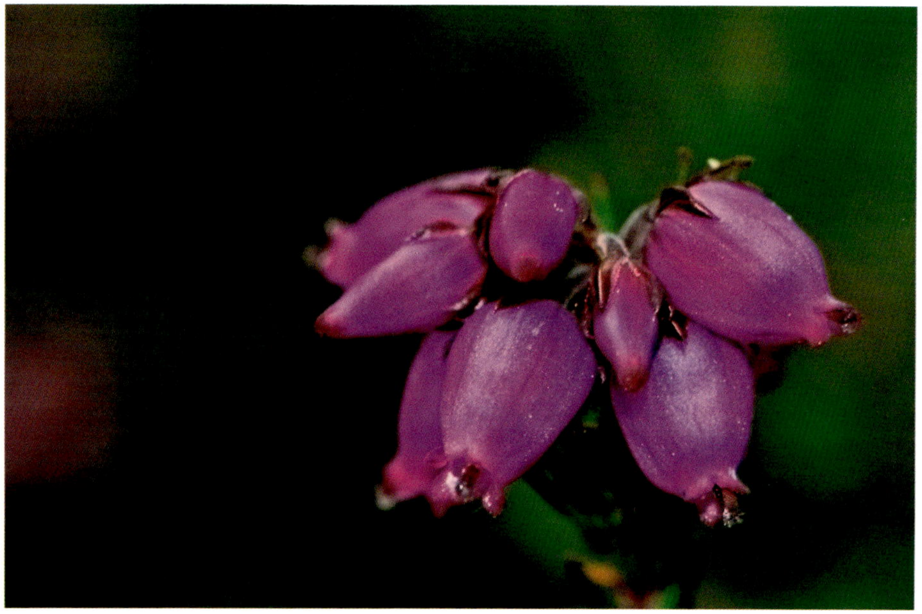

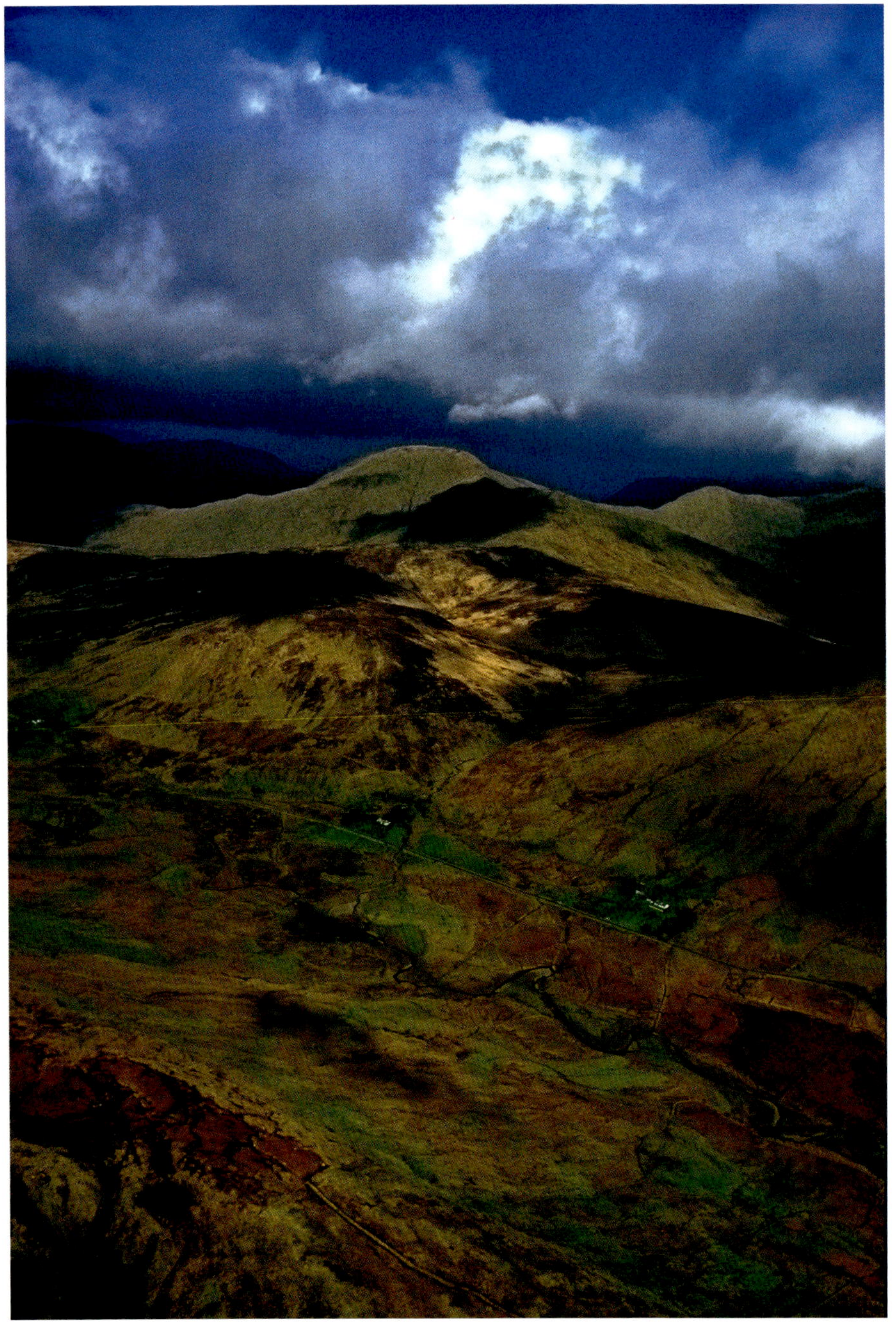

On a sunny day, a traverse of sections of a ridge, such as the Derryclare–Bencorr horseshoe, has a quality of magic about it. The views from the ridges extend to the south over the lake-sprinkled wastes of Roundstone Bog, and eastwards to the islands of the ocean. In reality, these are low hills, but in winter with snow underfoot, or in fog, this is a serious place to walk in.

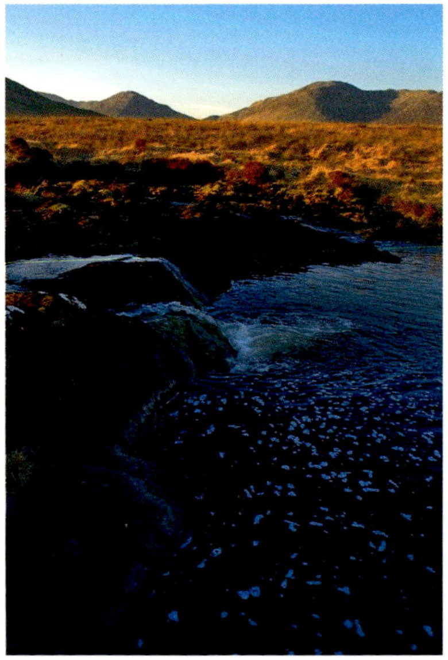

LEFT An aerial view of the Bens from the southeast.

ABOVE The Maumturks.

OPPOSITE The Twelve Bens seen to the north across Roundstone Bog.

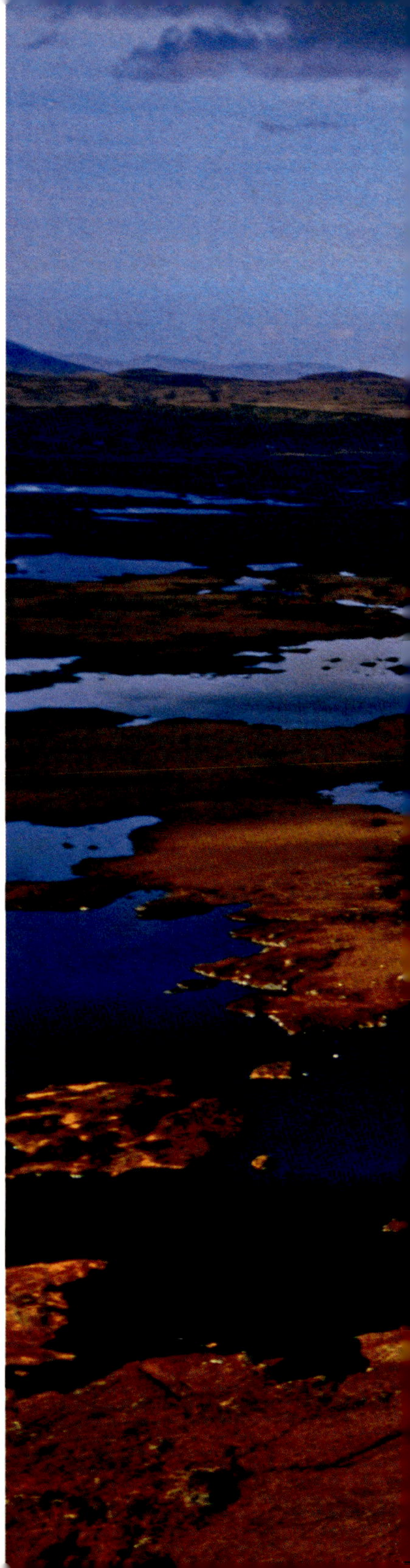

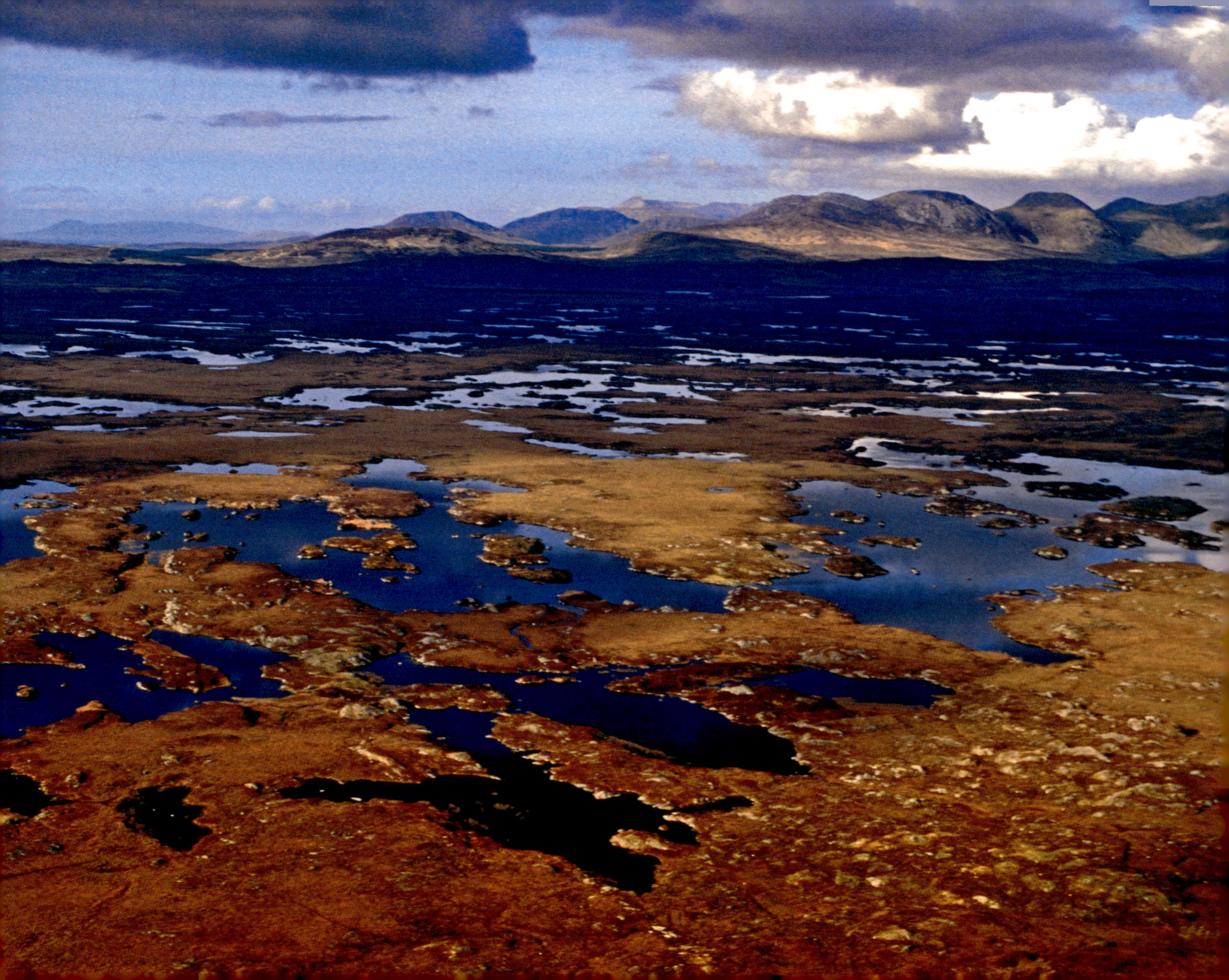

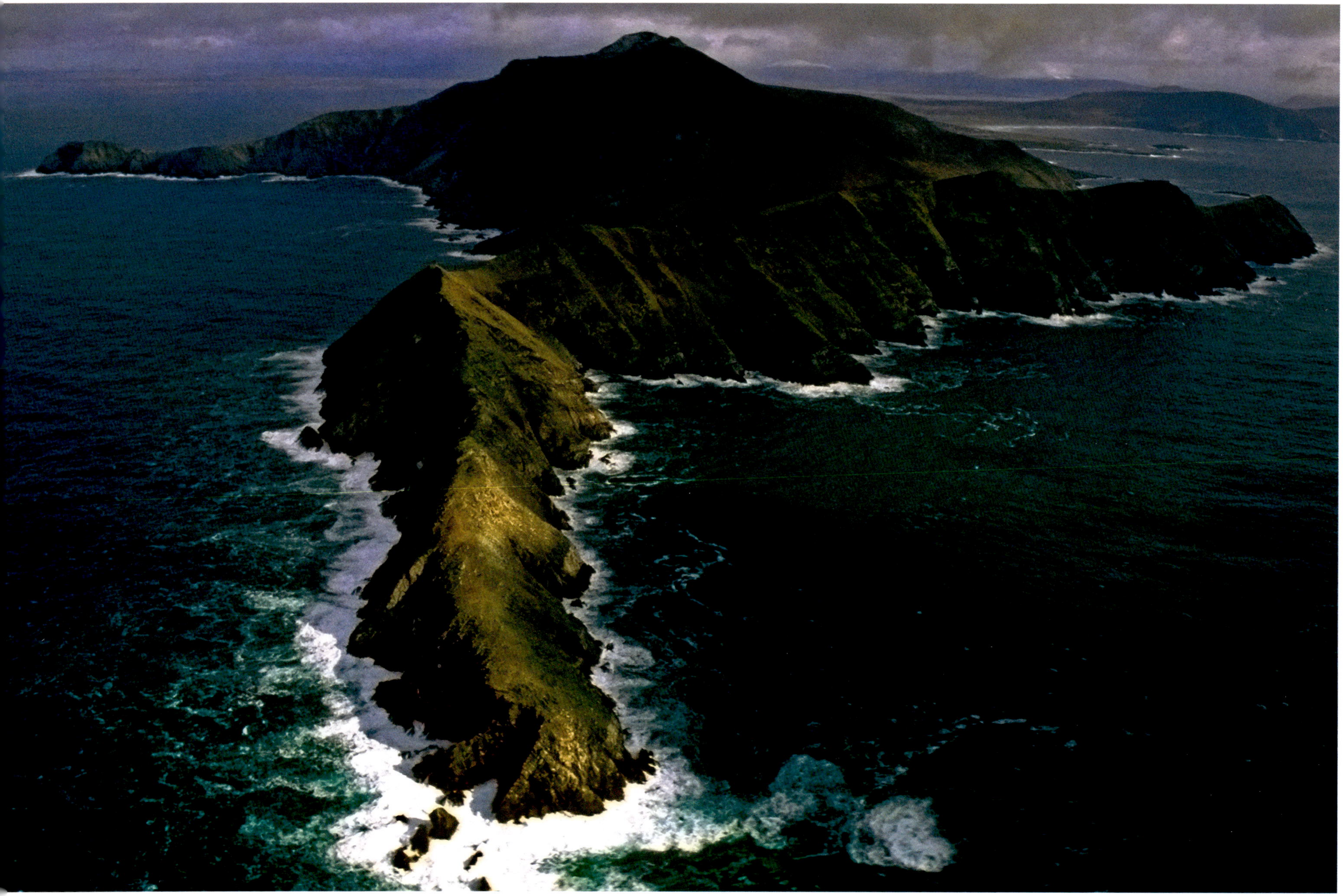

MAYO

This huge, empty region is moulded from the bog, lifting into ranges of rounded hills in the Partry Mountains, the Sheeffry Hills, the Nephin Beg Range. In the south, above Killary Harbour, lies the great bulk of Mweelrea, rising to 817 metres above a beach of golden sand to the west, and falling to the beautiful Dubh Lough Valley to the north. Farther north, on the southern shores of Clew Bay, stands the impressive fin of Croagh Patrick. The ridge can often be shrouded in cloud, but the way to the summit is clear on the broad thread of the Pilgrims' Trail; on such occasions, a sudden clearing of the cloud can leave one astonished at the sheer drop to the sea. To the northwest of Clew Bay the land reaches out into the spectacular Achill Island, scarcely separated from the mainland, and rising to 688 metres on the peak of Croaghaun.

OPPOSITE Achill Island. The long westerly ridge of Croaghan reaches out into the ocean.

RIGHT The spectacular fjord of Killary Harbour at Leenane, seen at dawn. Here we leave behind Connemara's Twelve Bens to move into the remote, boggy wildness of western Mayo.

FAR RIGHT Croagh Patrick, with its summit church poised 764 metres above Clew Bay. Each year on the last Sunday in July, ('Reek Sunday'), pilgrims walk the rough trail barefoot to the church.

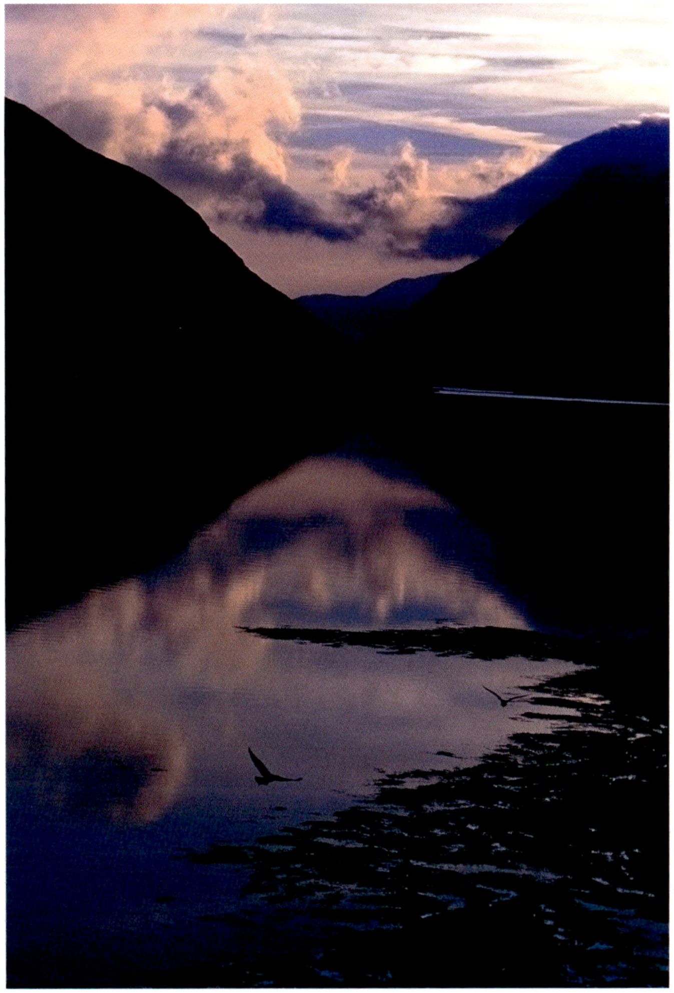

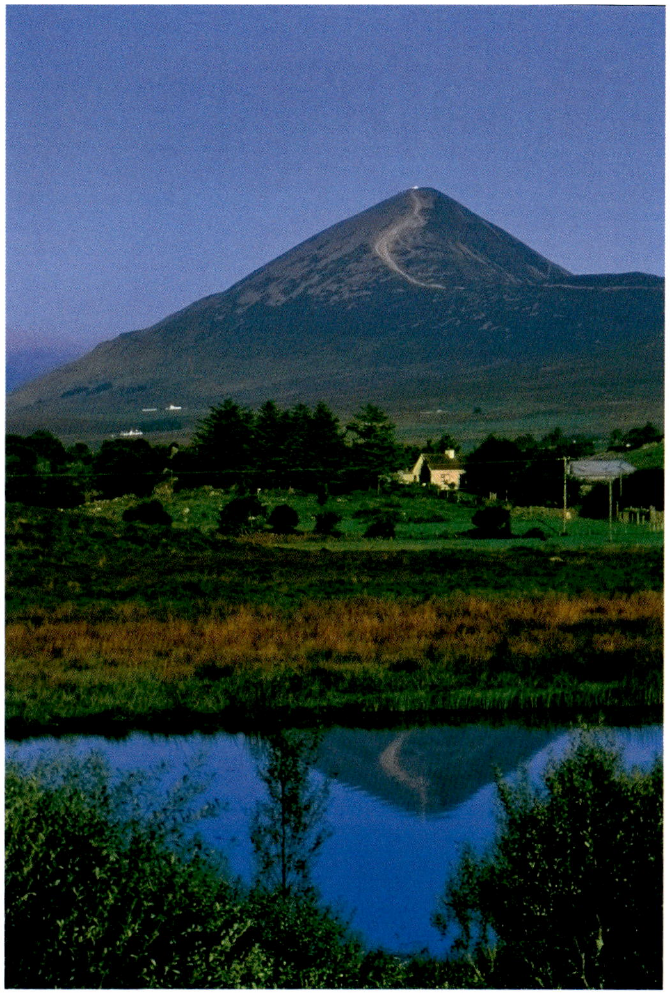

SLIGO

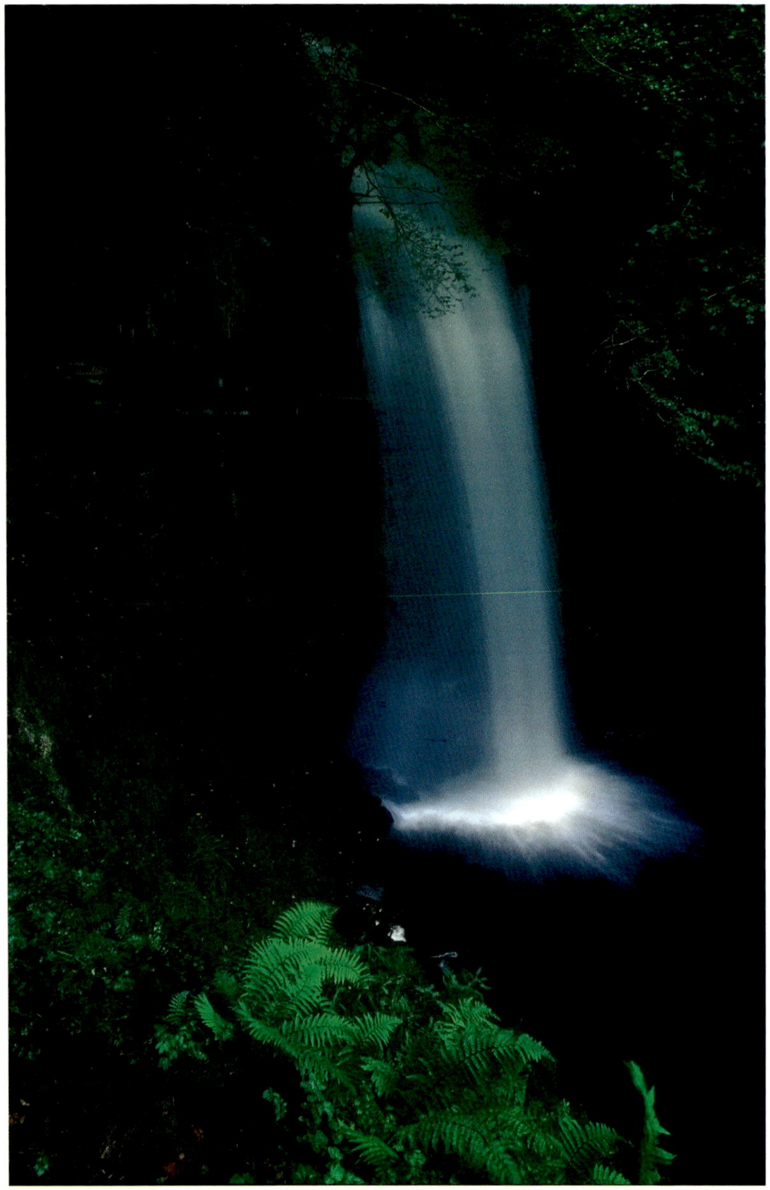

The startling profiles of Ben Bulben, King's Mountain, and Truskmore, reaching a height of 647 metres, dominate the whole of north Sligo. Few easy routes penetrate the encircling cliffs of water-eroded limestone, giving the summit plateau a great sense of remoteness, and requiring good navigation to descend in bad weather. Days spent on these shy uplands will almost certainly be in solitude. The northern aspect overlooks Donegal Bay, with Slieve League standing 50 kilometres away. To the south is the mellow, wooded valley of Glencar, with its tumbling waterfalls, and beyond, the romantic and famed Lough Gill, reaching into Leitrim.

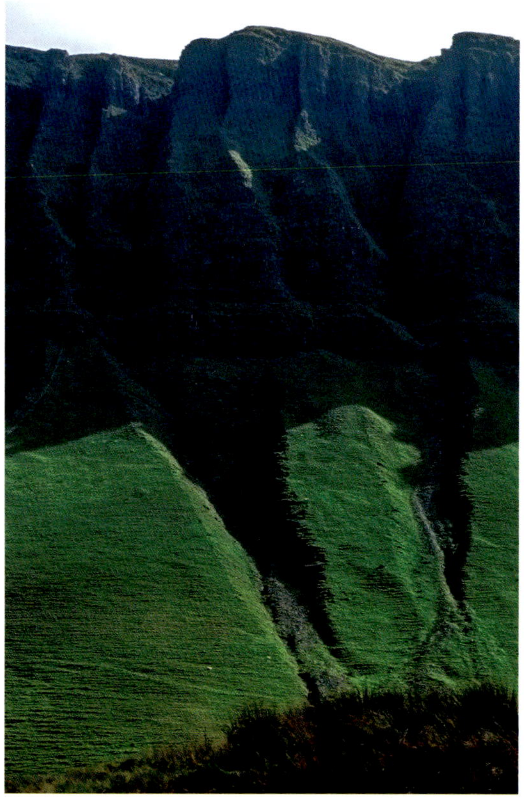

LEFT Water erosion has shaped the dramatic peaks of north Sligo. Here a fall plunges from the western edge of King's Mountain.

RIGHT Deep gullies cut into the north-west edge of Ben Bulben.

OPPOSITE Ben Bulben from the north.

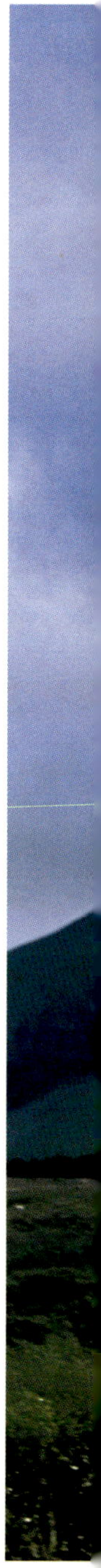

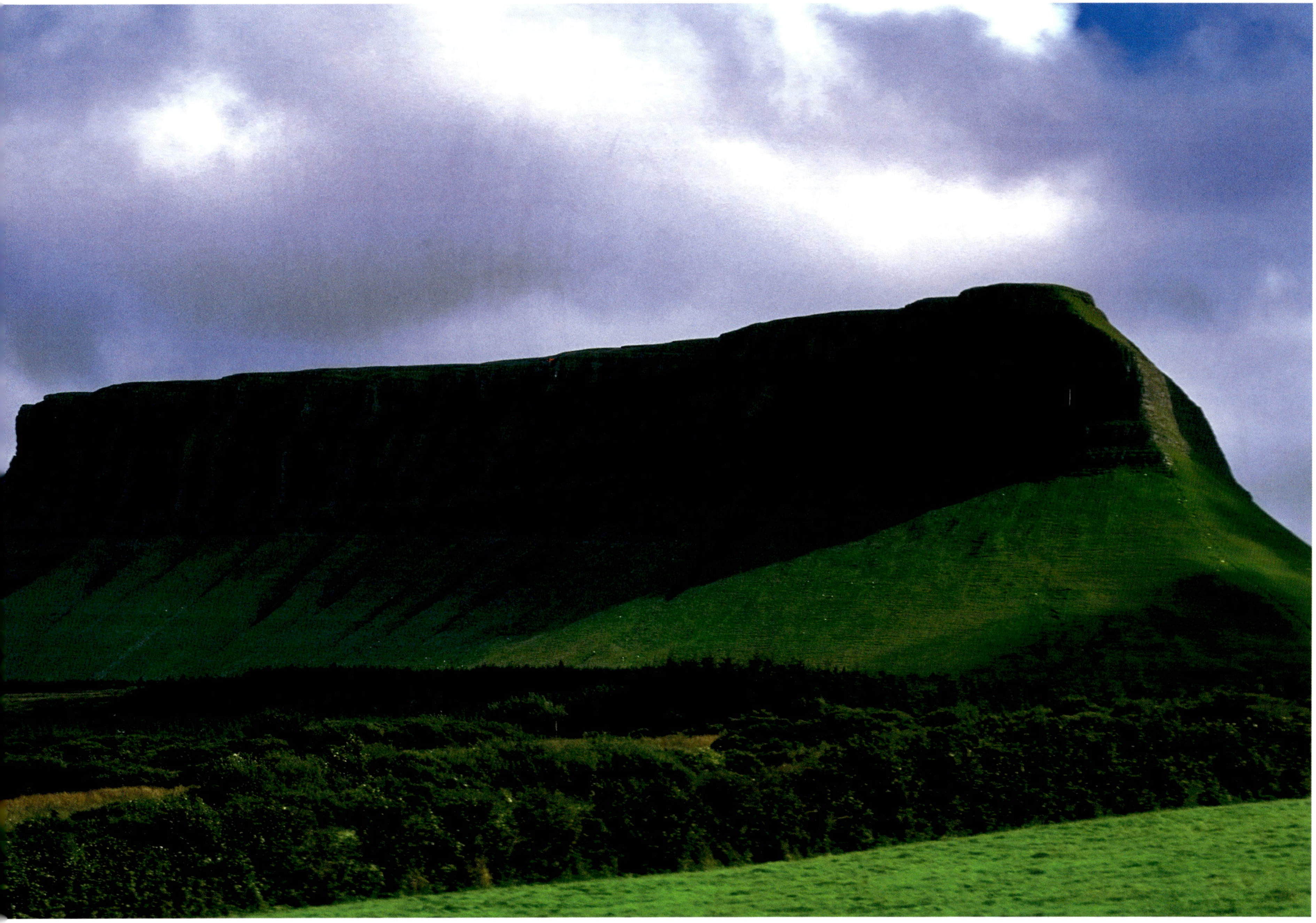

DONEGAL

Donegal, to me, is the jewel in the crown of Irish mountain areas. Here, there is a sense of purity and remoteness not to be found in any other area. The coastline in the south-west corner of the county rears up into the magnificent cliff of Slieve League, 595 metres sheer from summit to sea. A traverse of the ridge from east to west, crossing One Man's Pass to the summit, then returning by the Pilgrim's Path, is a wonderful outing. Further north lies the stunningly beautiful Glenveagh National Park, with the classic mountain profile of Errigal, at 752 metres to the west, and the long ridge of Slieve Snaght, with the spectacular coom of the Poisoned Glen, to the east. An ascent of the eastern ridge of Errigal in the late evening is an unforgettable experience. Rocky, and narrow at the summit, it feels like a real mountain. Linger here, and savour the beauty of mountains stretching to every side, and beyond, to the west, the ocean.

BELOW Cotton grass, or bog cotton, thrives in the wet areas surrounding the peaks.

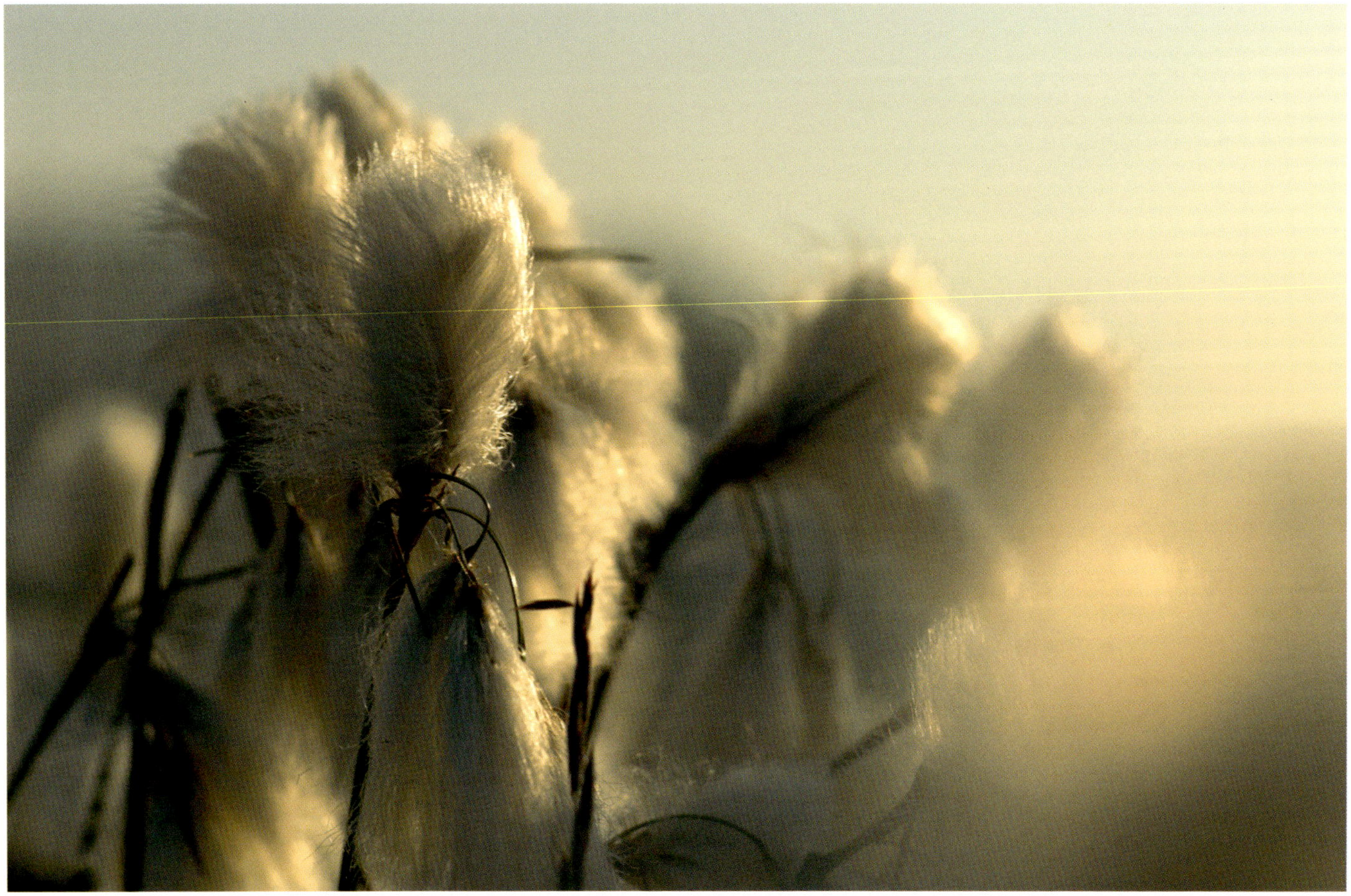

OPPOSITE Descending Errigal at sunset, looking northwest into the wonderful, remote purity of this amazing corner of Ireland.

OVERLEAF Errigal from the west at sunset, with the peaks of the Glenveagh National Park to the right.

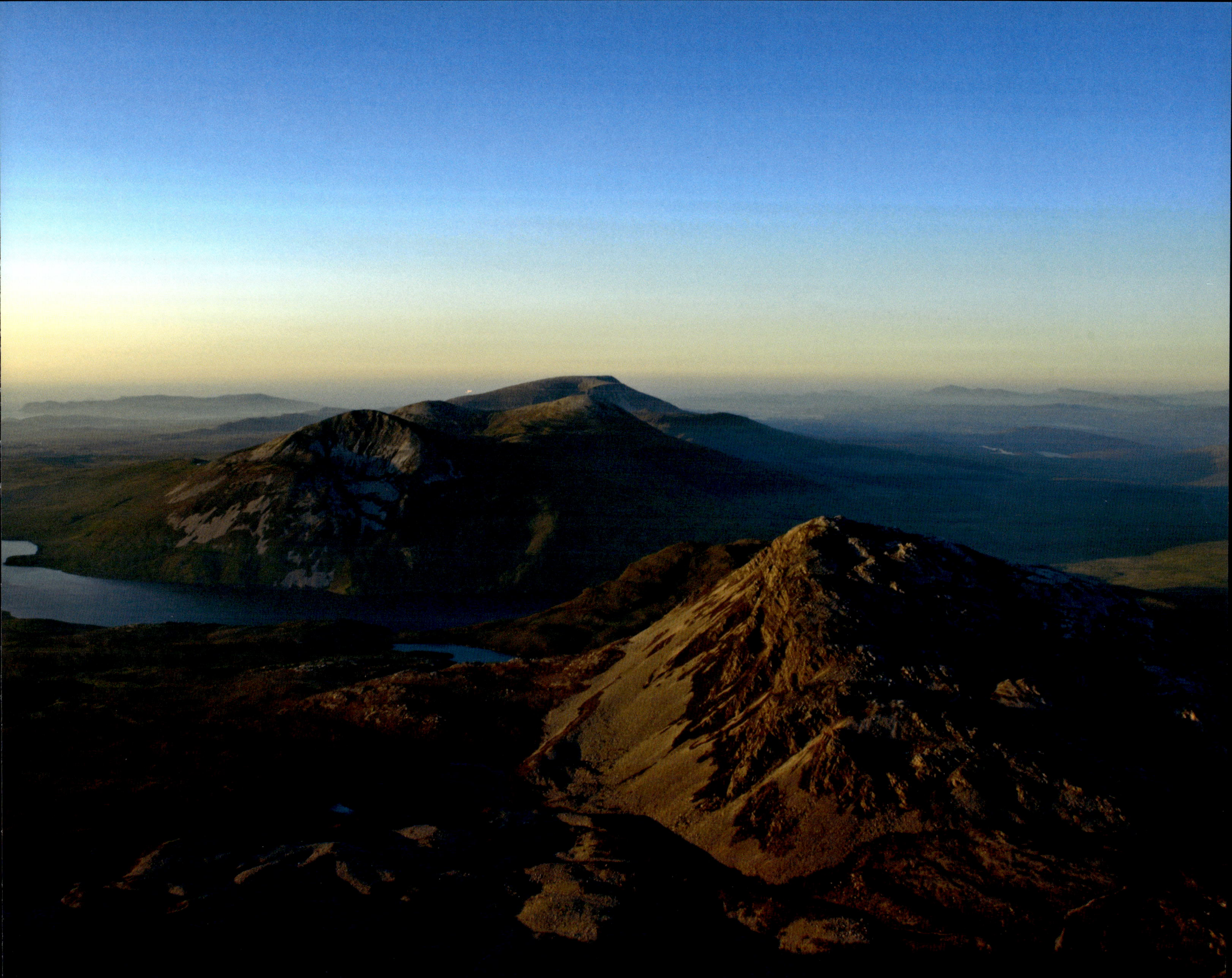

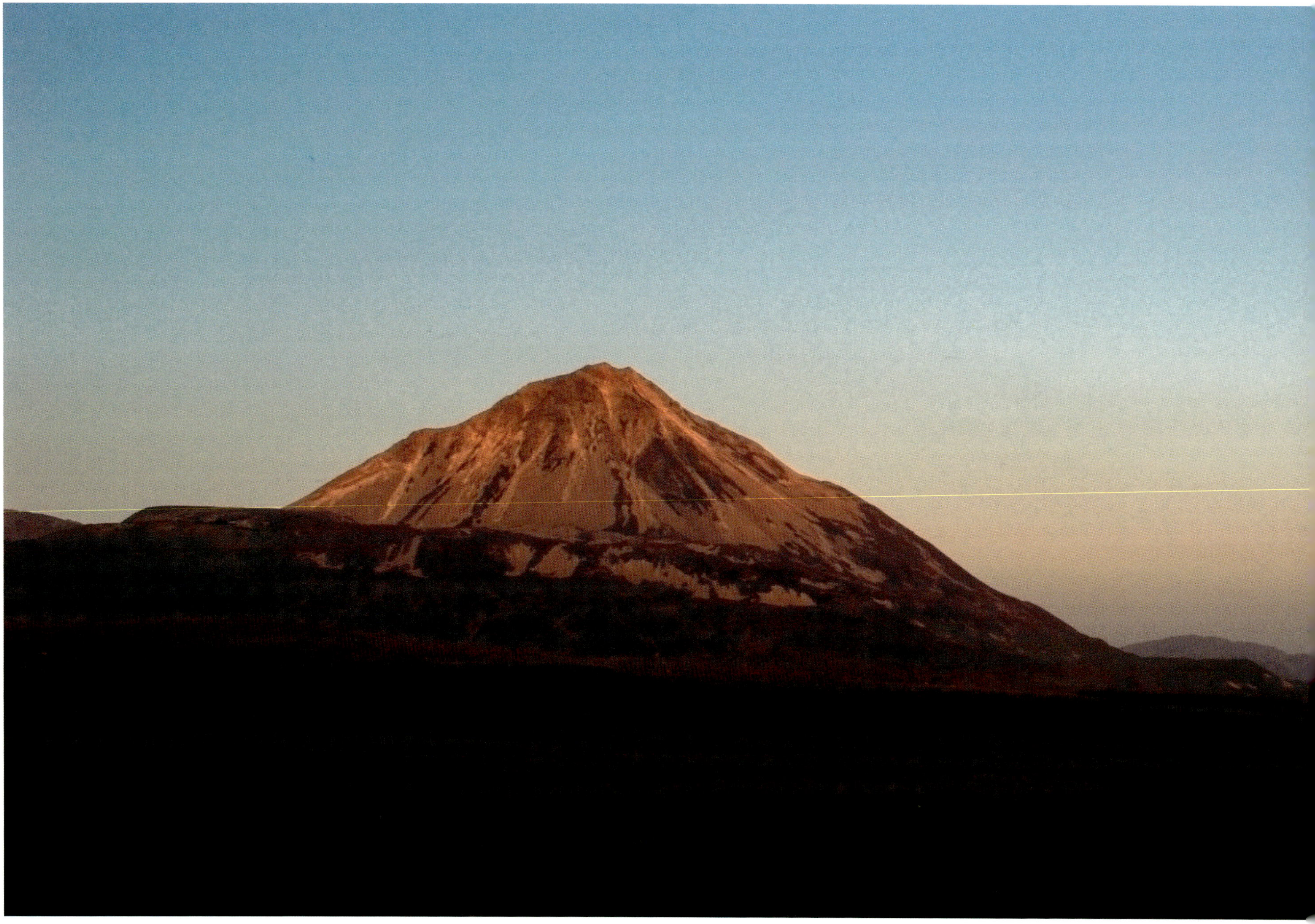

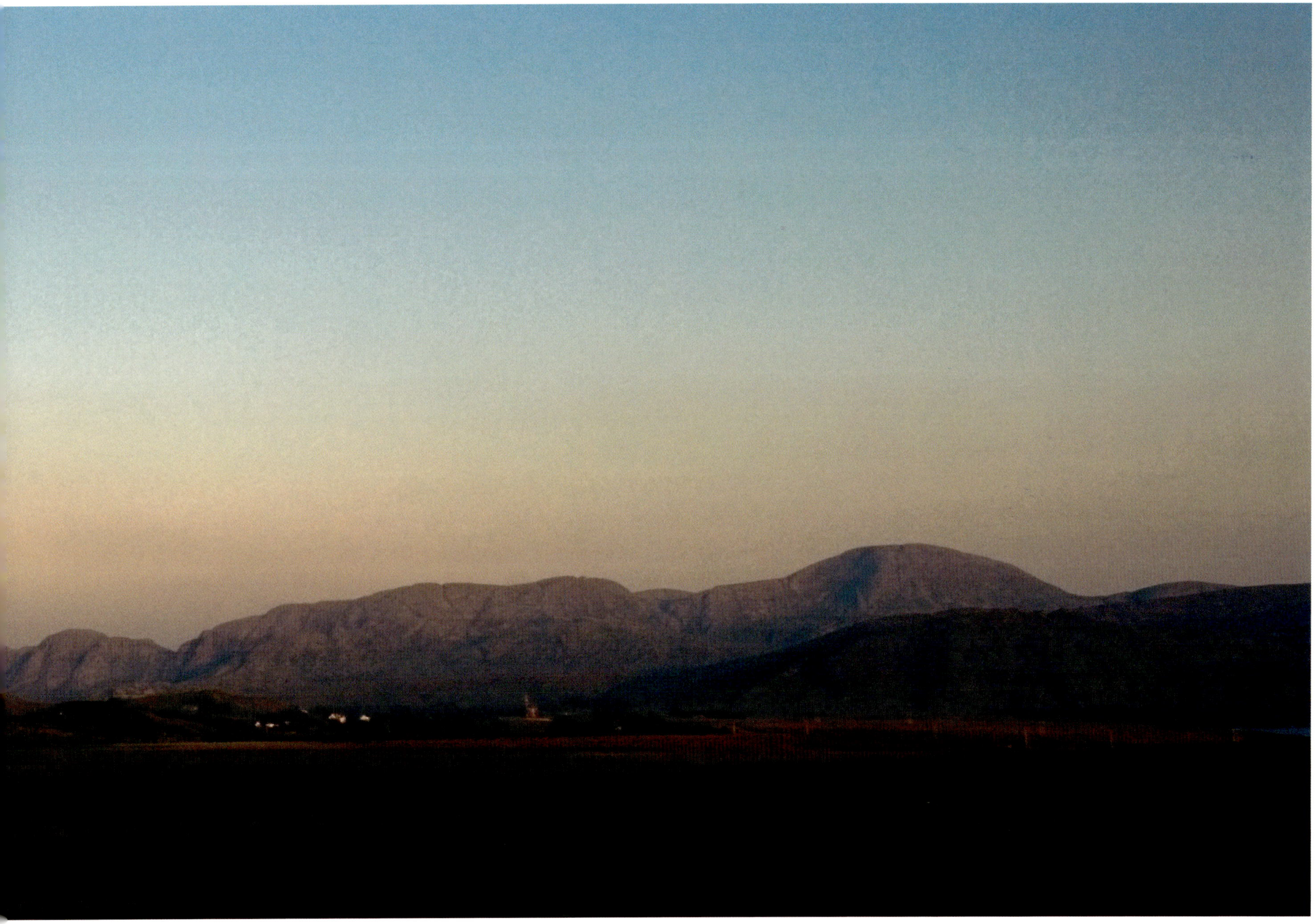

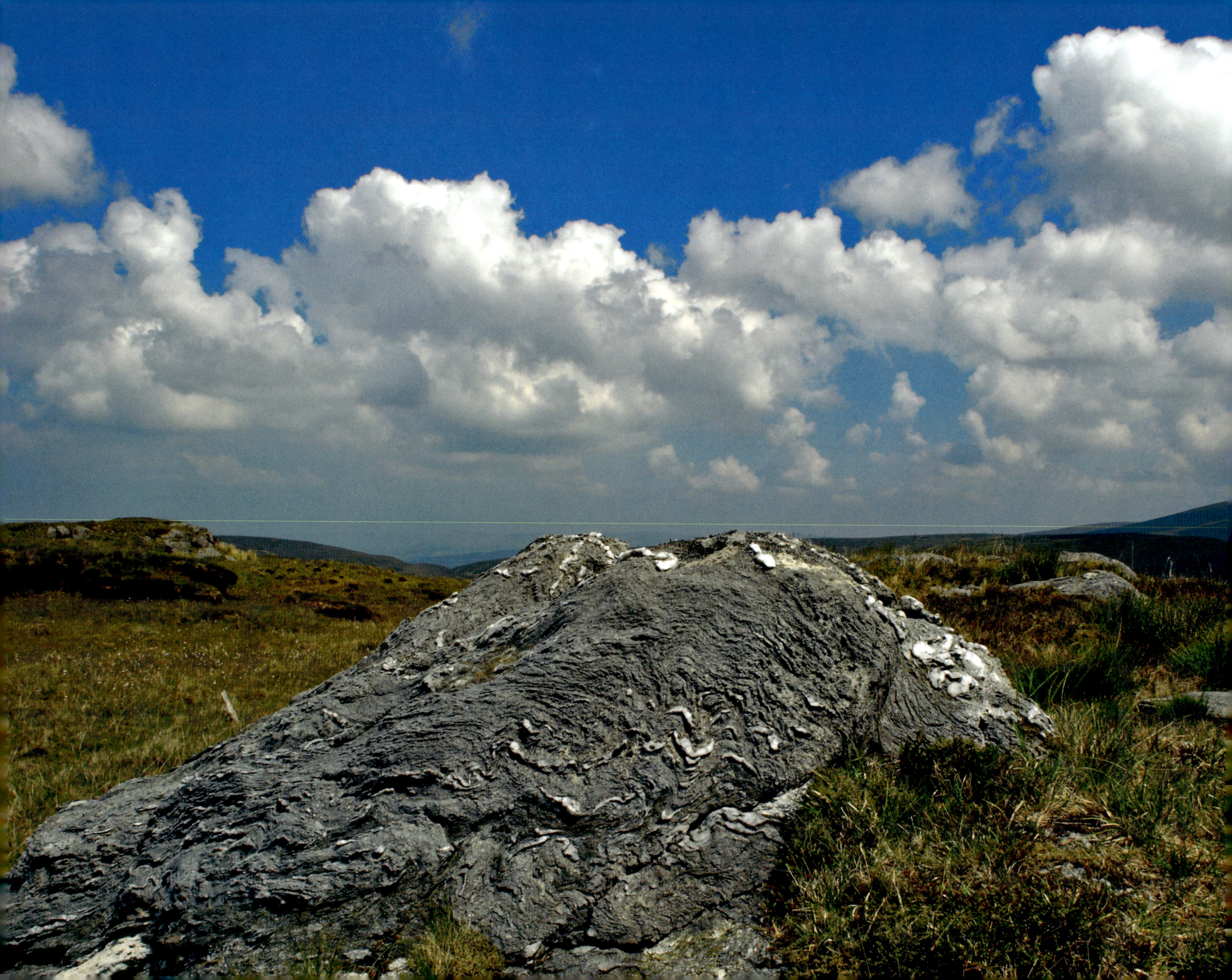

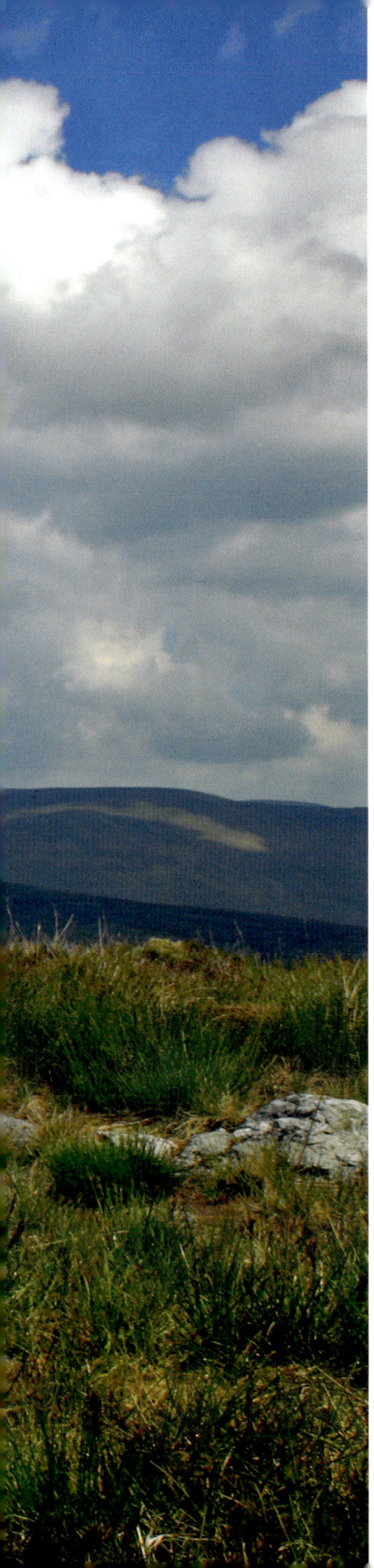

THE SPERRINS

In the Sperrin Hills, on the border of counties Tyrone and Derry, lies a subtle delight. These hills, insignificant looking from afar, have a special magic. The quartzitic rock is mostly clothed in wet peat bog, the hills are rounded and of easy gradient, but here is to be found a great peace of walking gently in quiet and solitude. A fragmentary path leads from the crest of the Cloghornagh Pass westwards over undulating moorland to the highest point at Sawel Mountain, at 678 metres. In bad weather the largely featureless terrain can make navigation difficult.

LEFT The Sperrin Hills on a sparkling June day.

RIGHT These hills are seldom dry, even in summer.

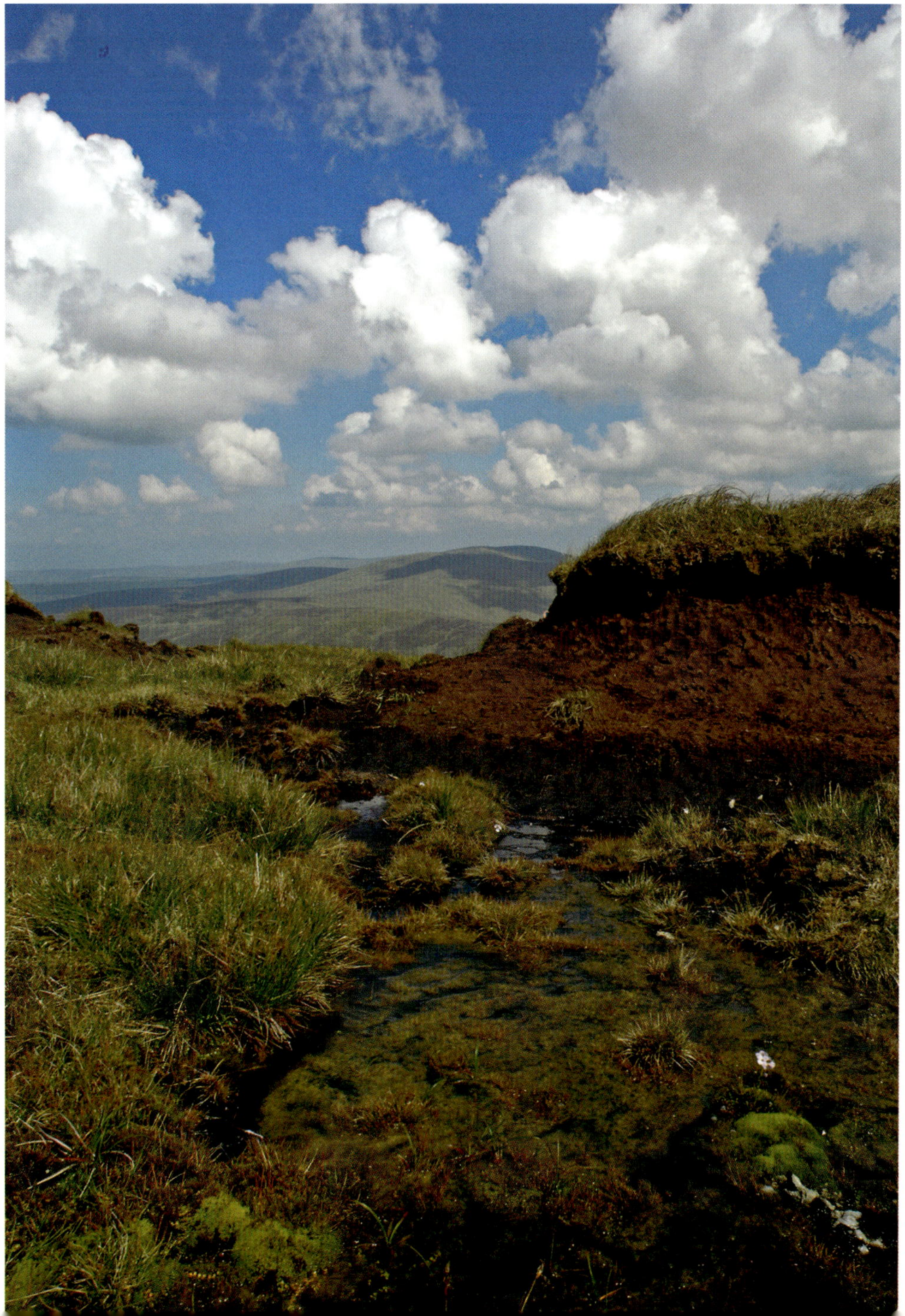

THE MOURNES

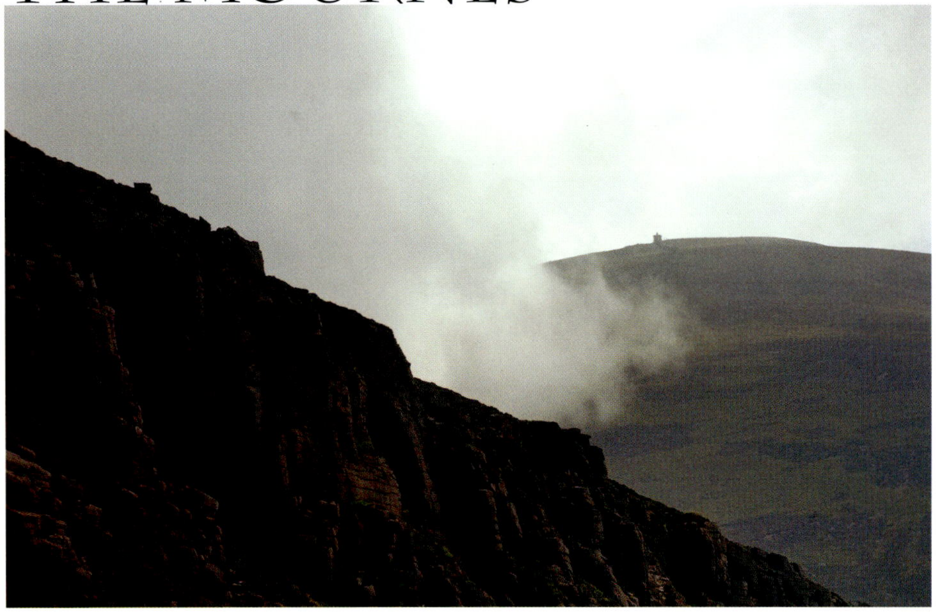

The granite massif of the Mourne Mountains, tucked away in the extreme south-east corner of Ulster, is a wonderfully atmospheric and uplifting place to walk. The main horseshoe of peaks is grouped around the Annalong Valley, where a bold trail leads into the heart of the mountains. To the right lies the highest summit, Slieve Donard, at 853 metres, reached by swinging to the east along the Mourne Way from the head of the valley. The ridge south along the west side of the valley leads over the spectacular natural feature of the Devil's Coach Road, with spectacular prospects into the 'Silent Valley', the valley of the Kilkeel River, and its two reservoirs. This valley has its own horseshoe of peaks, sharing the dividing ridge. A full traverse of either of these groups of hills is a magnificent, rugged, and remote mountain day.

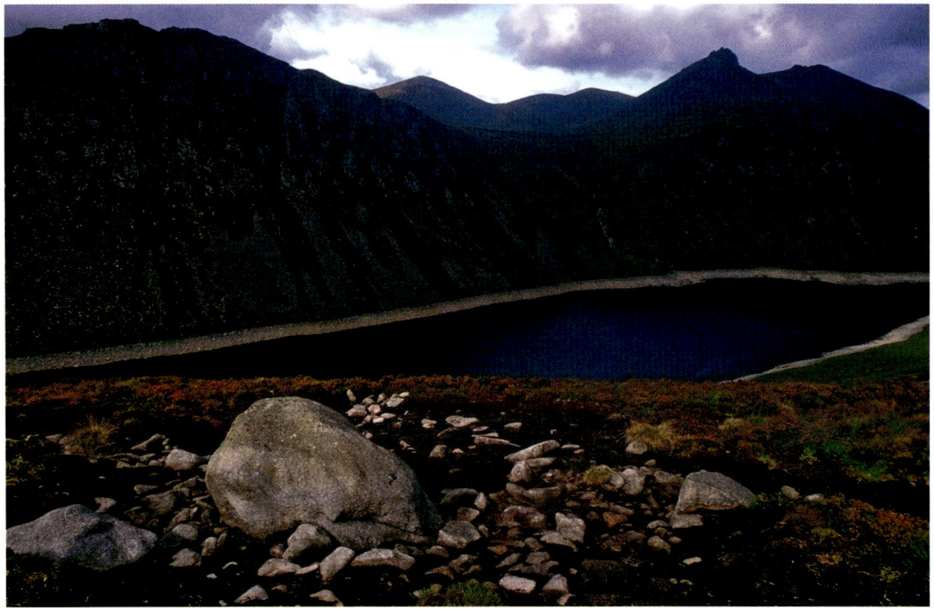

LEFT Looking from Lamagan Pass across Ben Crom Reservoir to the peak of Slieve Bearnagh at 739 metres, with Meelmore and Meelbeg to its left.

ABOVE LEFT Looking east past The Castles towards Slieve Donard, with its summit tower.

OPPOSITE The Mourne Way west to Slieve Bearnagh from the Slieve Beg Pass.

OVERLEAF The northerly peaks of the Mournes on a summer evening.

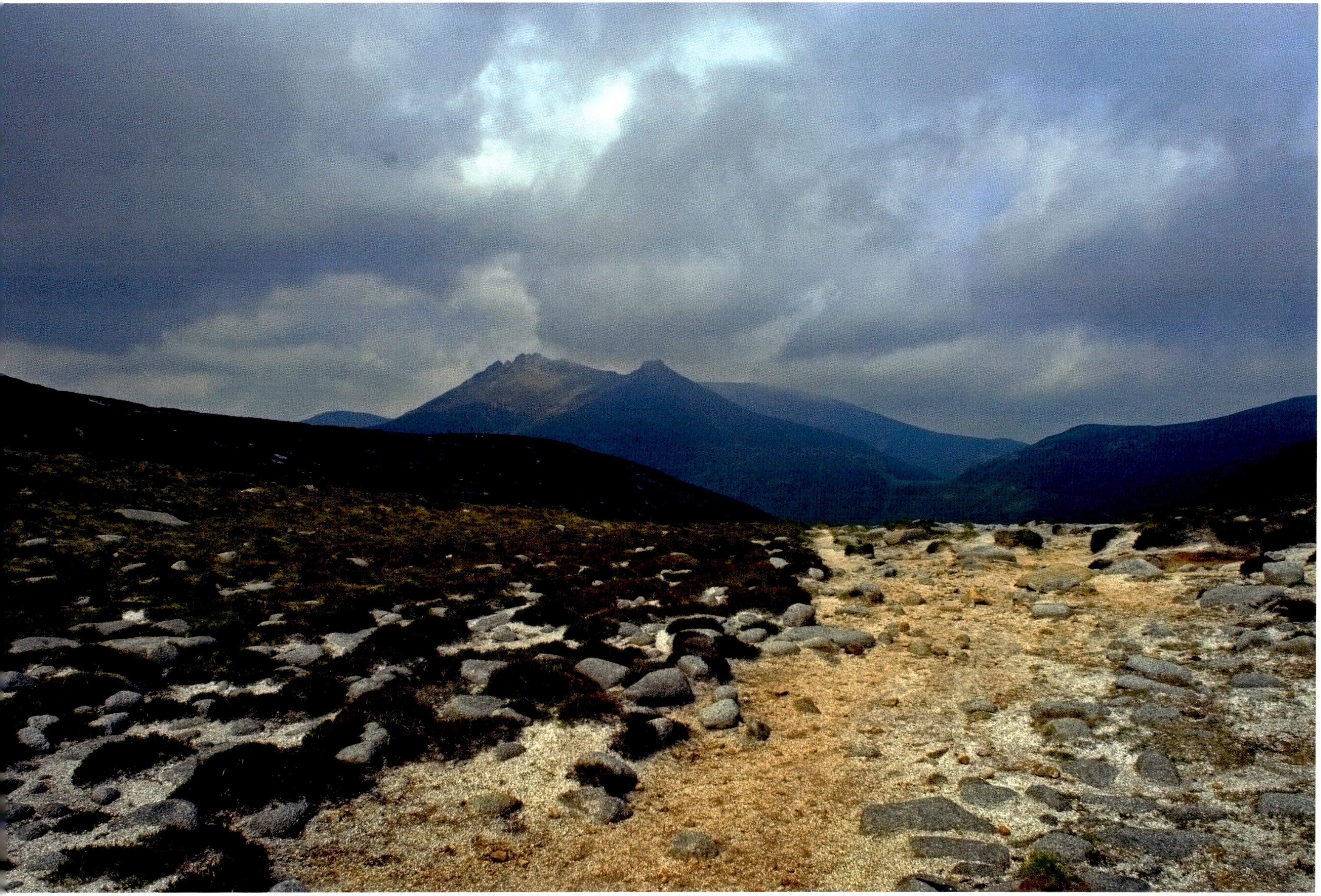

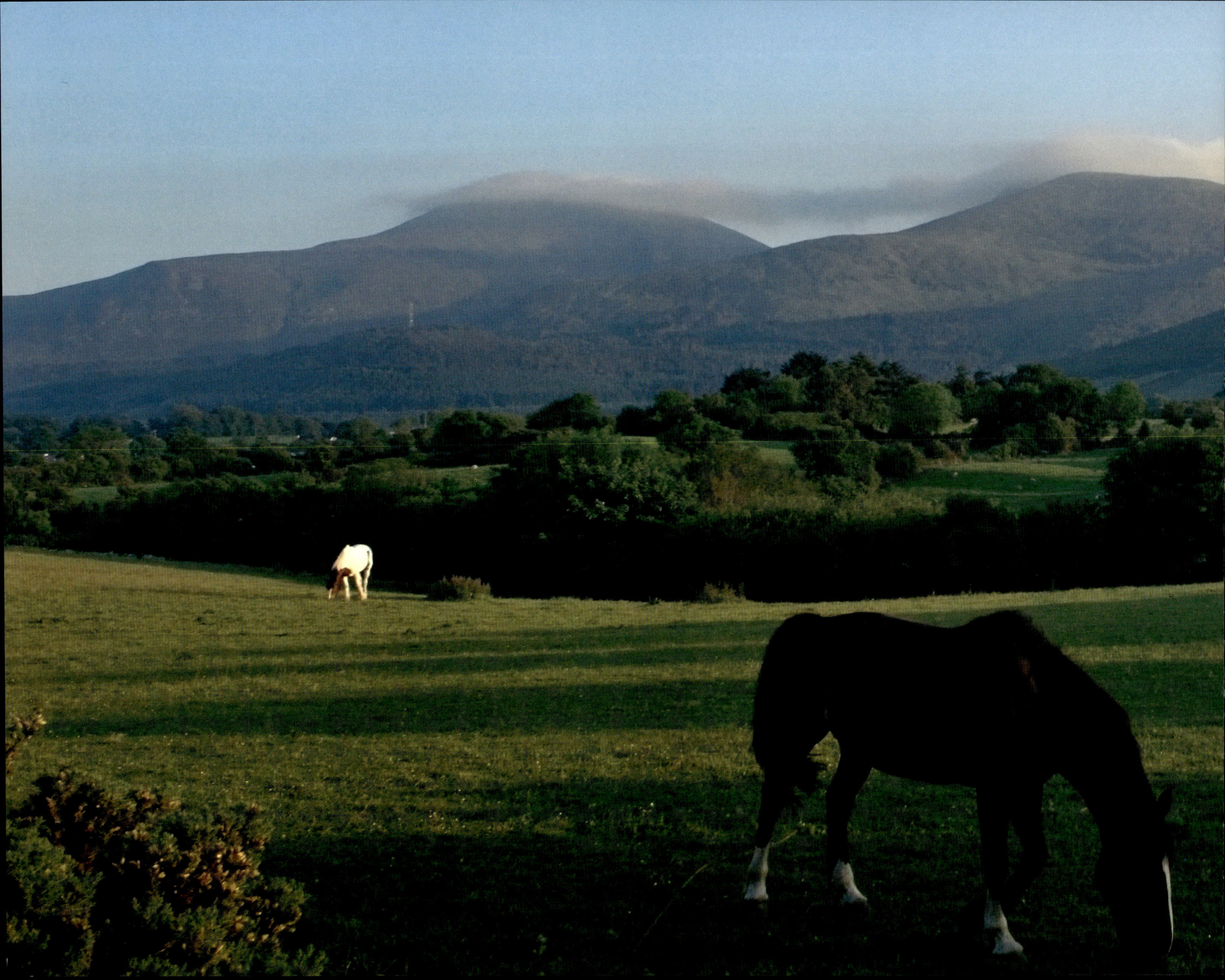

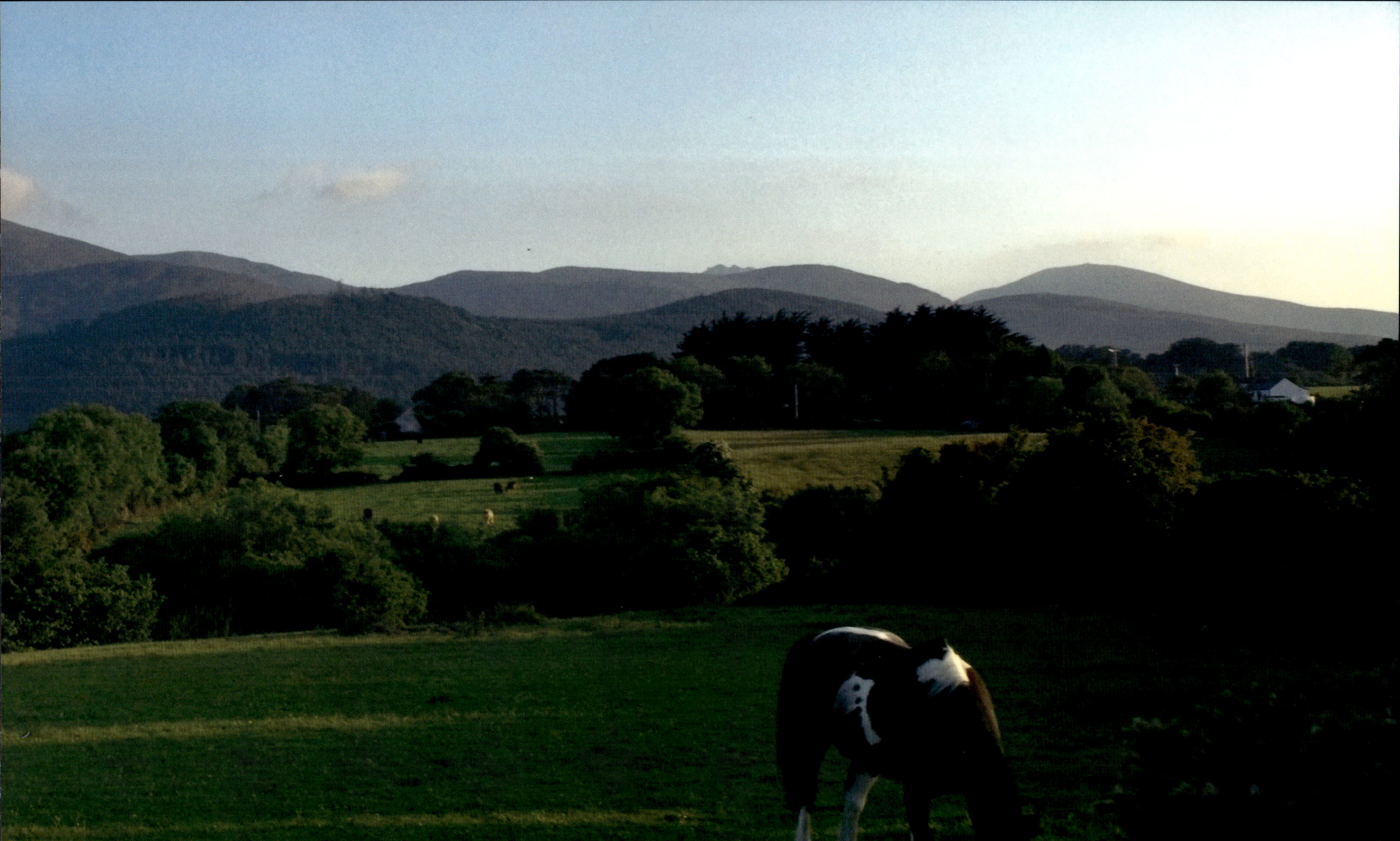

WICKLOW

This extensive region of bog-swathed granite uplands is a magnifcent recreational resource within easy reach of the city of Dublin. The two principal valleys, Glendalough and Glenmalure, give ready access to rich valley and high-level walks, and with connection to the Wicklow Way, which threads the whole length of the eastern side of the range. The highest peak in the area, Lugnaquillia at 925 metres, can be reached by two routes from Glenmalure, one from the north, the other from the east. It has a somewhat undistinguished summit, but has nevertheless a fine sense of remoteness, with the two unusual geographical features of the North and South Prisons edging the flat plateau. In Glendalough, the traverse of Spink to Lugduff is a good outing, made easier now by a series of railway-sleeper walkways, perhaps returning from the head of the valley across Camaderry, or by descending past the old lead mines. In the north-east corner of the region, Djouce Mountain, at 725 metres has a similar paved access from the road to Sally Gap. This pass, difficult to cross in winters of snow and ice, crosses a huge sweep of wild moorland, and gives access to further peaks north of the Wicklow Gap, an extensive area of upland wildernesss culminating in the summit of Mullaghcleevaun at 849 metres. These are not spectacular mountains in a visual sense, but the area as a whole has a splendid sense of atmosphere and character.

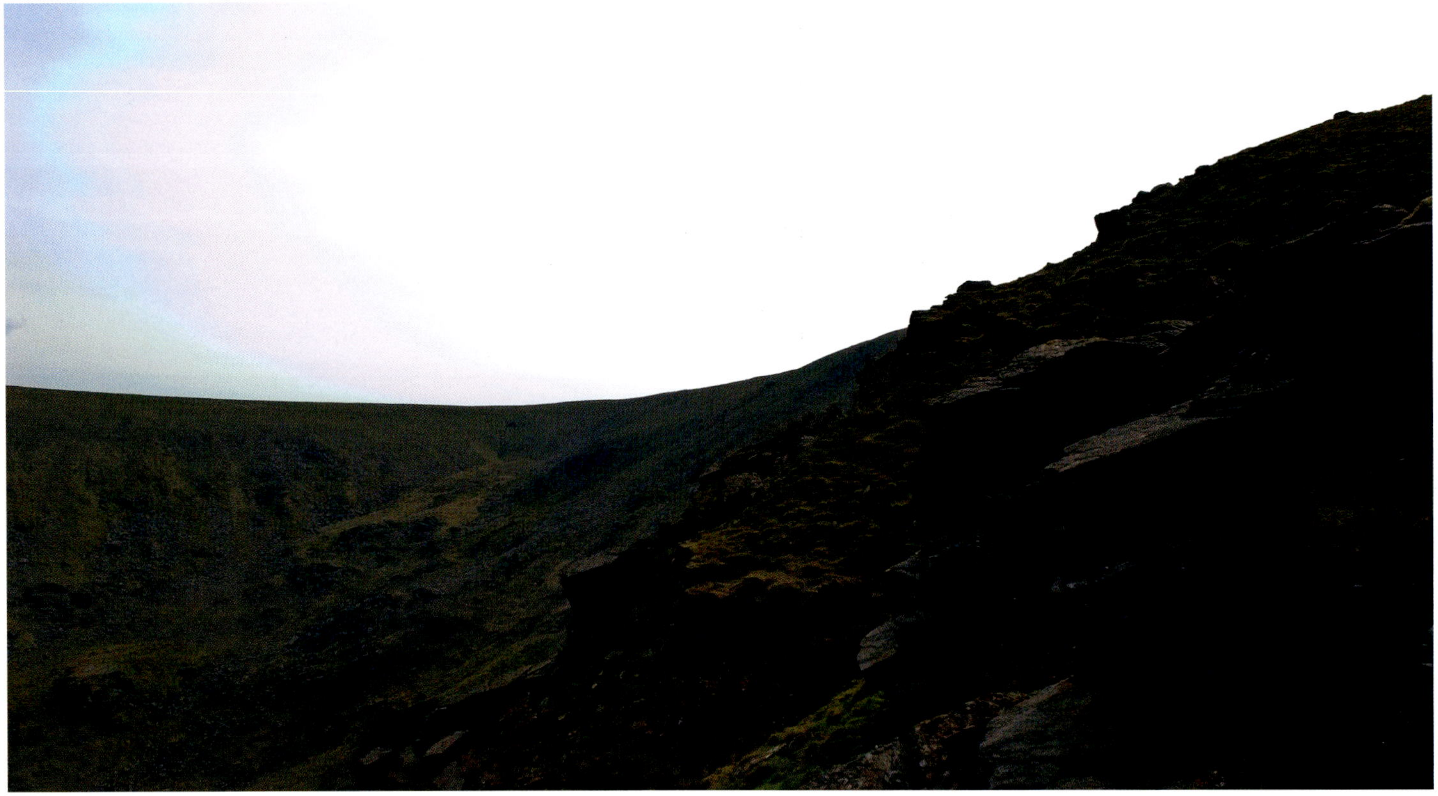

ABOVE The North Prison on Lugnaquillia, with the summit plateau to the right.

OPPOSITE The upper part of the beautiful and tranquil Glenmalure, with the slopes of Lugnaquillia rising to the left.

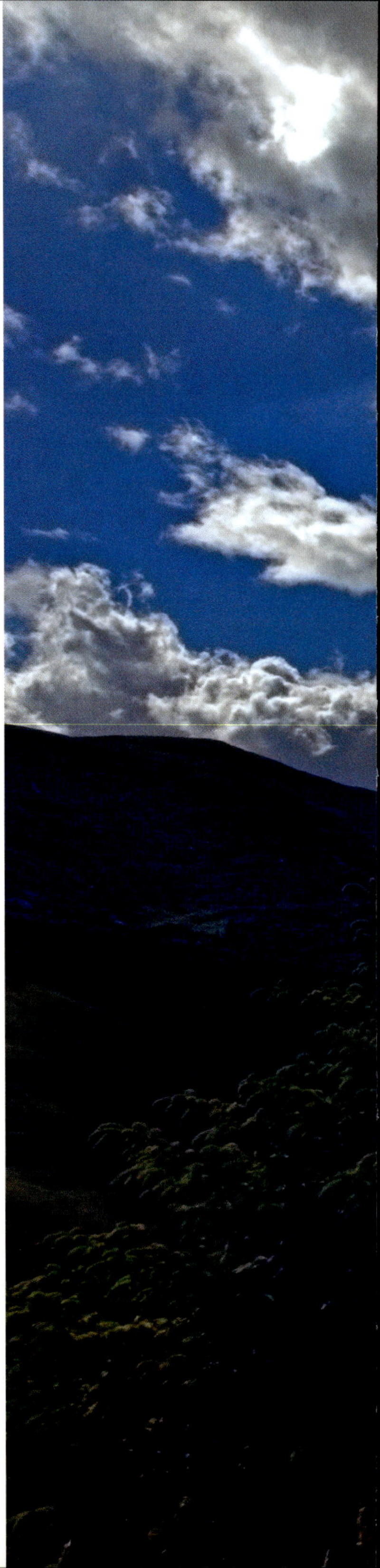

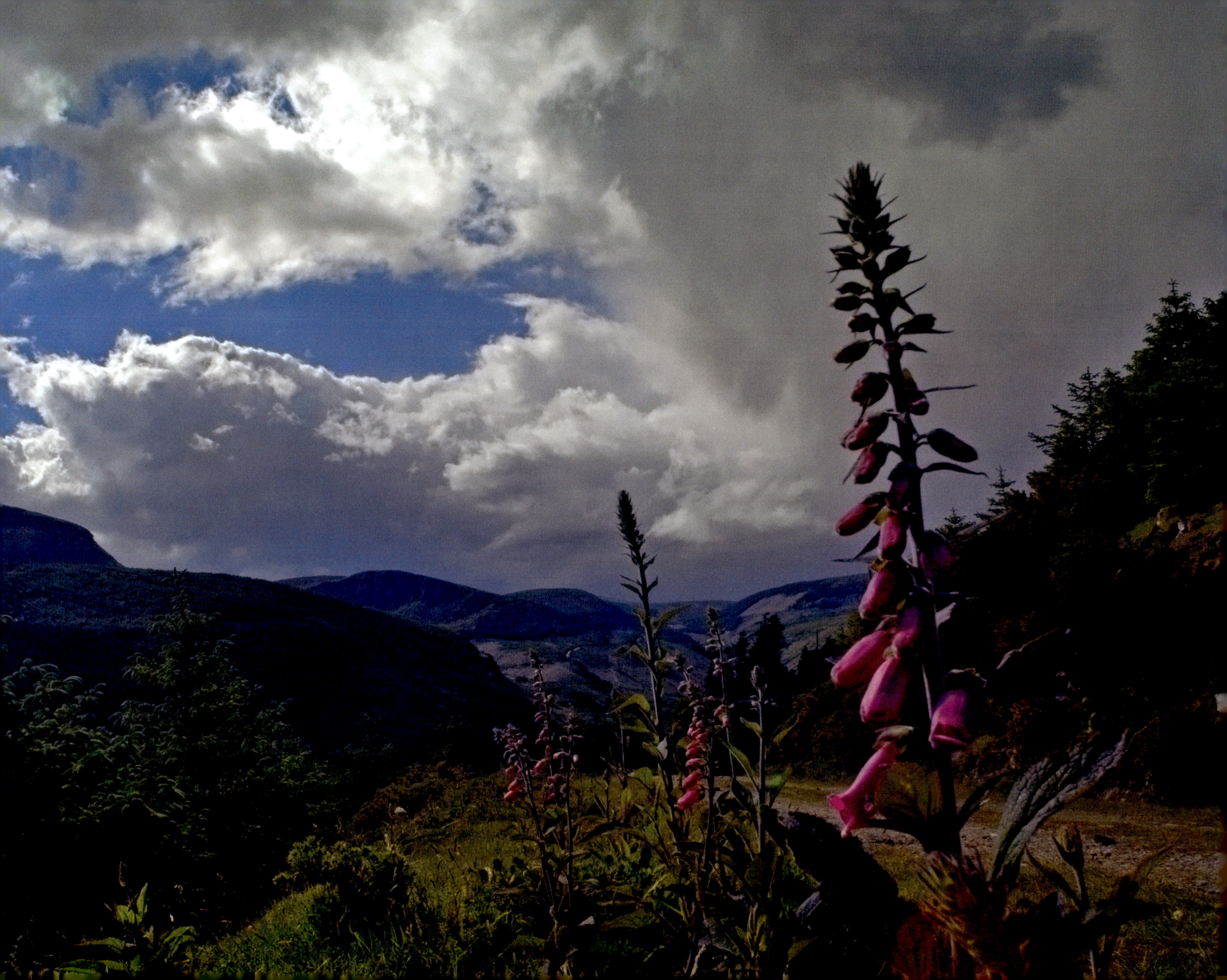

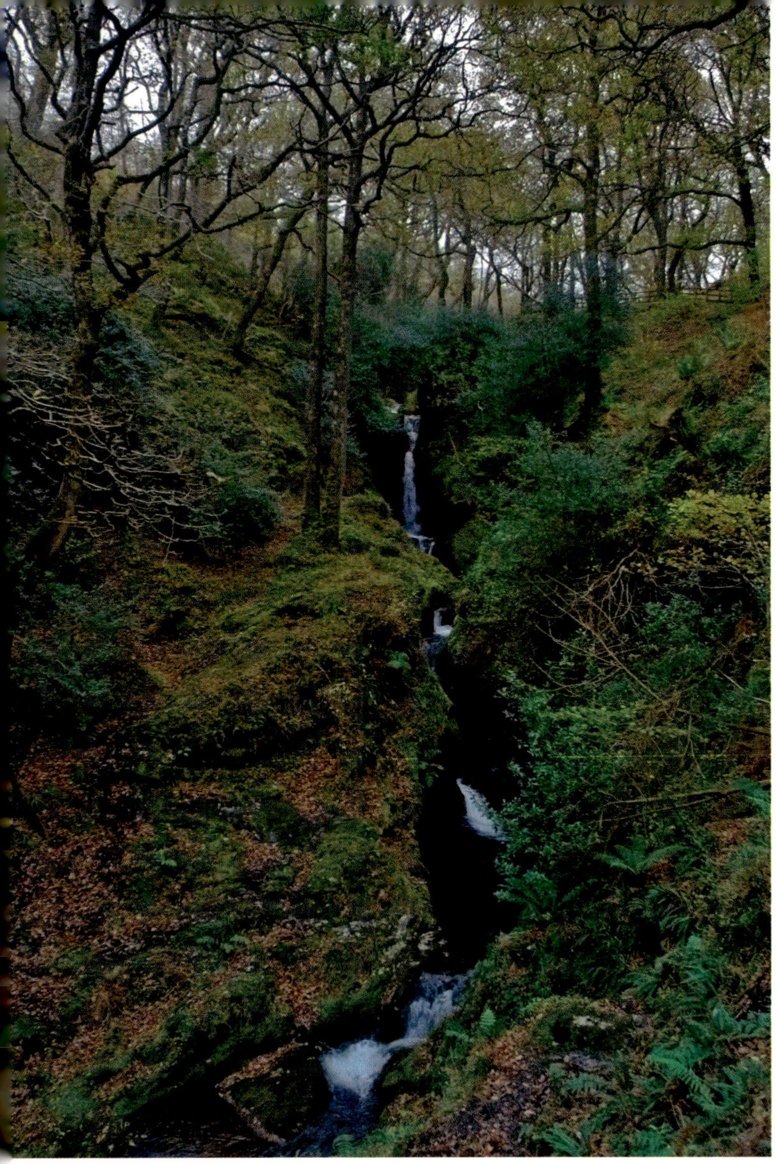

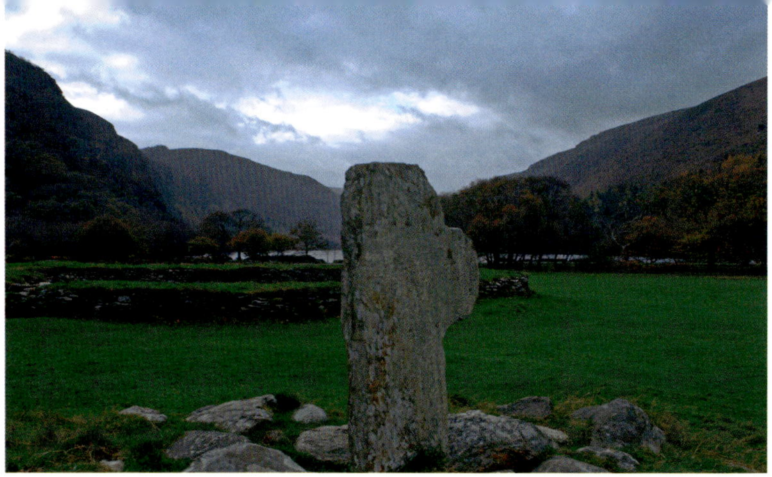

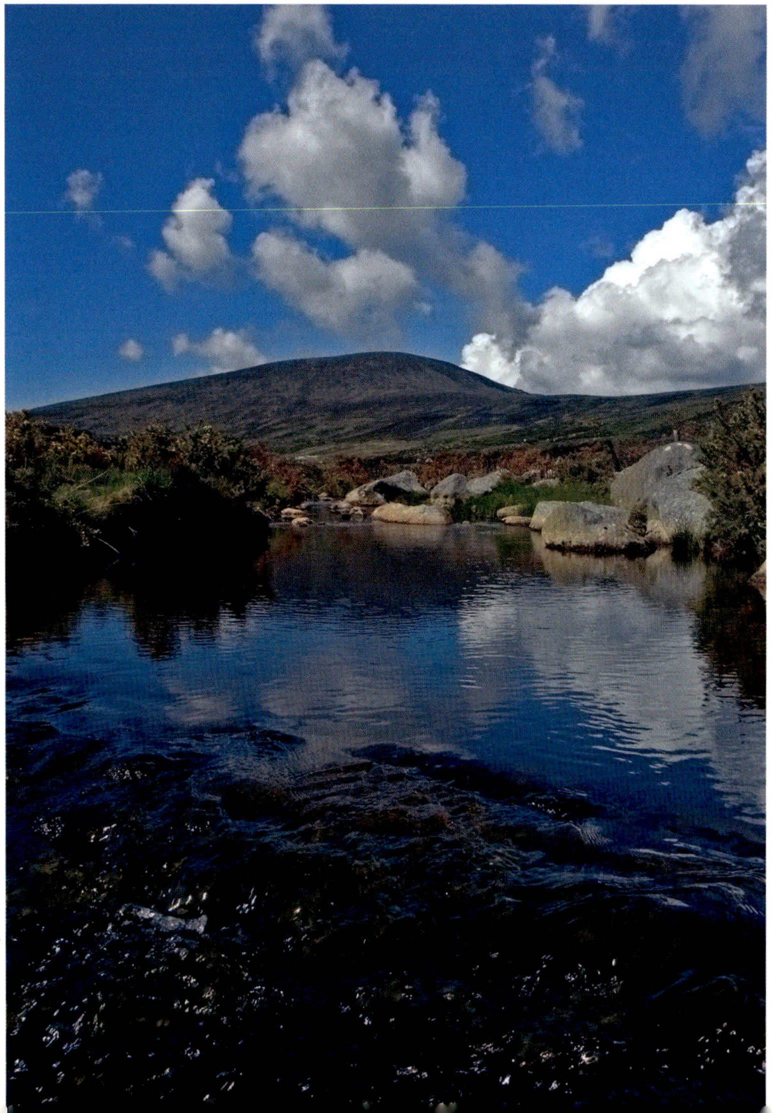

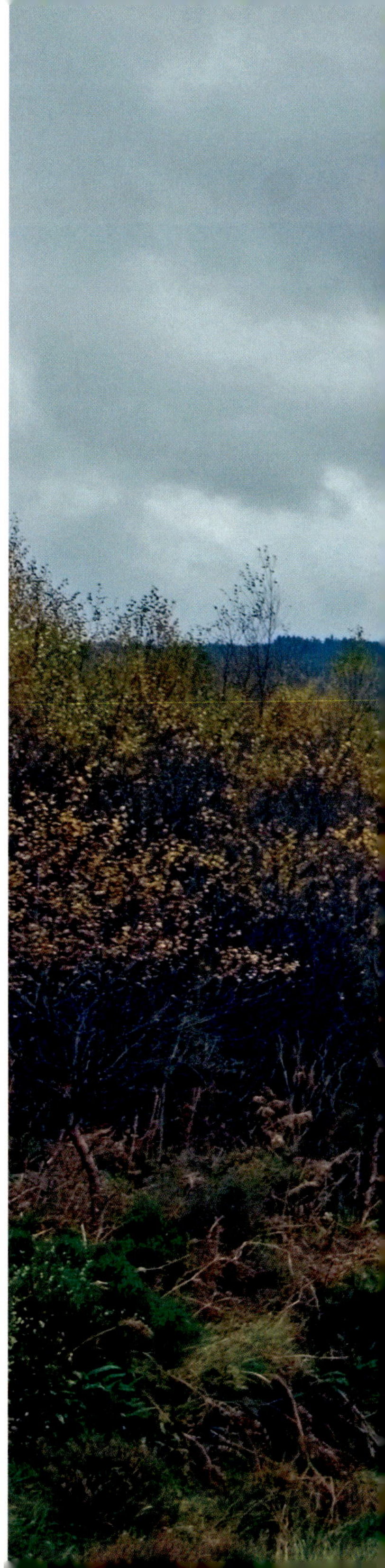

ABOVE Poulanass Waterfall, Glendalough.

ABOVE RIGHT Monastic cross below the Upper Lake.

BELOW RIGHT Tonelagee, 817 metres, from Wicklow Gap.

OPPOSITE The Wicklow Way, looking towards Spink.

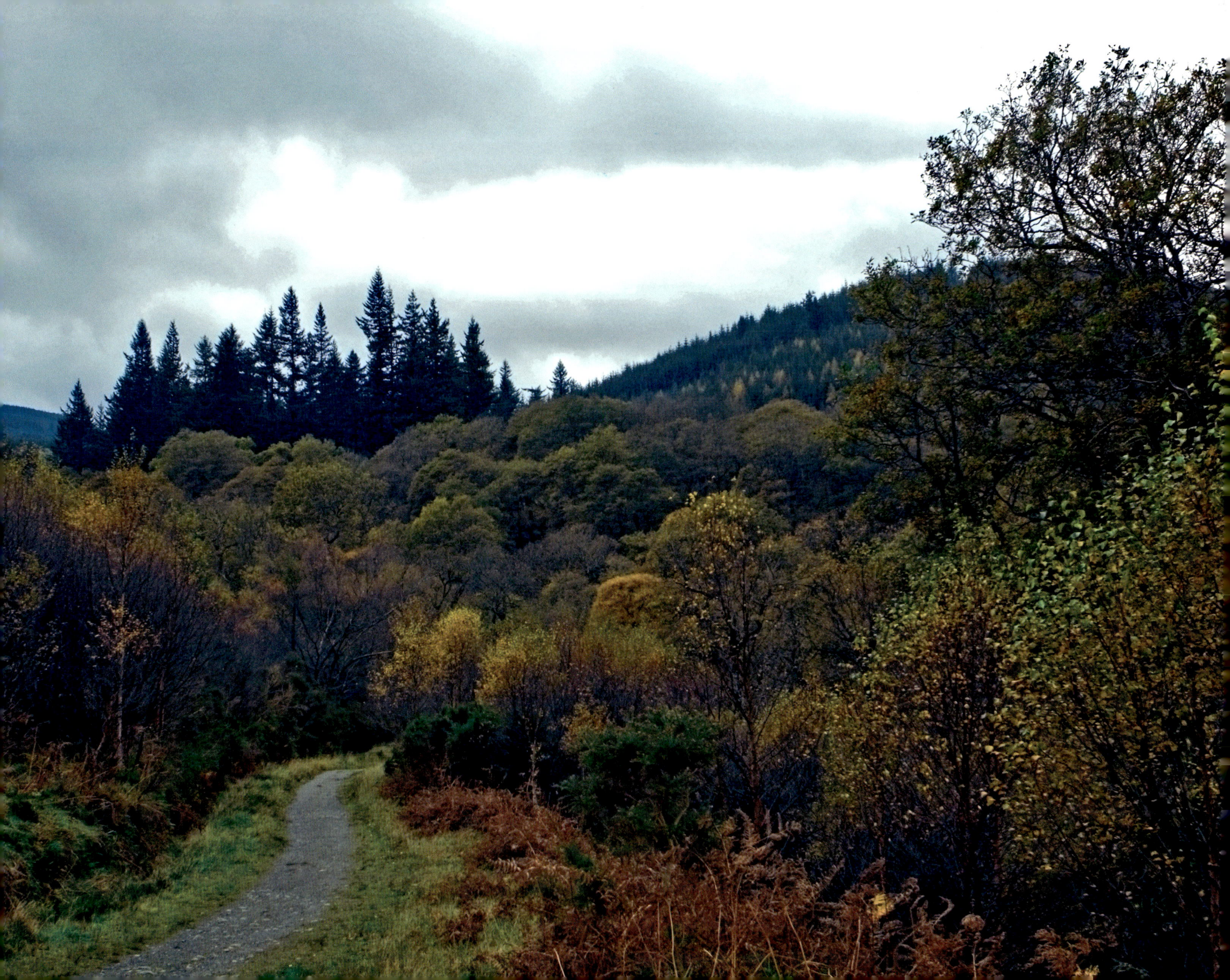

THE COMERAGHS

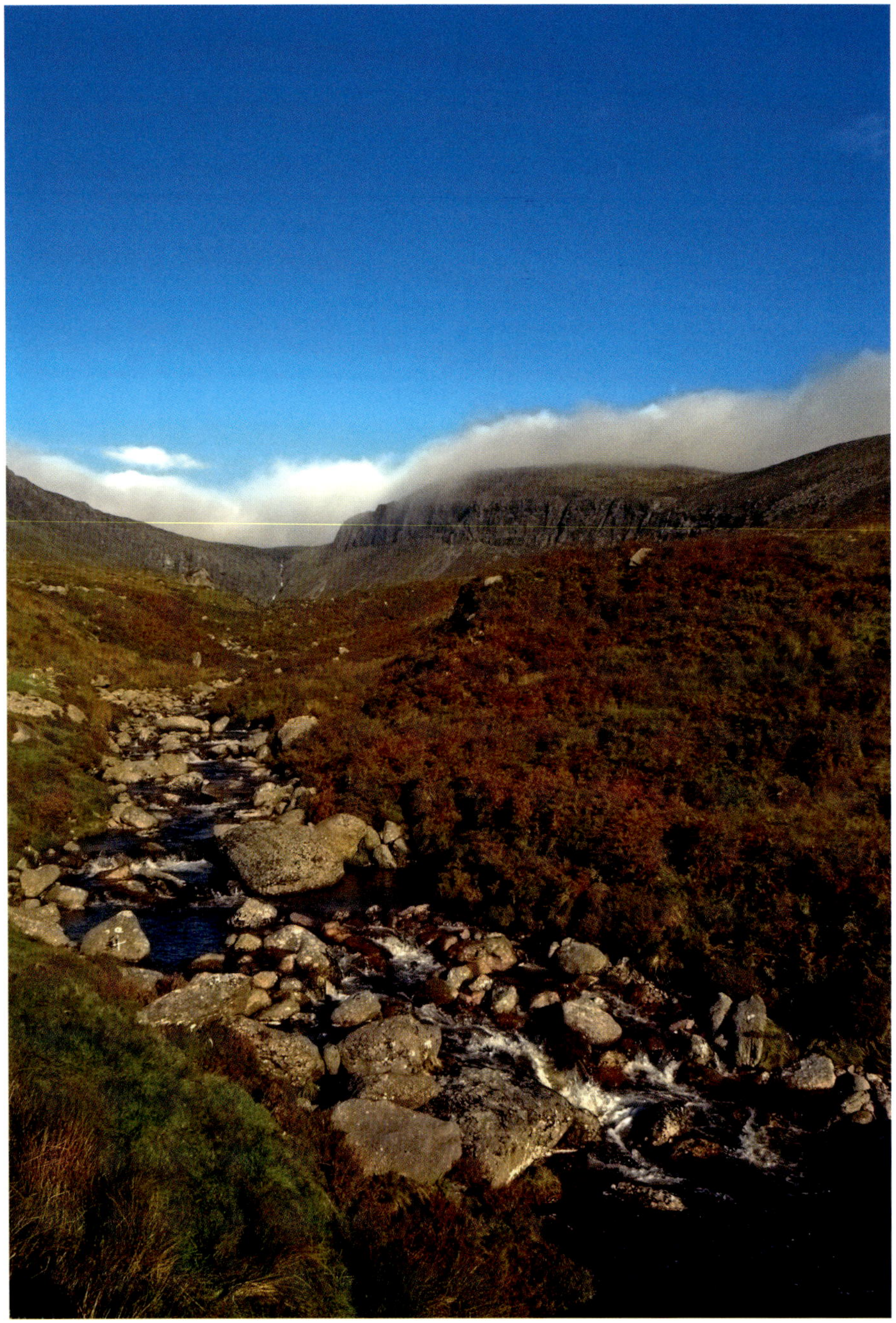

The Comeragh Mountains, bordering on the Monavullagh Mountains, lie a short distance to the west of Waterford in Ireland's south-east corner. The main summits are Knockaunapeebra, at 789 metres, and Seefin, at 725 metres. It is a region of peat moorland edged by spectacular cliffs, and speckled with lochans. It is fine remote country, made more exciting by the presence of rock. Approach can be made in two main ways. A narrow road in from the southeast gives ready access to a simple but beautiful walk to the vigorous Mahon falls. The walk can be extended by steep scrambling to reach the ridge from Coumfea to Knockaunapeebra, to return in either of these directions, left or right. Access to the northern area can be made from the Nire Valley, easily as far as the fine saddle of The Gap. From here, a spectacular traverse of the cliff bounded ridge of Carrigshaneun southeastwards leads to Knockaunapeebra, and then on over Coumfea to complete a fine circuit.

LEFT The river below Mahon Falls on a vivid late summer's day.

OPPOSITE The Mahon Falls, with the cliffs of Knockaunapeebra above.

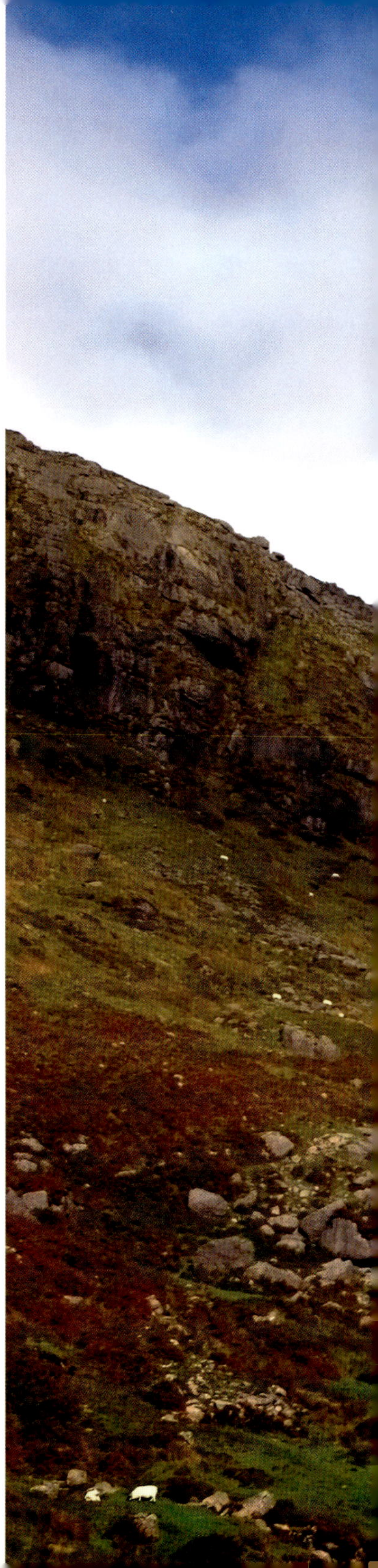

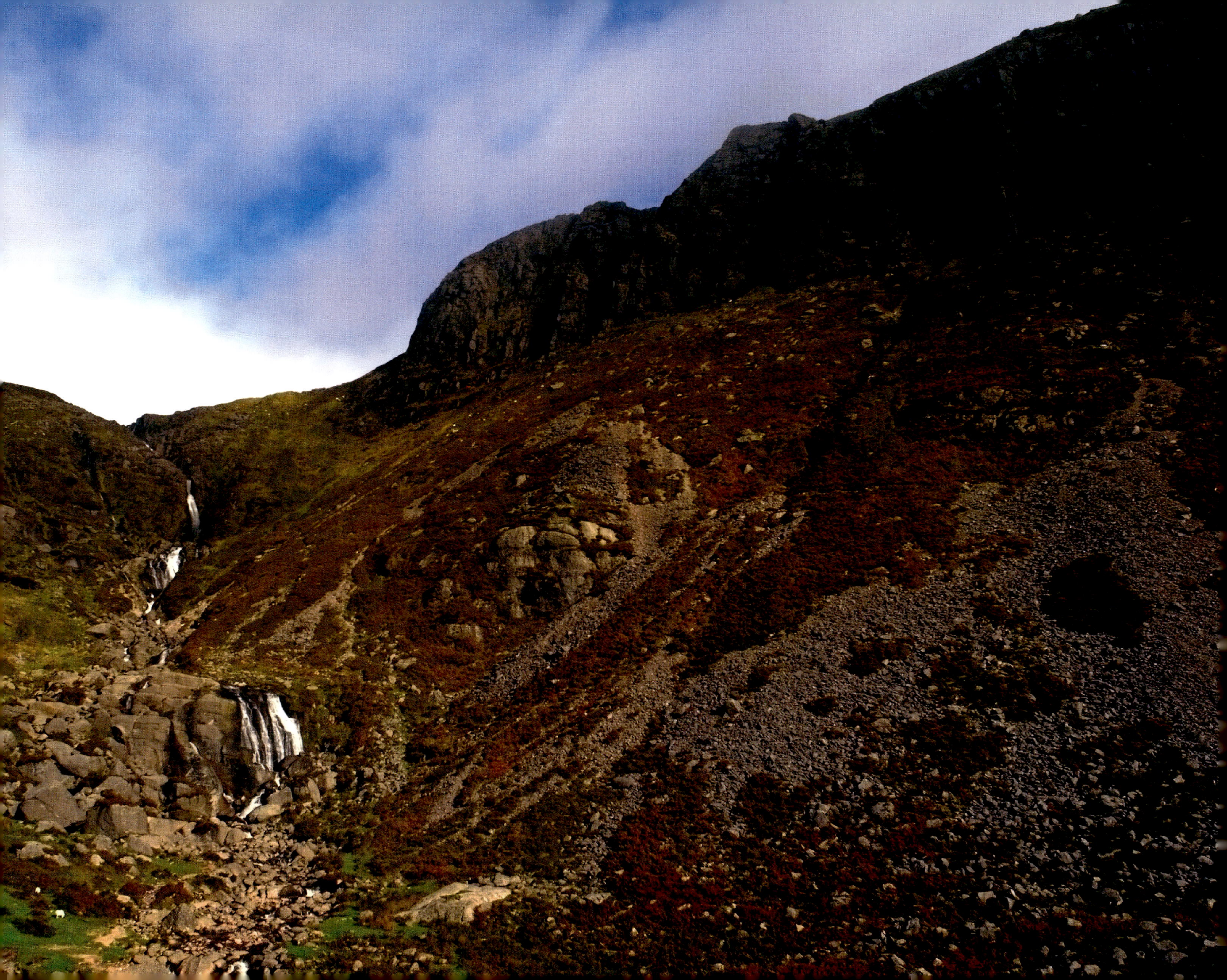

THE GALTYS AND KNOCKMEALDOWNS

The Galty mountains stand improbably above the low country to the south of Tipperary, reaching the exceptional height, for Ireland, of 919 metres on Galtymore. This is an outstanding piece of high landscape, with broad ridges interlocking intimately with the lake-filled cooms which cut steeply into the northern slopes. The ridge can be reached quickly from the south by a well-made path, which gives way to the steep summit slopes. The ridge offers in excess of 15 kilometres of lofty walking on largely firm, springy ground, with views dropping away to the valley far below, and across to the neighbouring Knockmealdown Mountains, which themselves reach a height of 793 metres.

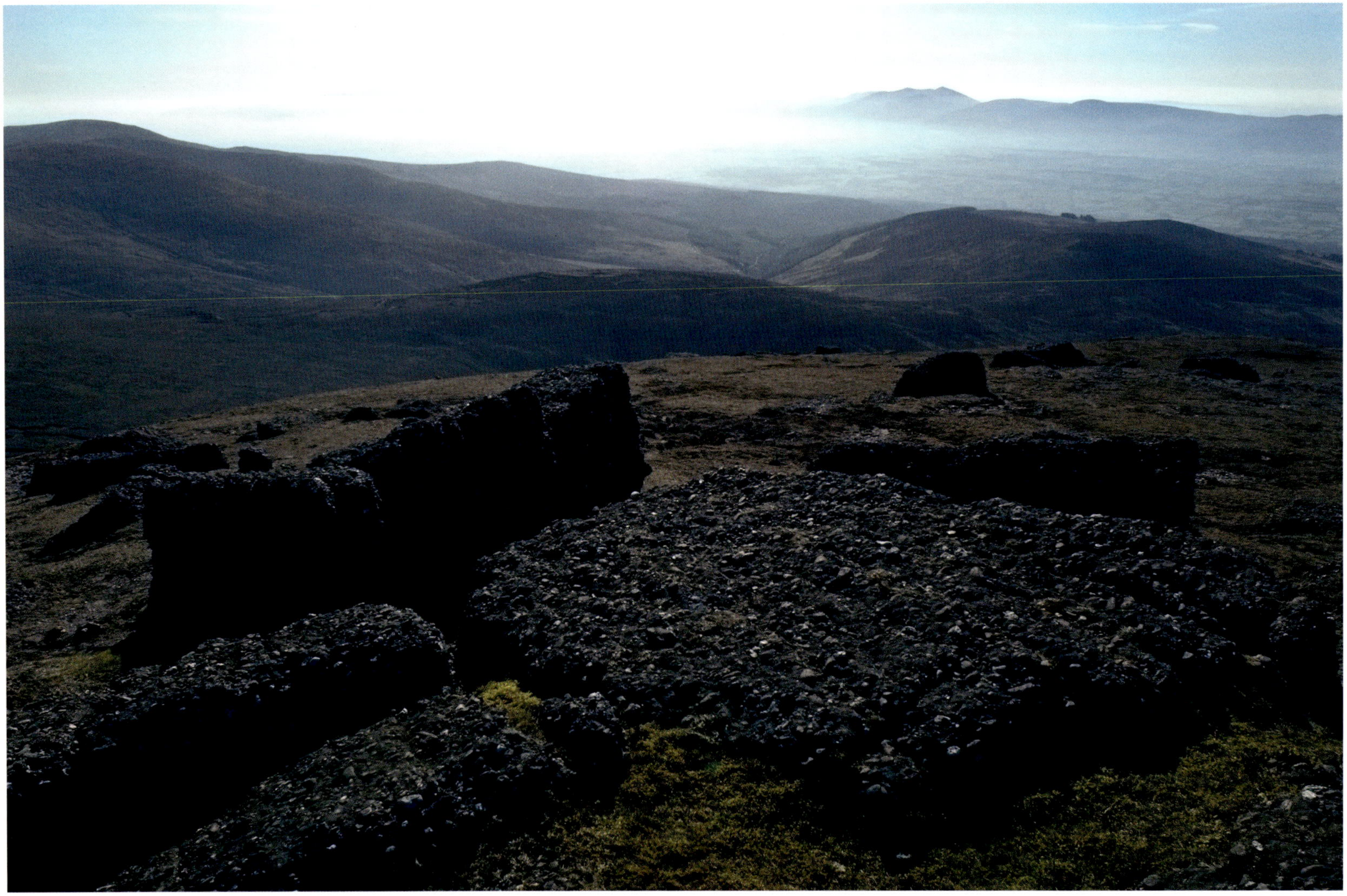

Near the summit of Galtymore looking southeast to the Knockmealdowns, early on a beautiful spring morning.

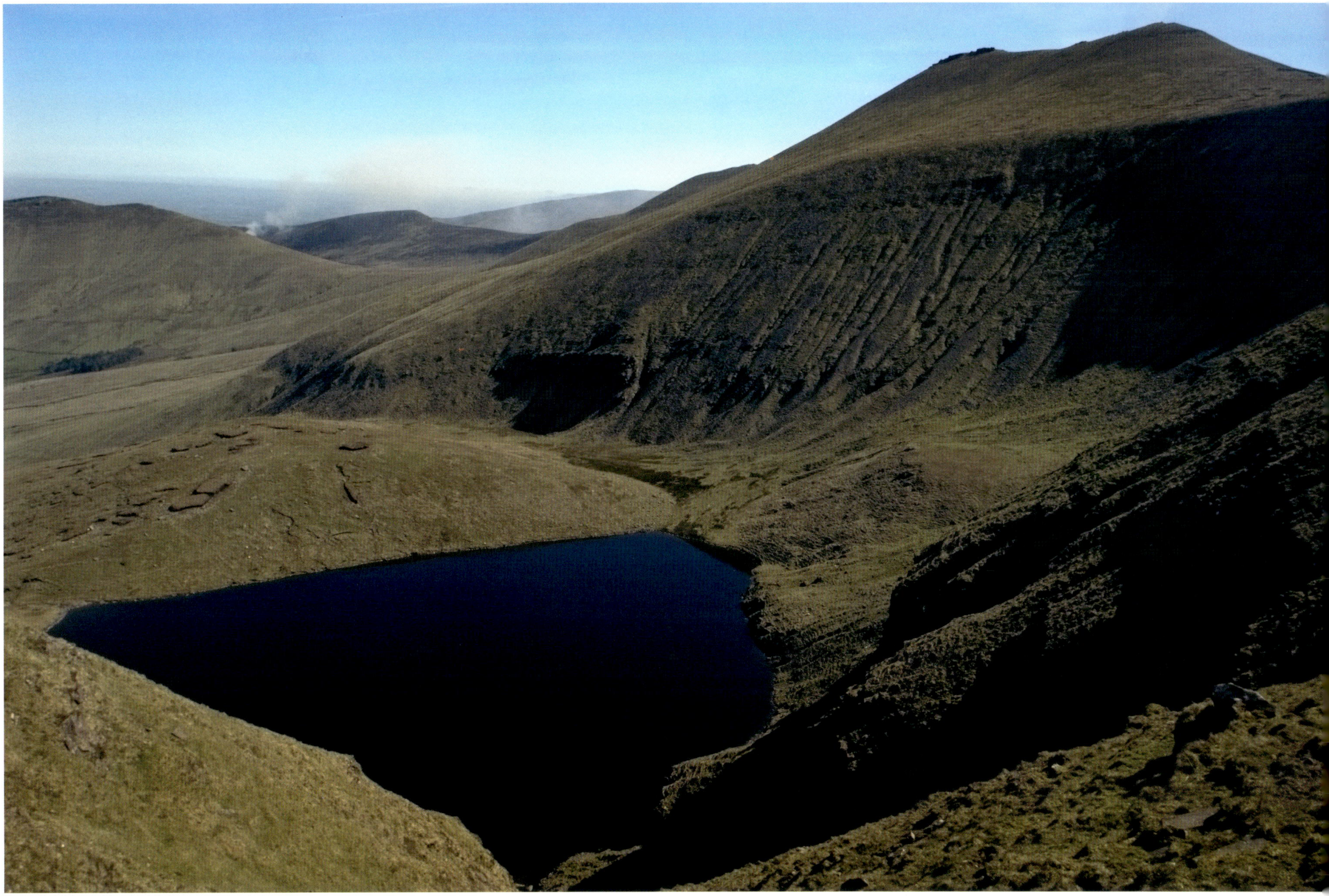

Looking towards Galtymore across Lough Curra. A spectacularly abrupt landscape.

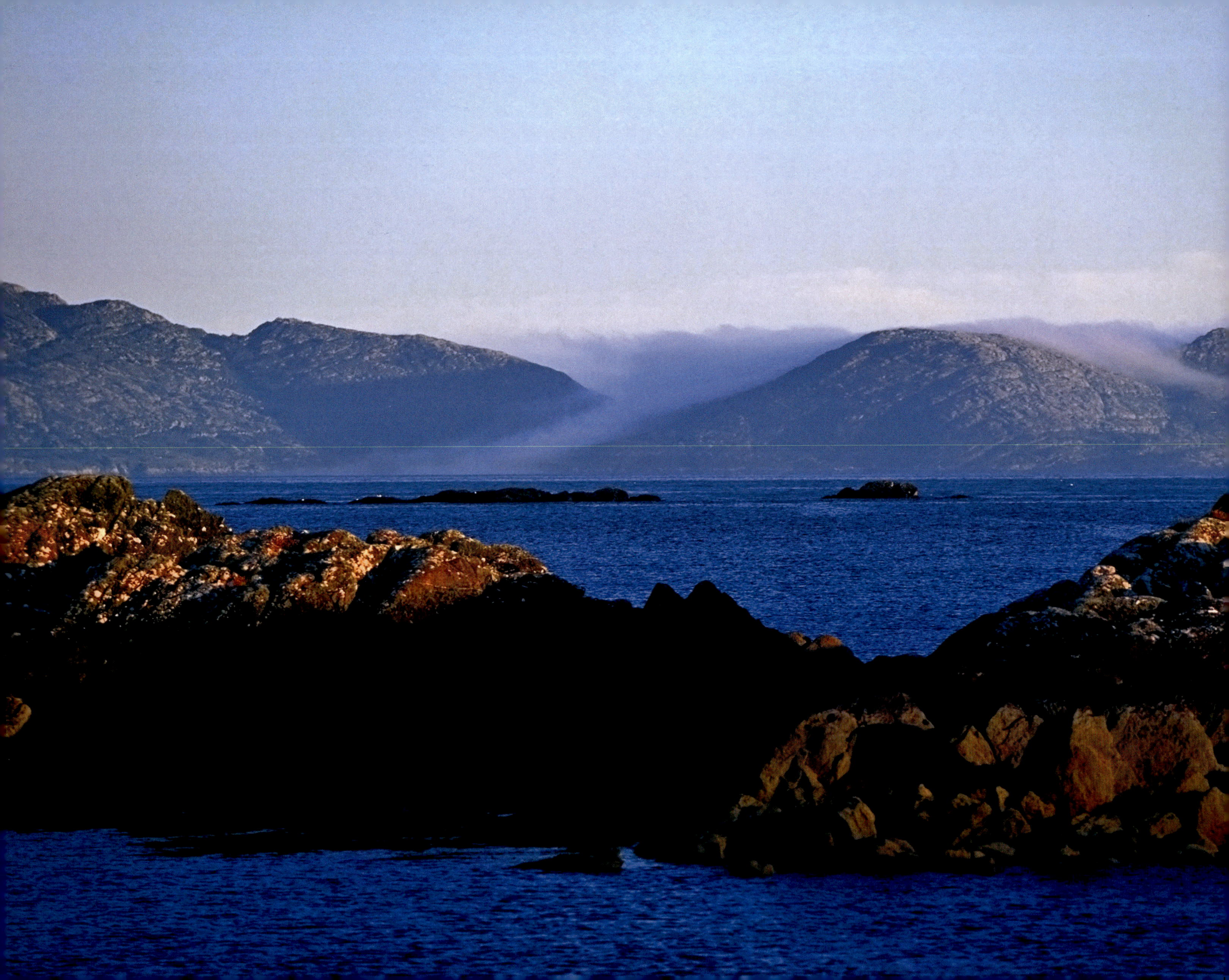

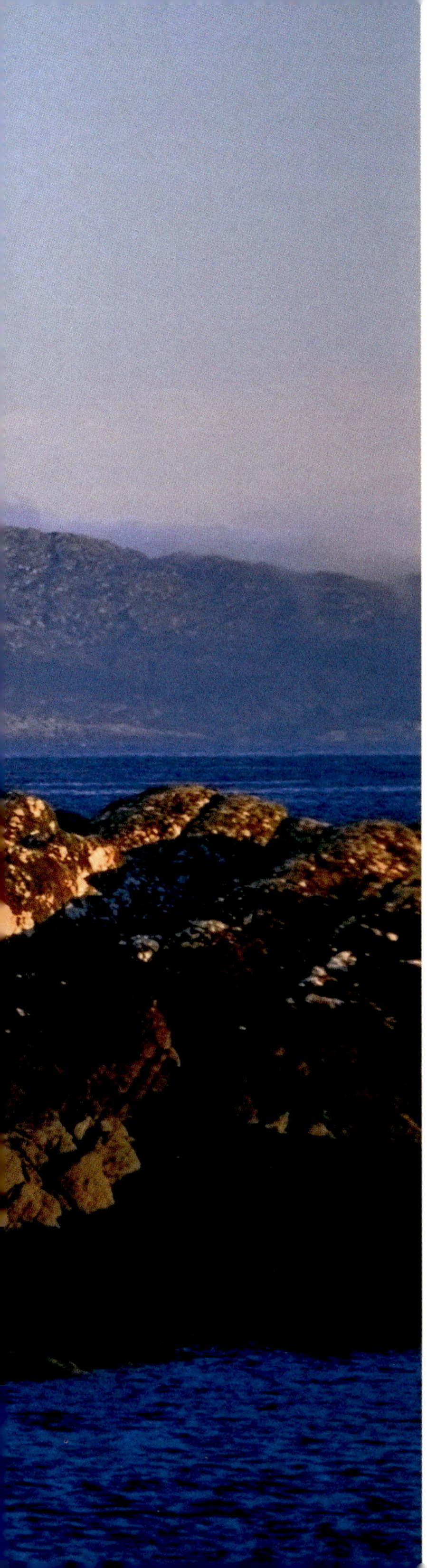

THE BEARA PENINSULA

The Beara Peninsula, stretching from Glengarriff in County Cork to Dursey Island, and including in the north a portion of south-west Kerry, has probably the greatest area of exposed rock in the whole of Ireland. It is a rough region of wonderfully bold peaks, rising spectacularly from the brink of the ocean. Sugarloaf, a mere 573 metres, but with a classic mountain profile, dominates the eastern end of the peninsula. The dramatic Healy Pass crosses the spine of the Caha Mountains to Laragh, with impressive prospects to the southeast across Glanmore Lake to the ring of peaks which culminates in Hungry Hill at 685 metres. The crest of the pass gives convenient access to the spine of the mountains, but not to easy walking: there is little of that in Beara. Beyond Castletownbere, the Slieve Miskish Mountains run their fairly low, but rocky spine as far as Allihies. This is exceptional country, standing ruggedly in the face of Atlantic weather, and having walking that requires much focus to negotiate the rocky terrain. Beara is a true wilderness experience.

OPPOSITE The exposed rock of the Beara Peninsula, seen from the Iveragh Peninsula.

BELOW The town of Allihies nestles under the western end of the Beara Peninsula.

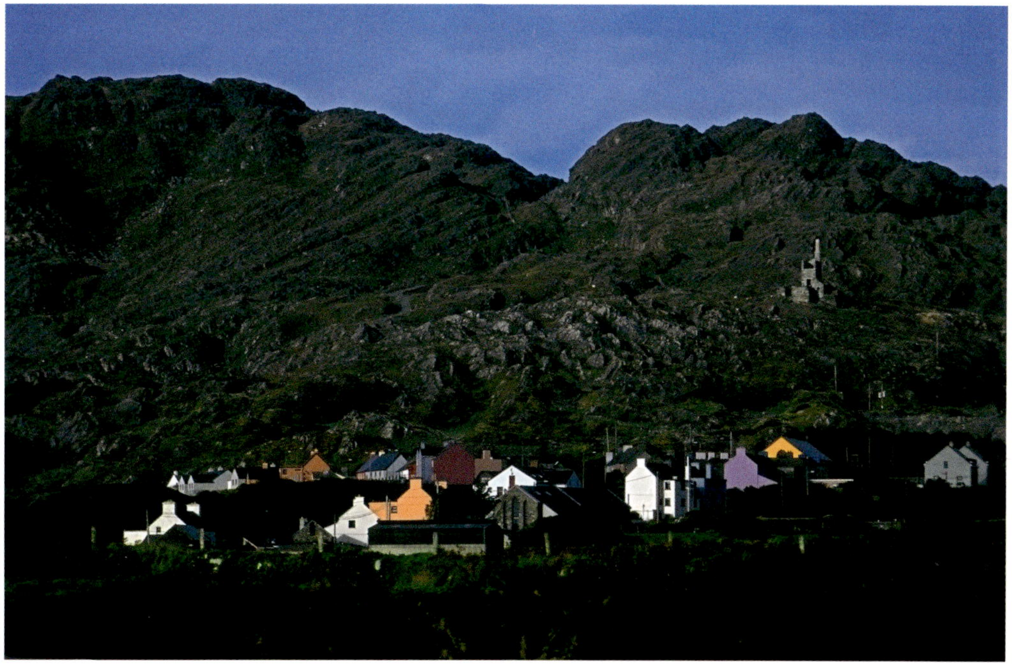

SEA TO MOUNTAIN, MOUNTAIN TO SEA

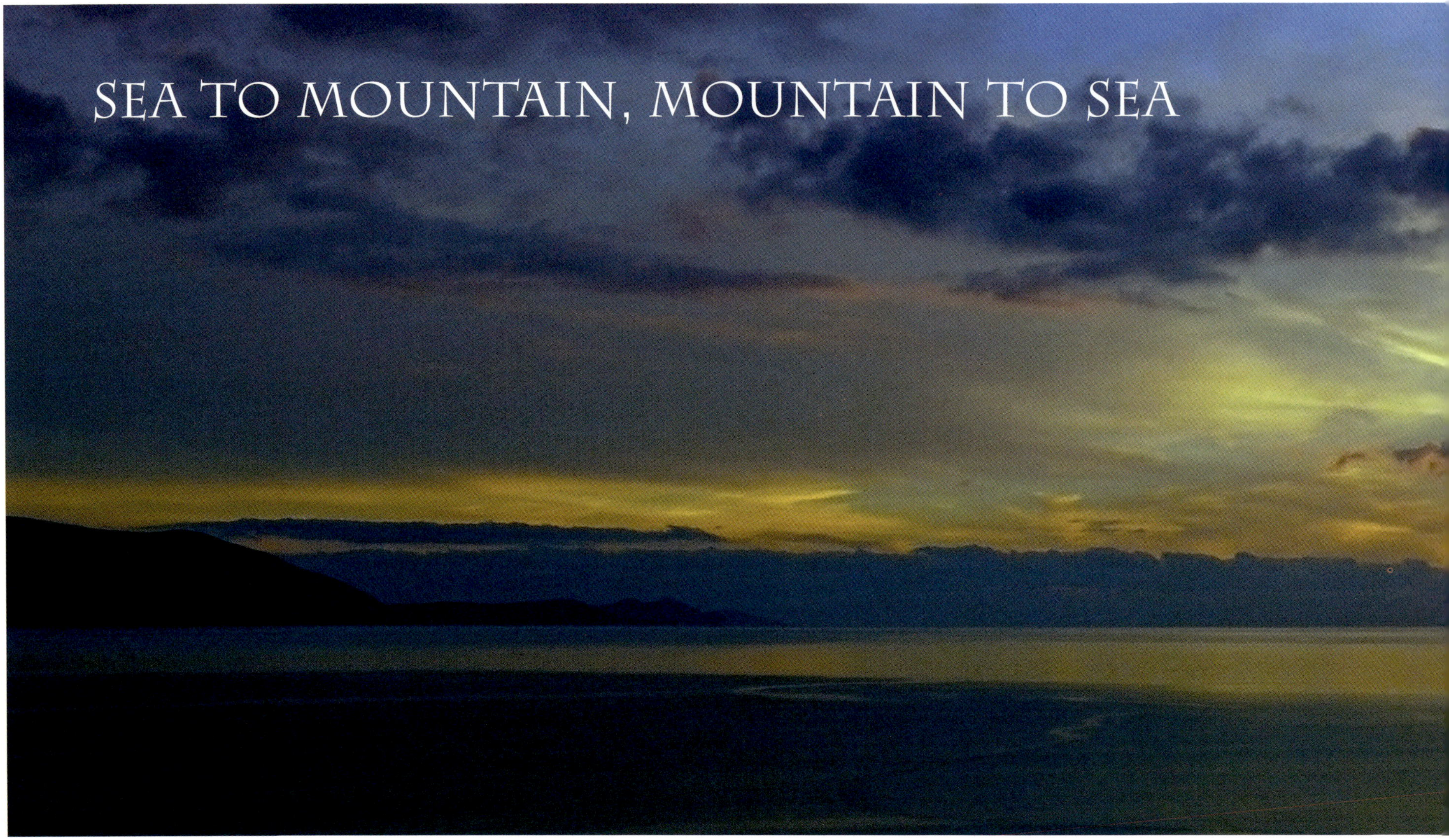

We may stand and gaze at the uplands and describe what we see rising in front of us as a mountain, but in truth the mountain is all of its height, from the level of the sea until the ground starts to go down again. A mountain stretches from the sea to the summit, and from the summit to the sea. It rests with its feet on the shore, and its head in the sky. The mountain shape has been created by water, which still tumbles down its surface in trickles and streams, in fall and river. Every fold and crease of its bulk is clothed with life, with grasses and flowers and trees, with birds and animals and insects. Ireland sits on the western edge of Europe, open to every flurry and furrow of Atlantic weather. The weather shapes both the form and the feel of its mountains. More than any other nation in Europe, it has atmosphere in vivid and swiftly changing variety. Each day is a surprise; the moment is to be seized whilst it is here. The chance is that it will be different tomorrow.

The mountains of the Dingle Peninsula meeting the ocean.

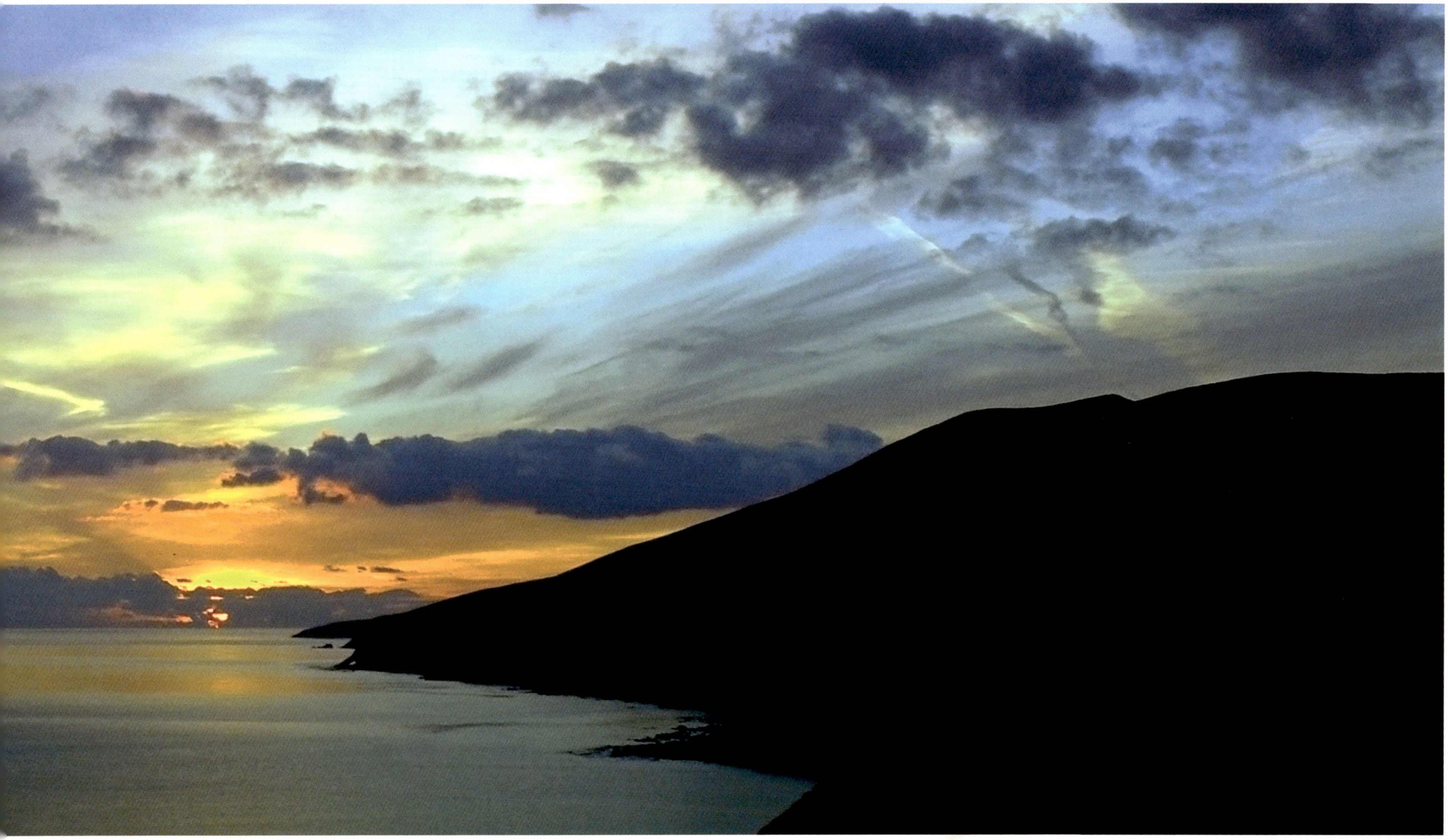

In this eternal flow and change lies much of Ireland's beauty. The proximity of the ocean to the majority of the mountainous regions lends a special presence to days spent there. The Dingle Peninsula in particular has sea and mountain intimately interwoven. Why then is it neccesary to climb the mountain when much of this pageant can be observed in comfort from the valley, or even through a window? One may suppose that such an elevated place as a summit could provide unlimited and uninterrupted views not available from lower down, and that perhaps this is the main benefit of reaching the top. The satisfaction of making the last step to the highest point is the sum of many things, which, if we were to arrive there from above, would leave us short of major parts of the experience. In the following pages we will explore the wealth of detail which is available for us to experience on every outing, and explain why we might want to repeat the apparently futile process of struggling up a hill over and over again.

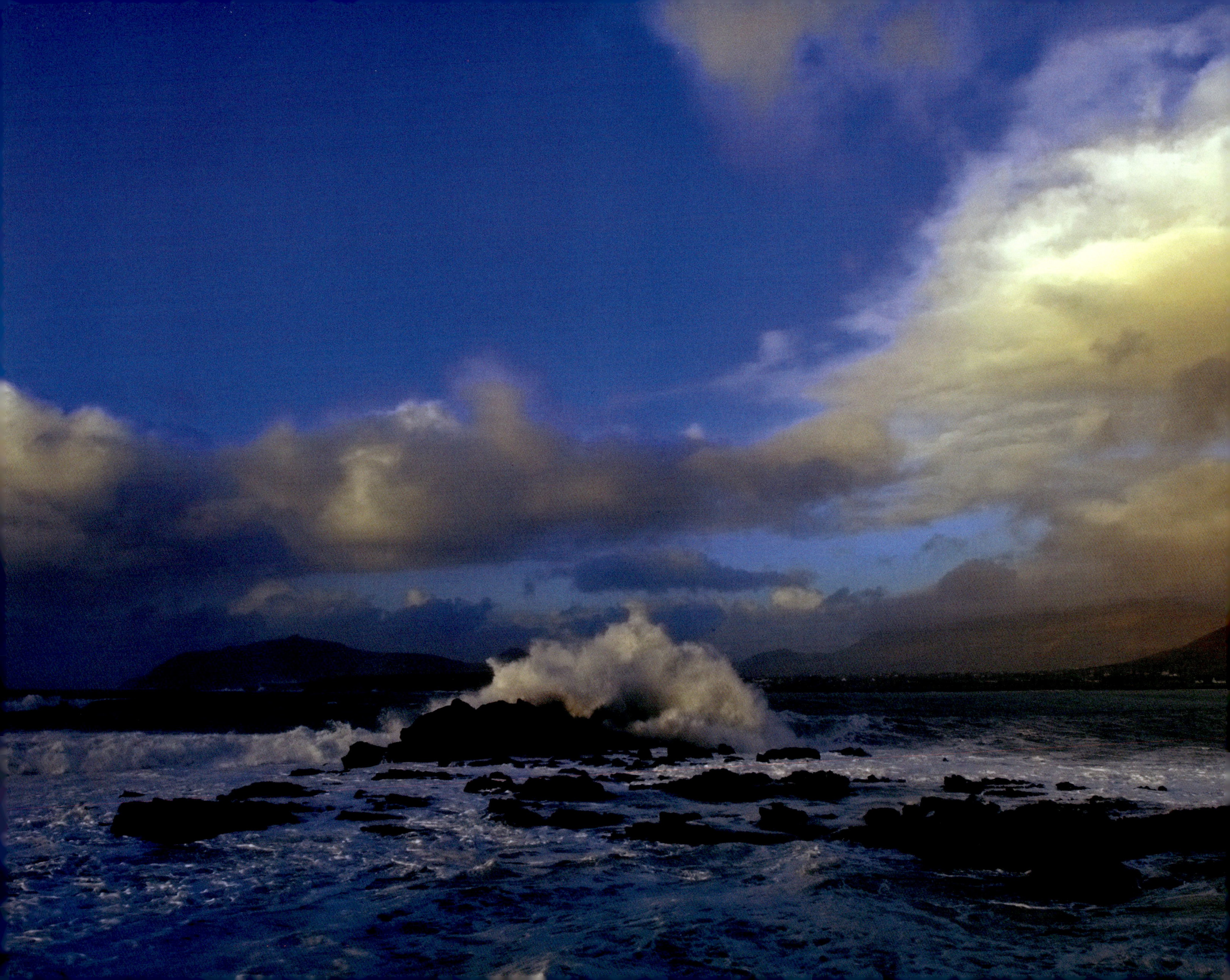

OPPOSITE Smerwick Harbour on the north side of the Dingle Peninsula. Cloud is created over Mount Brandon as humid air from the Atlantic begins to rise.

BELOW LEFT At Brandon Bay, Dingle Peninsula, where the two principal rock types of the region, sandstone and limestone, can be seen together.

BELOW RIGHT Hungry Hill on the Beara Peninsula in the early morning. Bare rock is seen in abundance here.

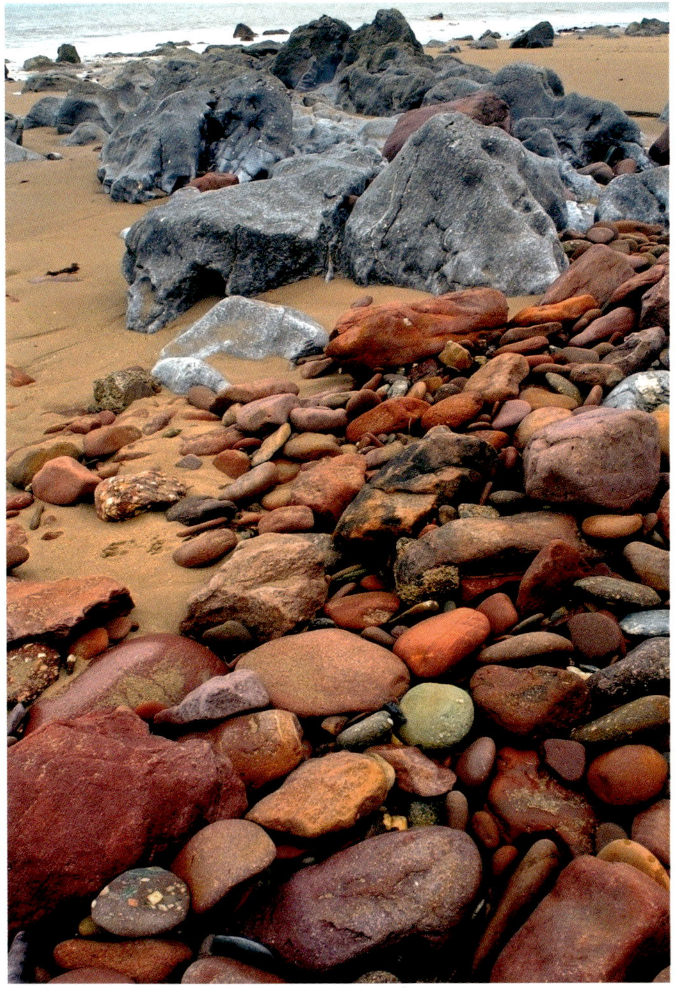

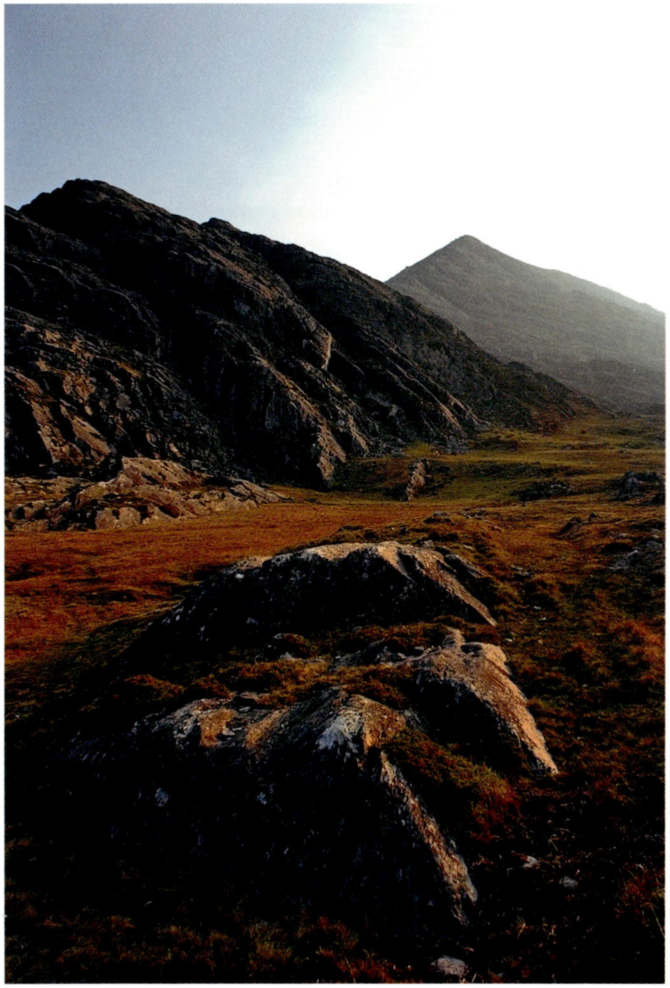

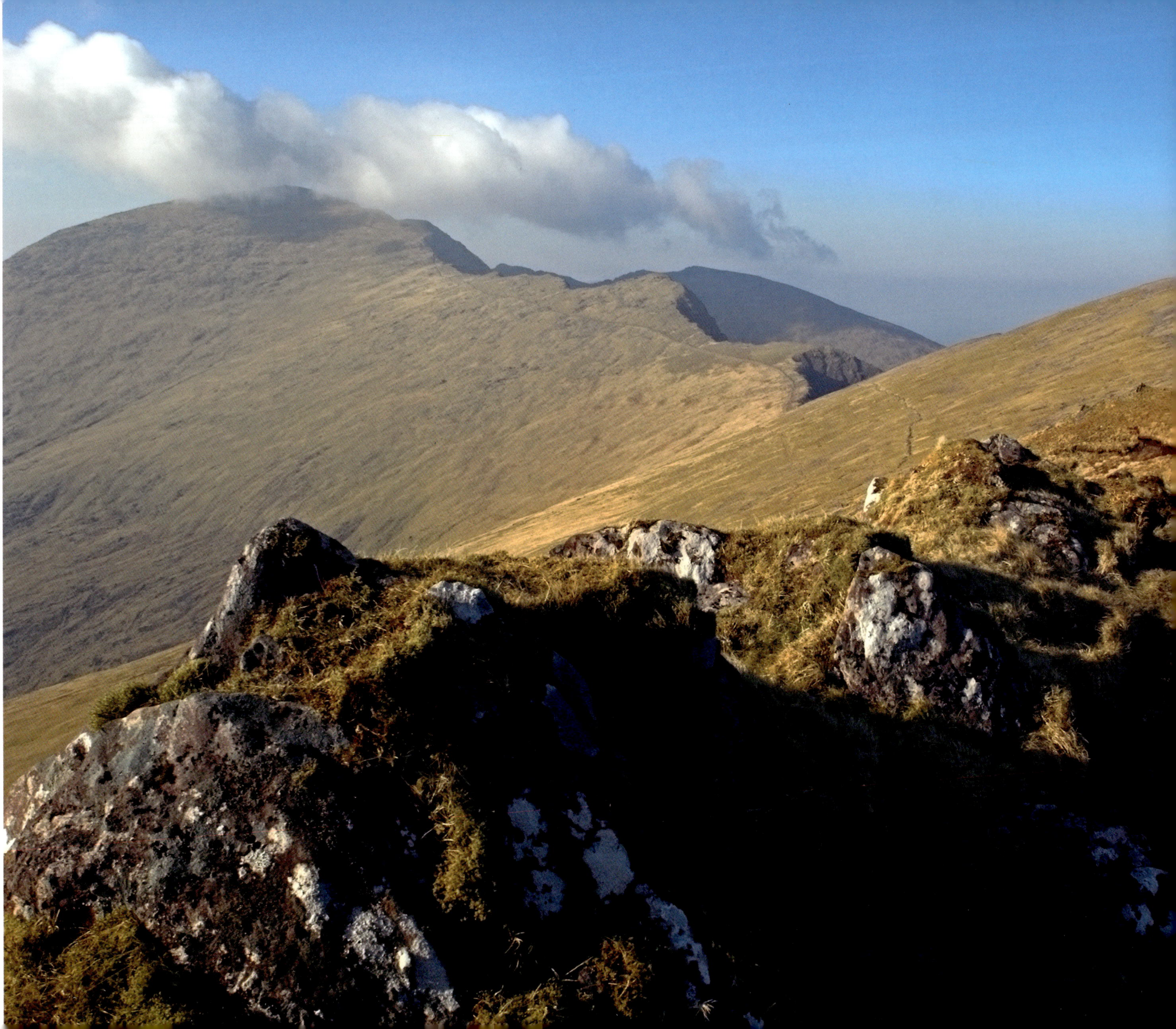

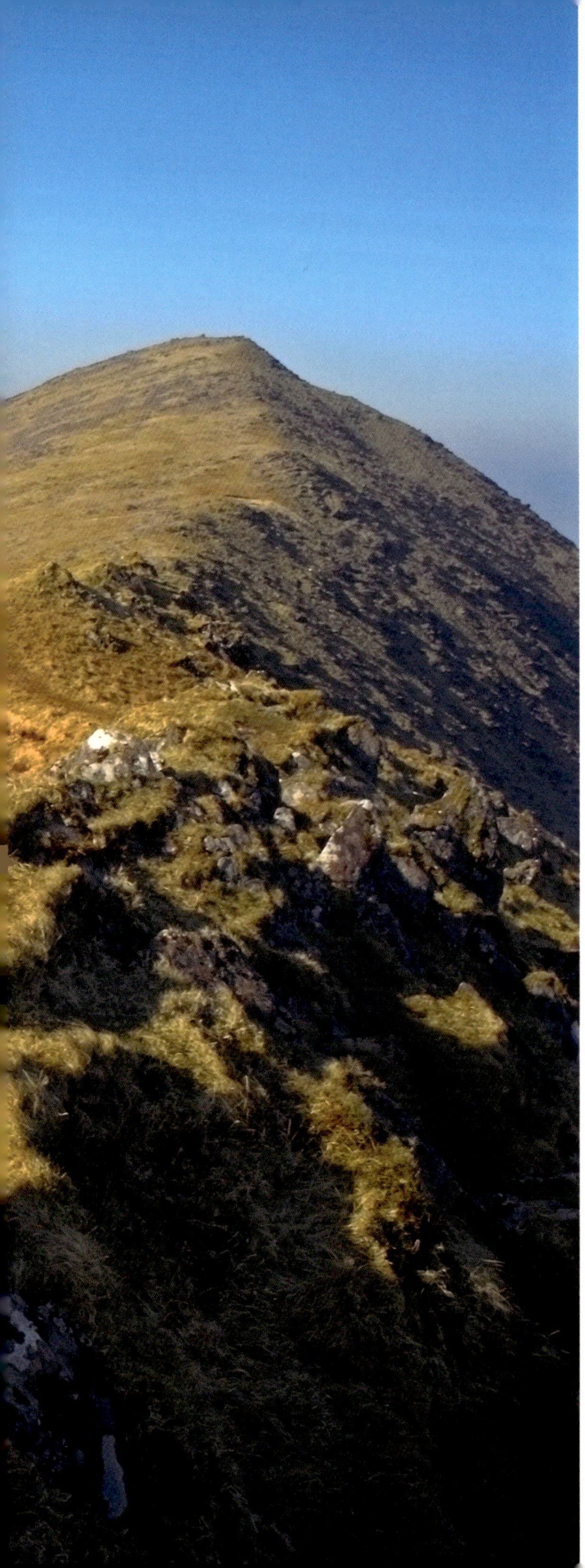

TO THE MOUNTAIN

OPPOSITE The ridge to Mount Brandon from the south passes over Brandon Peak. This route to the summit has superb views in all directions.

RIGHT A small flurry of winter has settled on the slopes of Ballysitteragh, near Dingle.

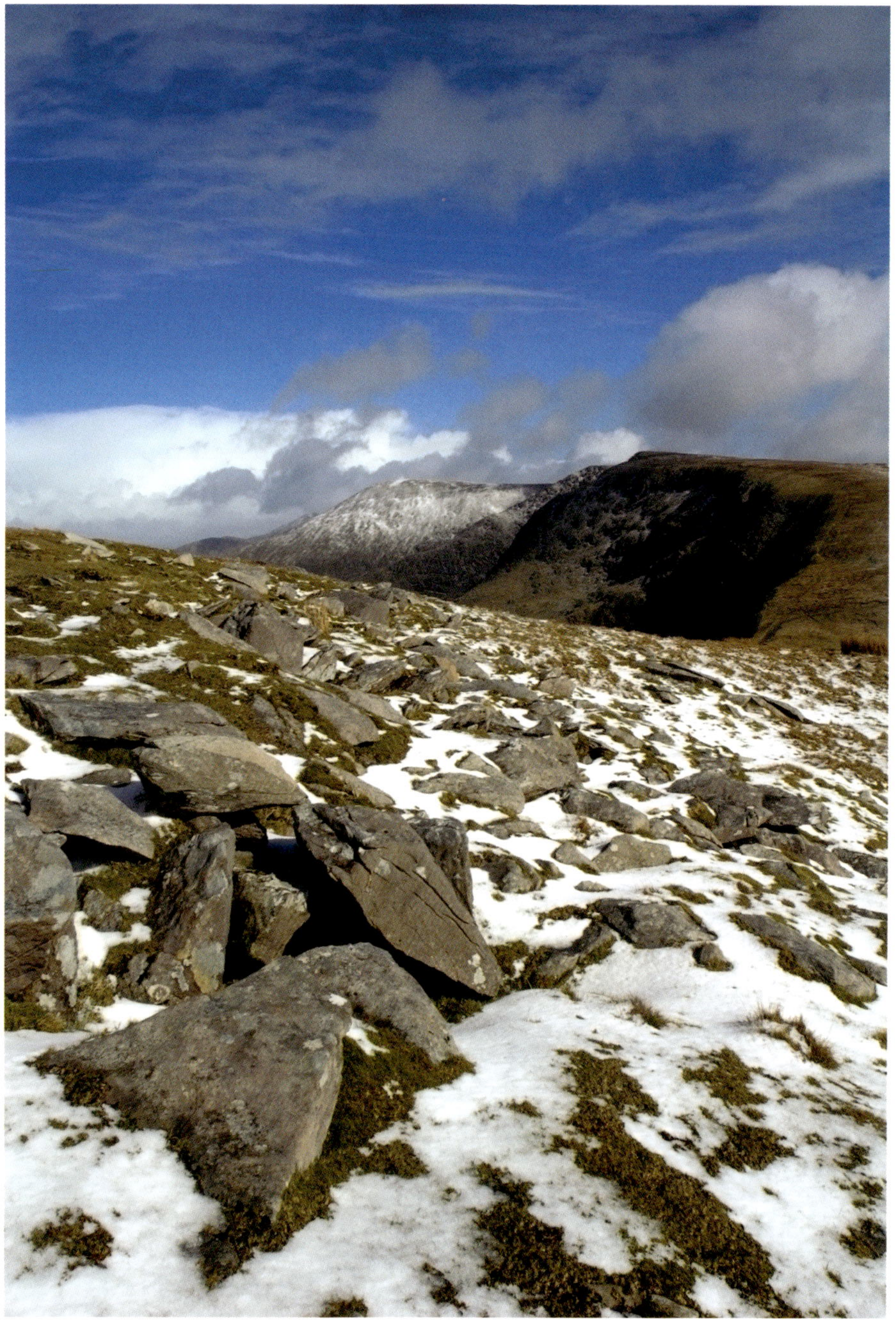

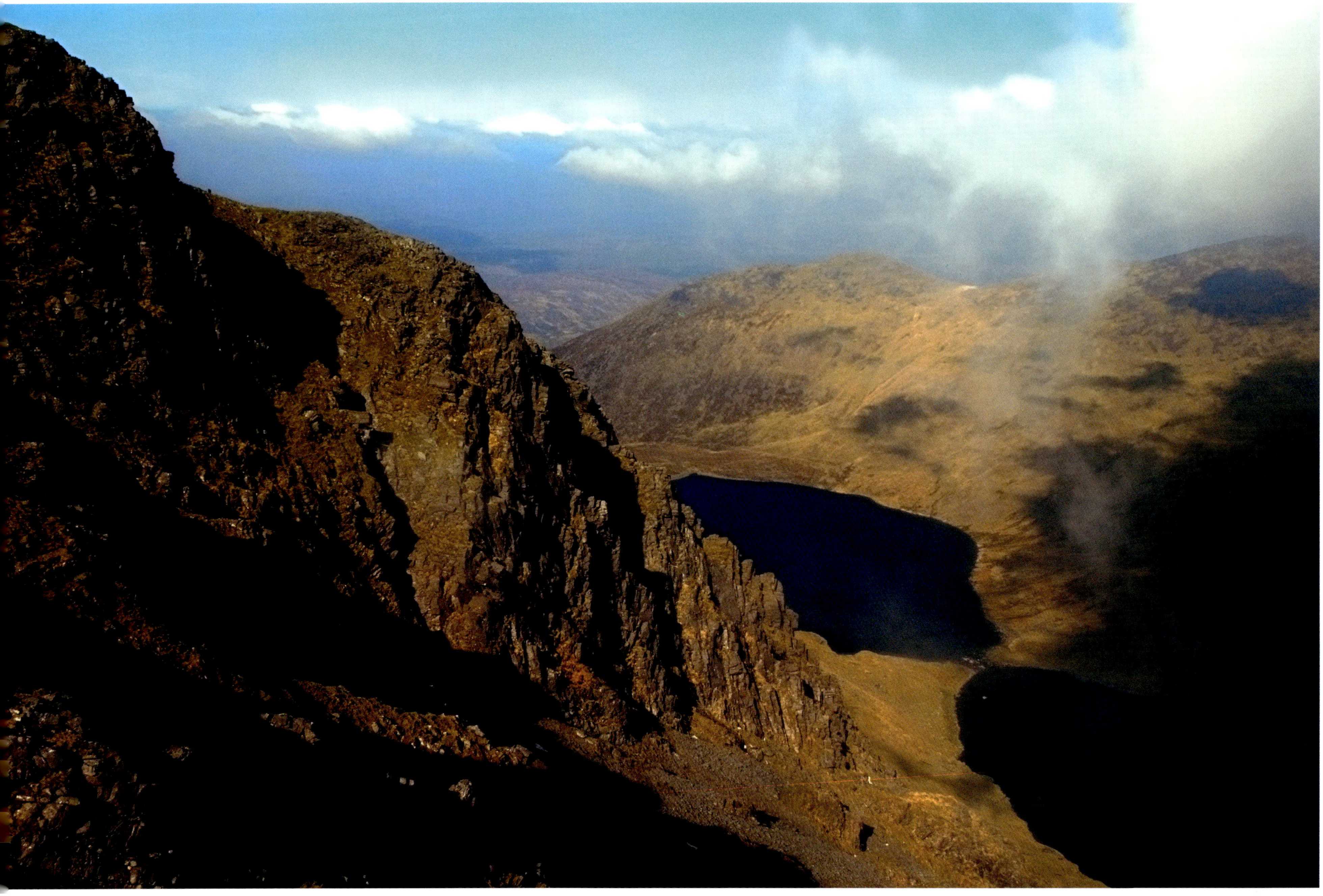

OPPOSITE Looking towards Lough Eagher, on the right, and Lough Coomloughra, from high on Caher in the western Macgillycuddy's Reeks.

BELOW The ridge of Caher leading left to the summit of Carrauntouhil, seen from Lough Coomloughra.

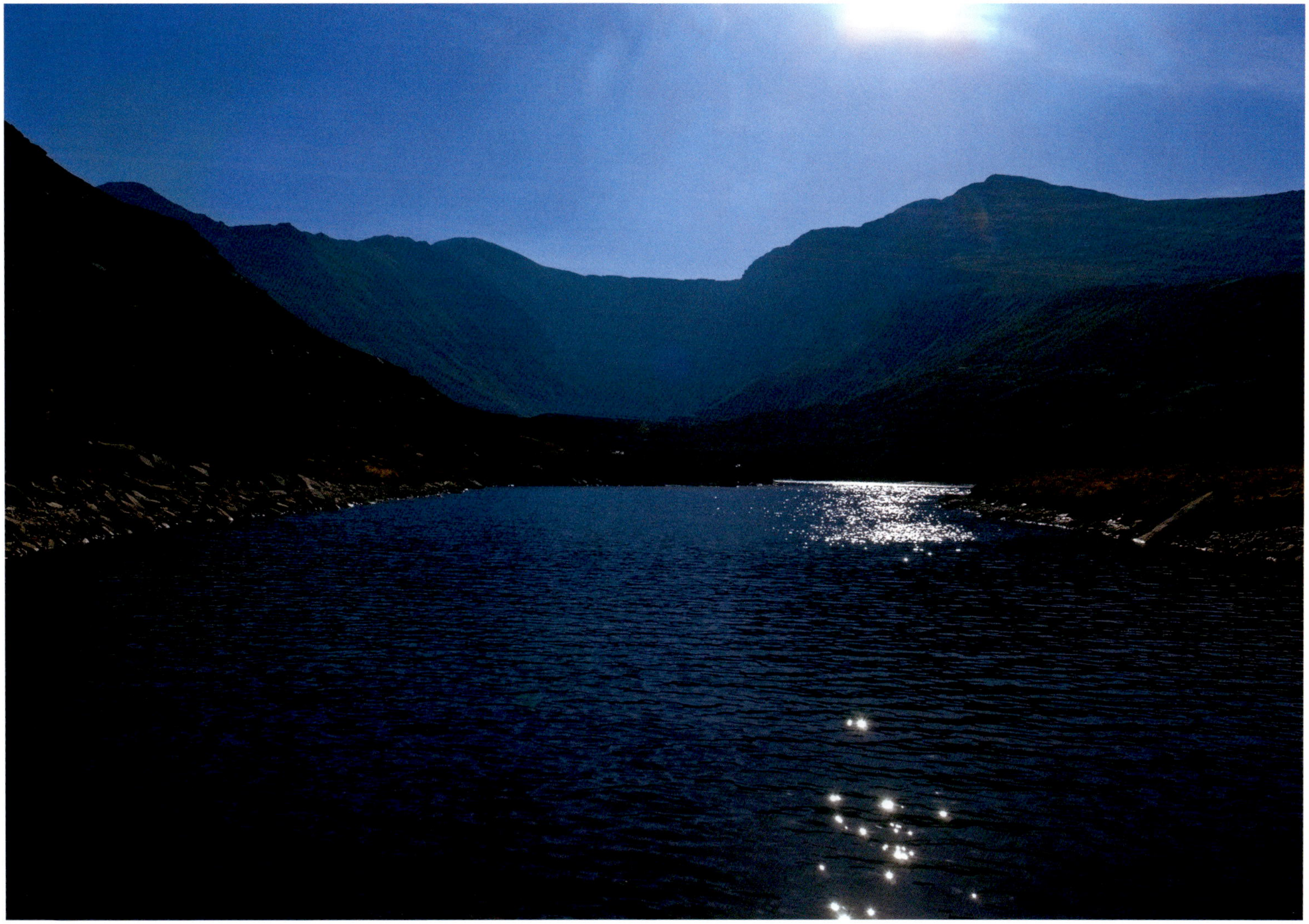

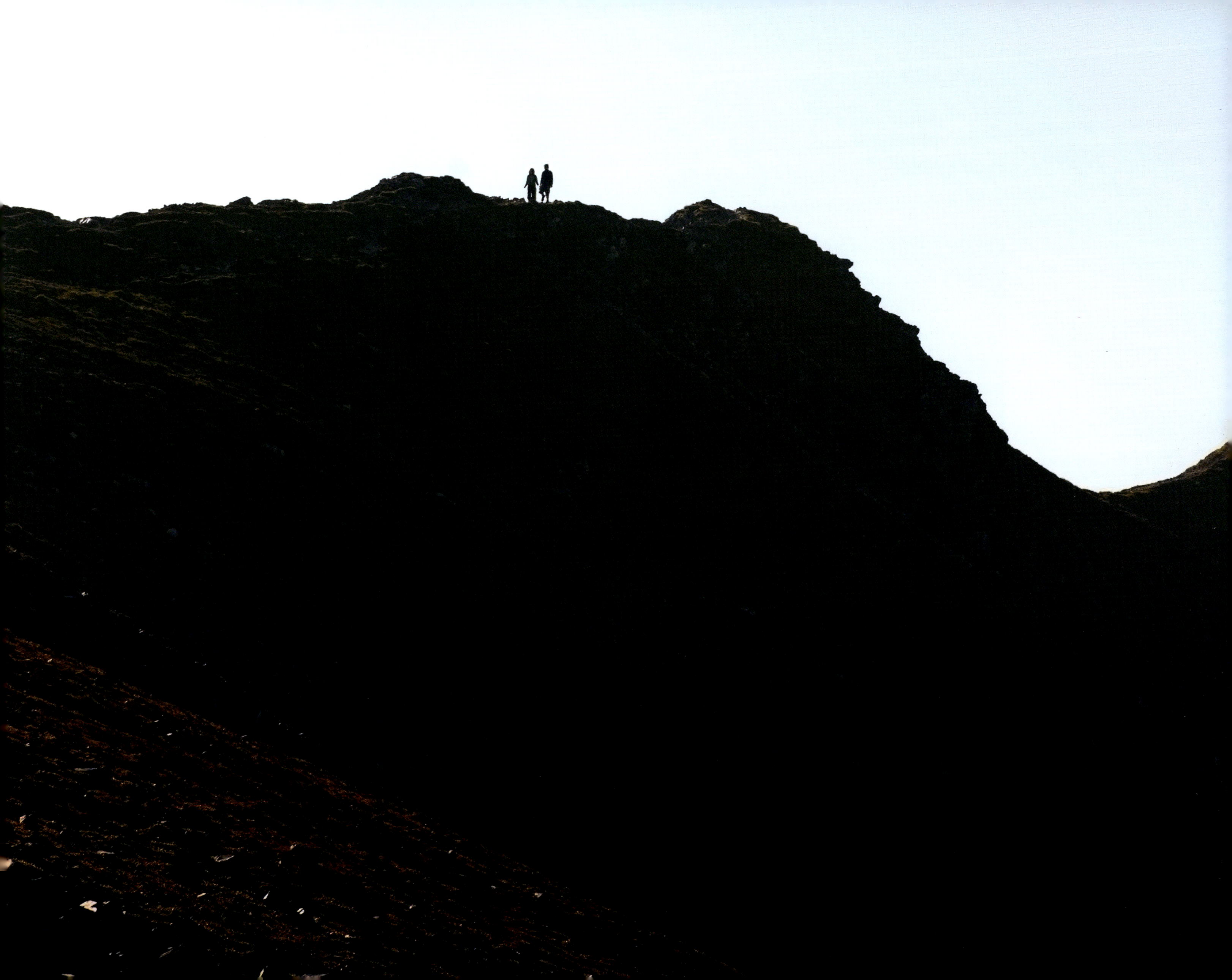

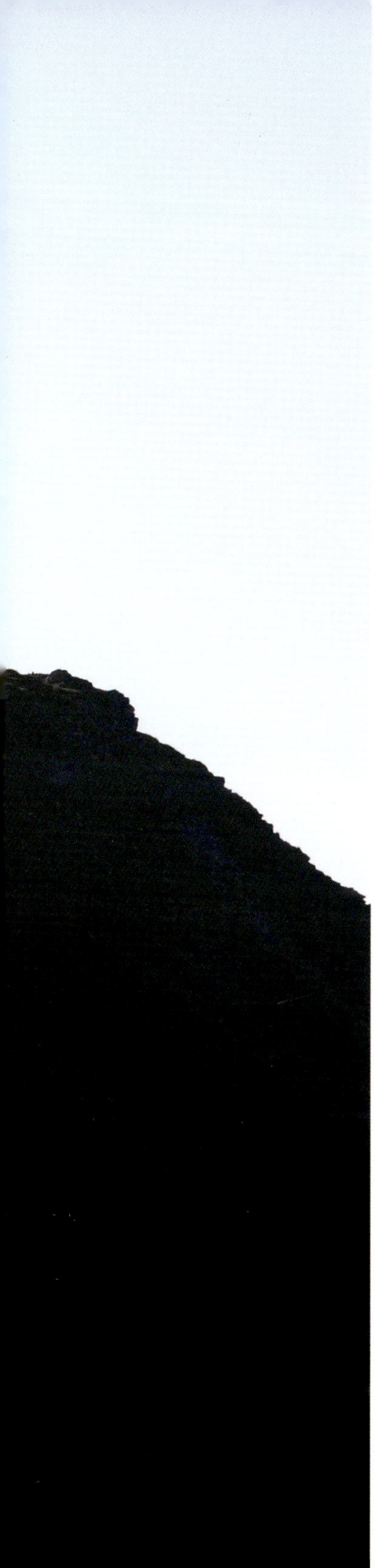

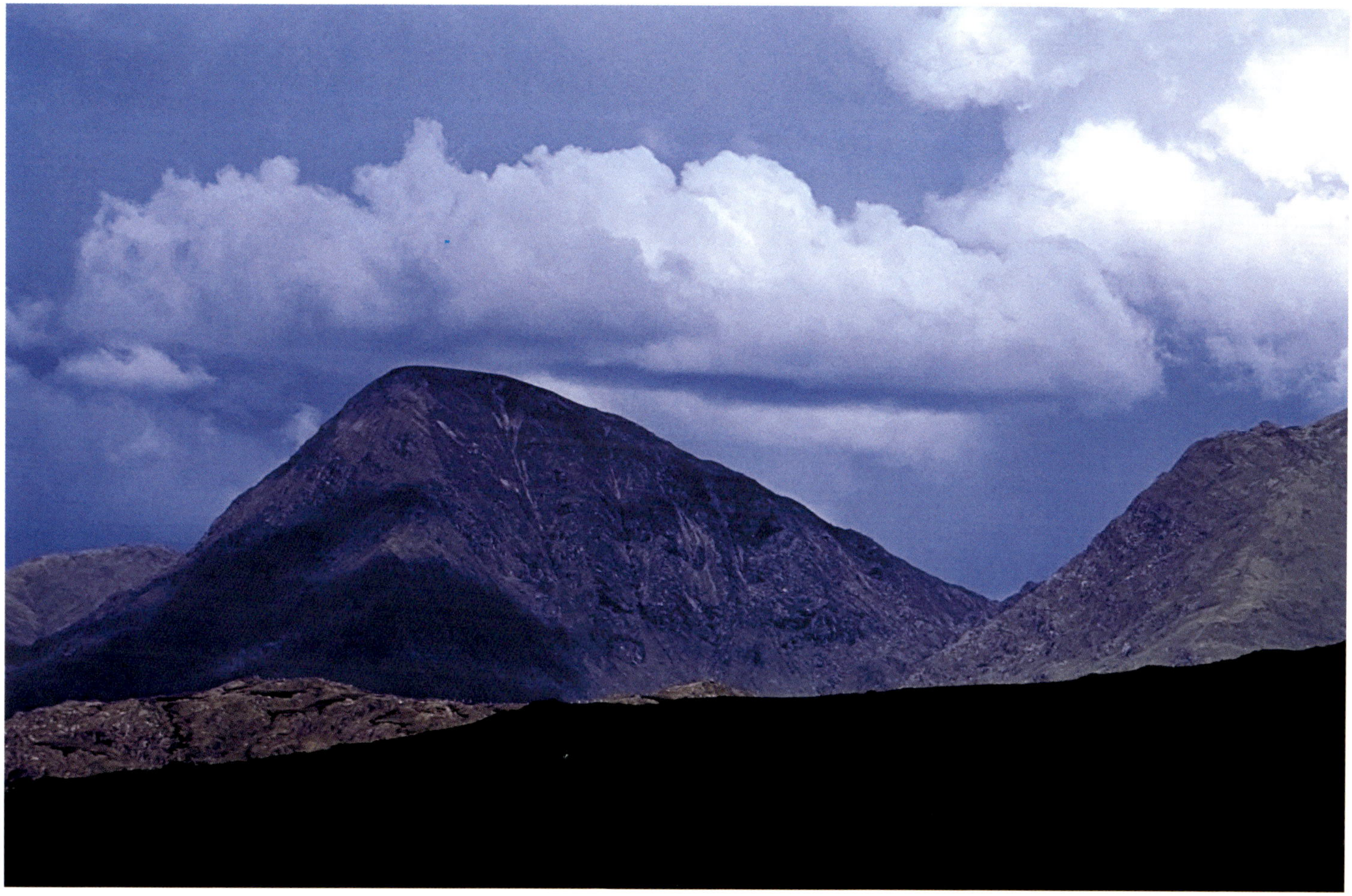

HIGH ON THE MOUNTAIN

OPPOSITE Climbers on the ridge of Caher in the Macgillycuddy's Reeks.

ABOVE The spectacular peak of Broaghnabinnia, 745 metres, stands at the head of the Black Valley, to the south of the main ridge of the Macgillycuddy's Reeks.

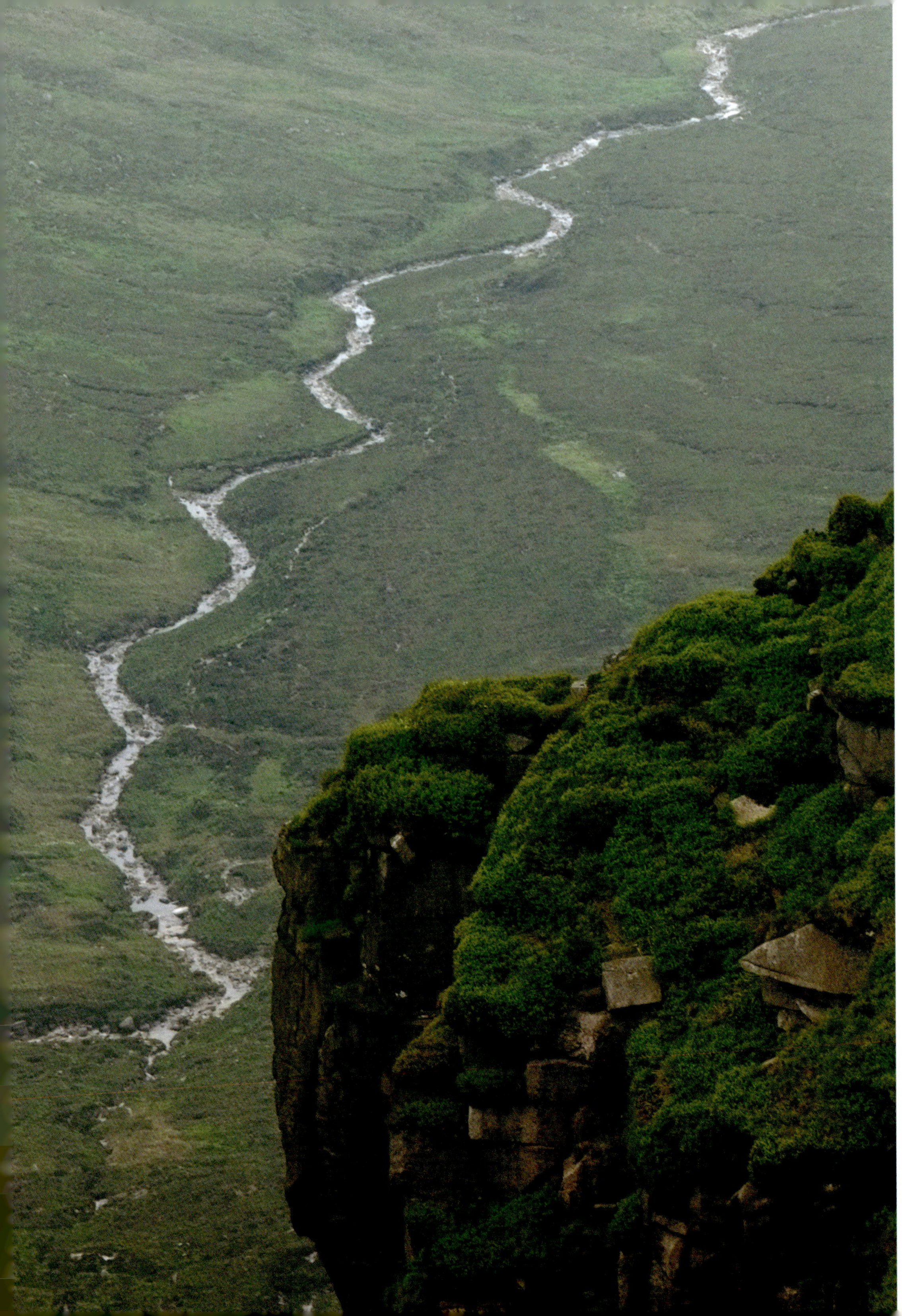

SPACE AROUND US

LEFT The abrupt end to the Devil's Coach Road, high above the headwaters of the Annalong River, in the Mournes, County Down.

OPPOSITE Looking across to Stradbally Mountain, from Ballysitteragh in the Dingle Peninsula.

OVERLEAF Mount Brandon, County Kerry, from the air as early mist clears from the peak. Smerwick Harbour lies in the distance, with Mount Eagle in the cloud beyond. Sea and mountain lie so close to each other here.

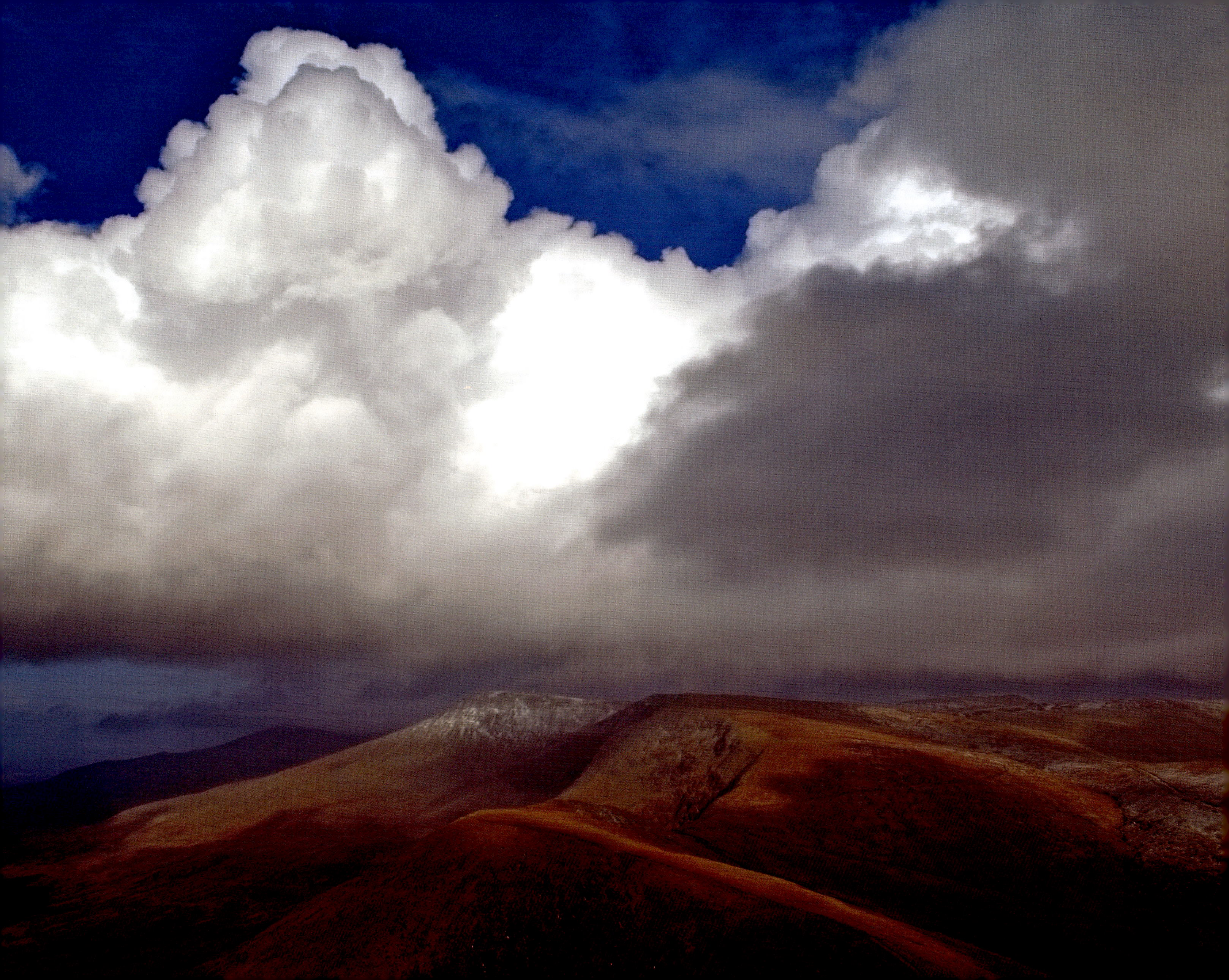

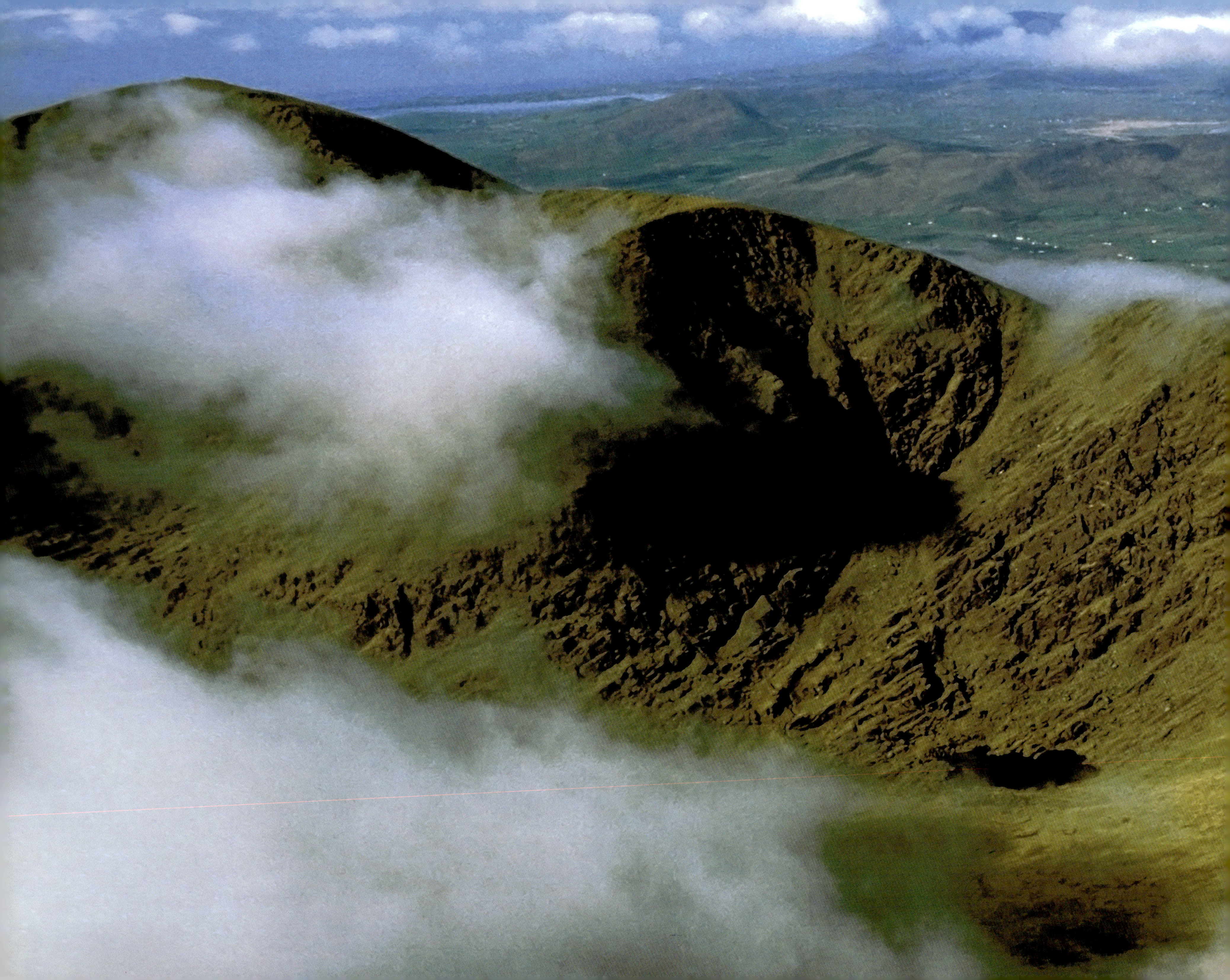

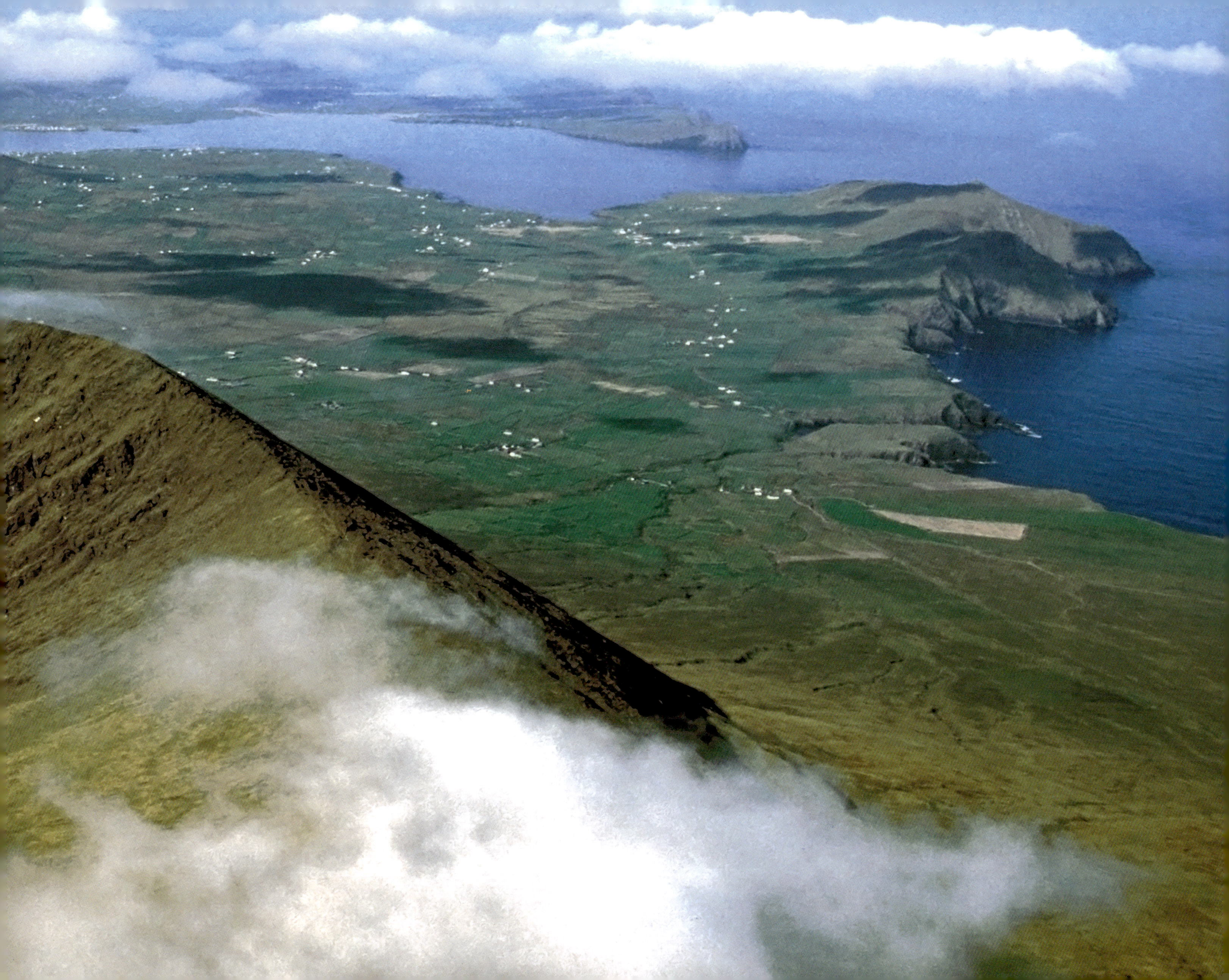

BELOW Heather growing in a crack of quartz-streaked rock: a small echo of the greater scene.

OPPOSITE The Twelve Bens in County Galway from the air, looking across the peaks of the Derryclare Horseshoe to the Maumturks.

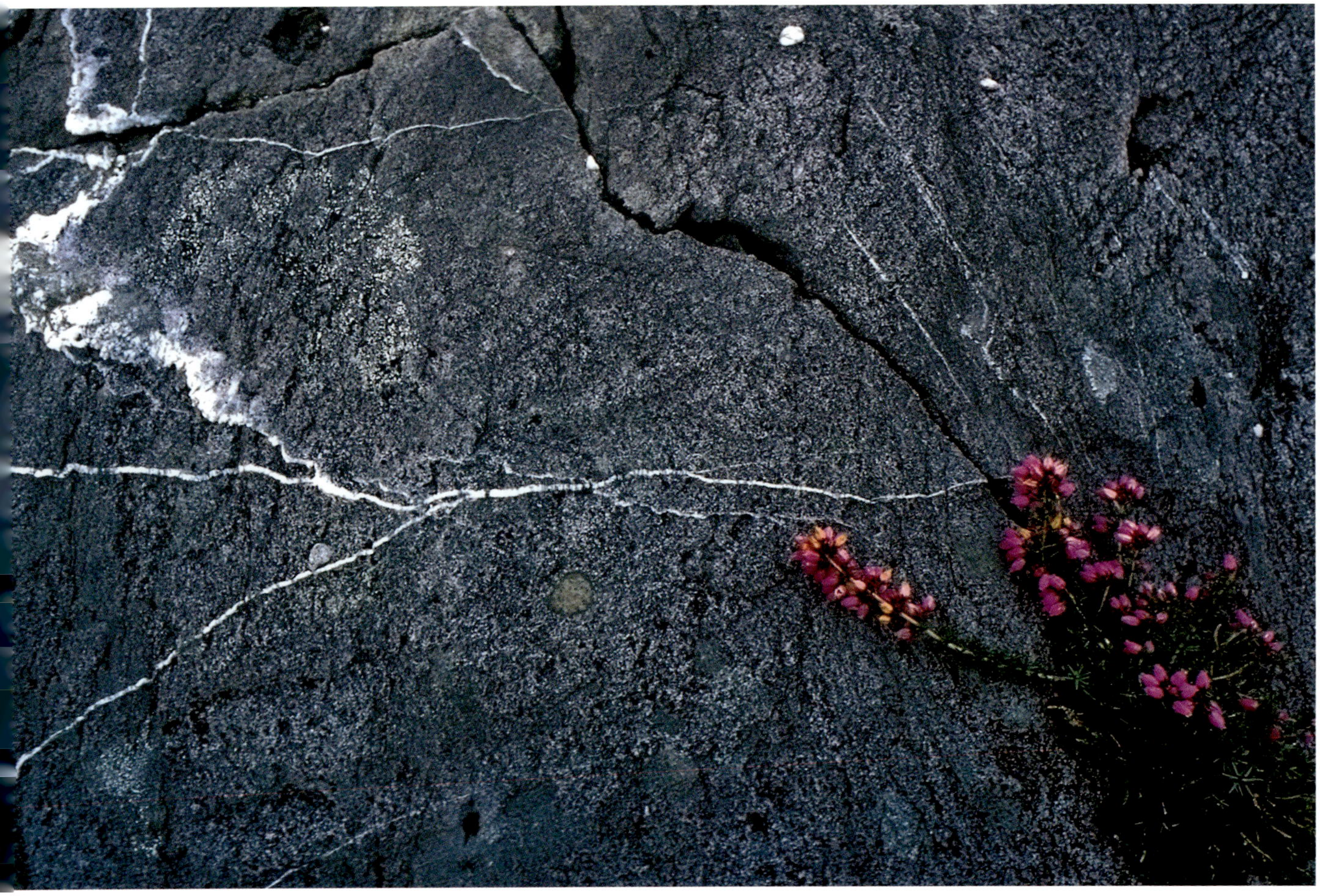

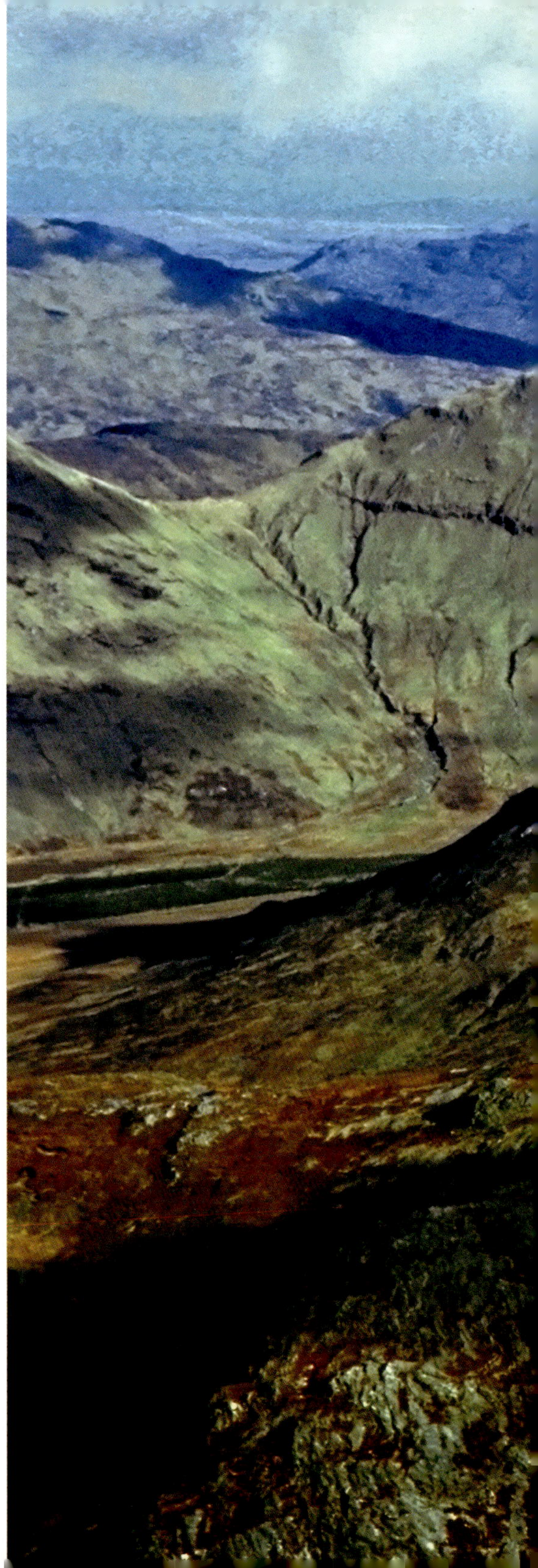

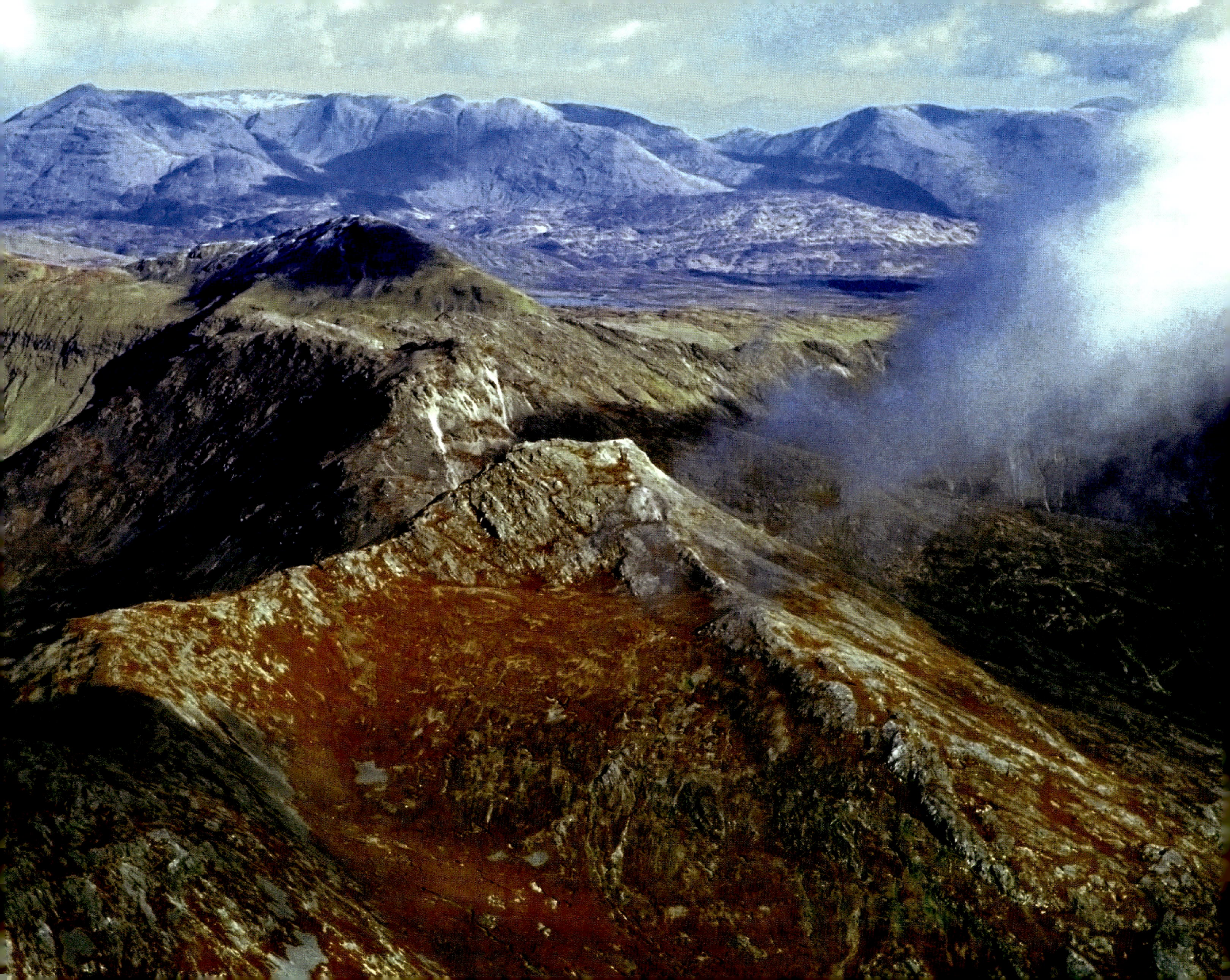

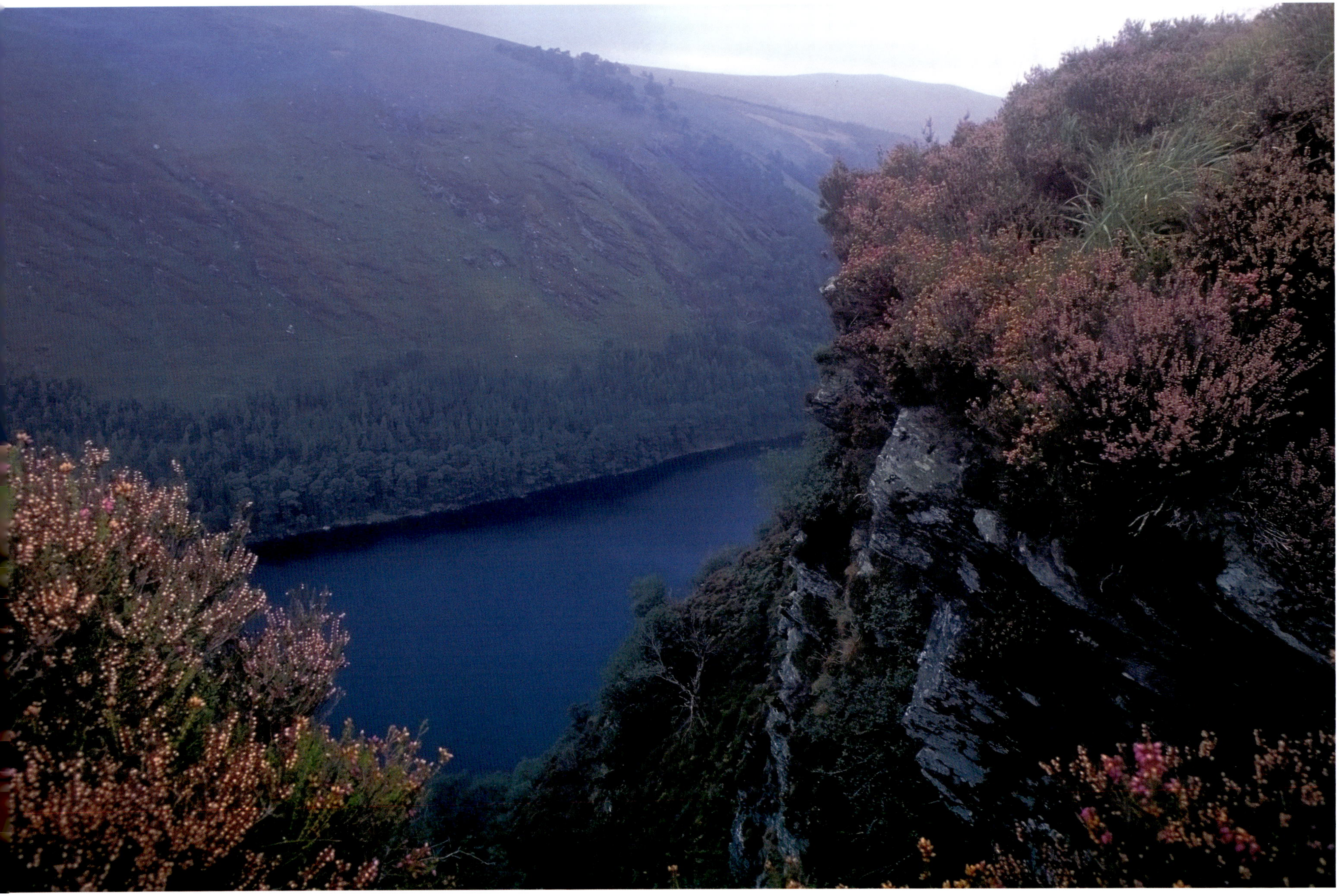

OPPOSITE Looking down to the Upper Lough at Glendalough, County Wicklow, and across to the slopes of Camaderry, from Spink Mountain.

BELOW Cotton grass, or bog cotton, grows in profusion in the wet moorland below Errigal, County Donegal.

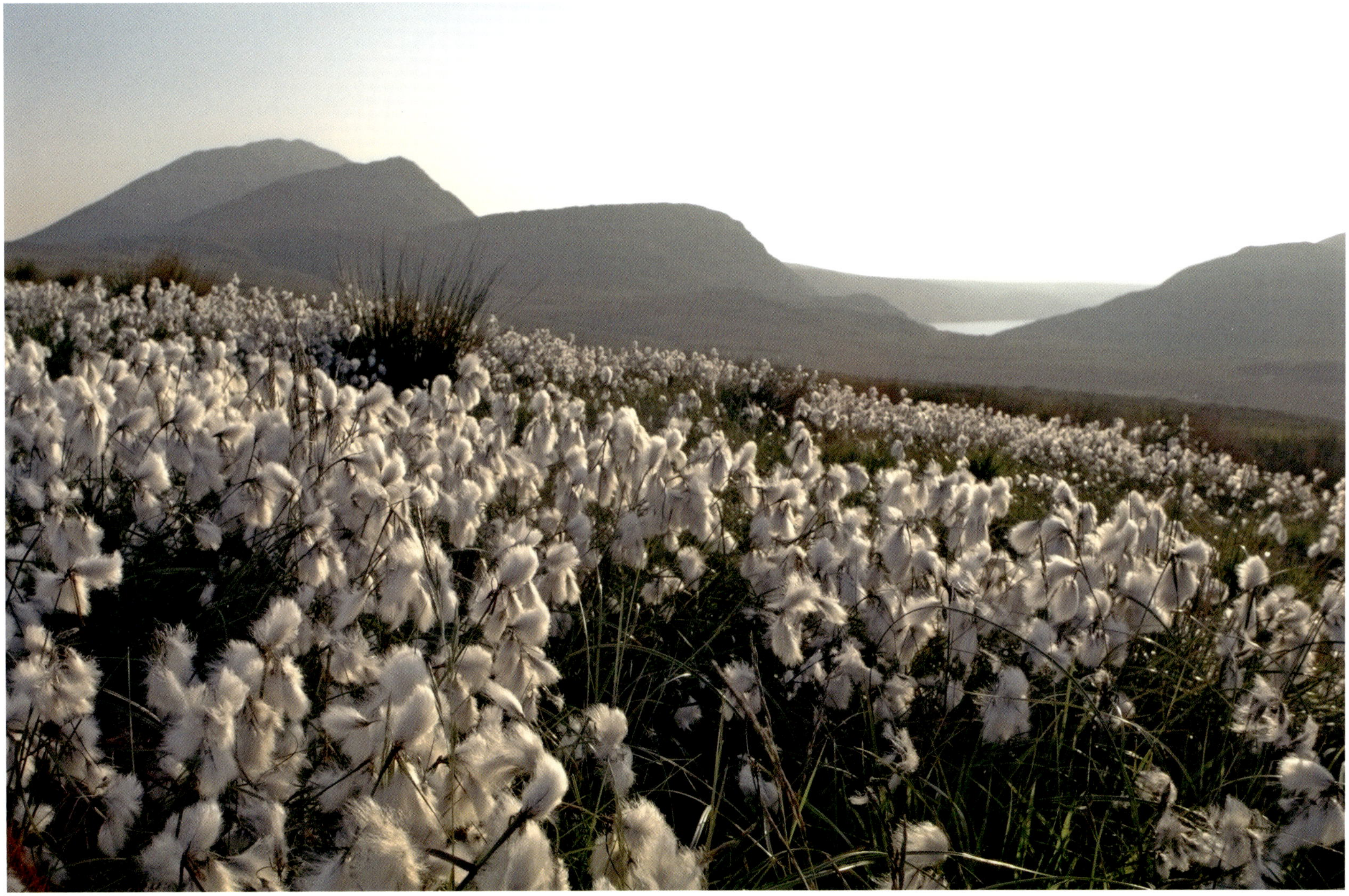

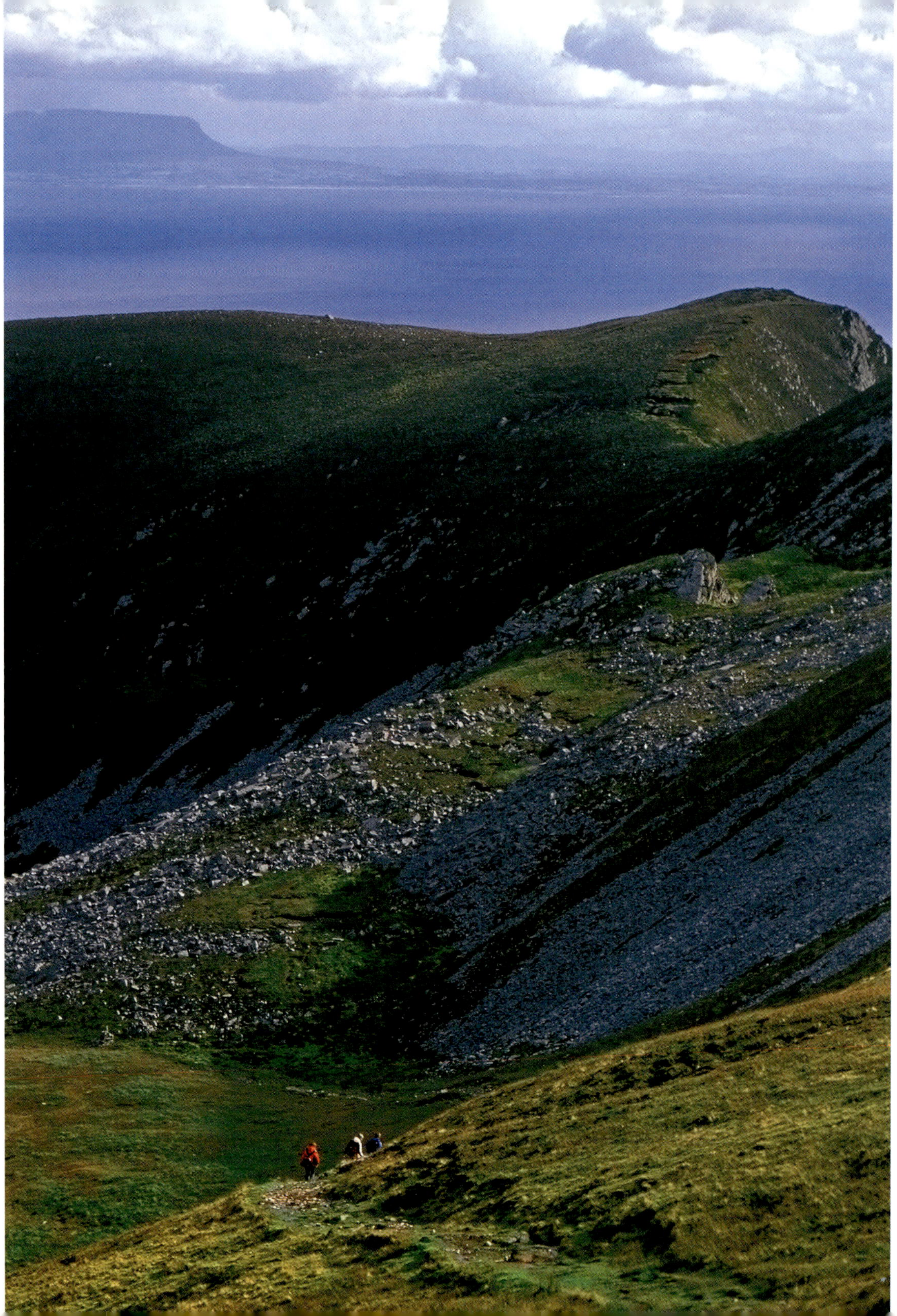

DESCENDING

LEFT Descending from Slieve League on the Pilgrim's Path. Ben Bulben, in North Sligo, can be seen across Donegal Bay.

OPPOSITE A waterfall on Caherbarnagh Mountain, 681 metres, at the eastern end of the Killarney Mountains in County Cork.

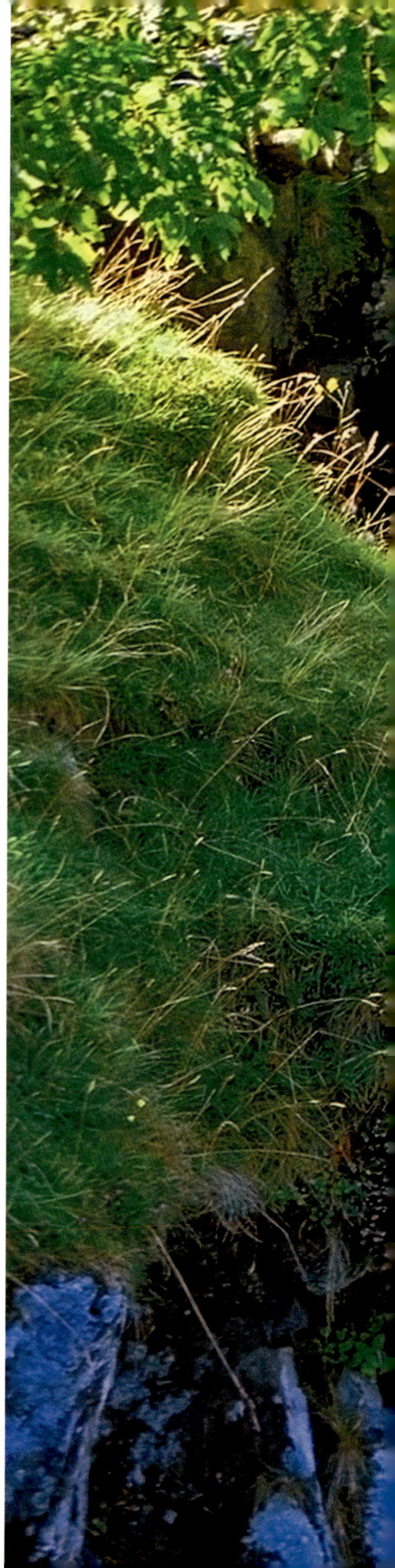

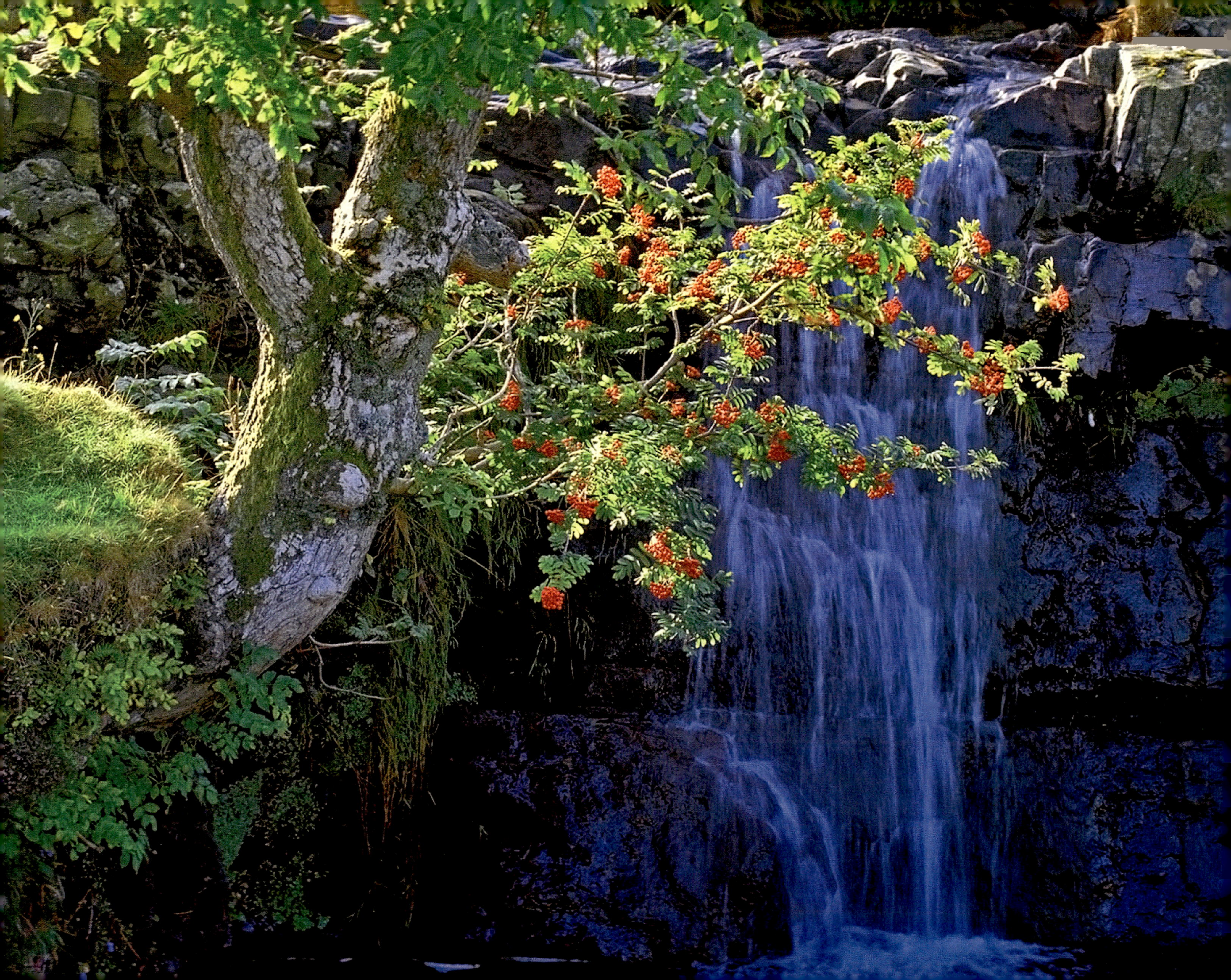

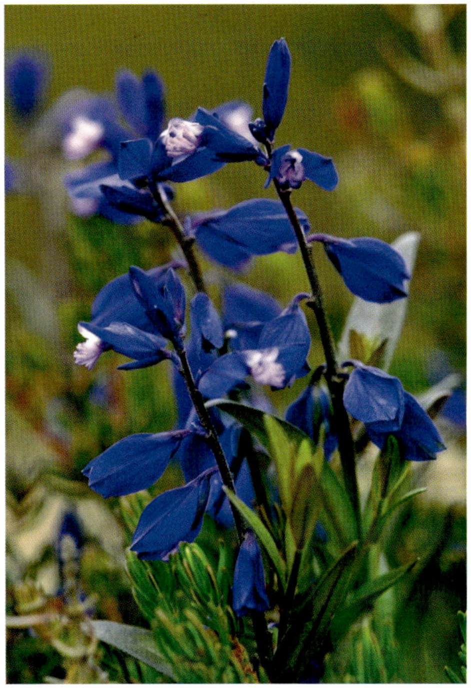

NEARING THE VALLEY

LEFT The delicate flowers of milkwort stand out from the brown of the boggy hillsides.

OPPOSITE The frothing brown waters of the Scaul River, plunging down the dramatic valley of Coom Dubh, near Annascaul on the Dingle Peninsula.

BELOW The water of Mahon Falls running from the slopes of Knockaunapeebra in the Comeragh Mountains, County Waterford.

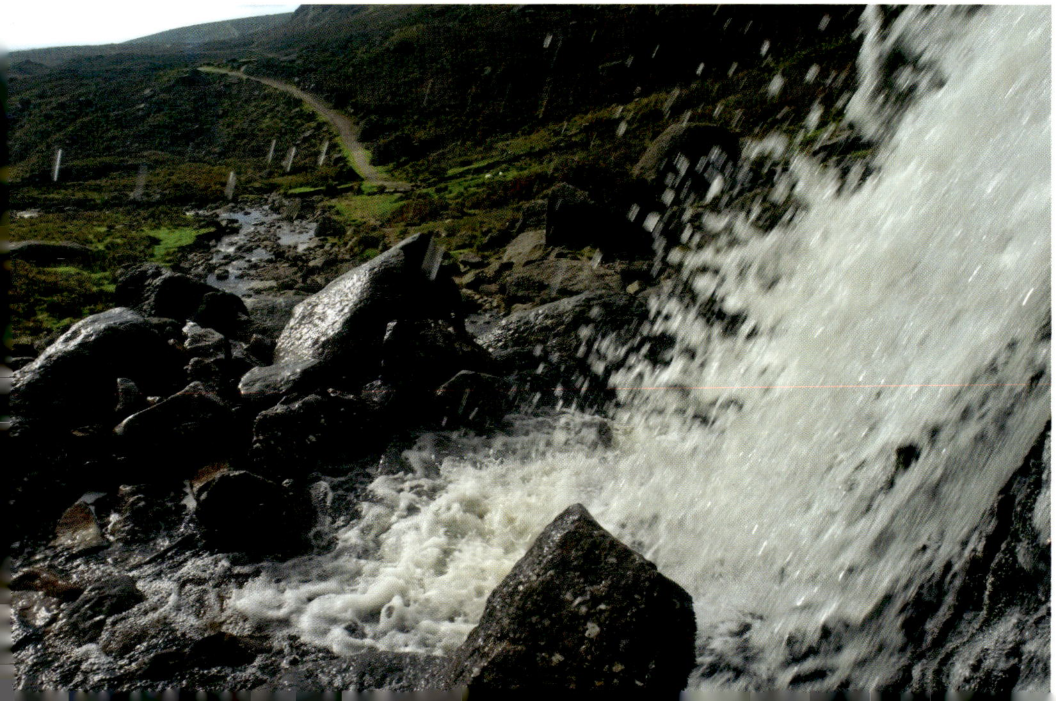

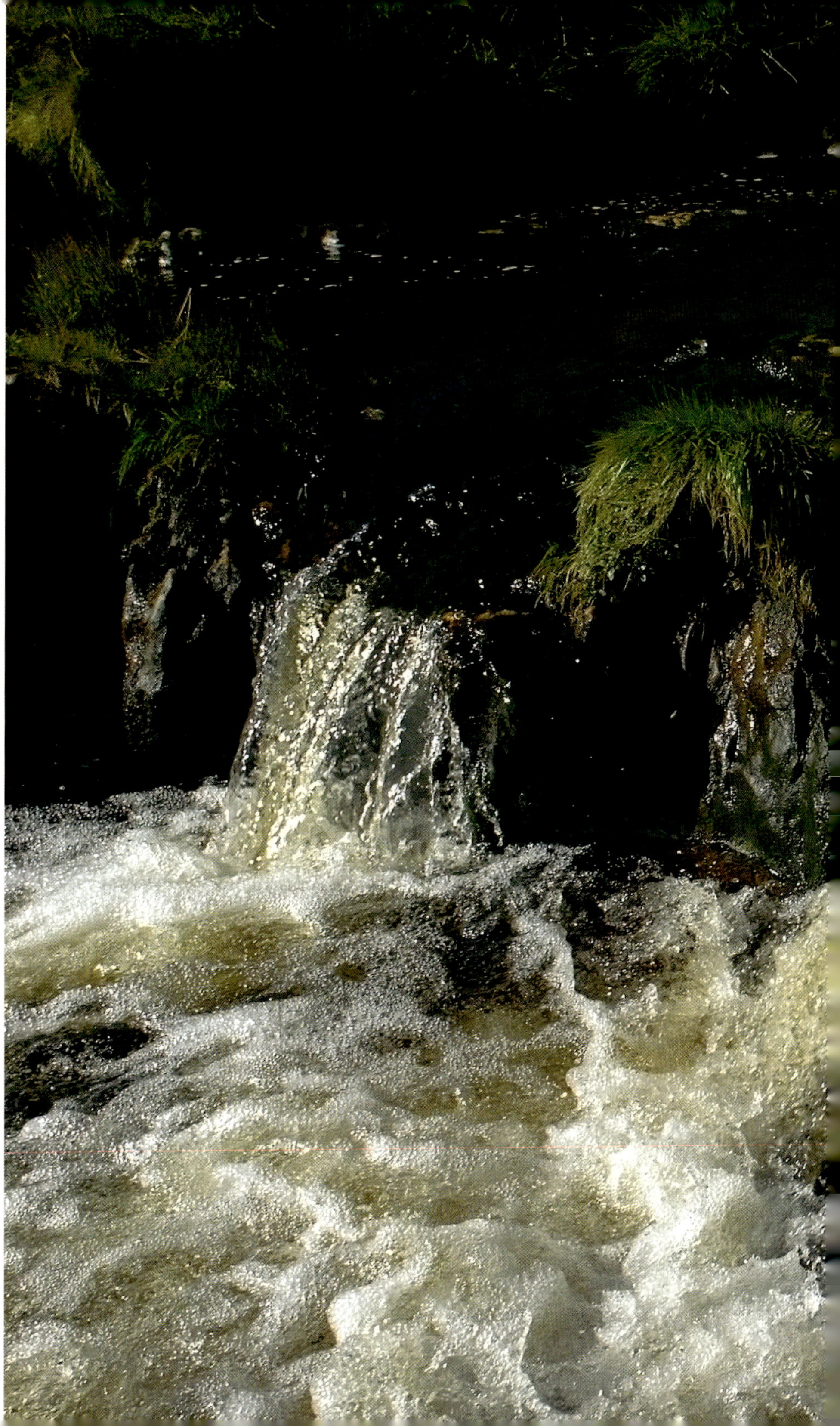

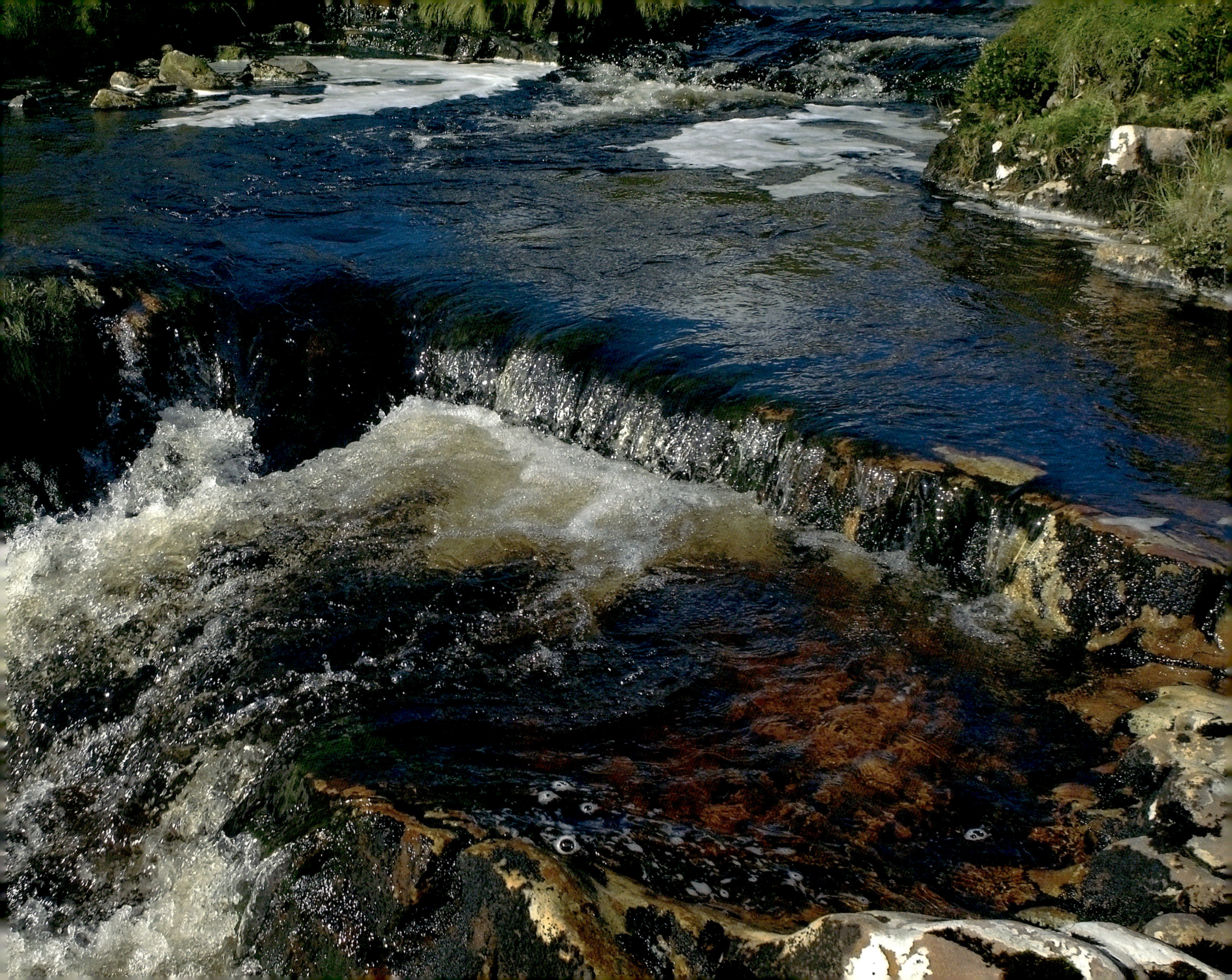

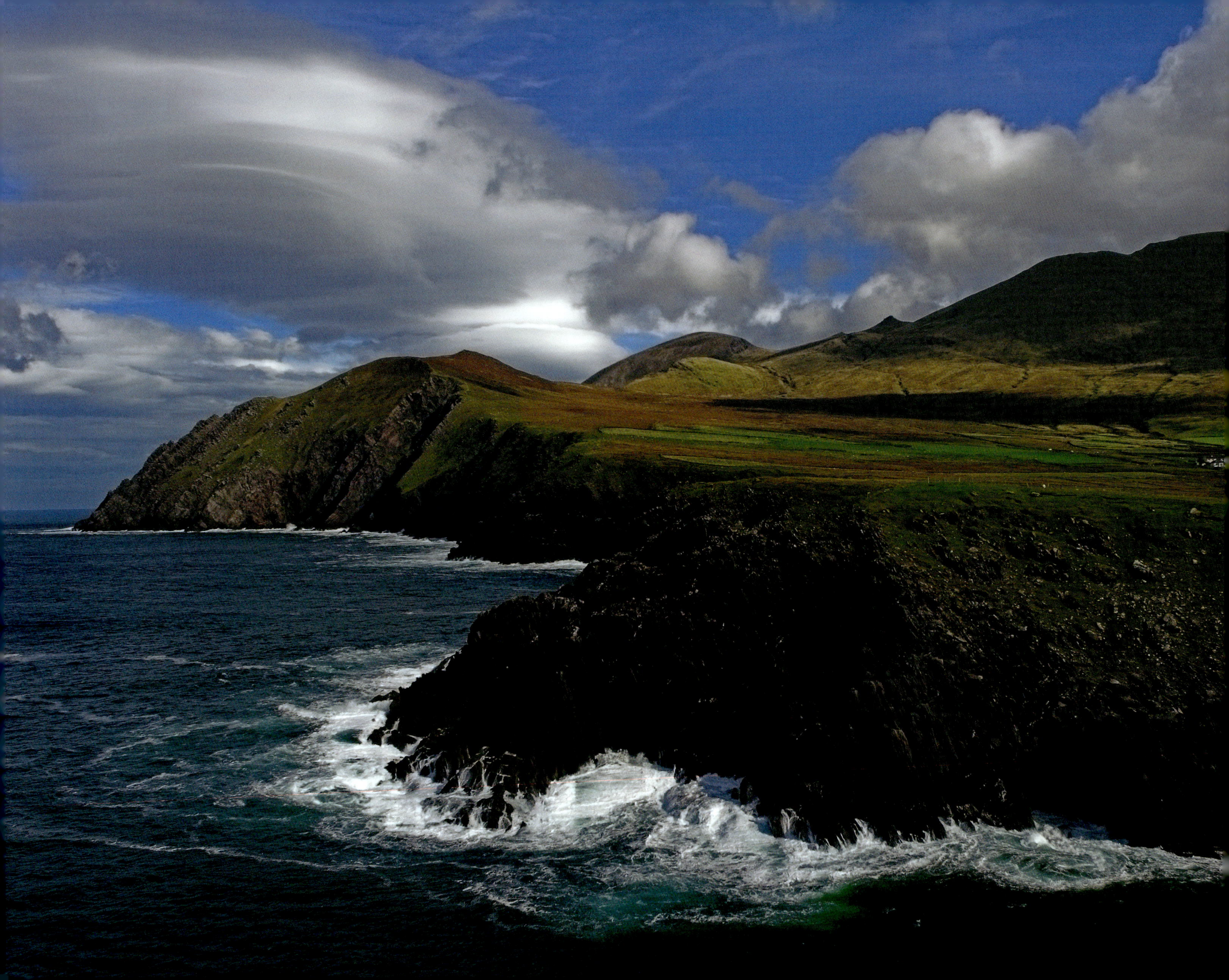

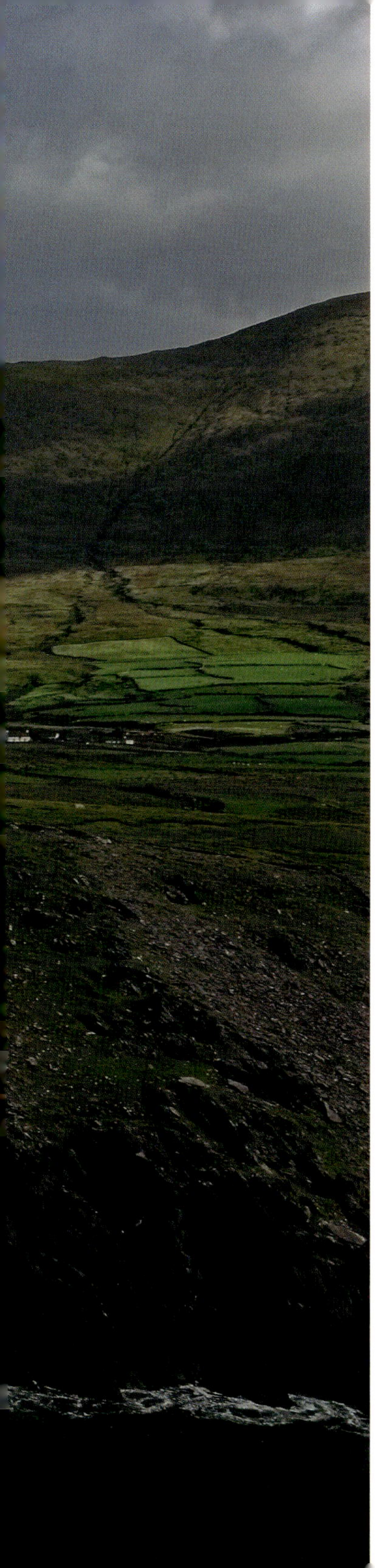

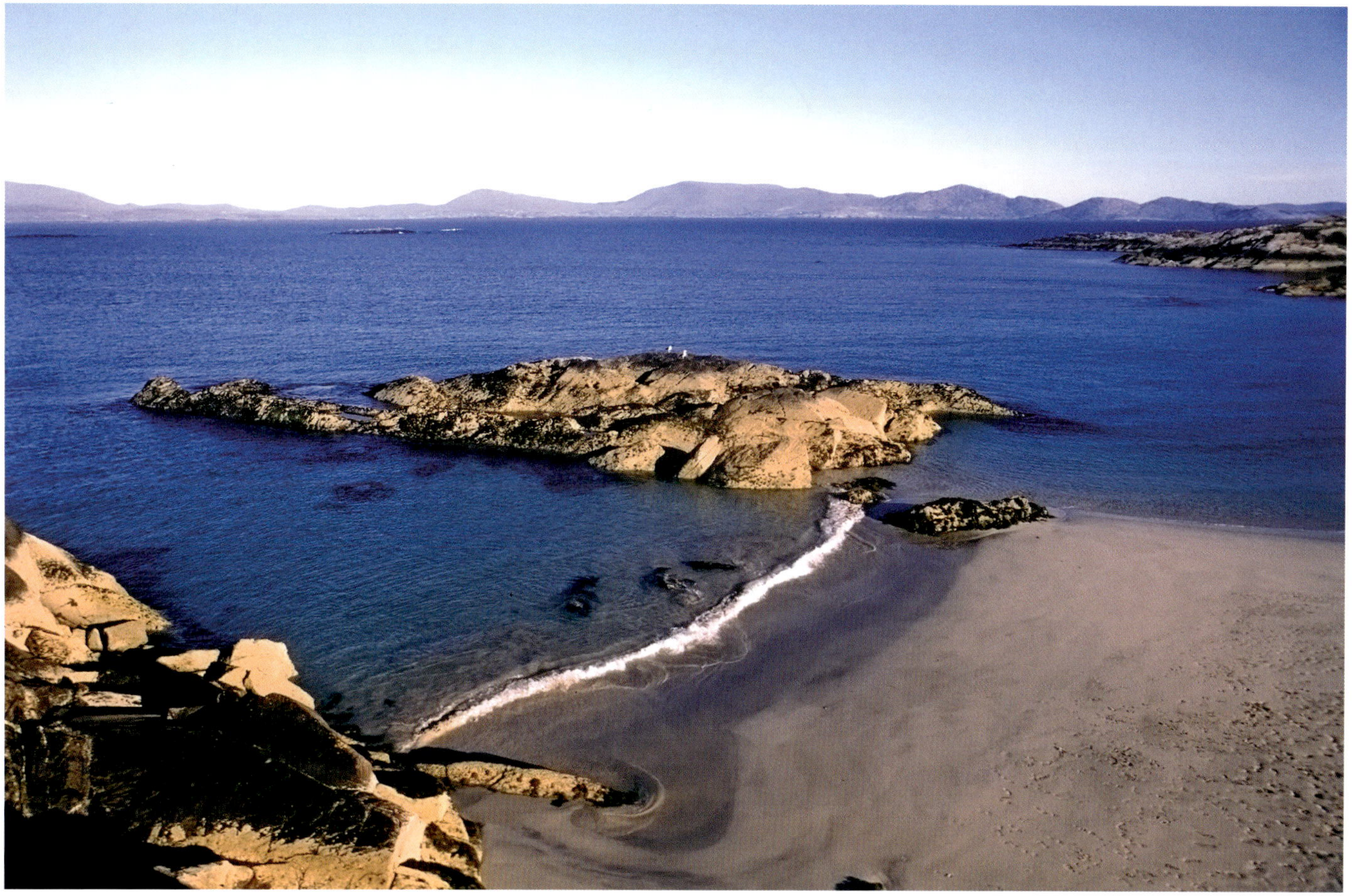

RETURN TO THE SEA

OPPOSITE Mount Brandon slides into the sea at Brandon Creek, County Kerry, where St Brendan set off for America in a leather boat.

ABOVE Church Cove, on the Iveragh Peninsula, County Kerry, looking across to the peaks of the Beara Peninsula.

THE BEAUTY OF FORM

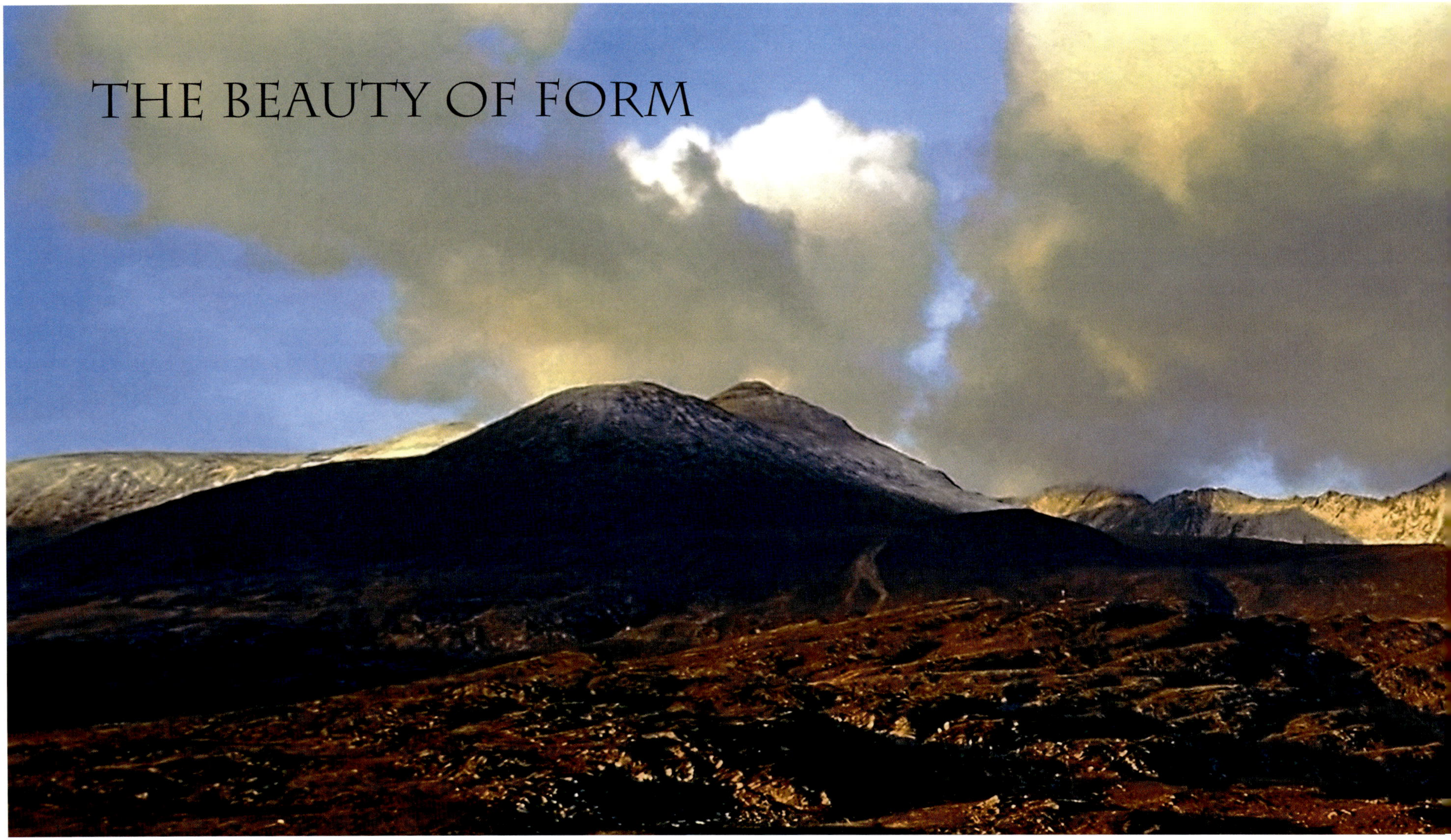

The succession of days draws in endless variations of light and shade, of cloud and sky, of calm and storm, each change representing to our eyes a landscape which is fresh and unique. Every part of a day has its own quality; at dawn, when the air is clear, shades of red and purple flood the sky and light up cloud. This time, not often seen in summer, when first light may be as early as 4.00 a.m., has a delicately beautiful quality, coloured also by the anticipation of the opening of a day, with all its unknown possibilities; the mysteries of night ebb with the advance of light. The growing fullness of sunlight, as the morning progresses, gives contrast between light and shade, and accentuates the features and texture of landscape. This etching of detail happens particularly strongly in winter, when the angle of light is low throughout the day, as the sun describes a much shallower arc across the sky. The middle parts of the day show themselves as they are, straight, in all their detail; little is hidden.

The Coomloughra Horseshoe, Macgillycuddy's Reeks, County Kerry.

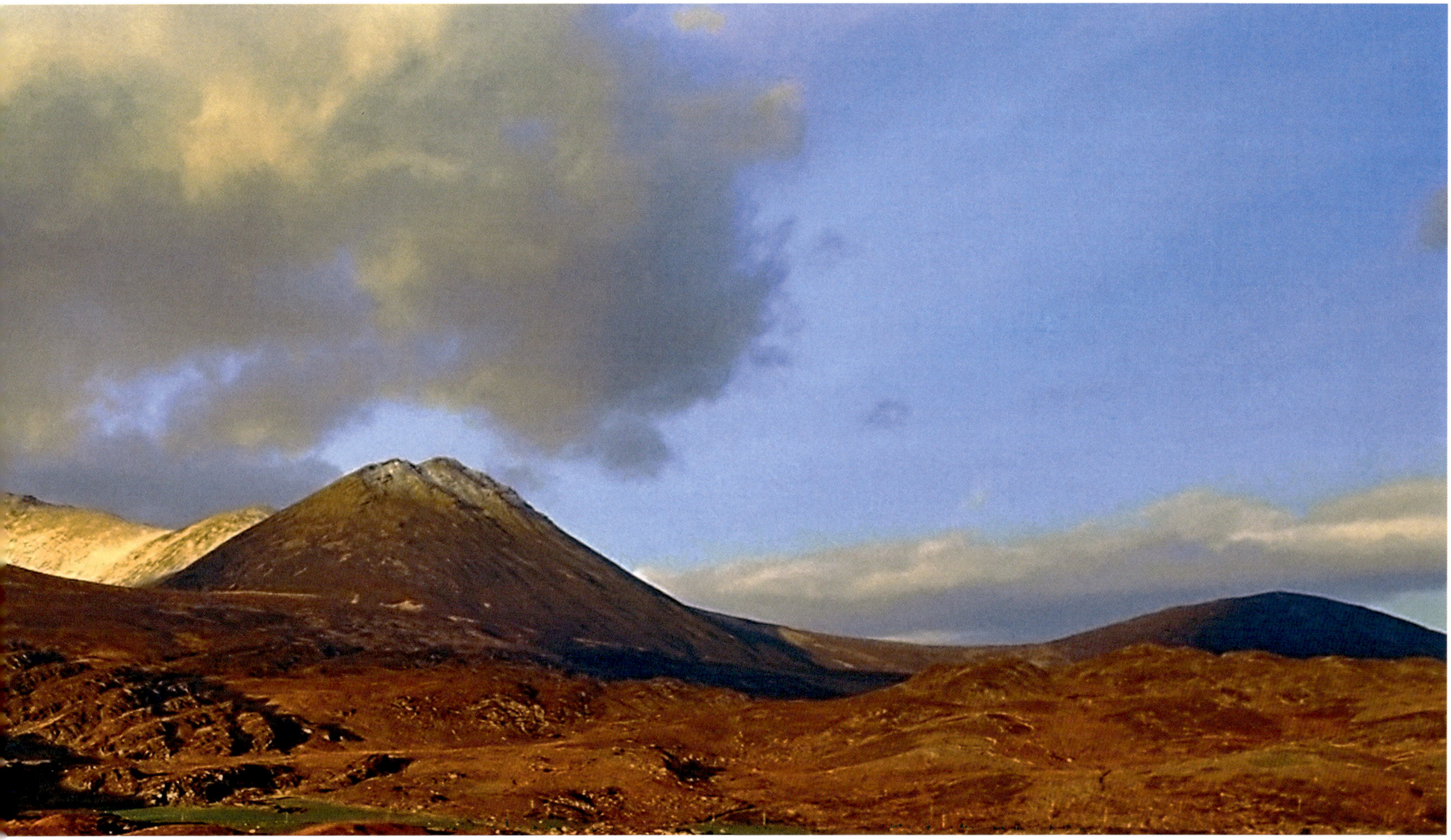

At the same time, and intertwined with the progress of the day, the body moves through its cycle of increase and decline of energy, so that by the time the red and yellow colours of late evening seep into the sky, the body is tending towards rest. From this state, sunset feels very different from dawn; our perception of what we see has changed, with the alteration of the colour and clarity of light, and with our own lower energy. And after the sun has set comes the dusk, a special time when magic emerges from the shadows. Whilst we may witness dawn, with a special effort, we very rarely see the pre-dawn as the very first light gathers in the east; at dusk, however, we often have the opportunity to savour this very special part of the day as the light declines to darkness. These short cycles are reflected in a greater one as the ebb and flow of the year sweeps changes across the surface of the land in colour and texture, in the swell of streams, in the bloom of vegetation, in the smells of growth and decay.

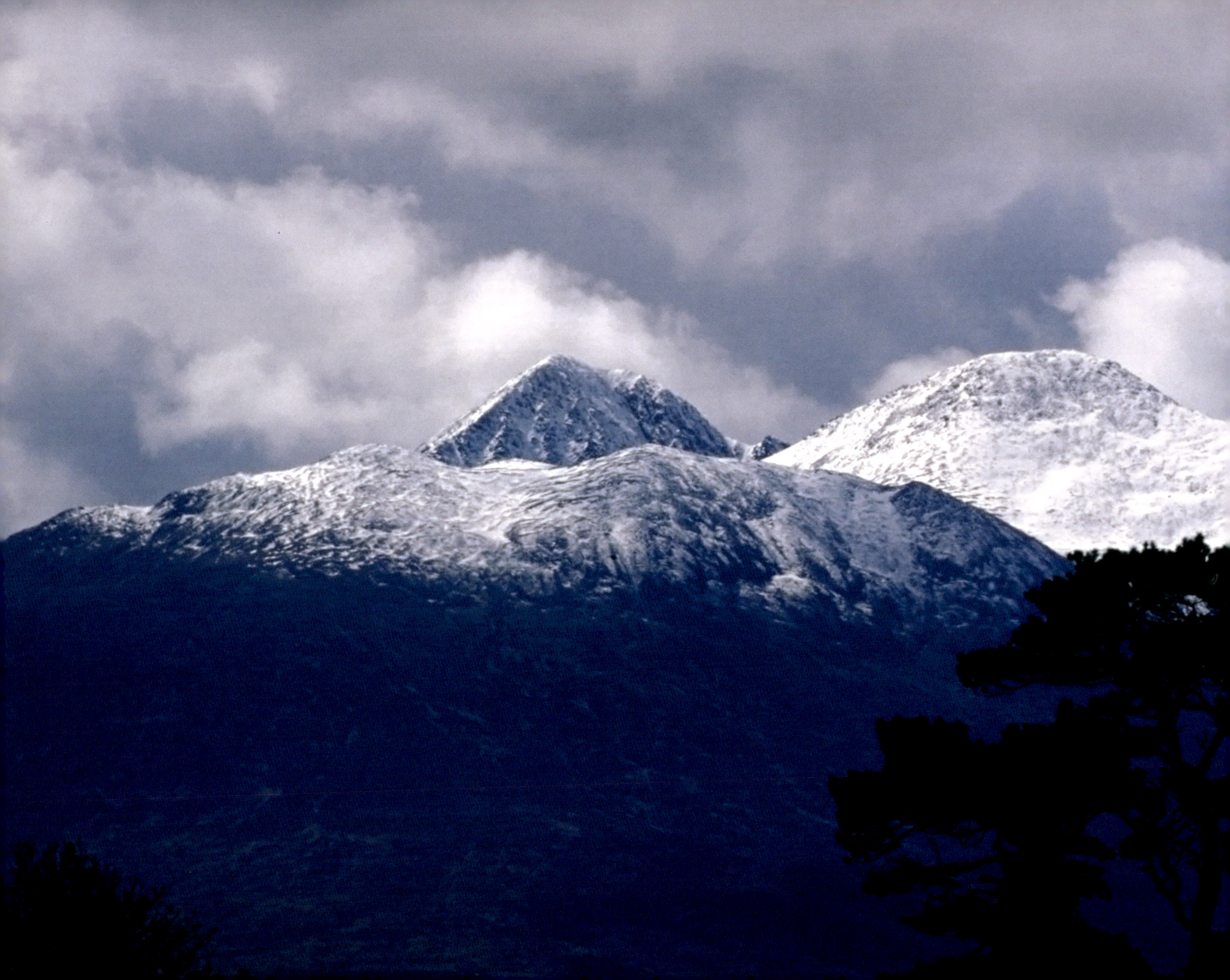

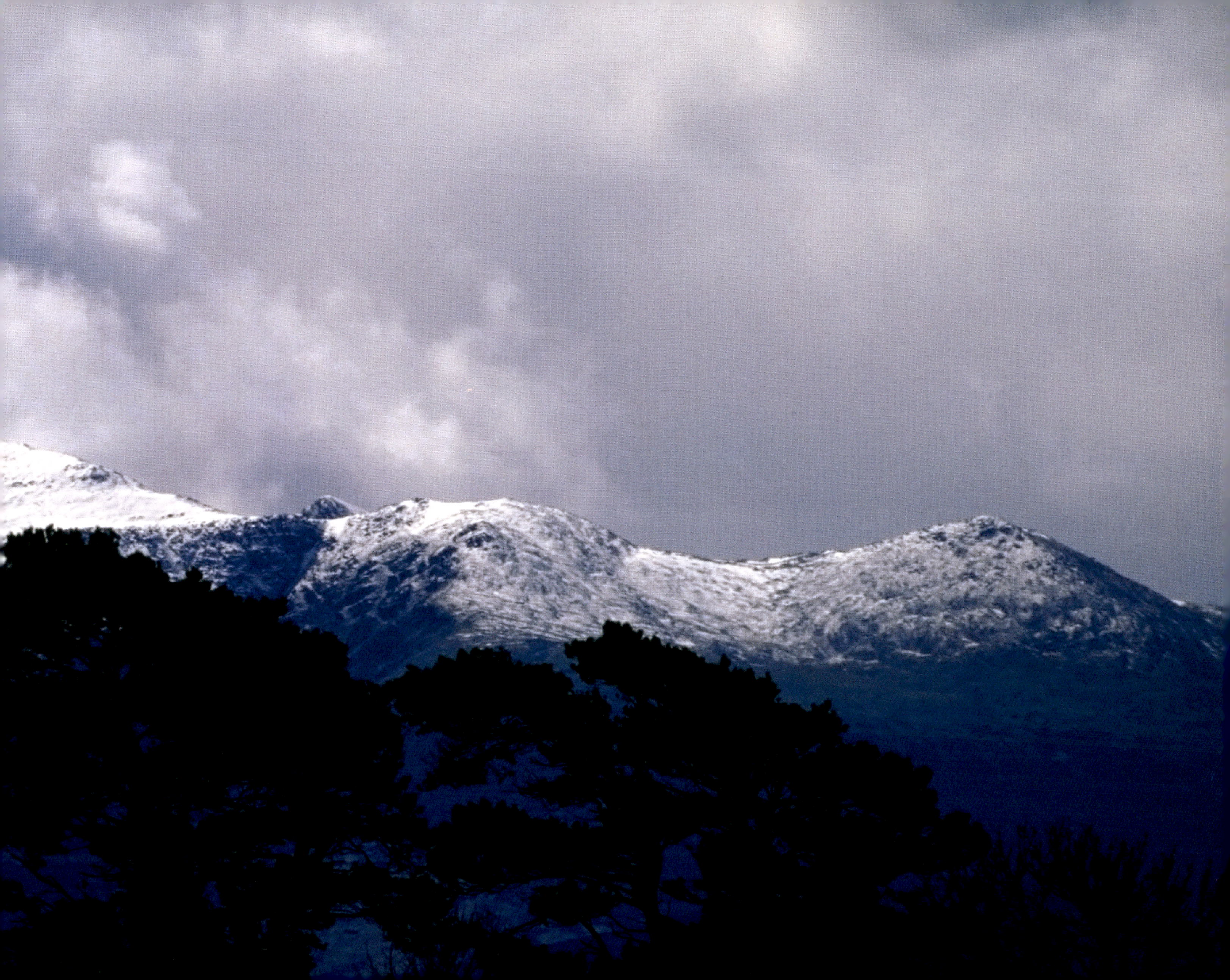

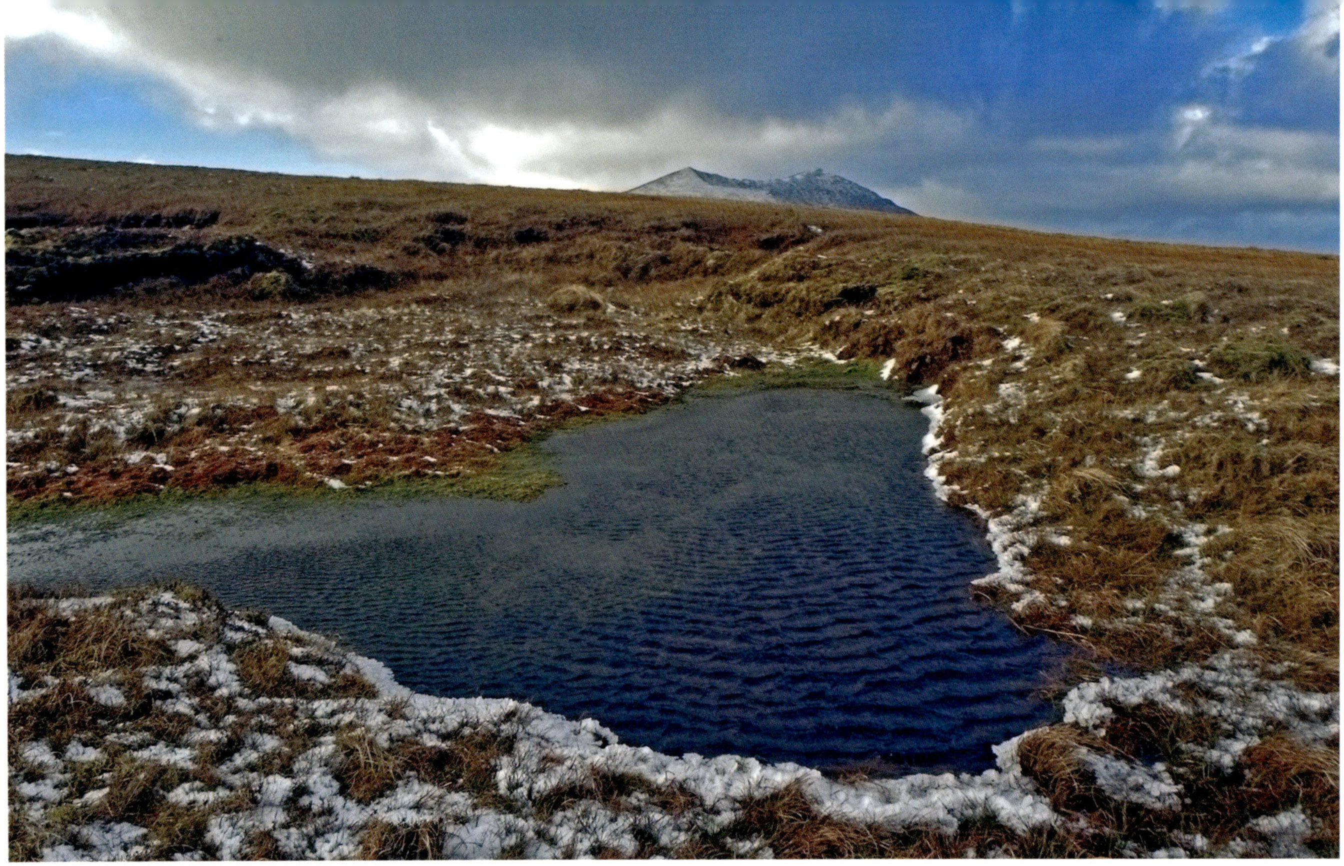

ABOVE Mount Brandon from Ballysitteragh on the Dingle Peninsula.

OPPOSITE The Macgillycuddy's Reeks from the Dingle Peninsula.

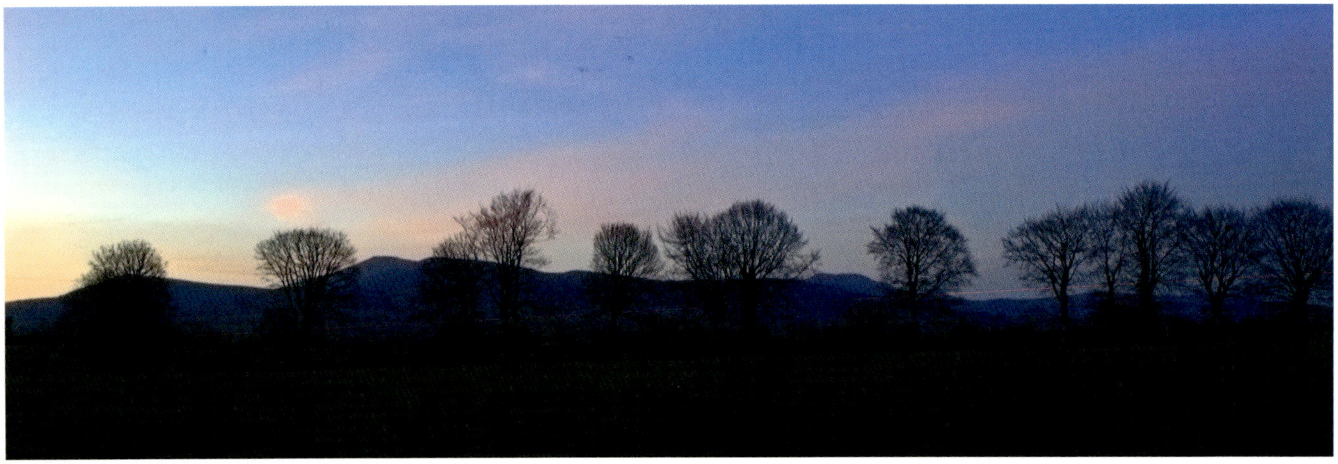

ABOVE Sunset behind the Galty Mountains.

PREVIOUS PAGE The Macgillycuddy's Reeks seen in rare snow cover, from Faha, near Beaufort, County Kerry.

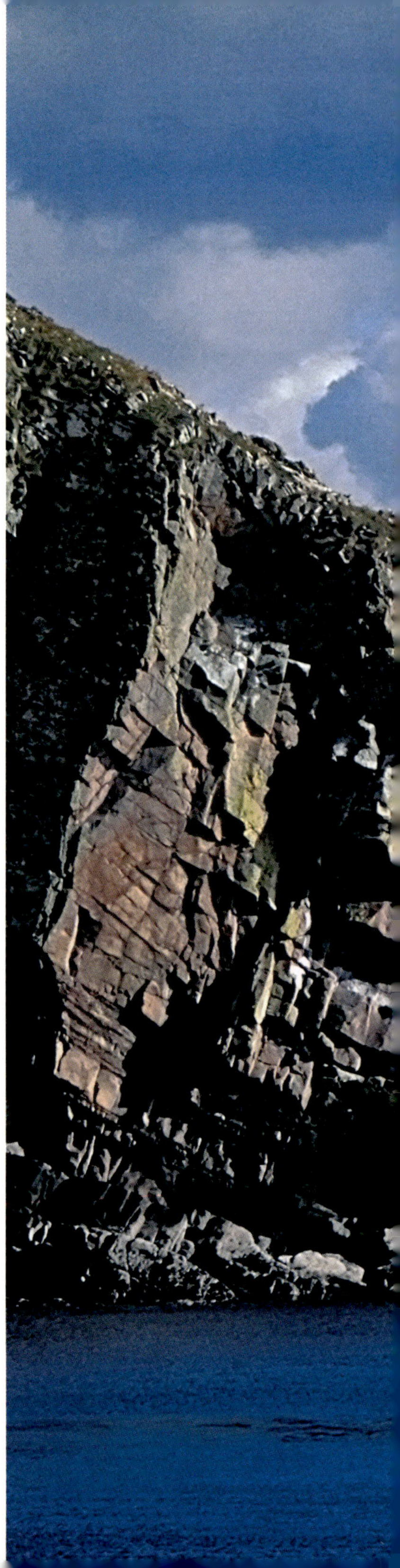

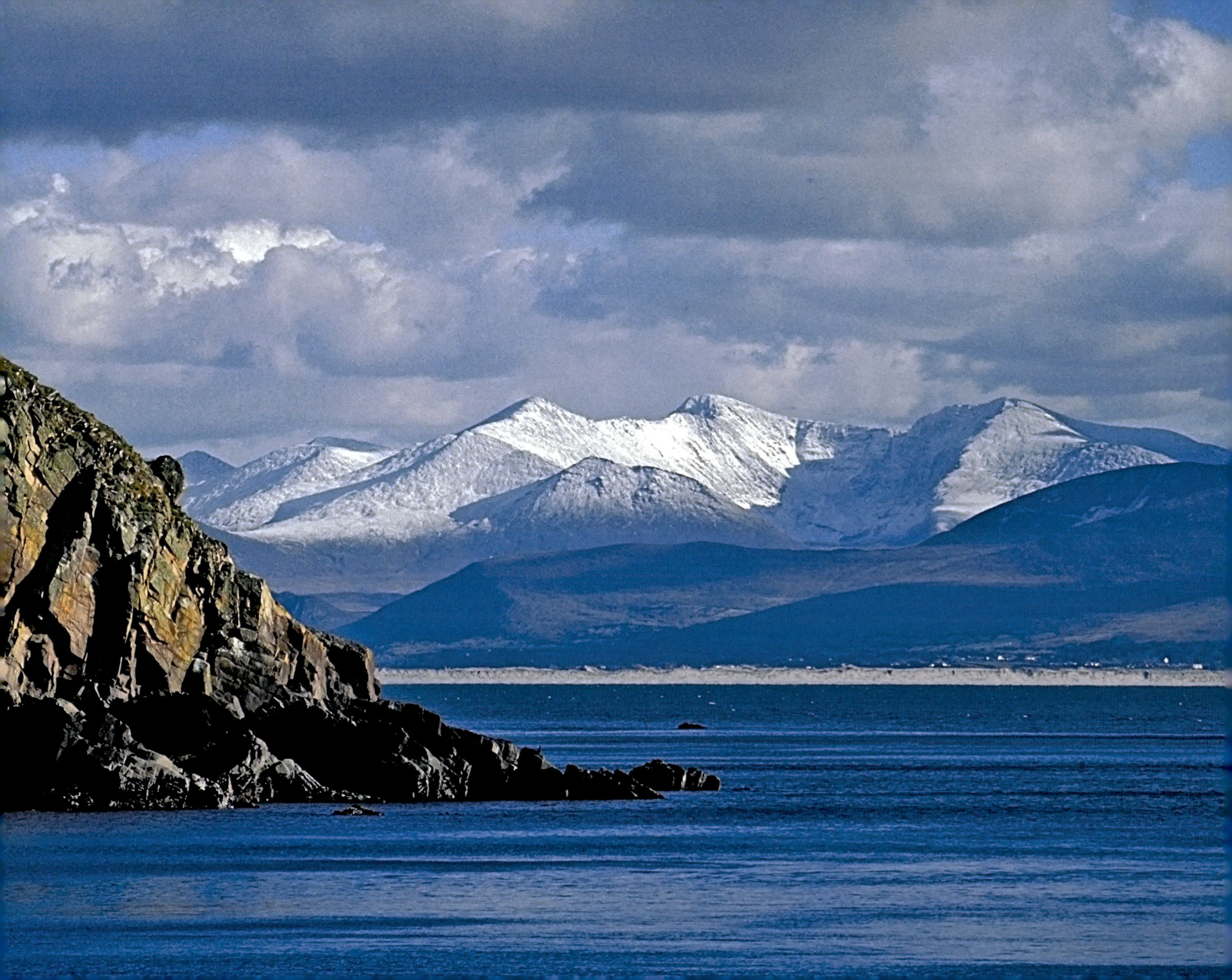

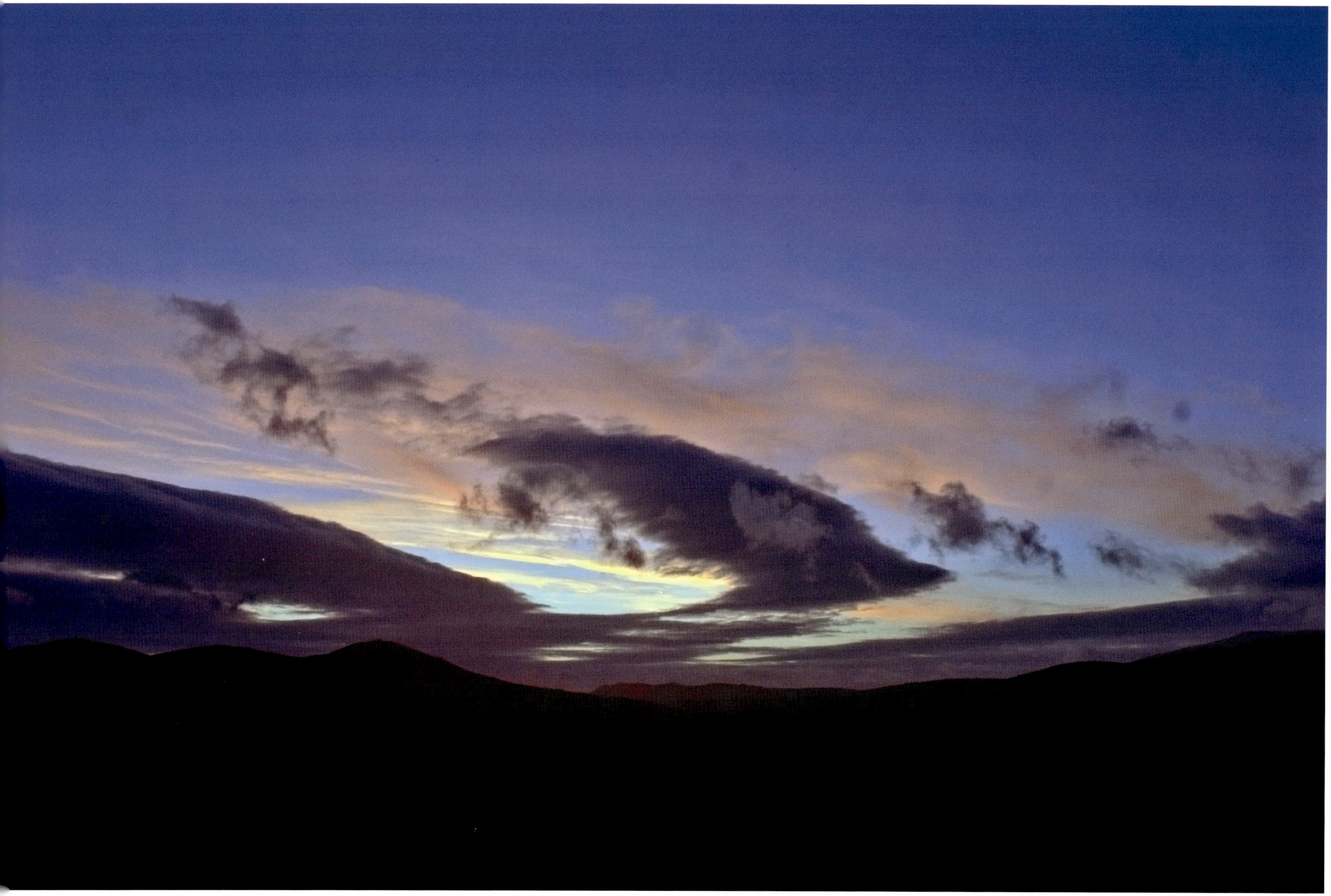

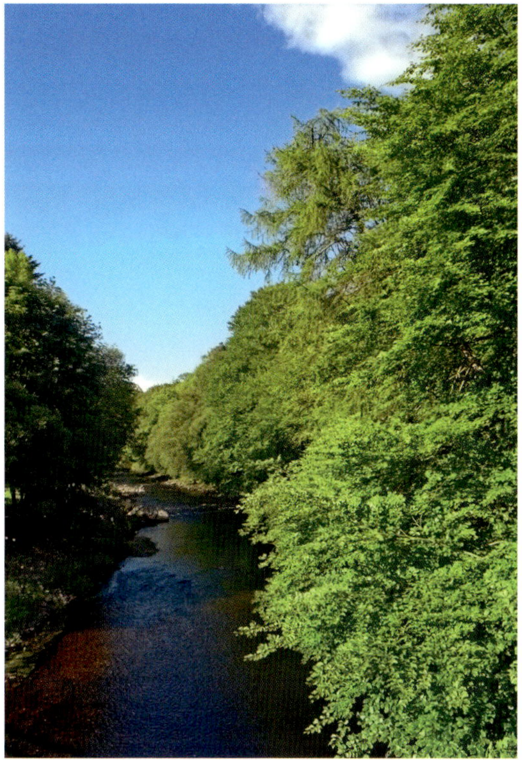

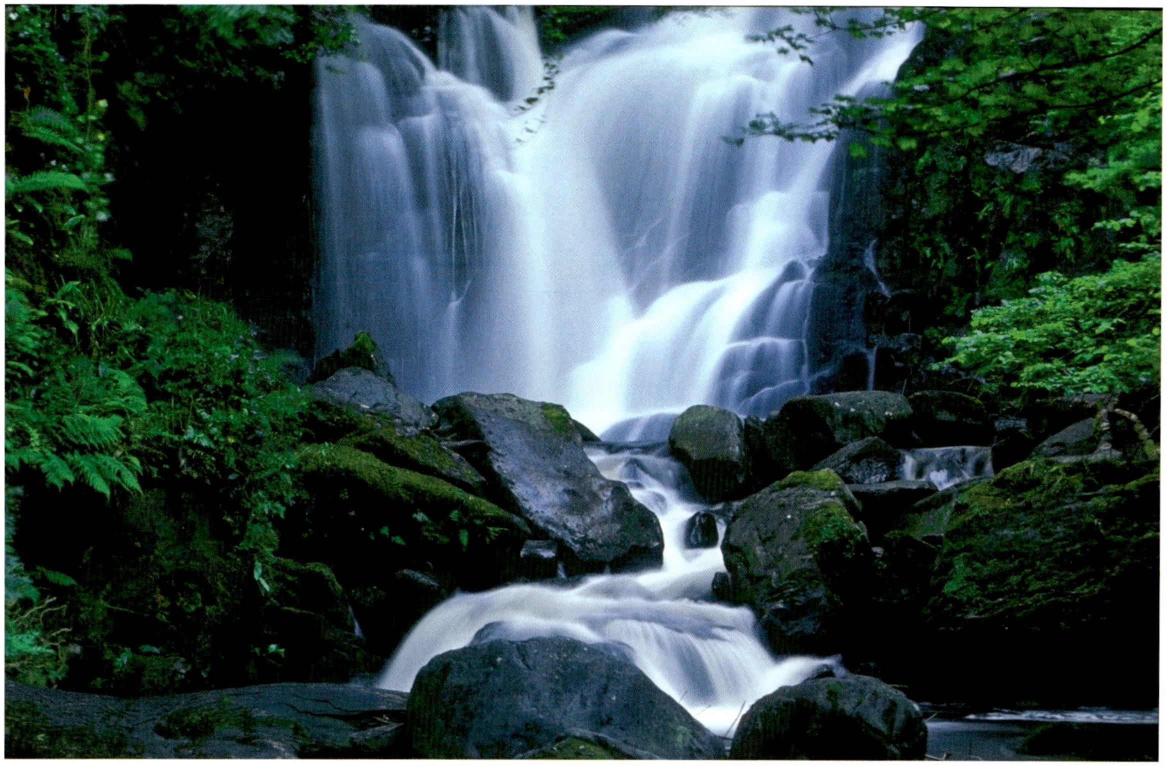

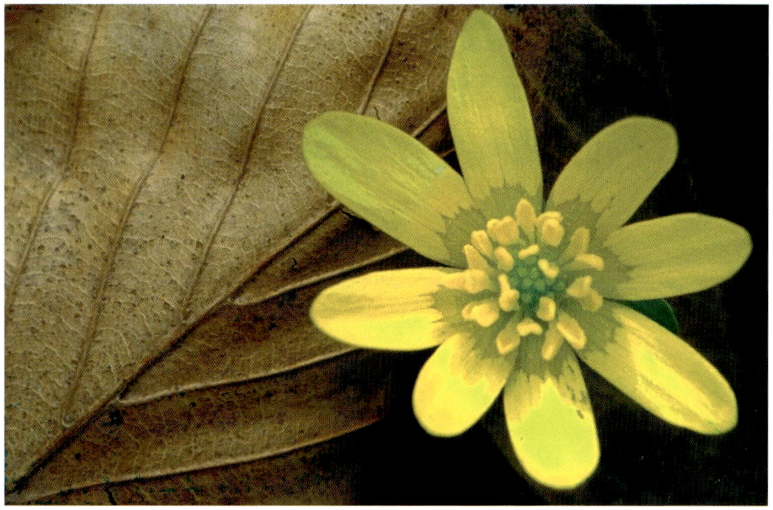

SPRING IN THE MOUNTAINS

OPPOSITE Dusk at Annascaul, the Dingle Peninsula.

ABOVE LEFT Avonmore River, Laragh, Wicklow.

ABOVE RIGHT Torc Waterfall, Muckross, Killarney.

LEFT Celandine growing through last year's beech leaves.

OPPOSITE Stepping stones at Cahir near Castlegregory, looking towards Stradbally Mountain, 824 metres, on the Dingle Peninsula, County Kerry.

BELOW Primroses.

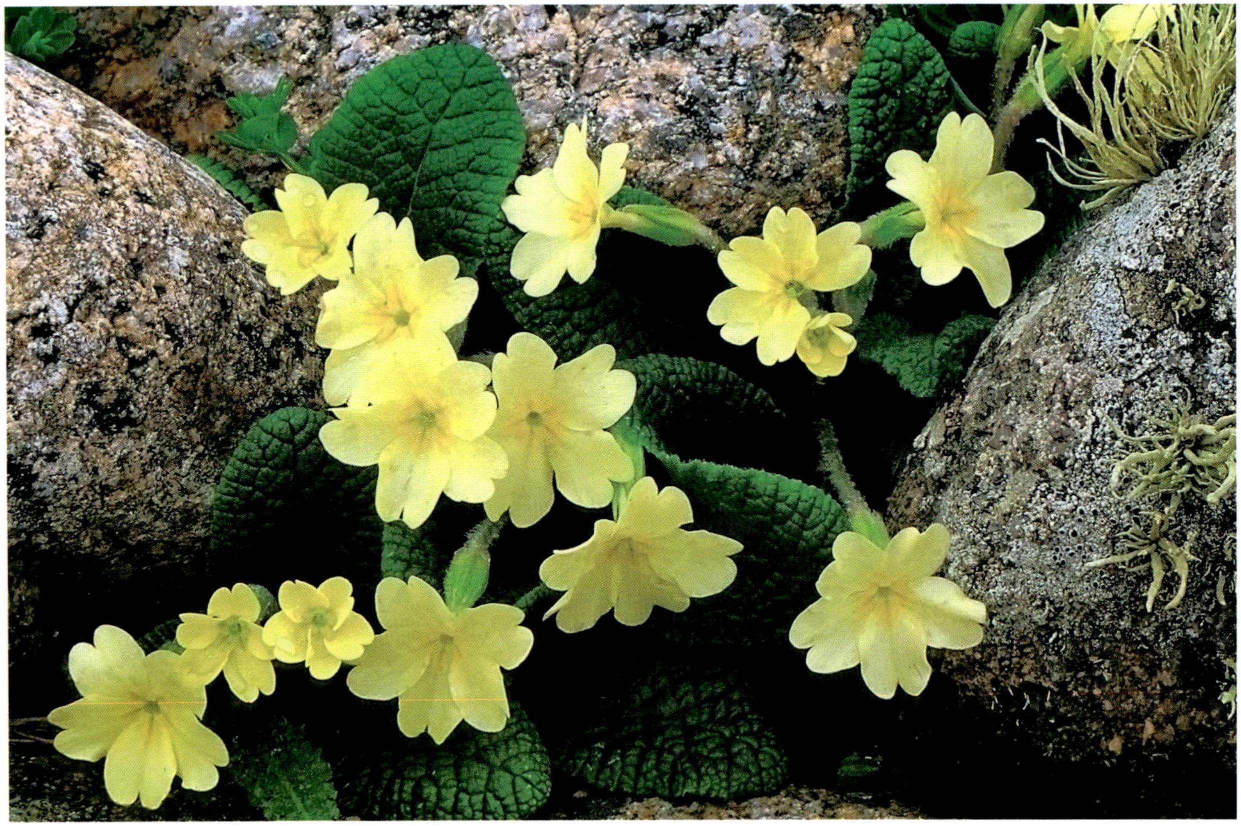

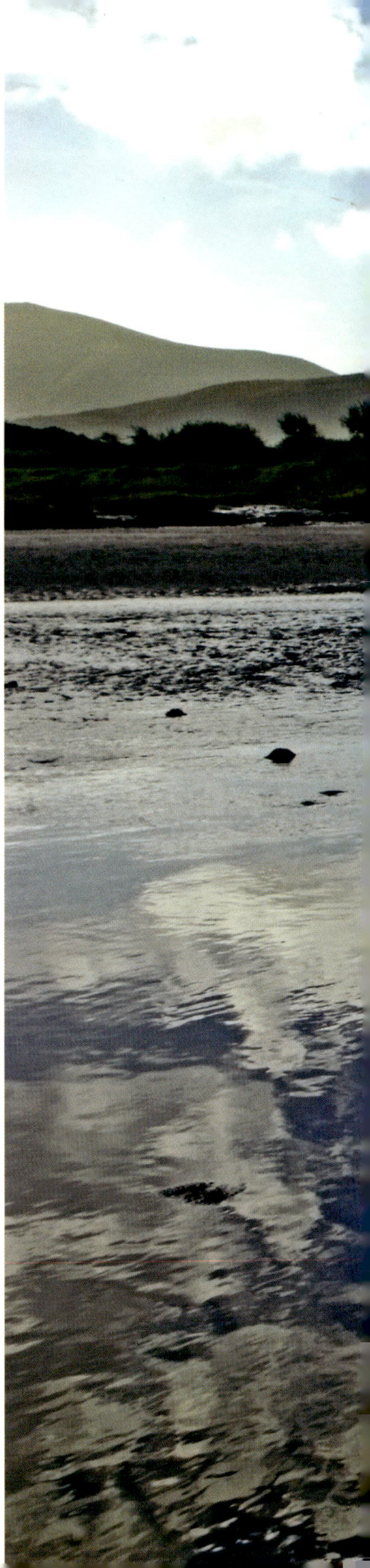

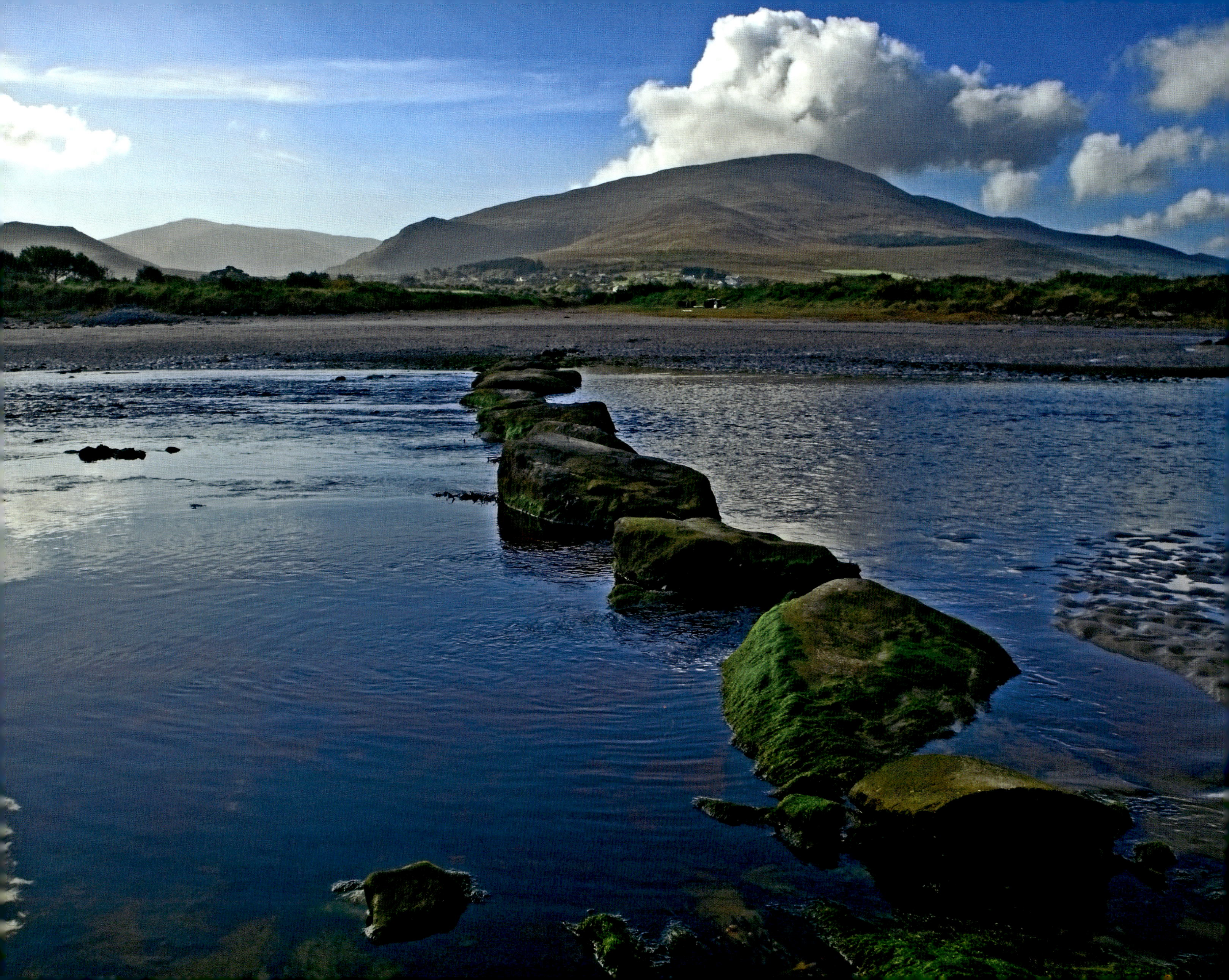

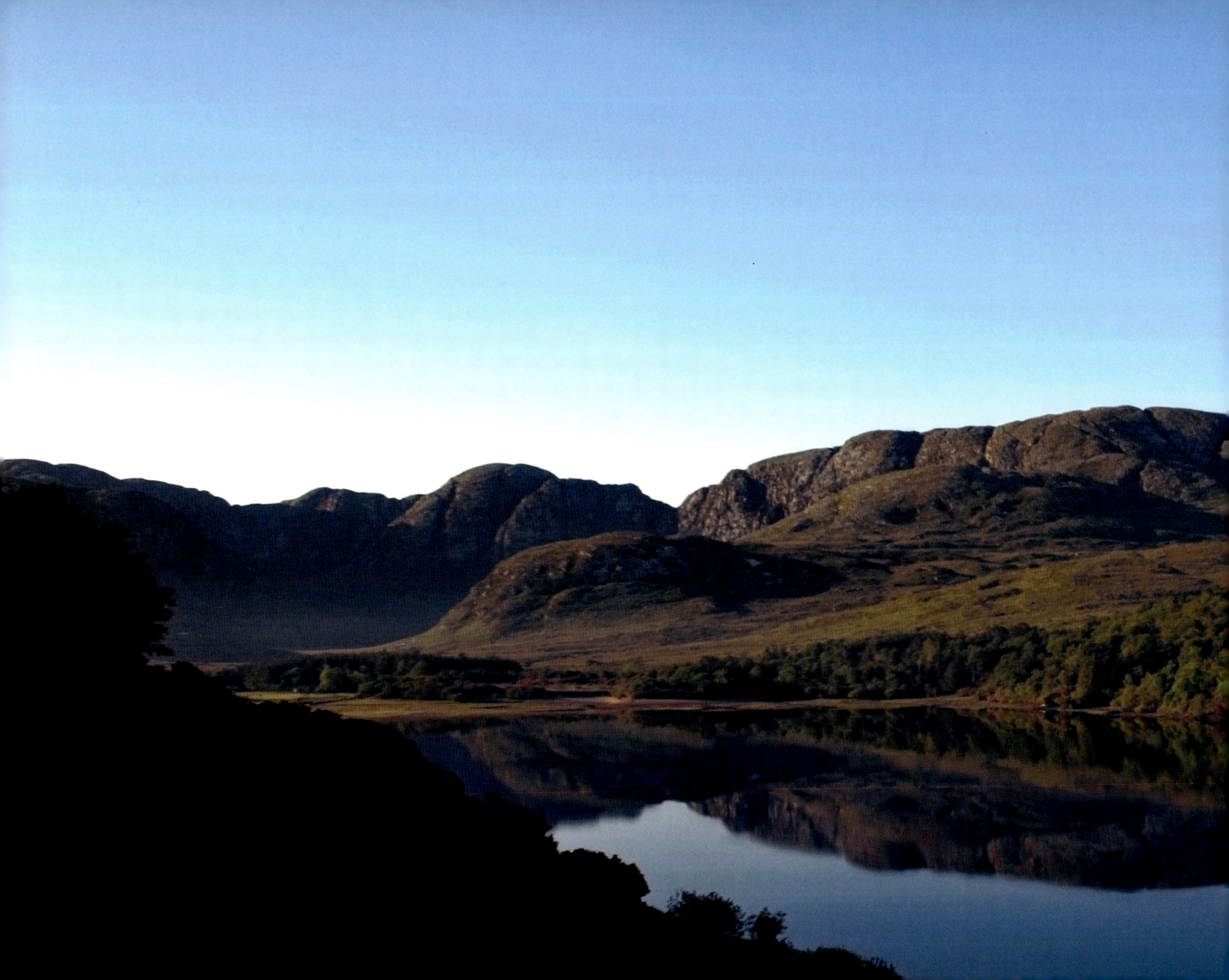

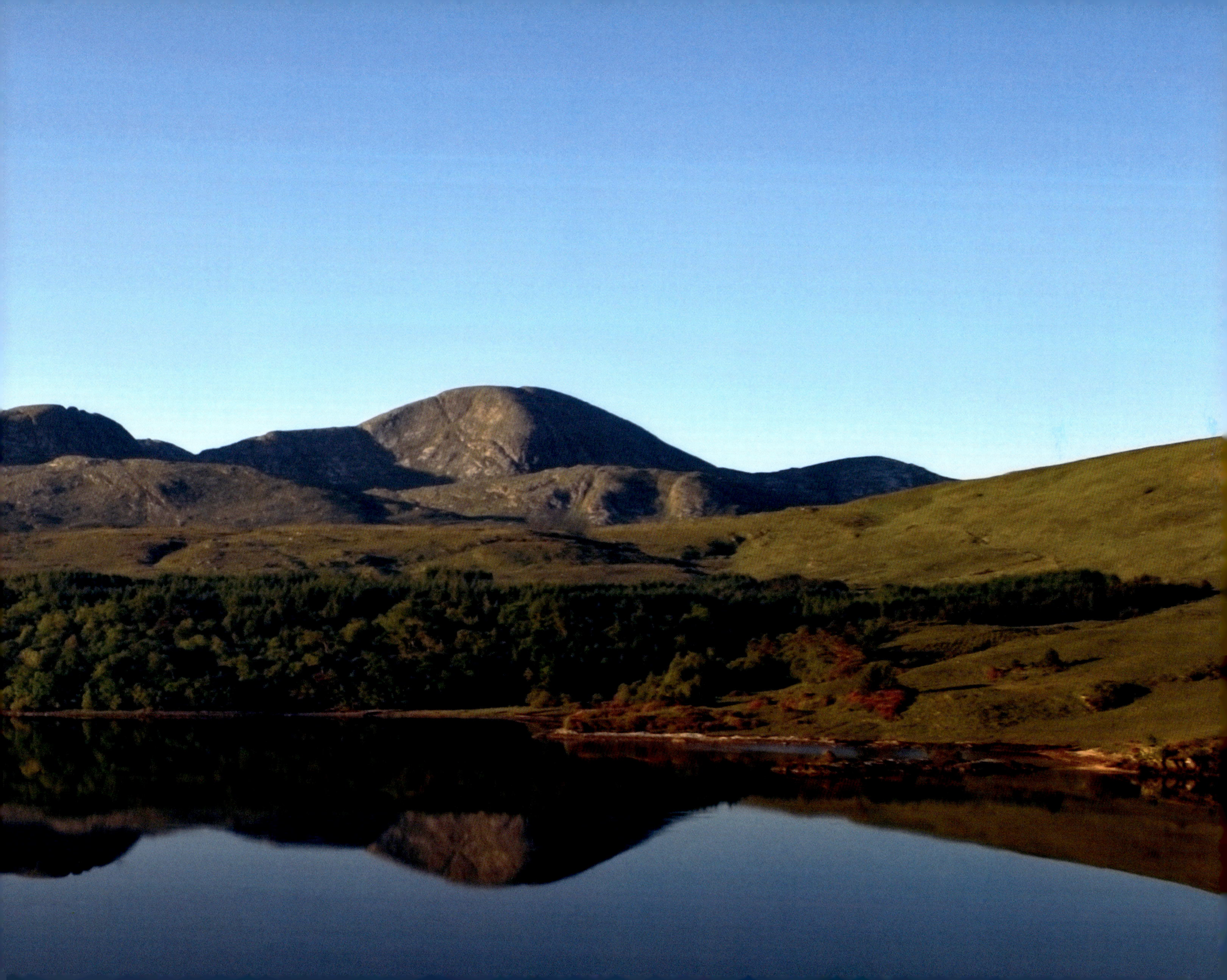

OPPOSITE In the Twelve Bens, Connemara, County Galway.

BELOW Ragged robin, a lover of wet meadows.

PREVIOUS PAGE Slieve Snaght, 683 metres, in the Derryveagh Mountains, Donegal.

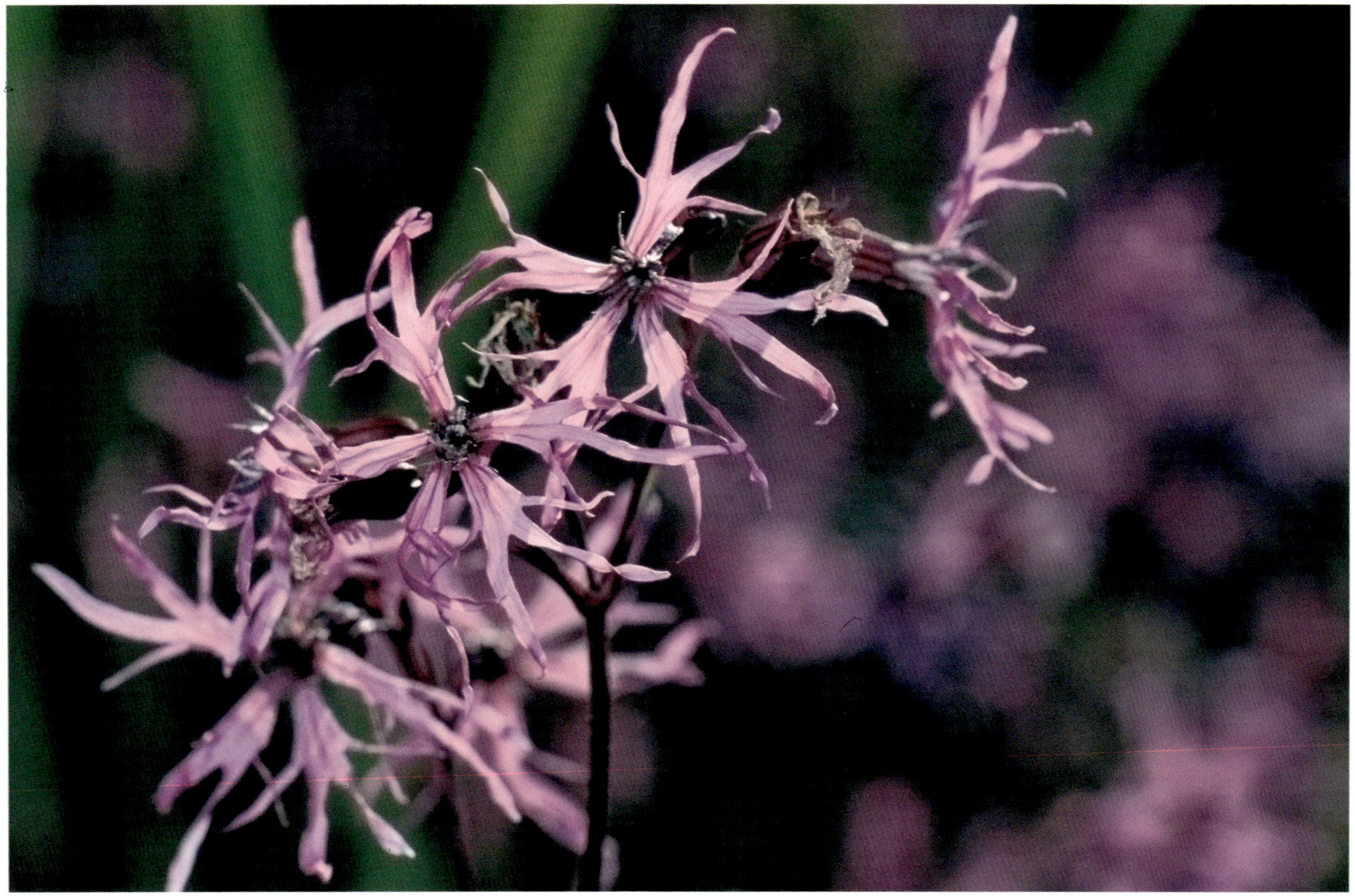

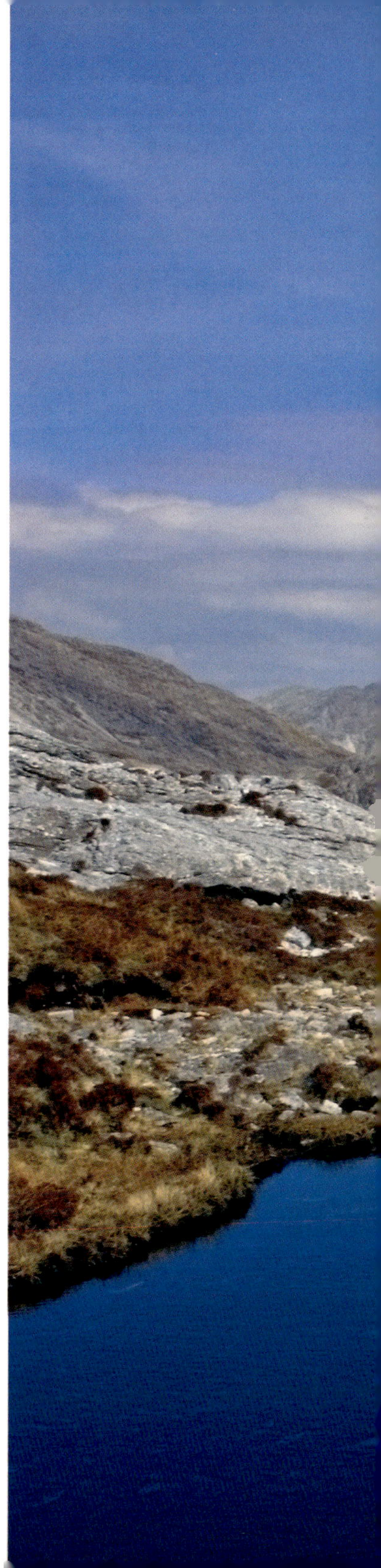

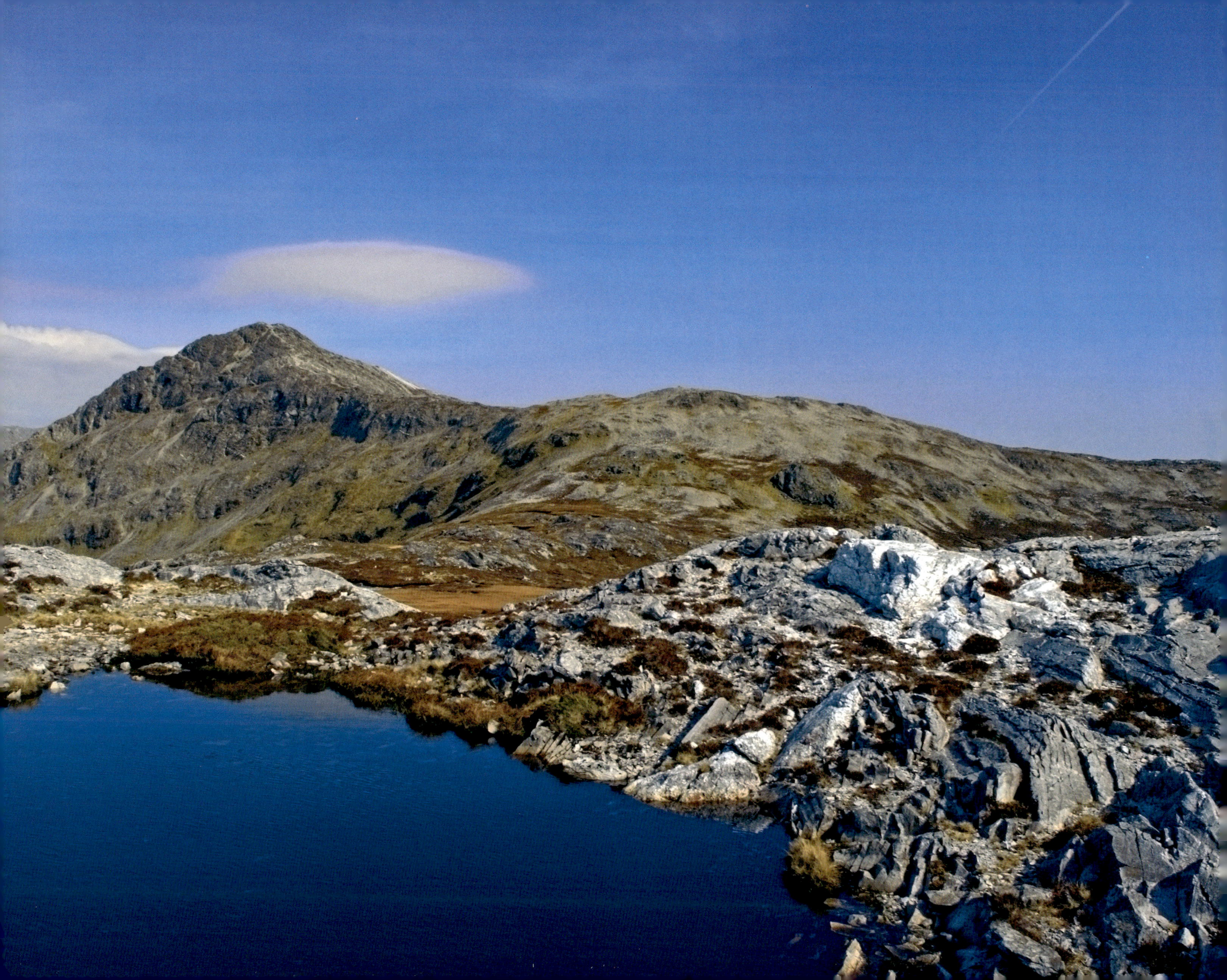

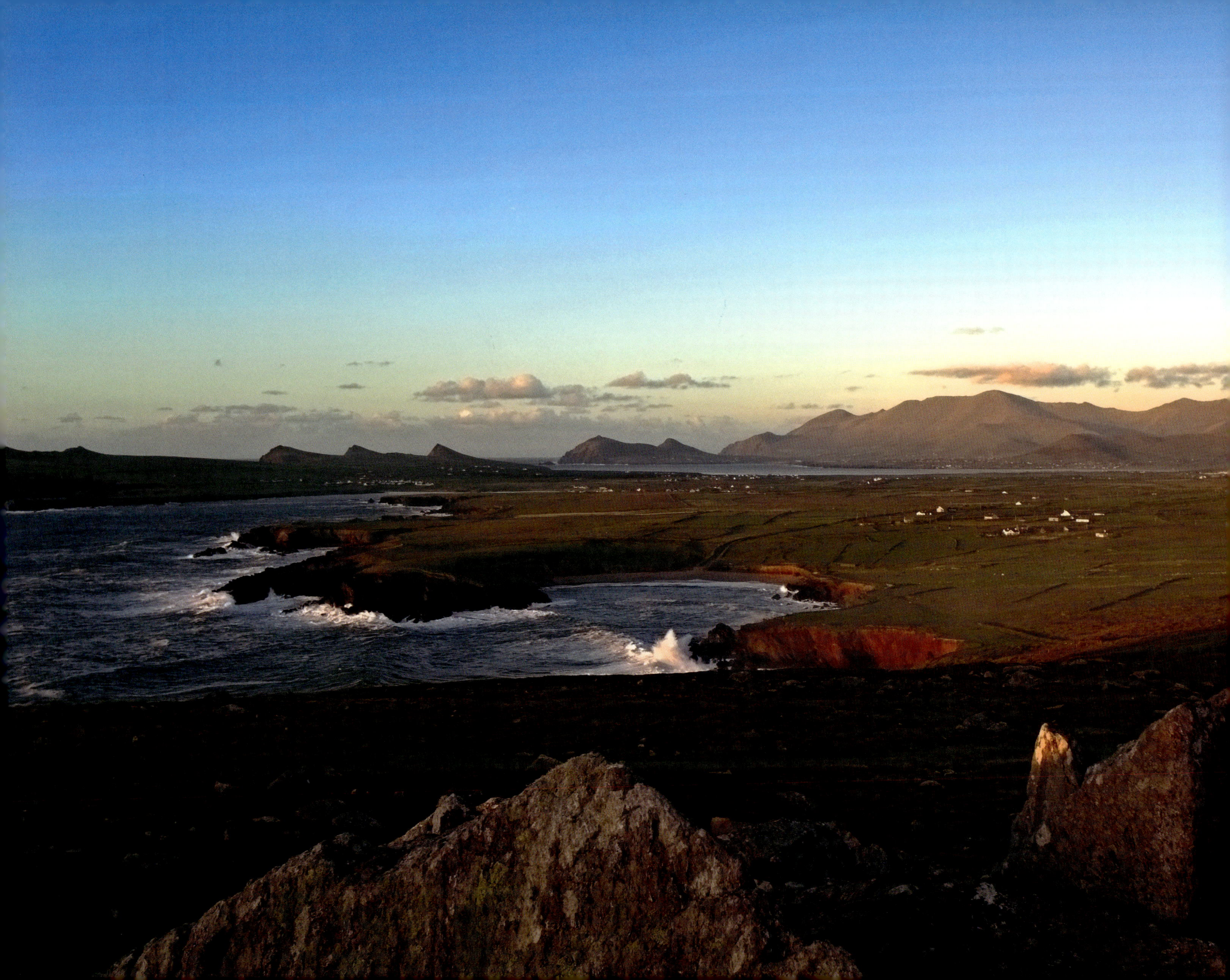

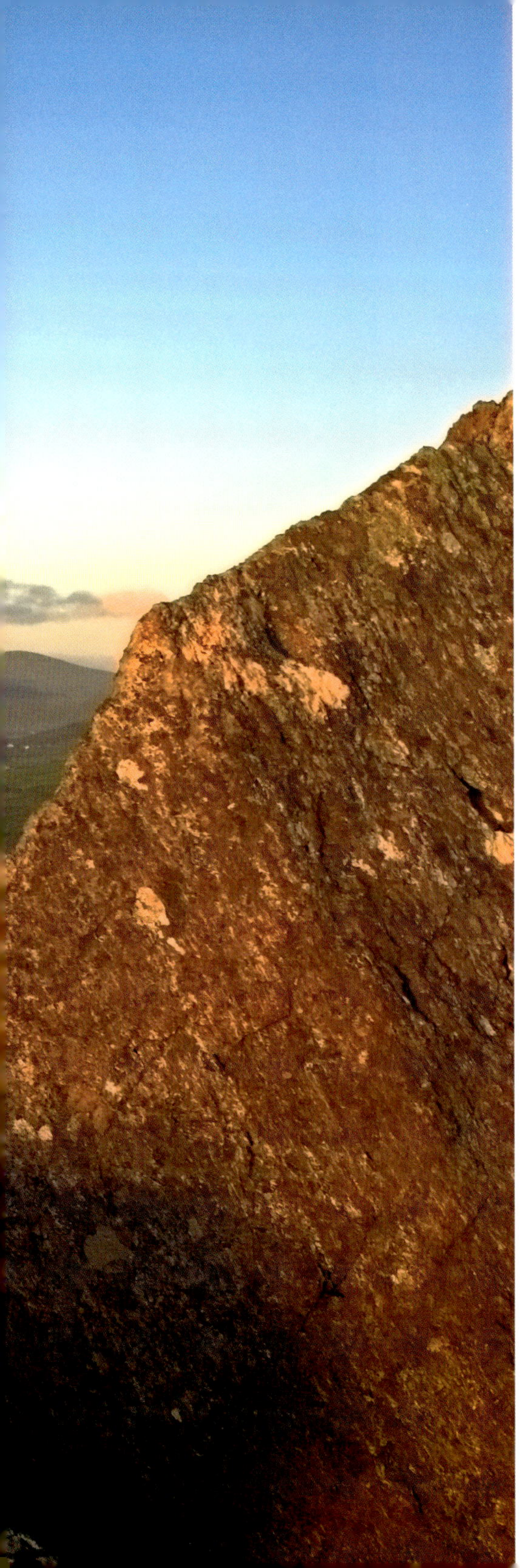

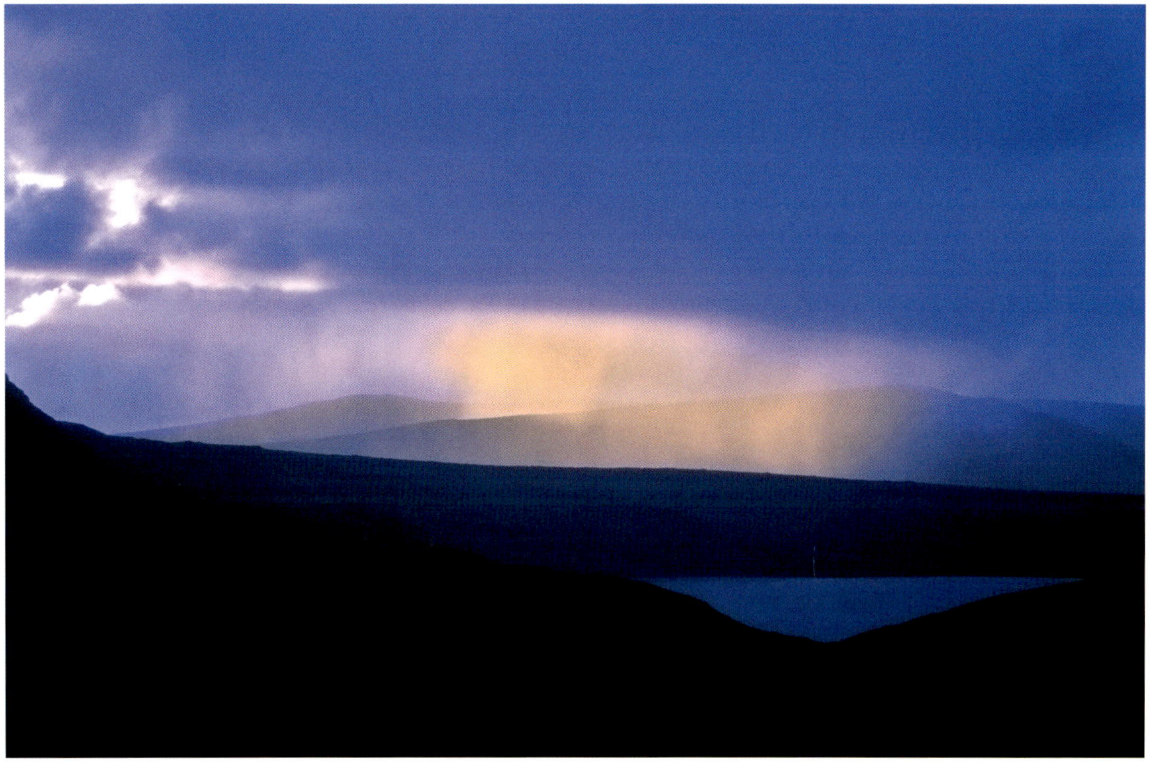

ABOVE Sunset clouds behind Errigal, Donegal.

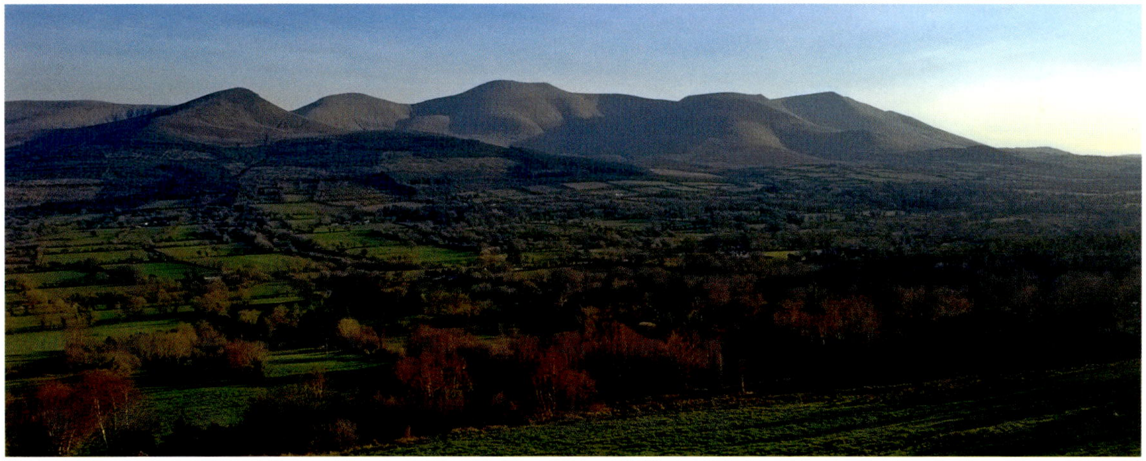

ABOVE The Galty Mountains from the north, standing above the Glen of Aherlow, County Tipperary.

OPPOSITE Late evening on Mount Brandon from Clocher Head, the Dingle Peninsula.

AUTUMN IN THE MOUNTAINS

OPPOSITE Upper Lough Leane, looking towards the Black Valley and the south side of the Macgillycuddy's Reeks, County Kerry.

BELOW Leaves in autumn.

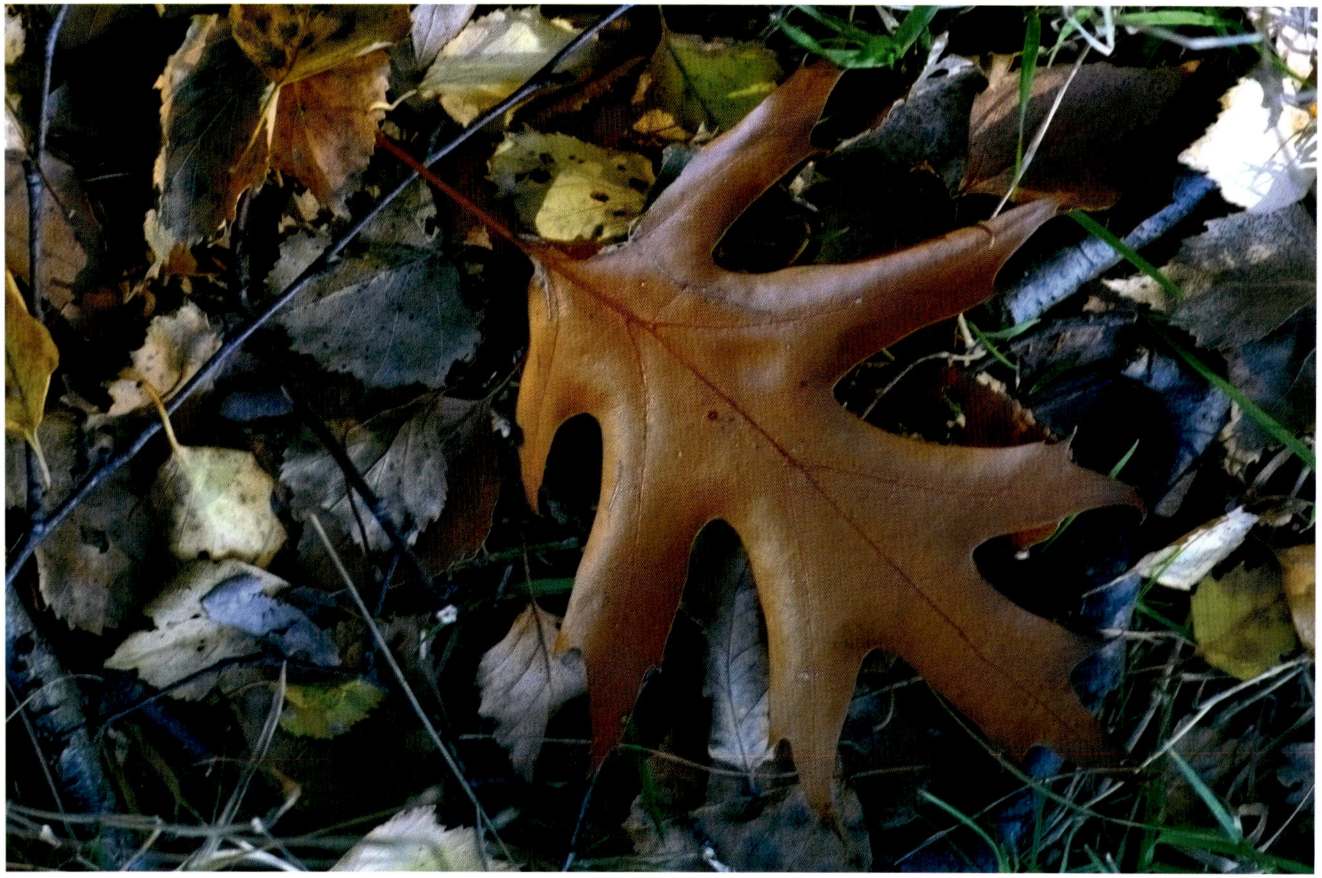

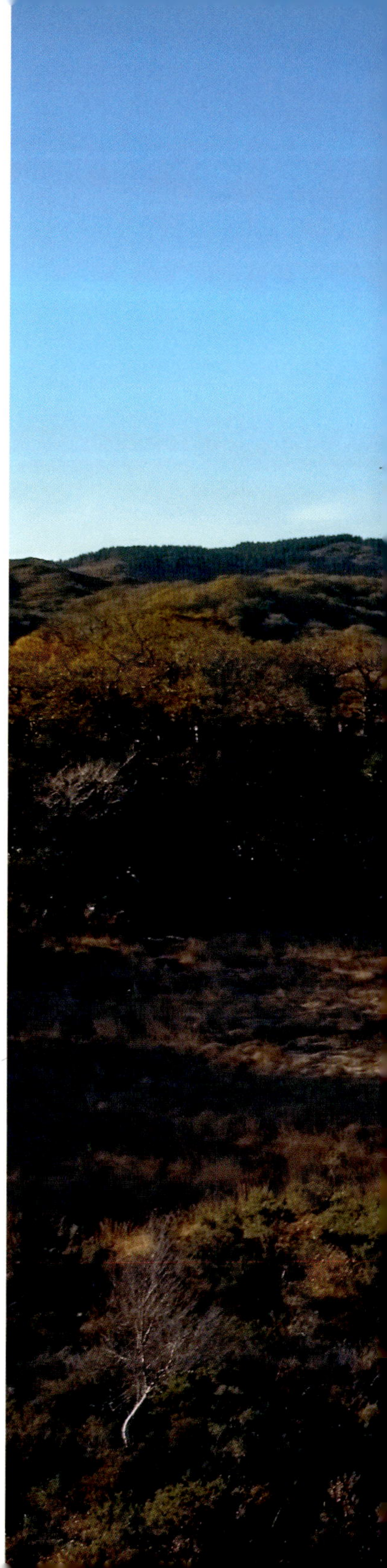

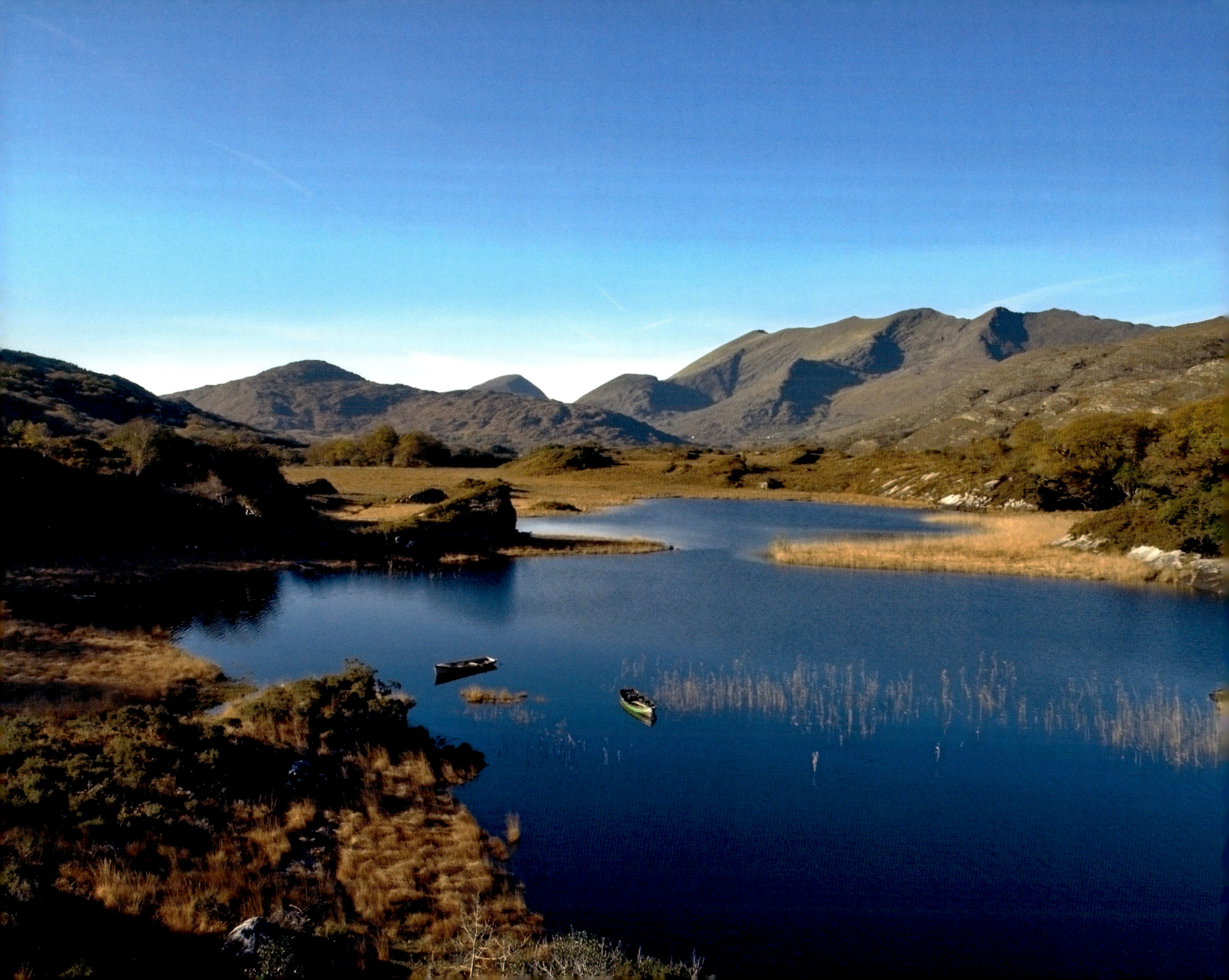

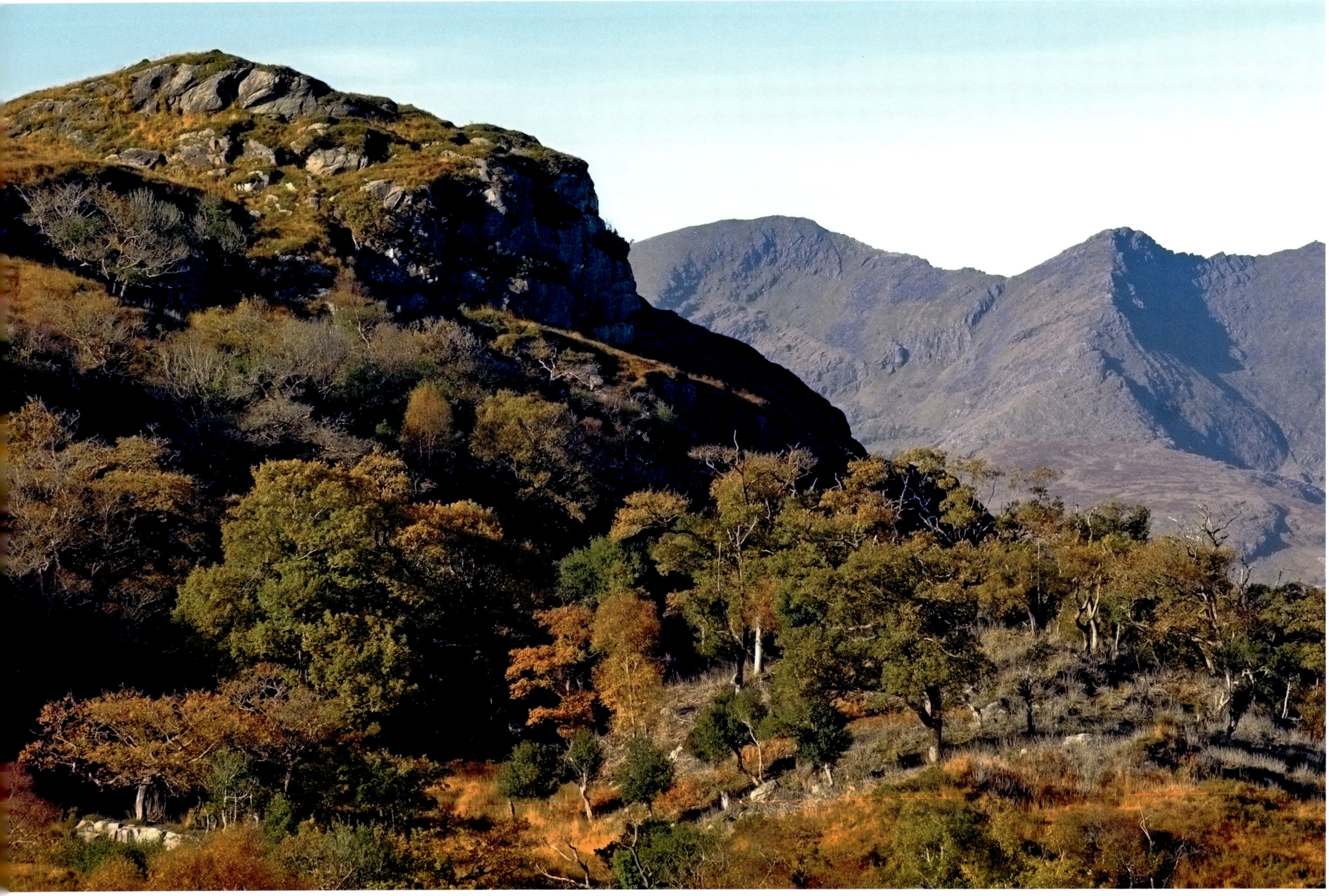

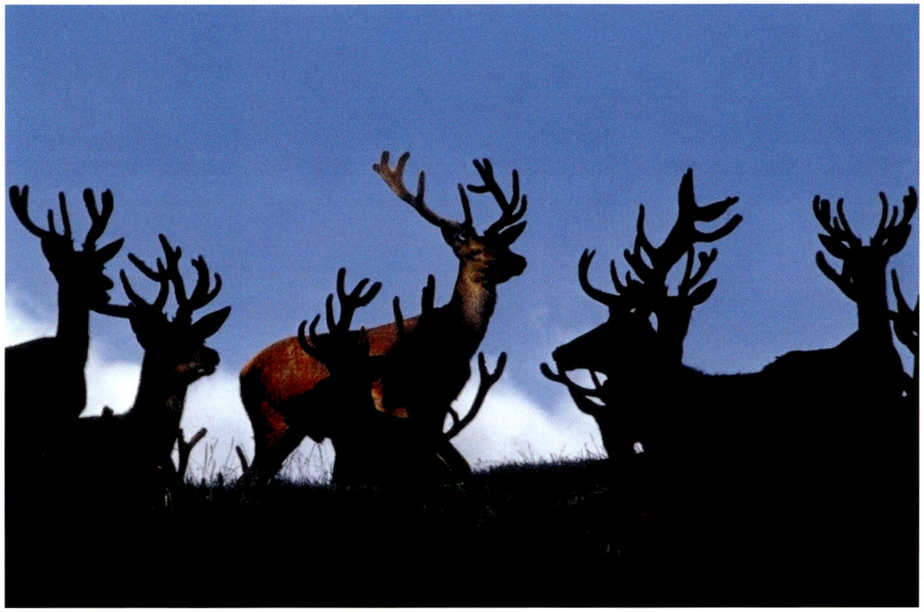

OPPOSITE The Macgillycuddy's Reeks from the Kerry Way at Galway's Bridge

LEFT Red deer roam freely on the mountains around Killarney.

BELOW Rowan, or mountain ash.

BELOW The Black Valley near Lord Brandon's Cottage, Killarney, County Kerry.

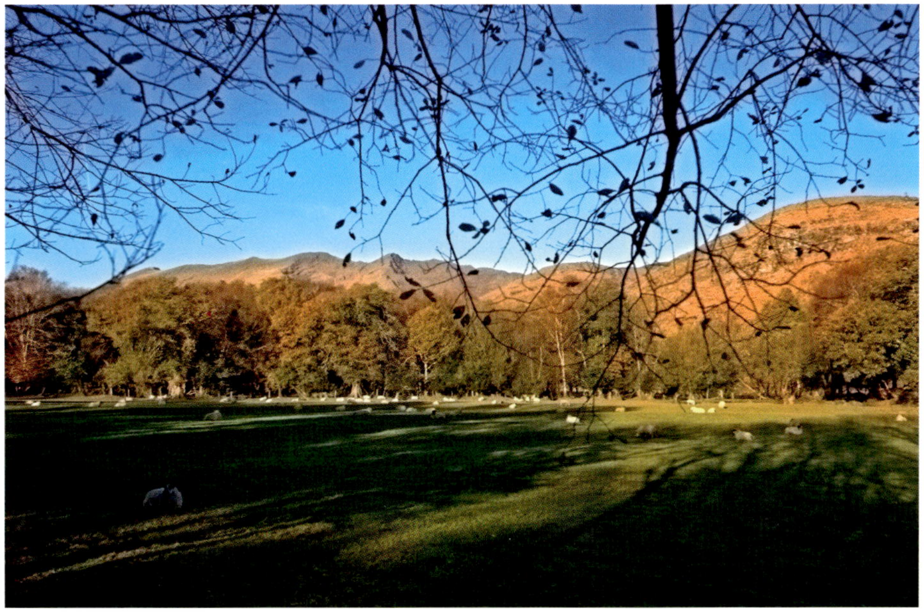

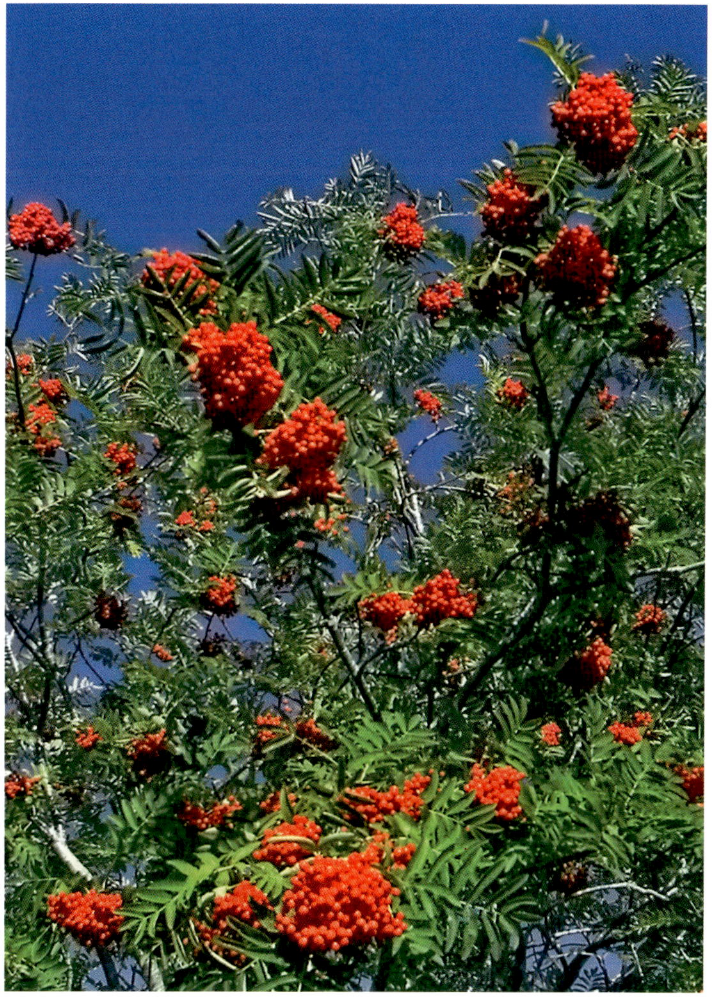

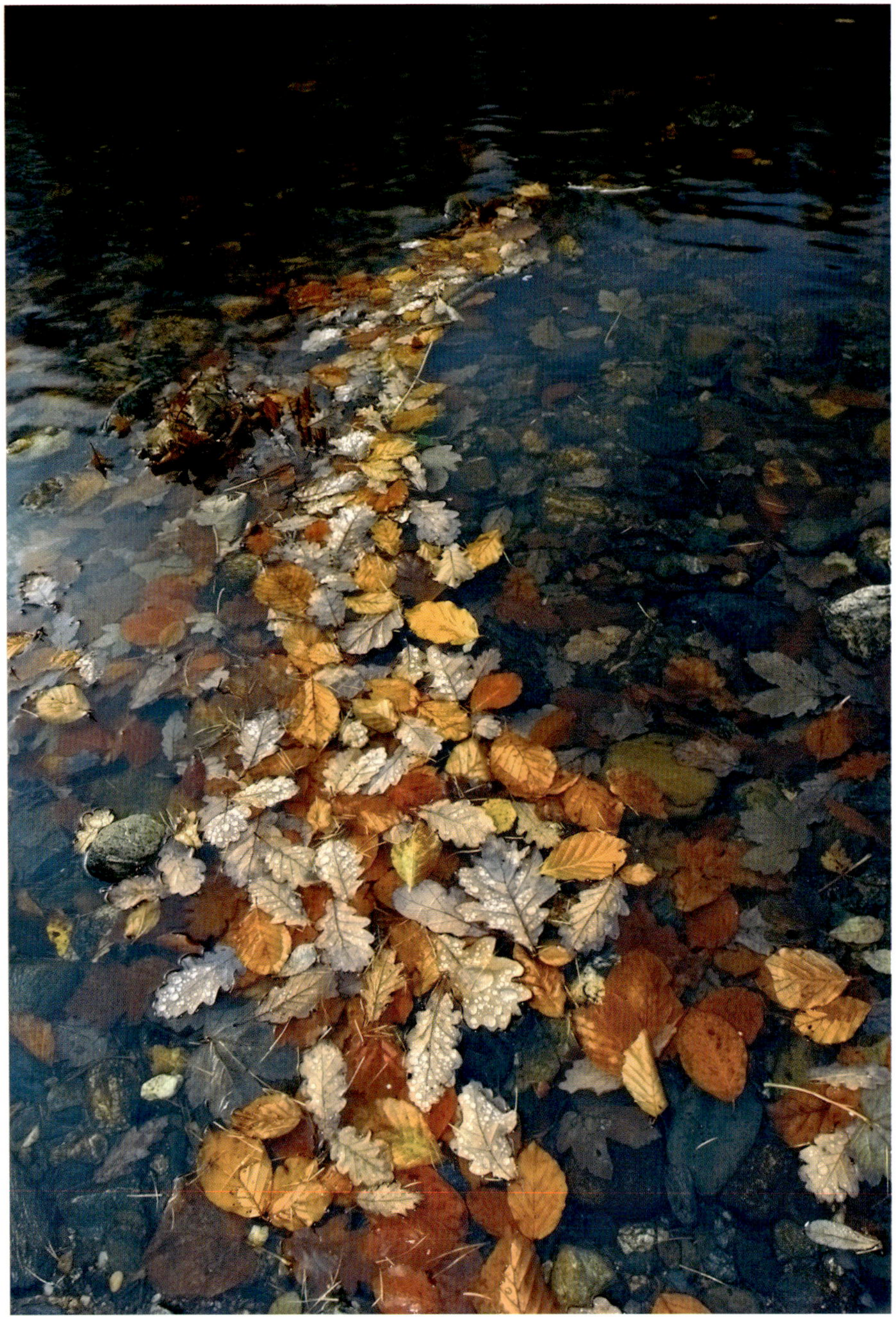

AUTUMN IN THE MOUNTAINS

LEFT. A drift of oak and beech leaves in the Avonmore River near Laragh, Glendalough, County Wicklow.

OPPOSITE Beech trees on the bank of the Avonmore River.

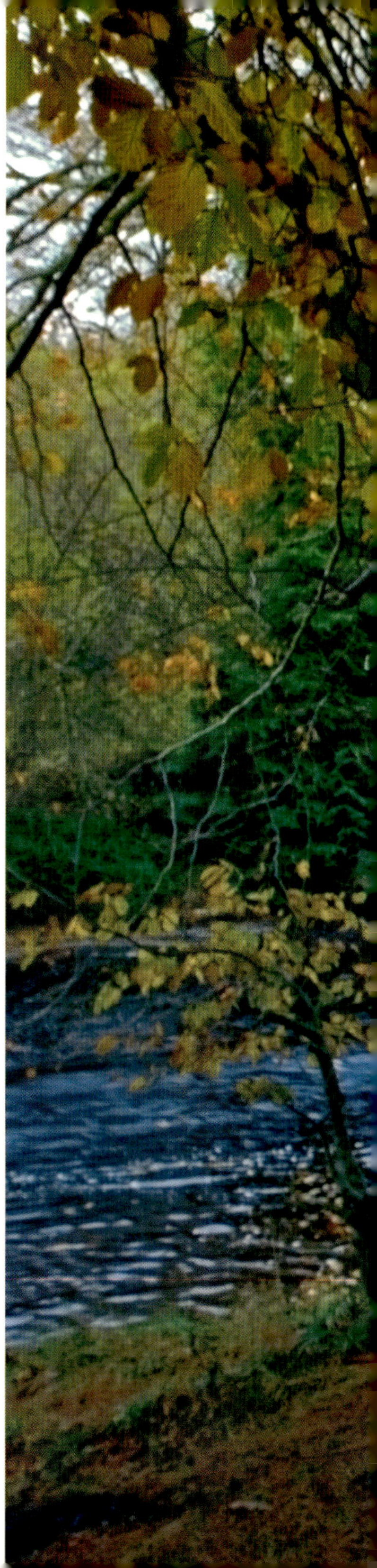

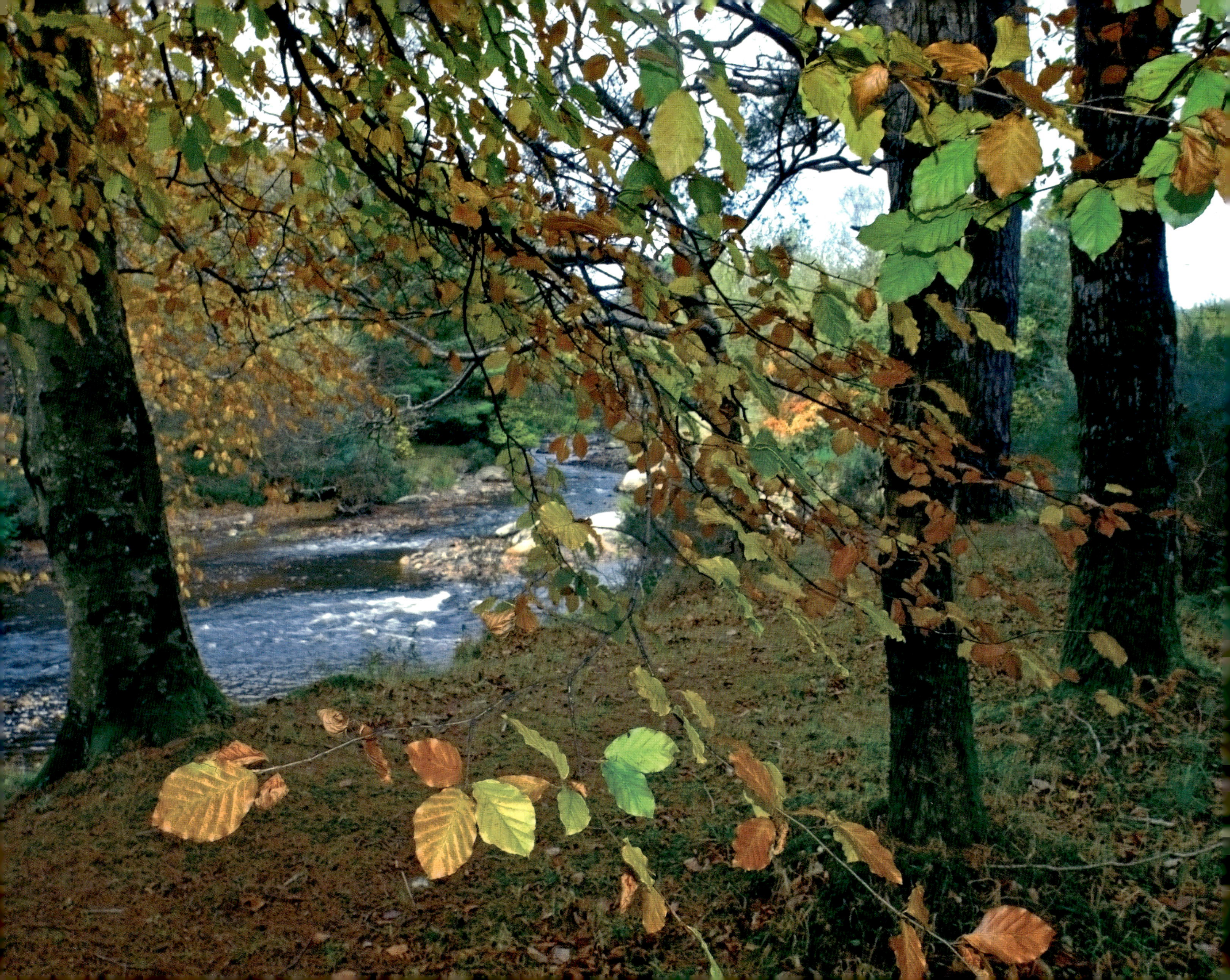

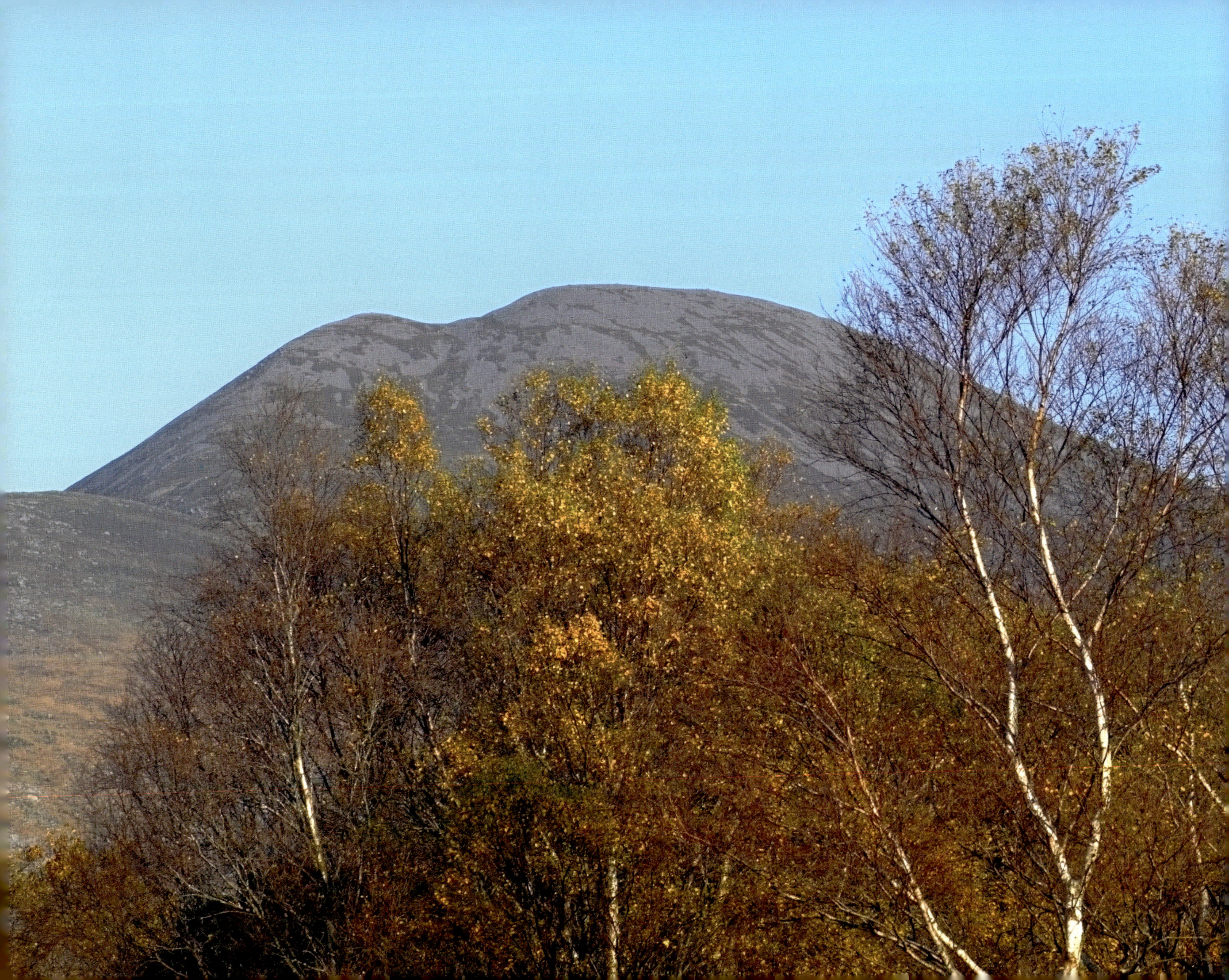

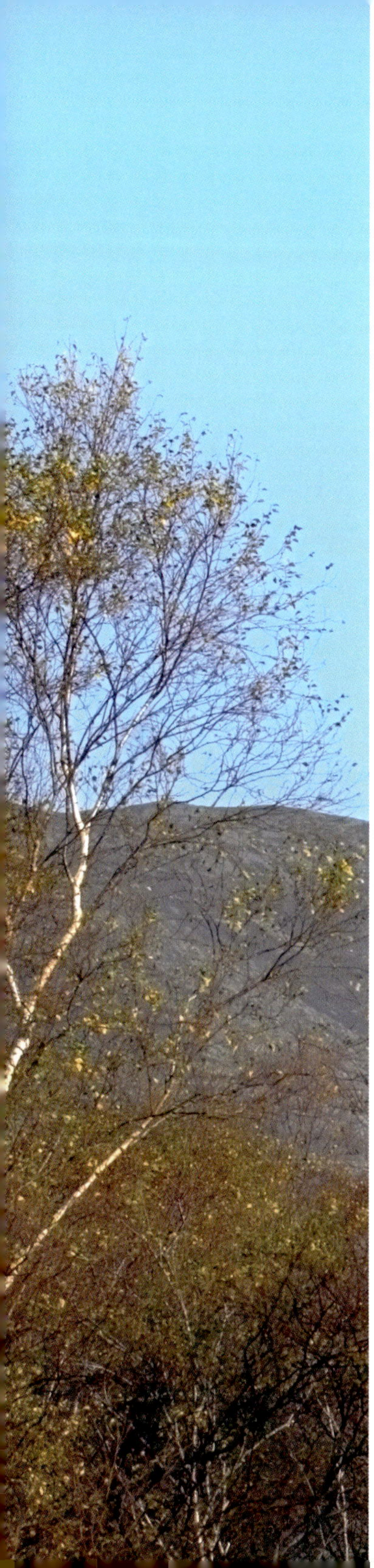

AUTUMN IN THE MOUNTAINS

OPPOSITE Birch trees in their fine late autumn colours, seen against Purple Mountain from Galway's Bridge, Upper Lough Leane, County Kerry.

BELOW Early morning mist on the Laune River at Beaufort, County Kerry.

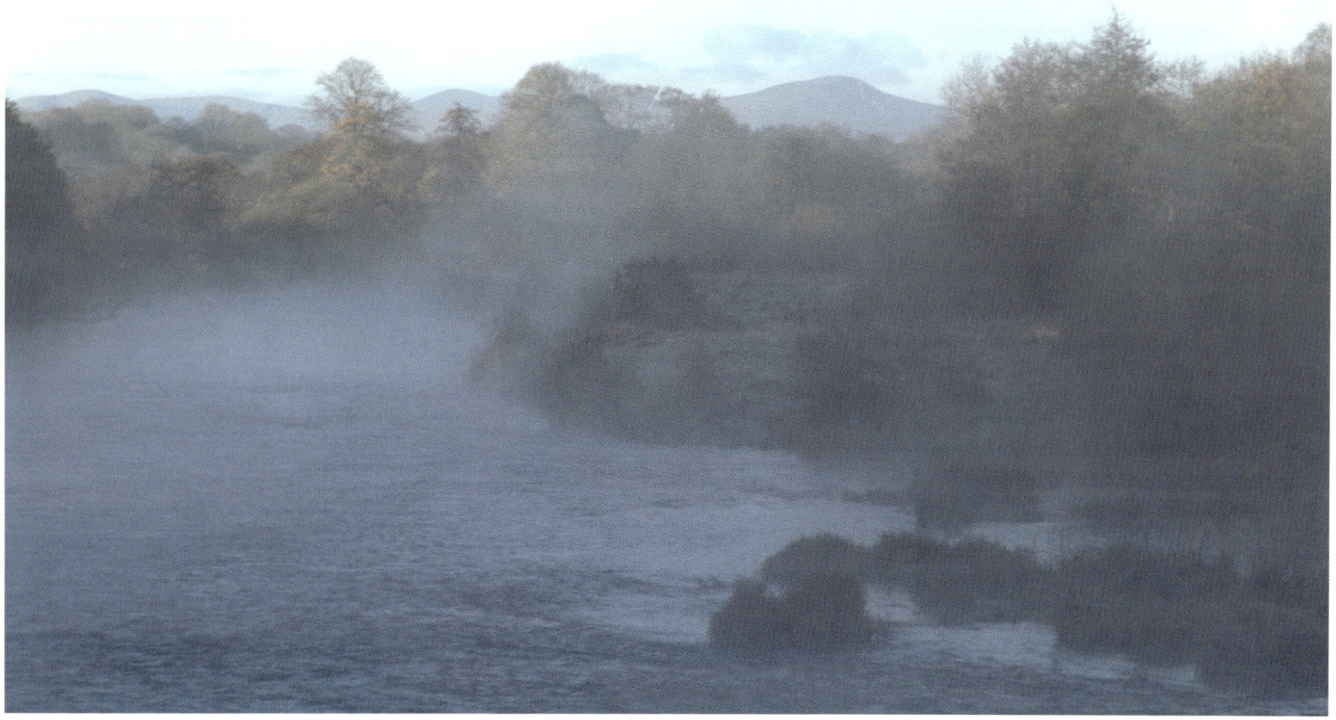

THE NATURE WITHIN

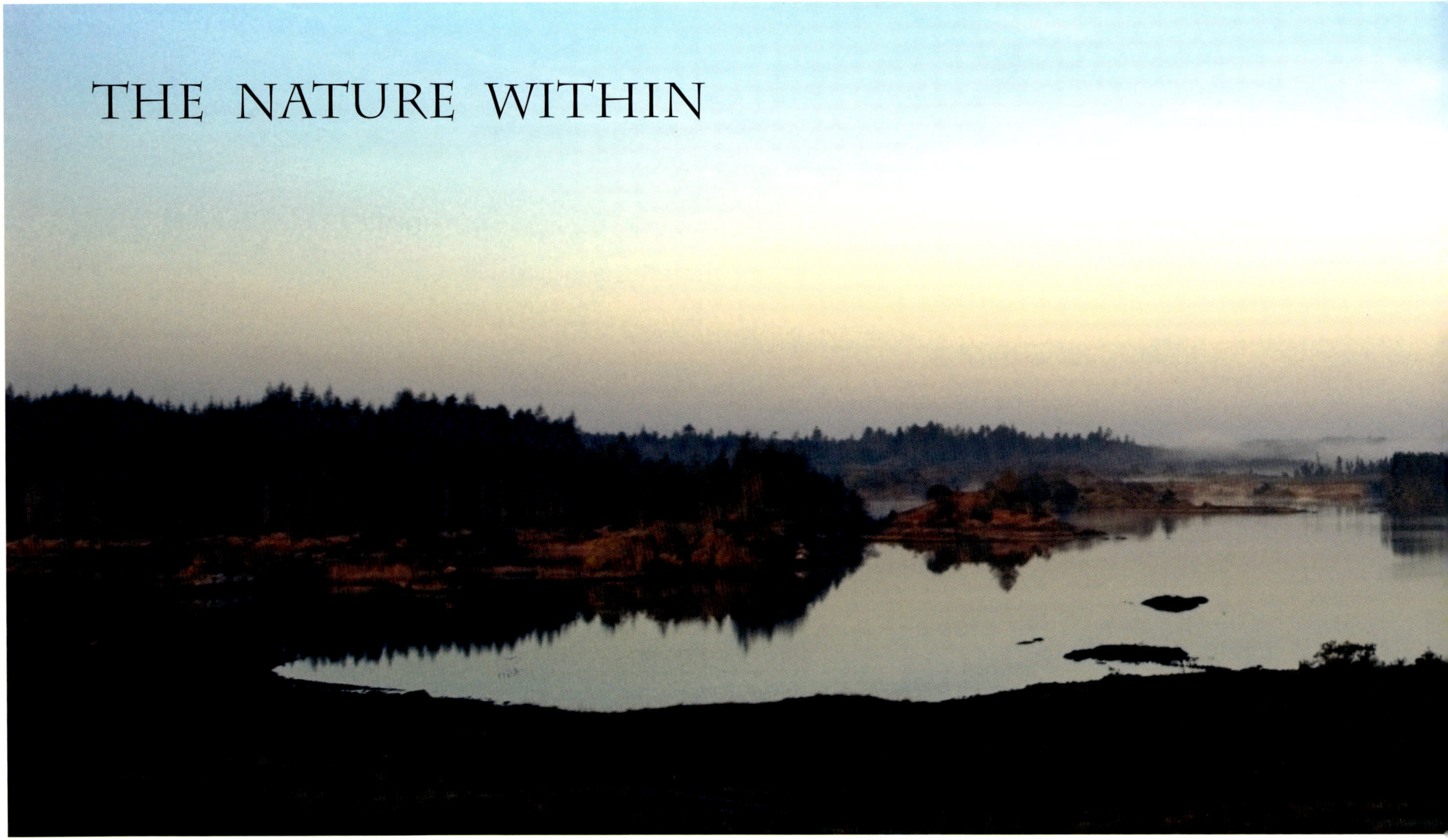

Beauty, the manner in which what we see strikes deep parts of ourselves, is very personal, yet at the same time, universal. Certain scenes may evoke feelings from our experience which are connected to good memories, that give us a sense of well-being. This response to beauty is specific; one person may respond emotionally to an image, another not at all. Underlying this individual identification with the fact of an image, the obvious associations with place or with subject, and the feelings that these may rouse in us, there is something more profound. There is a sense of an energy that we all vibrate to, perhaps felt as a pulse, that of life. Nature has within it an energy that has no separation from the energy of our own make-up; nature without is nature within. We are easily made restless; in our constant quest for stimulation from the magnificence of bigger, wider, higher, deeper, we can overlook the subtle impact of small details of the greater picture which may have a far greater effect on our senses.

Dawn over Lough Ballynahinch, Connemara.

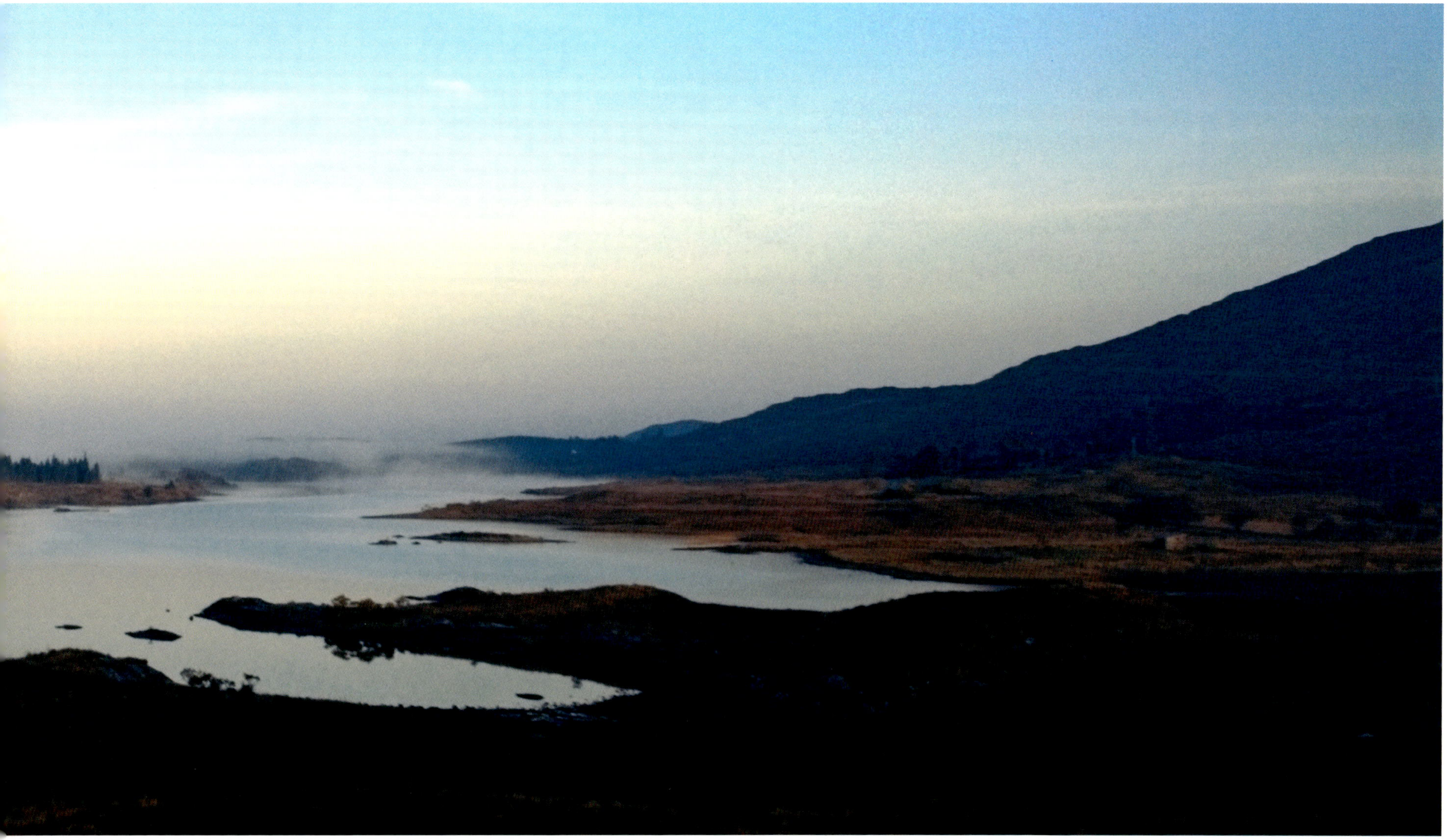

Truly, the 'spectacular in the ordinary' can amaze us with its grandeur. We may find that beauty is as much in the way in which we look at things as in the form of what we see. It is very easy to pass by with eyes as if closed, and be left only with a memory of a moment not really felt. We become accustomed to elements of what we see to the extent that our mind stores them as 'known', and we are then no longer surprised when we see them again, or perhaps do not see them at all. We can allow ouresIves to become open again, to see with 'beginner's mind', the eyes of a child, as if we had never seen this situation before. In this state, experiences do not become stale, and we no longer have the need to be engaged in the unfulfillable quest for the ultimate grand experience. Every experience, no matter how small, has the capacity to engage us fully over and over again; the smallest detail contains the essence of the greatest scene. Nowhere is this more true than in the subtle beauty of Ireland.

NATURE'S PATTERNS RESONATE AT MANY LEVELS

OPPOSITE Strands of high cloud lit by a dramatic summer sunrise behind Mount Brandon, seen across Smerwick Harbour, County Kerry.

BELOW A pool of rainwater on an oak leaf.

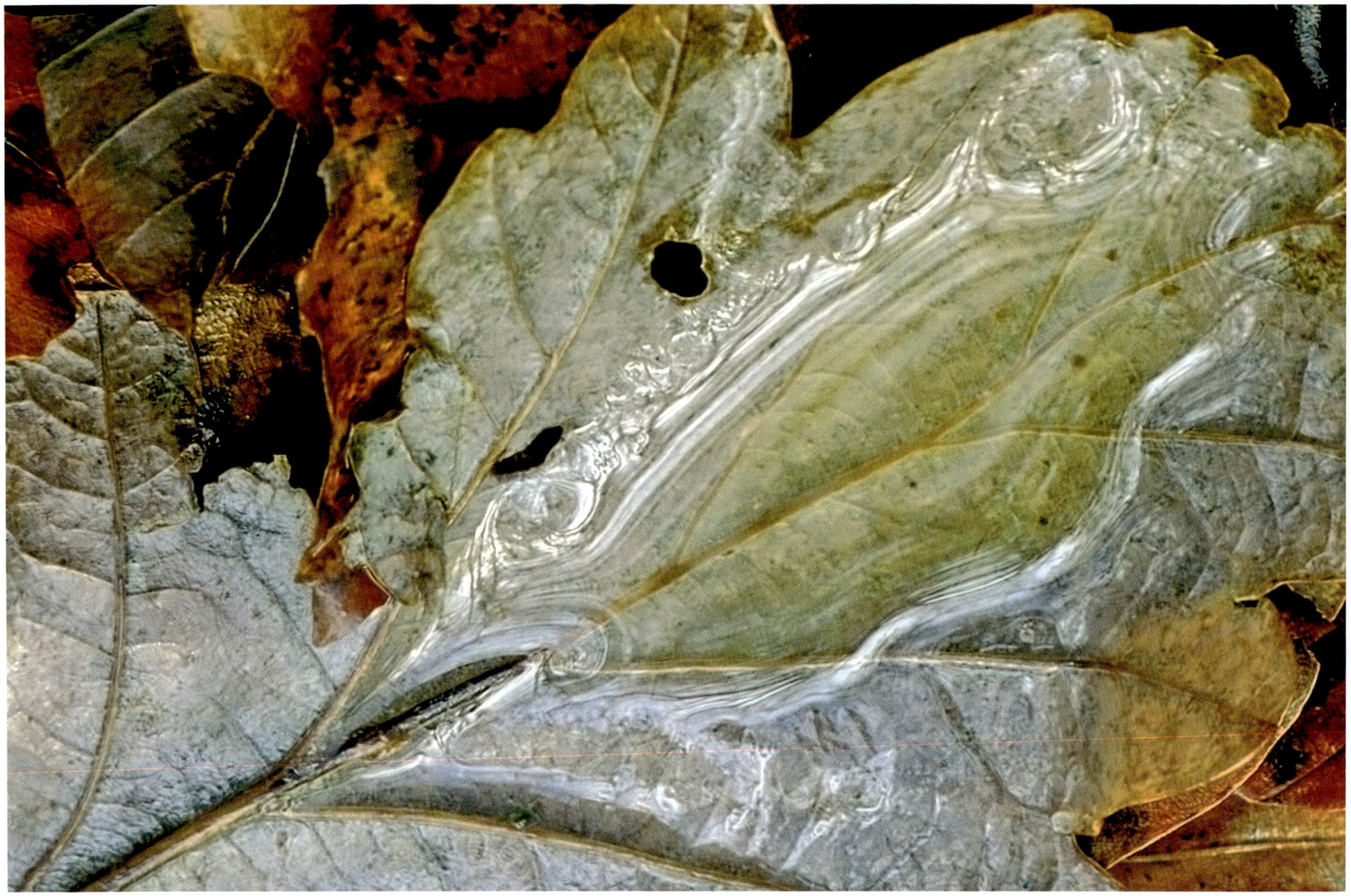

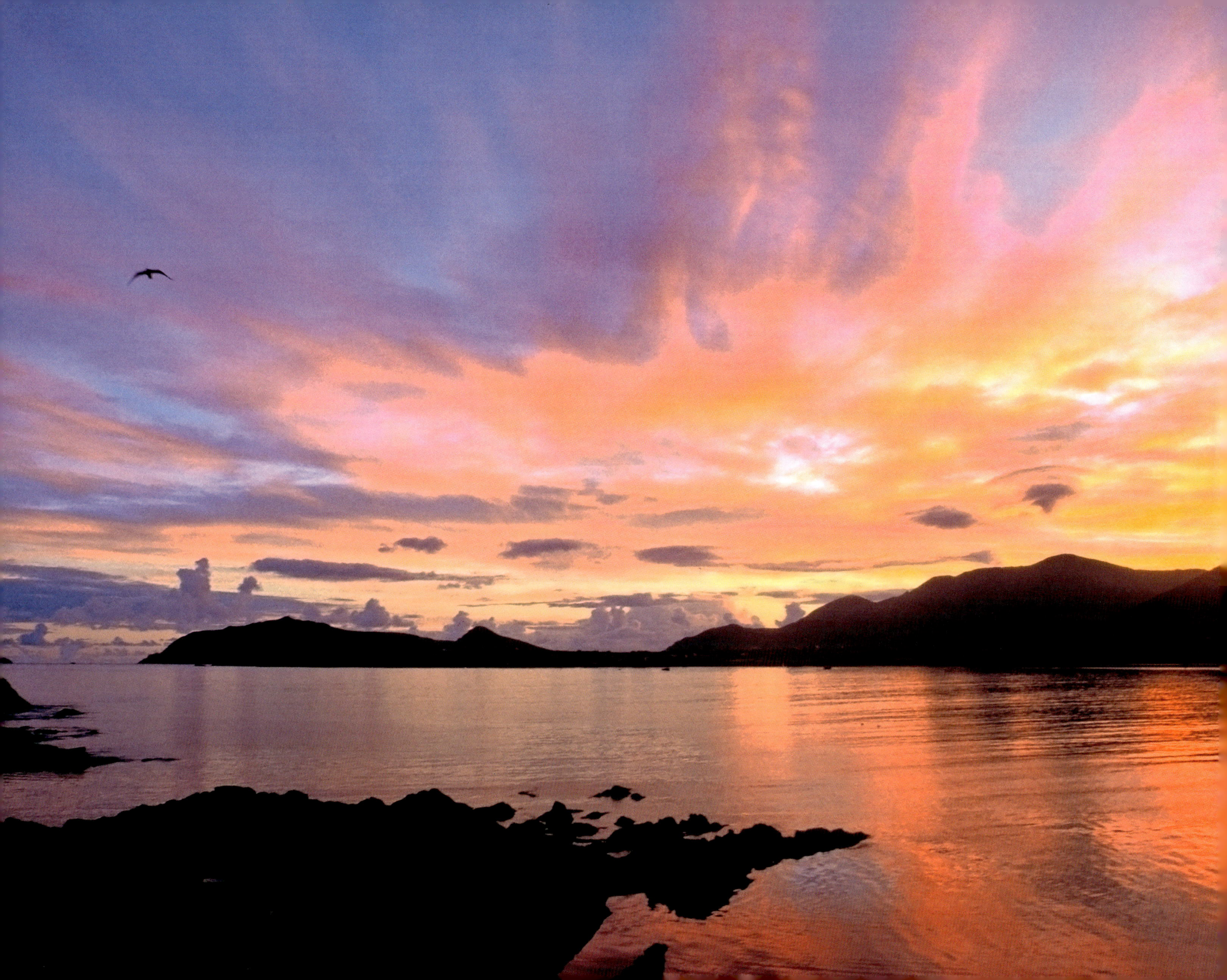

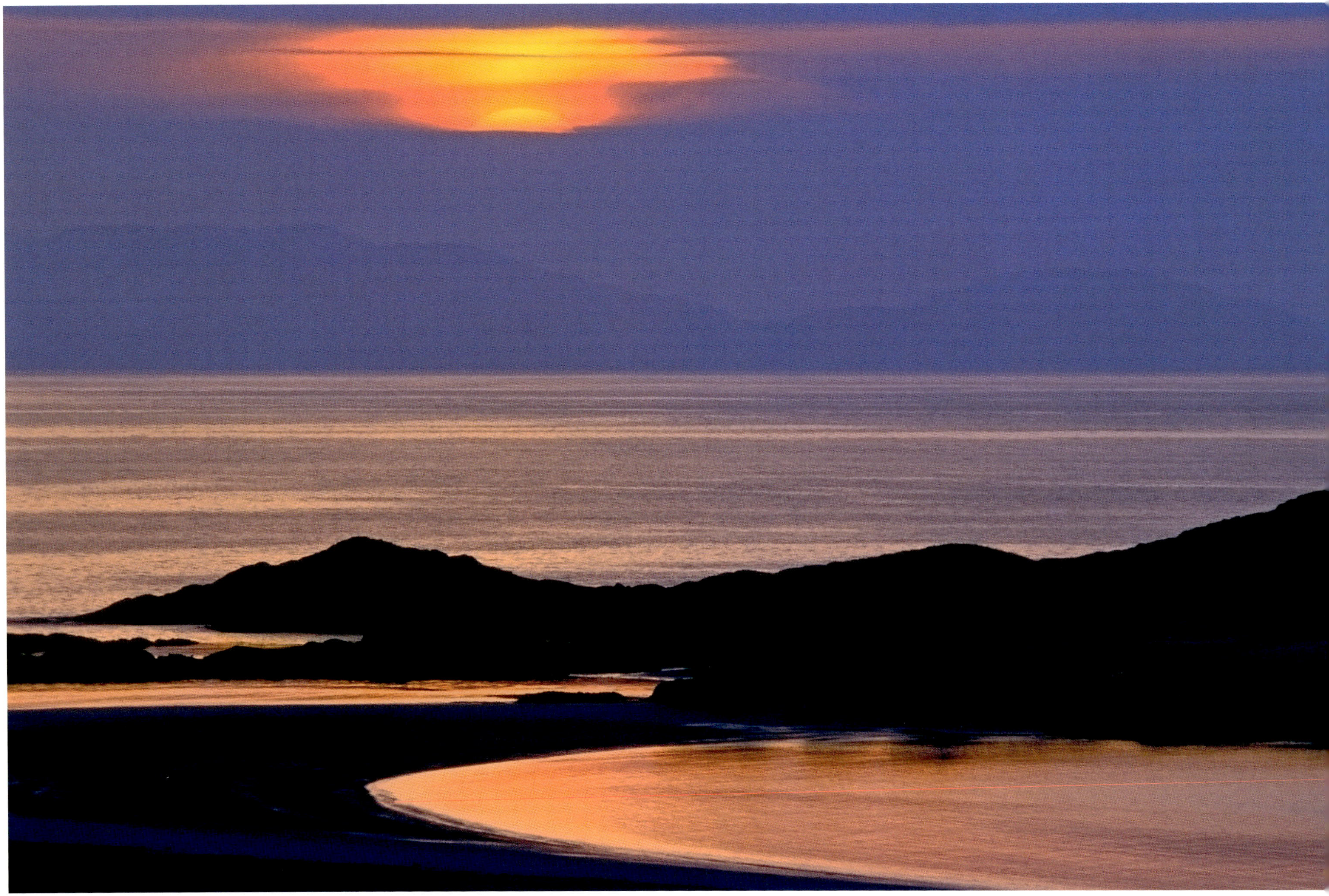

OPPOSITE Inis Glas, at the mouth of Killary Harbour, Connemara, County Galway.

BELOW Sun rising behind Errigal, Donegal.

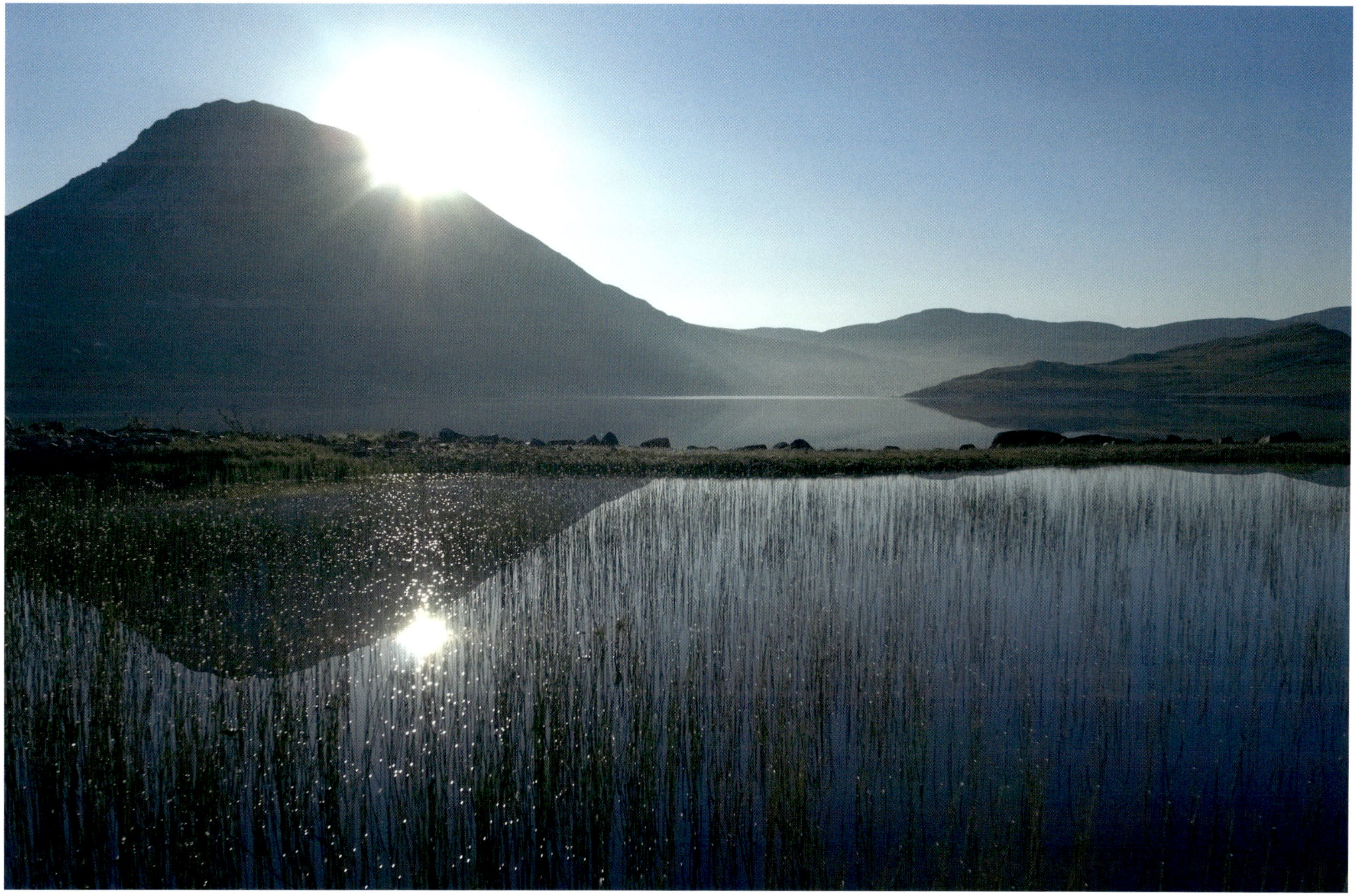

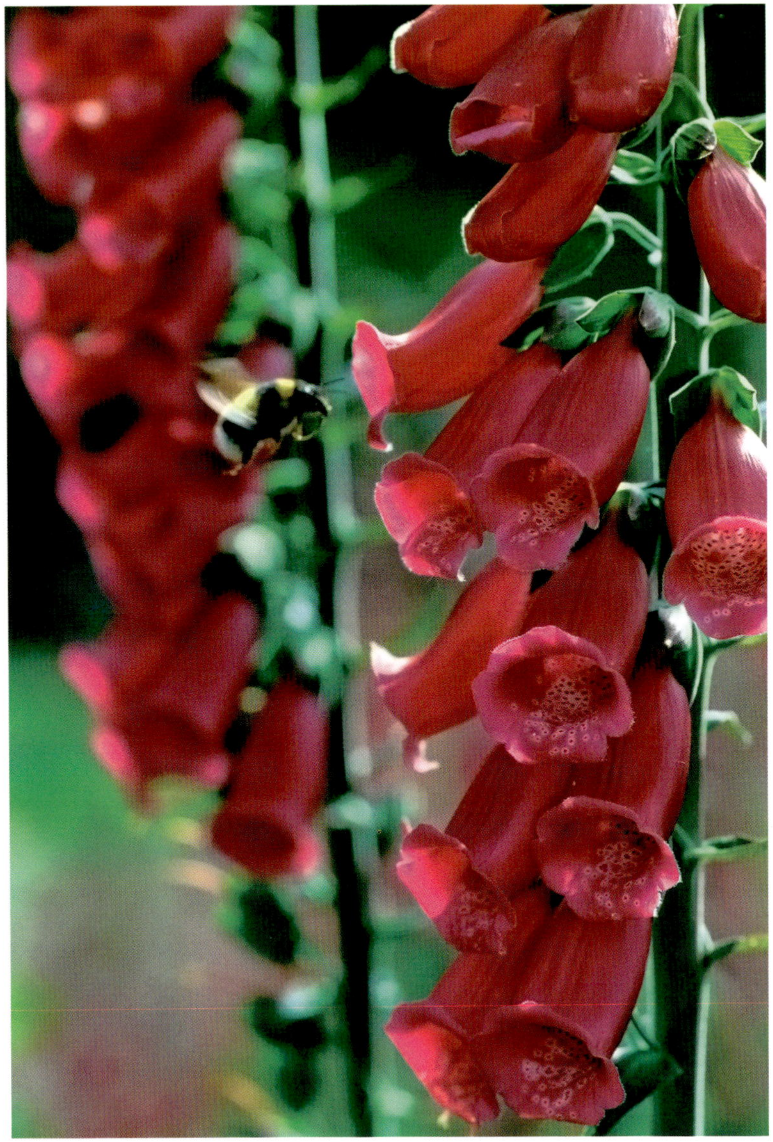

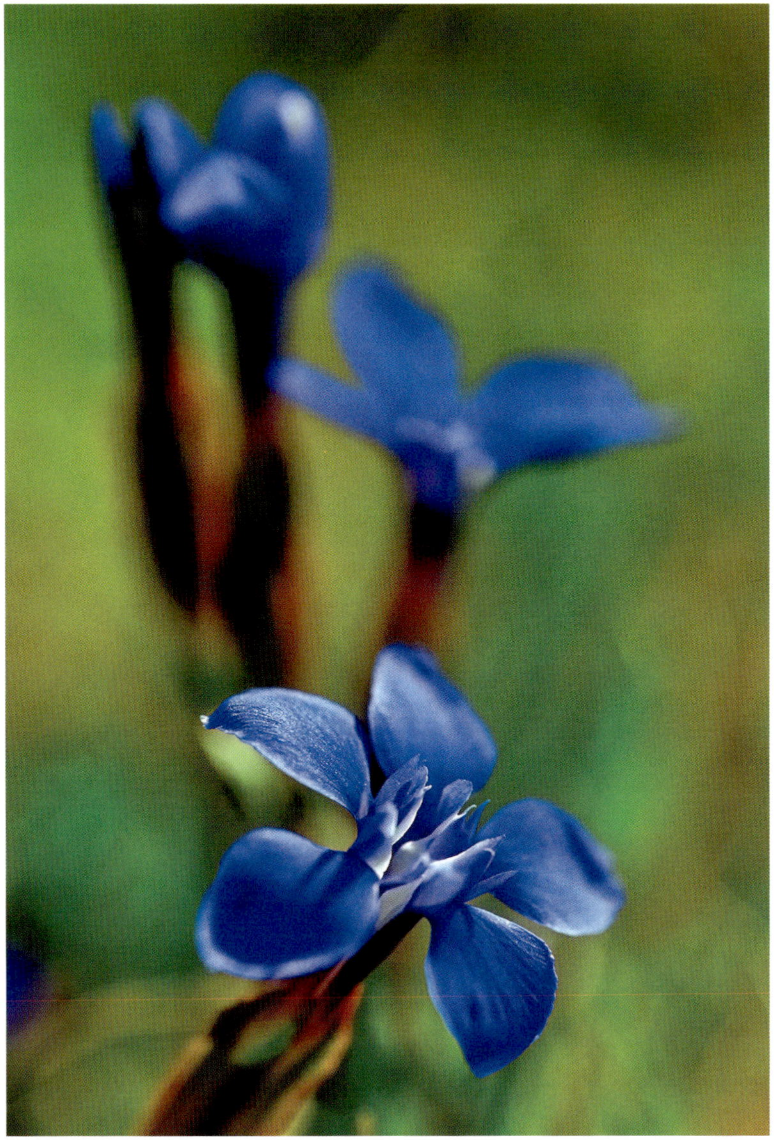

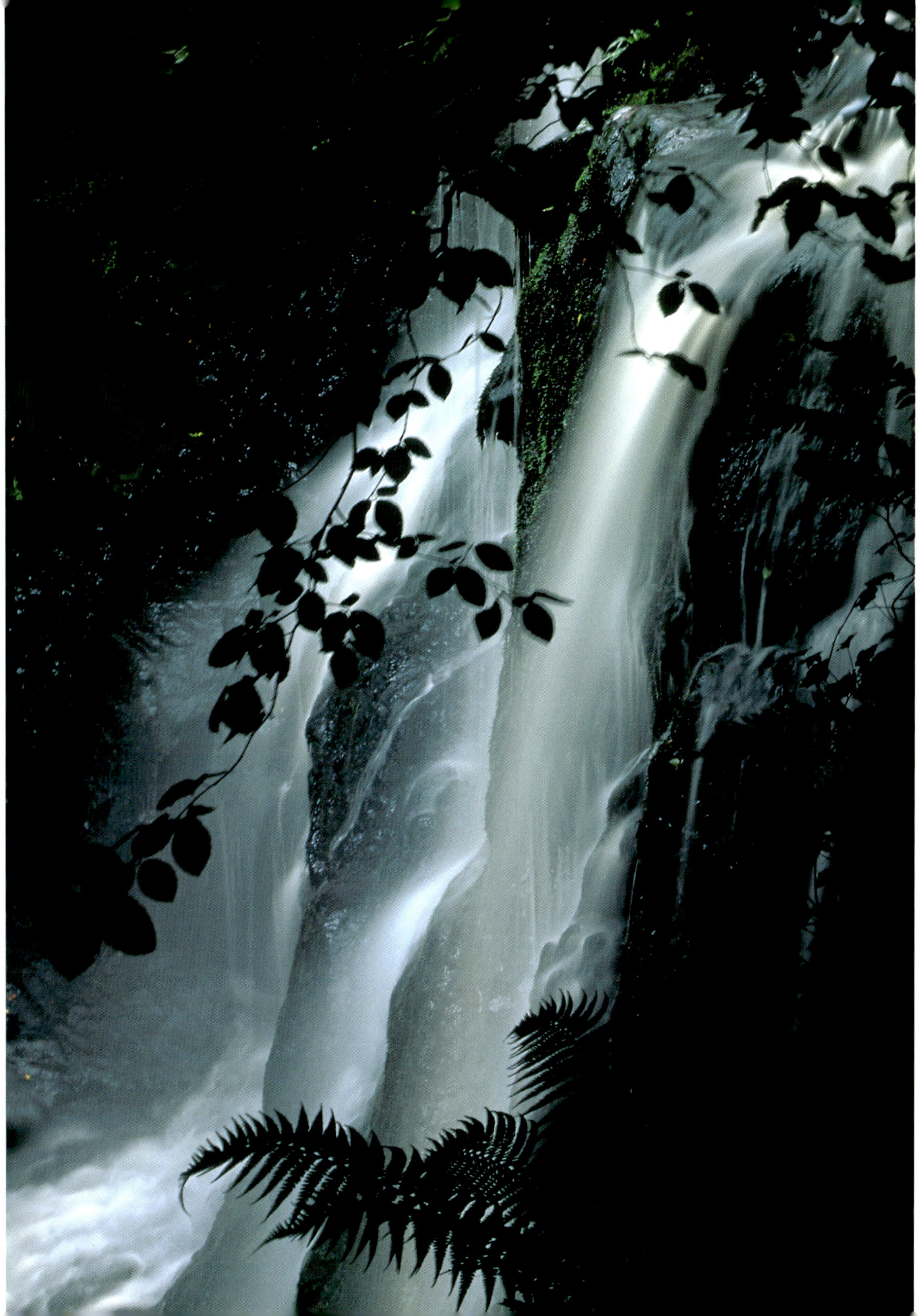

FLOW OF NATURE

OPPOSITE LEFT Foxglove.

OPPOSITE RIGHT Spring gentian in the Burren, County Clare.

LEFT Glenariff Falls, County Antrim.

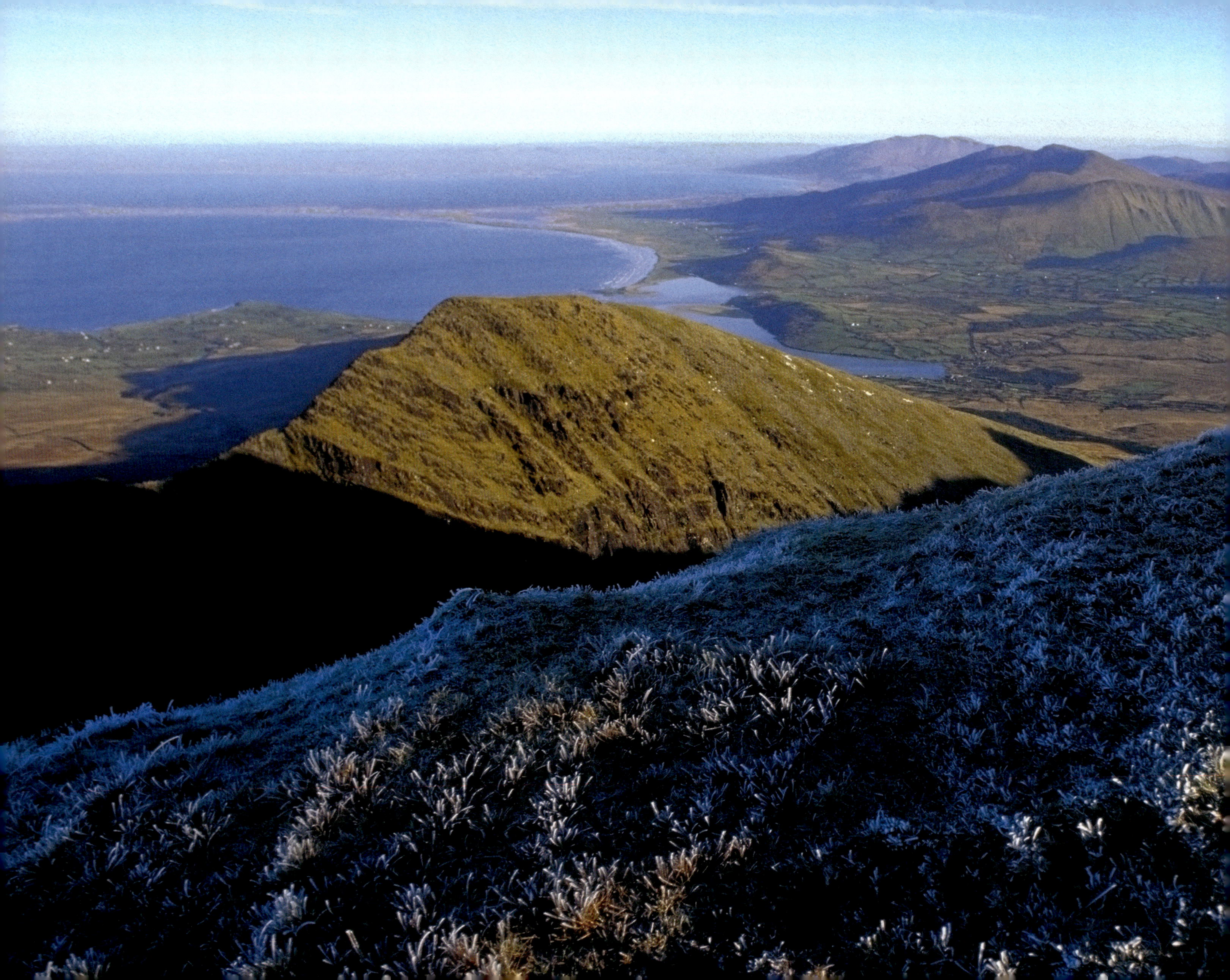

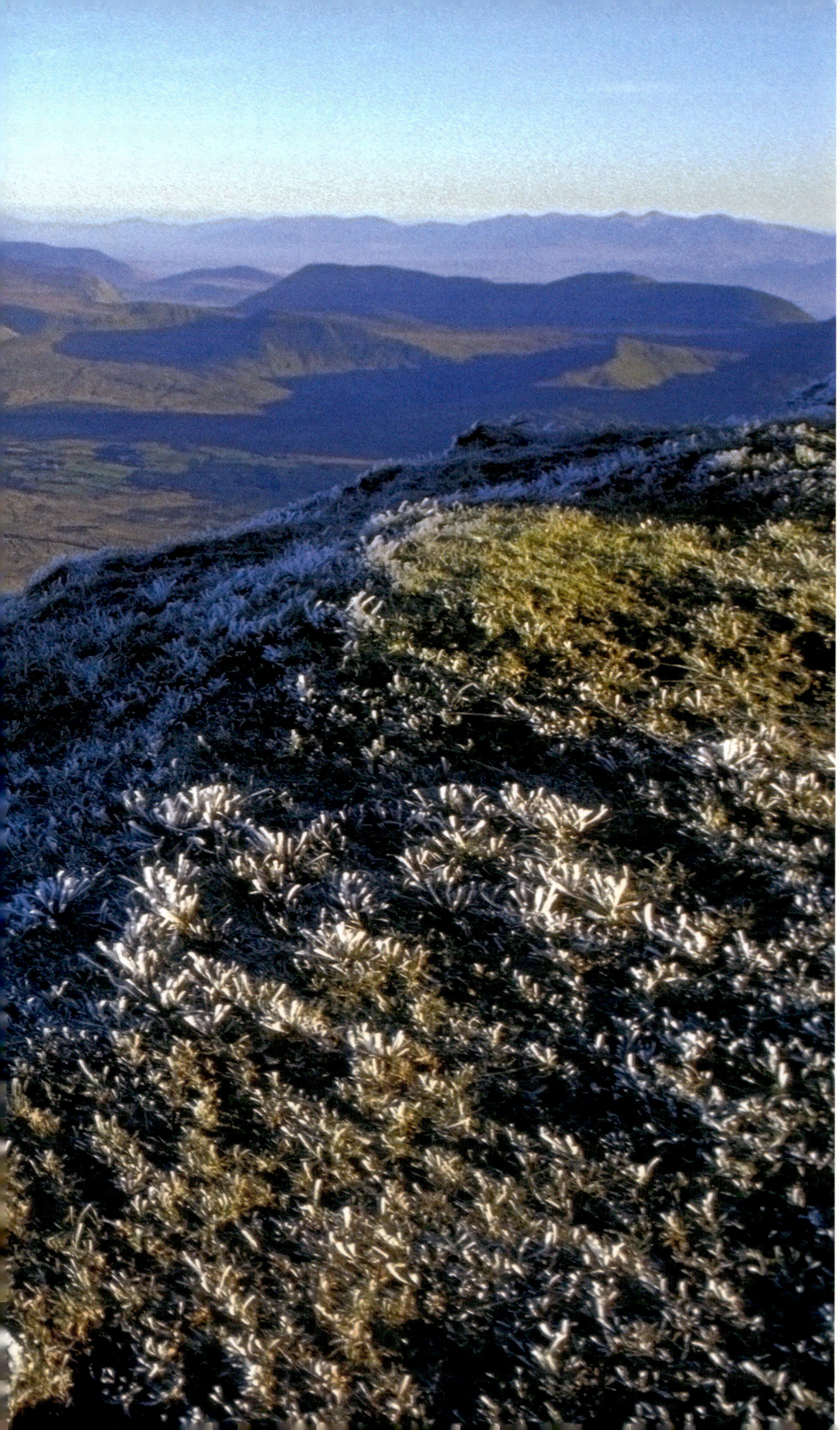

OPPOSITE Hoar frost on the summit of Mount Brandon, the Dingle Peninsula, County Kerry.

BELOW Frosted sycamore and hazel leaves.

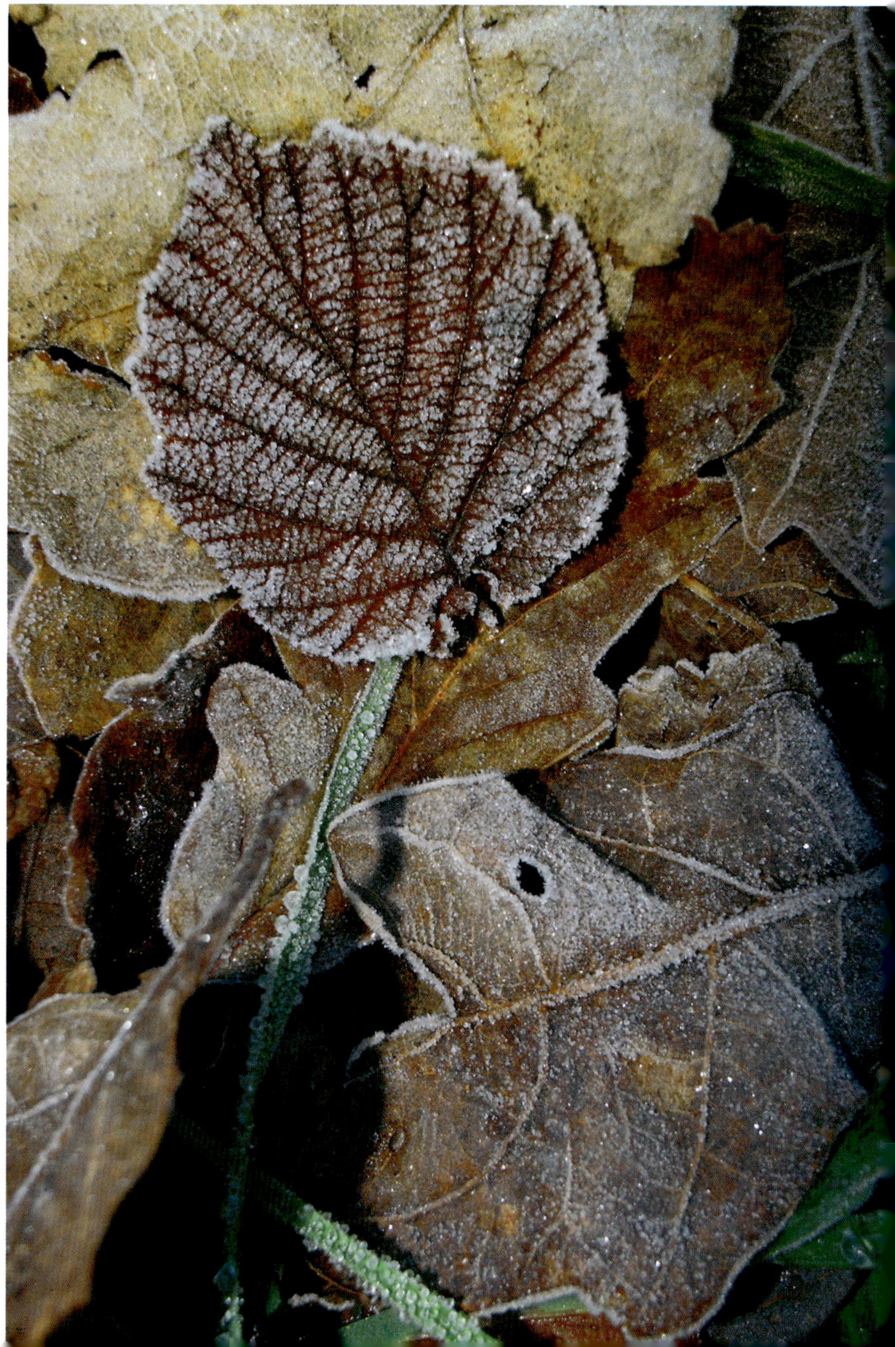

OPPOSITE The remarkable stone landscape of the Burren at Fanore, County Clare.

BELOW Harebells gather under the shelter of a stone post.

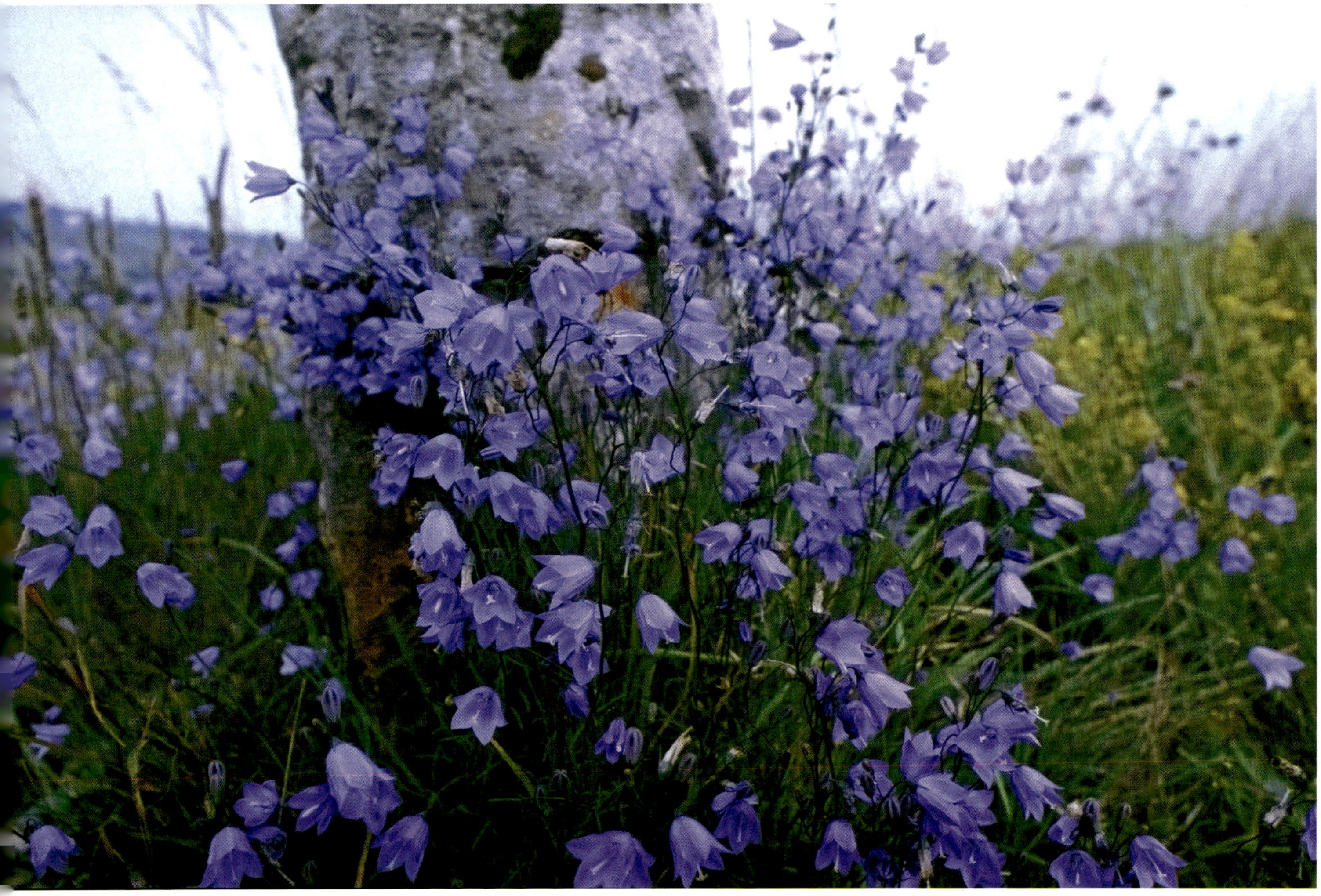

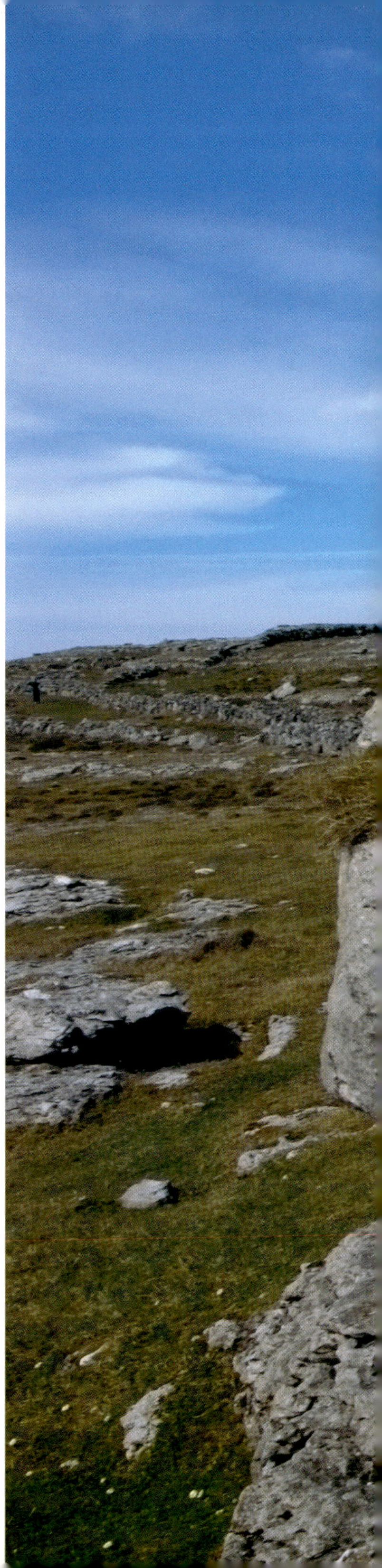

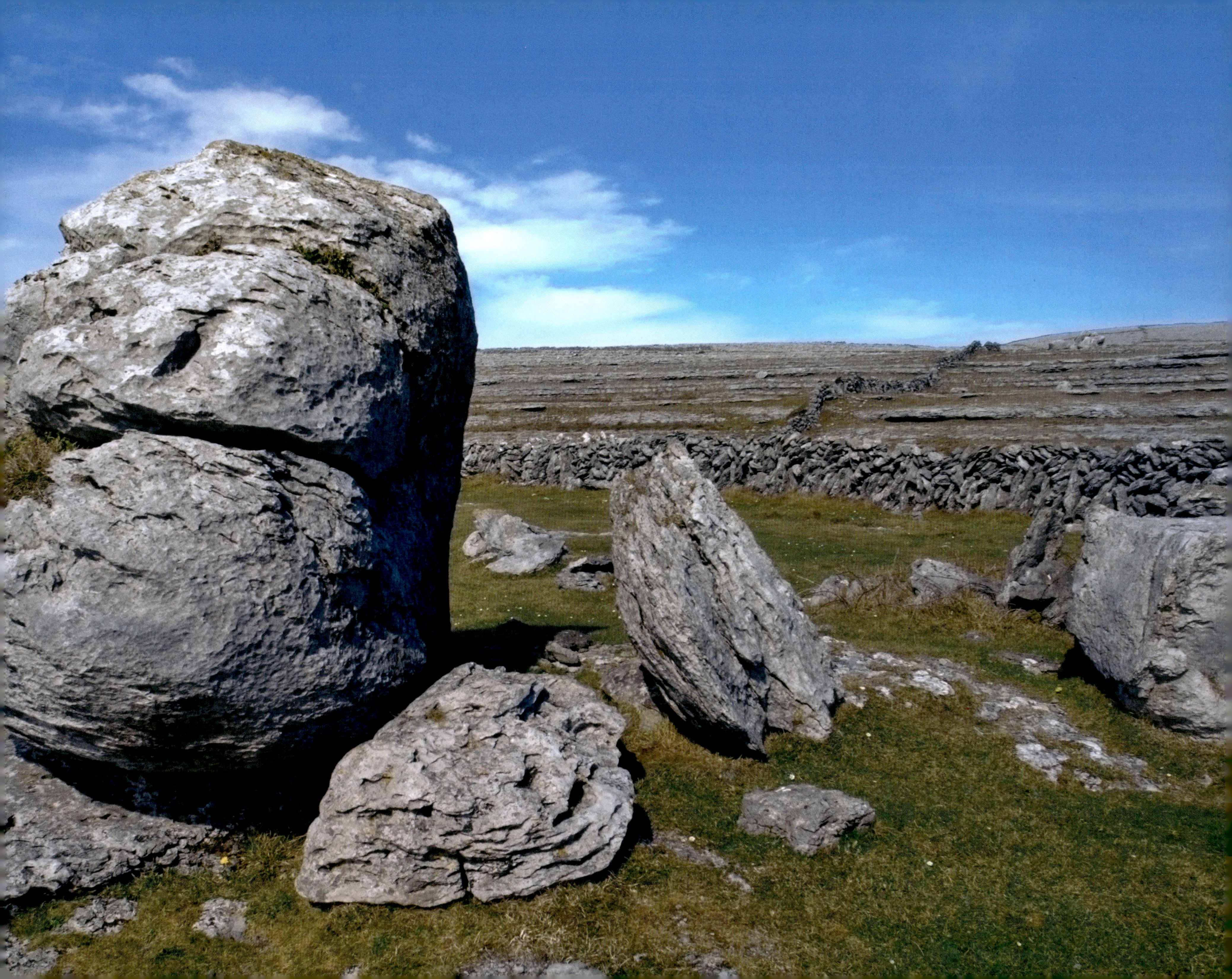

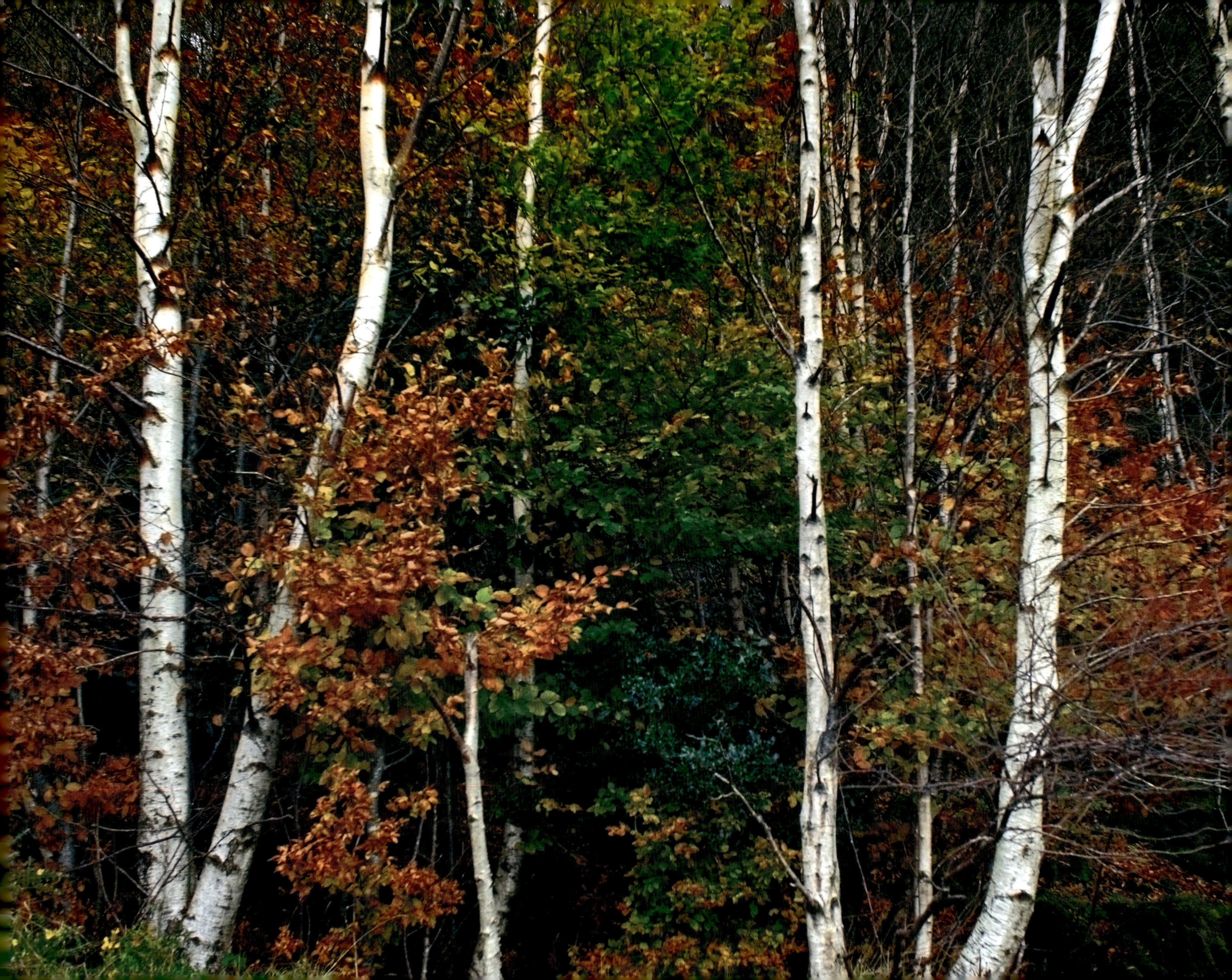

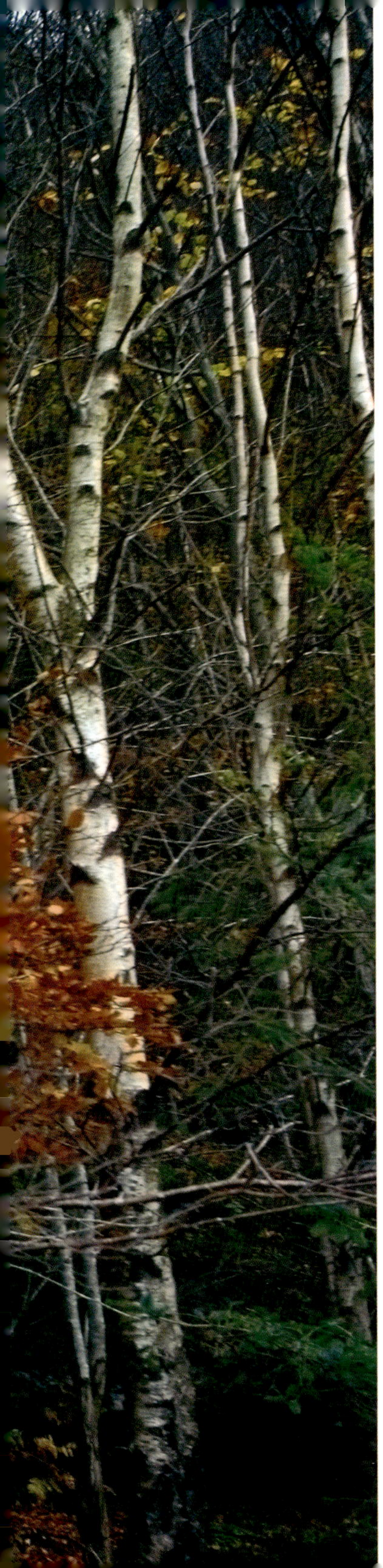

CONTRAST OF COLOUR AND TONE

OPPOSITE Young beech trees growing in birch woodland; light and dark juxtaposed.

BELOW Snow on the leaves of bramble.

OVERLEAF Sunset beyond the mouth of Dingle Harbour, County Kerry, with the peak of Cruach Mhárthain in the distance.

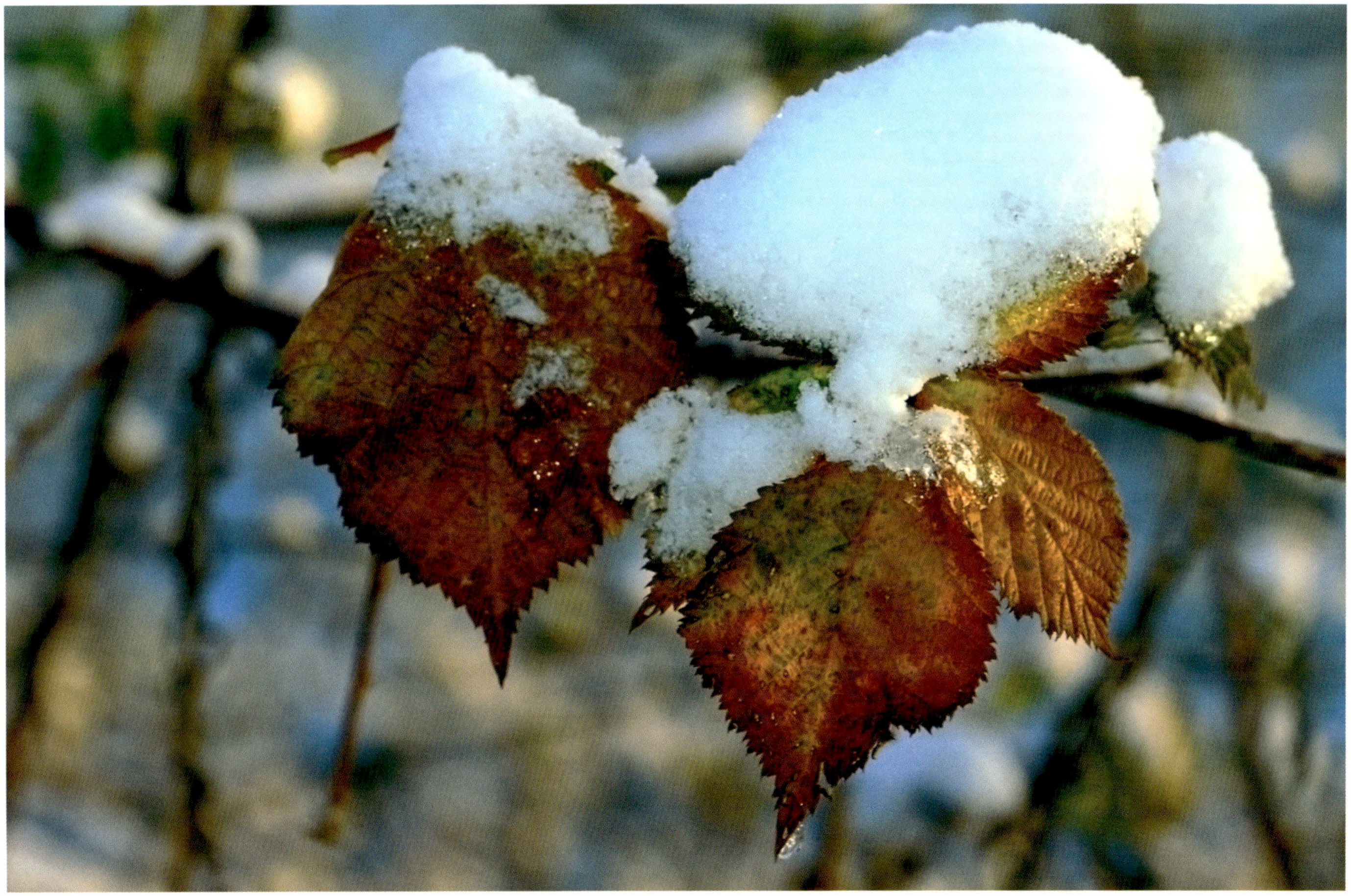

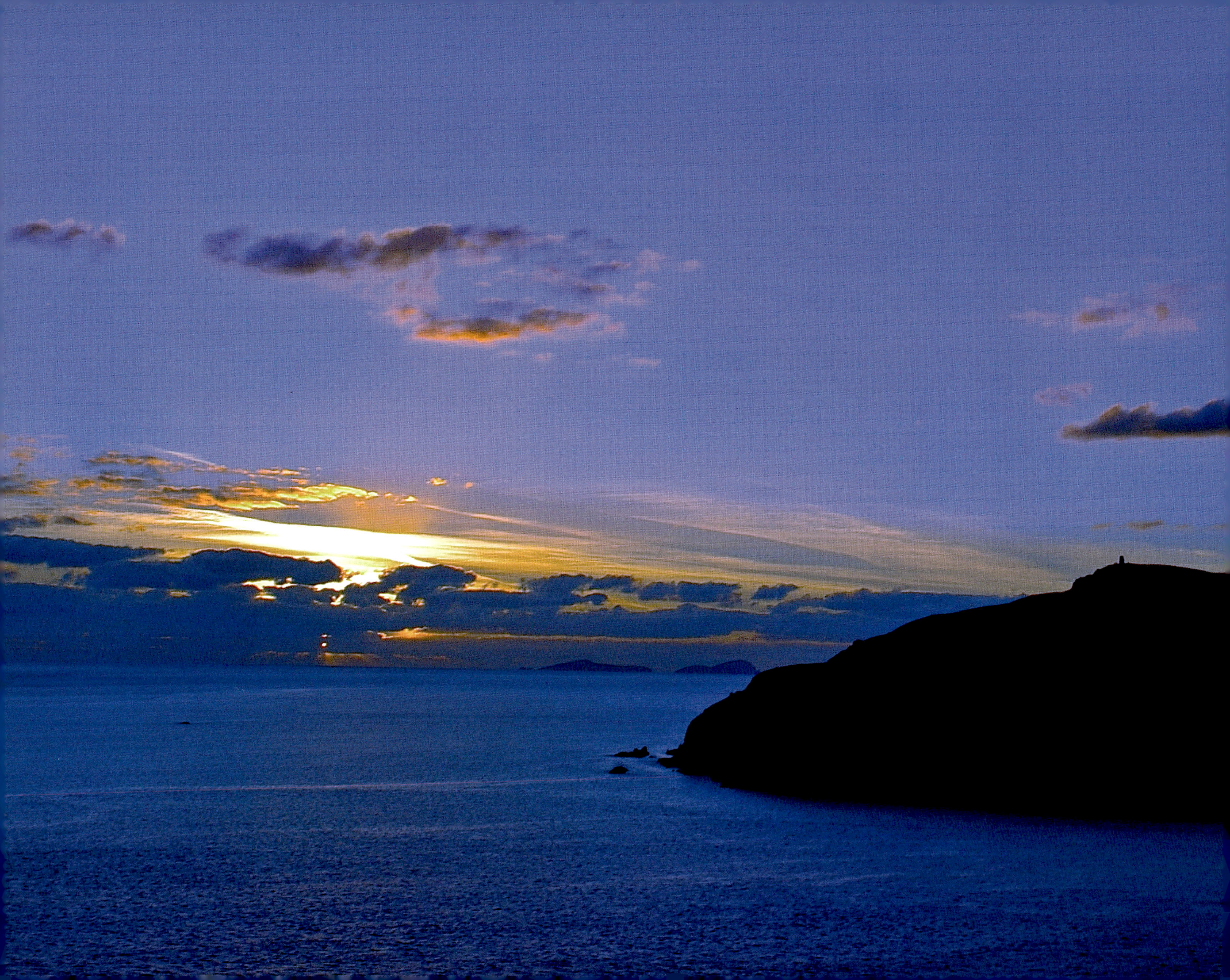

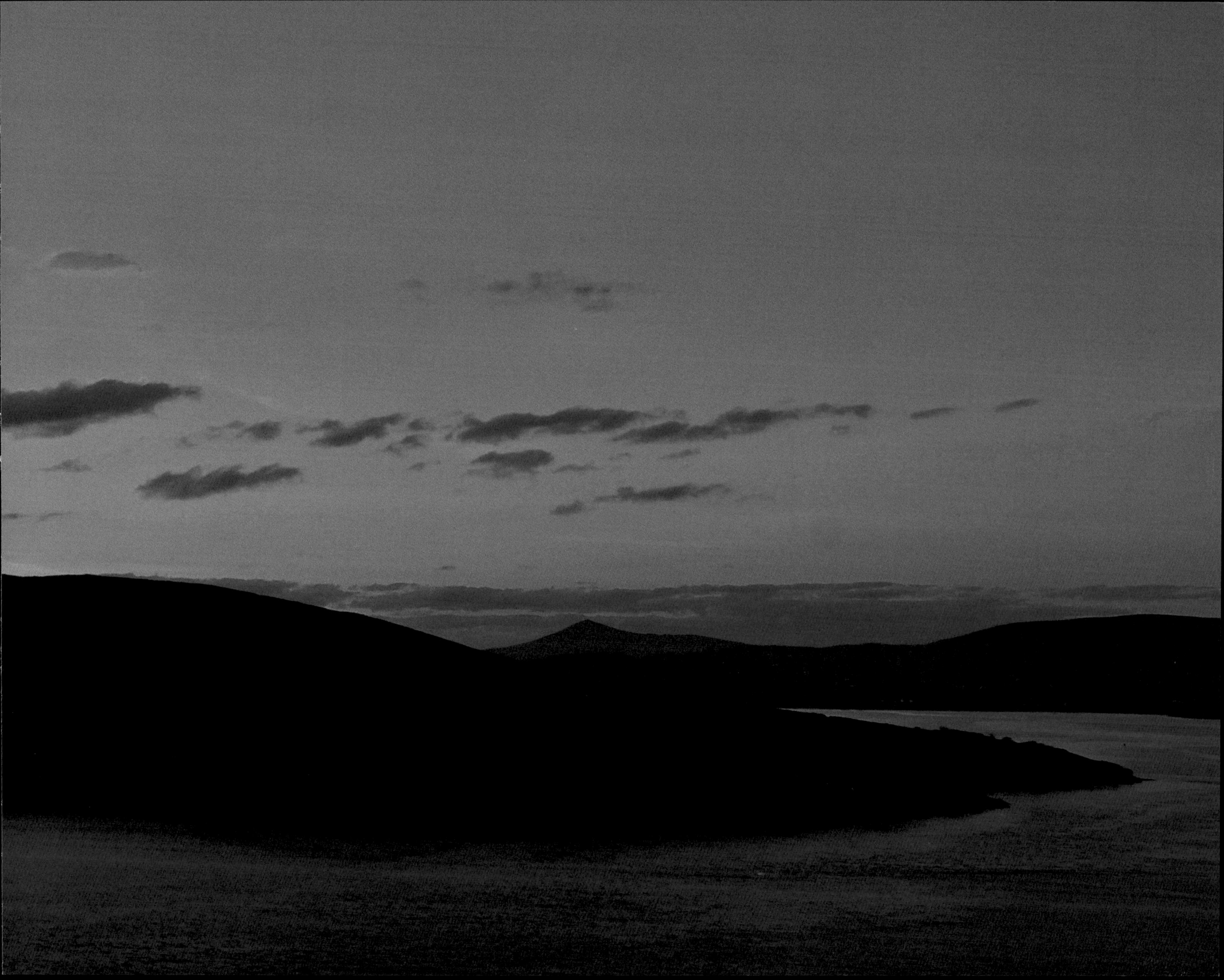

OPPOSITE Lamb's Head, near Caherdaniel, County Kerry, weathered by the Atlantic.

BELOW Rocky beach at Bun Inhir, Annascaul, County Kerry.

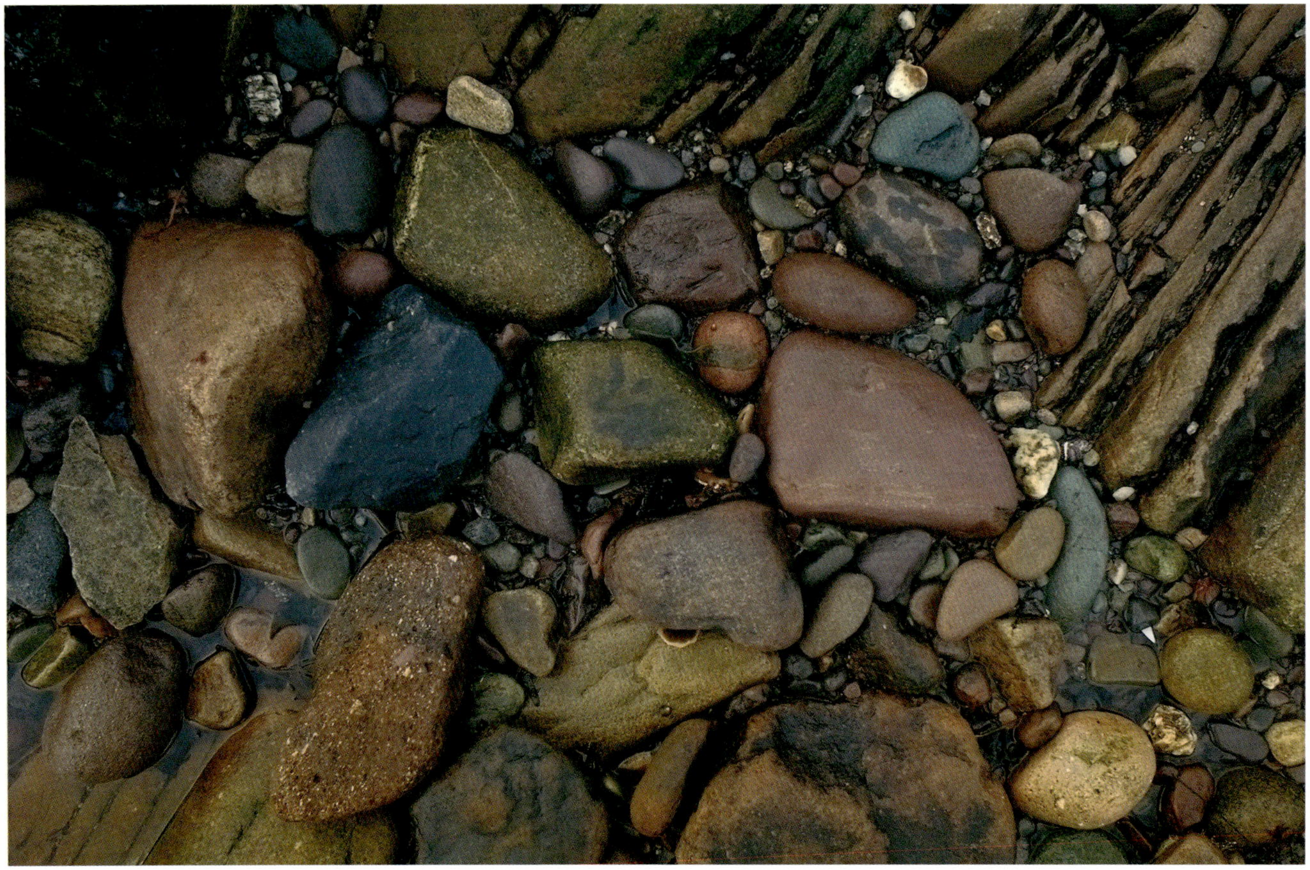

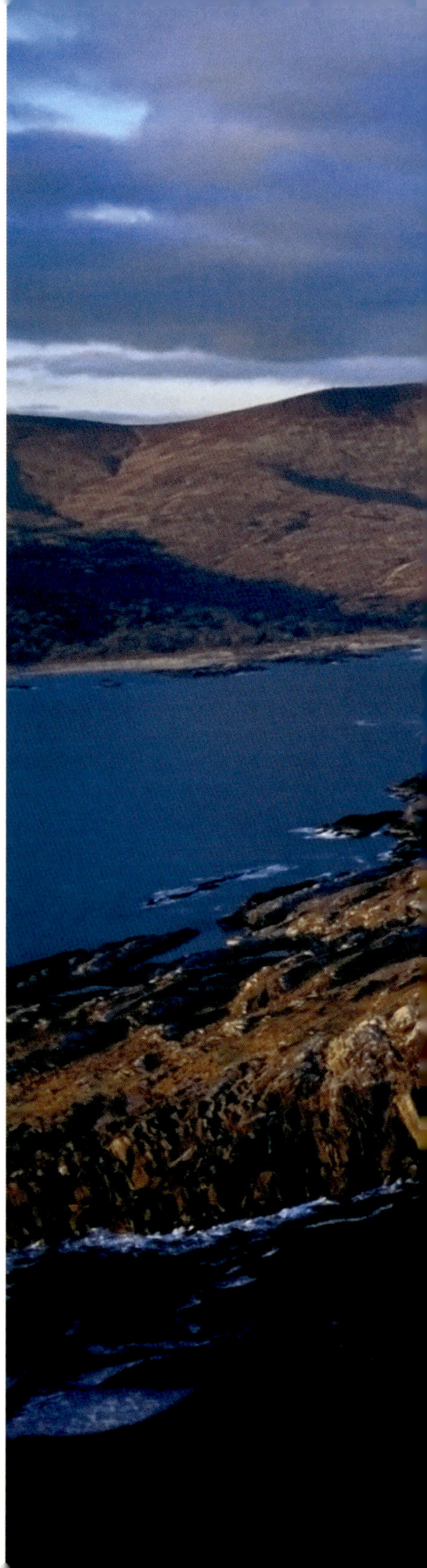

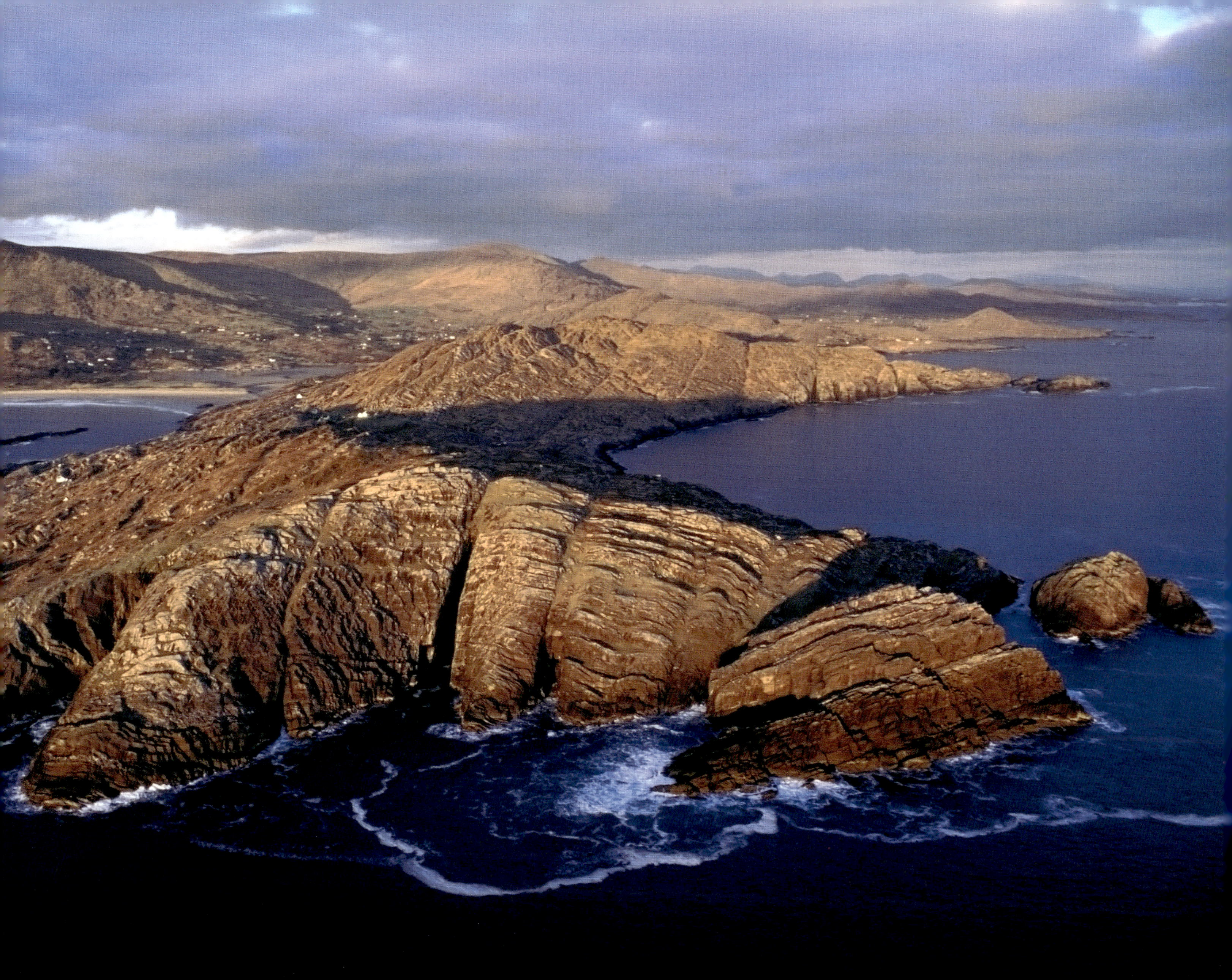

OPPOSITE Clew Bay, Mayo, looking across the many islands to Achill Head.

BELOW Late autumn lying on a pool, Killarney National Park, County Kerry.

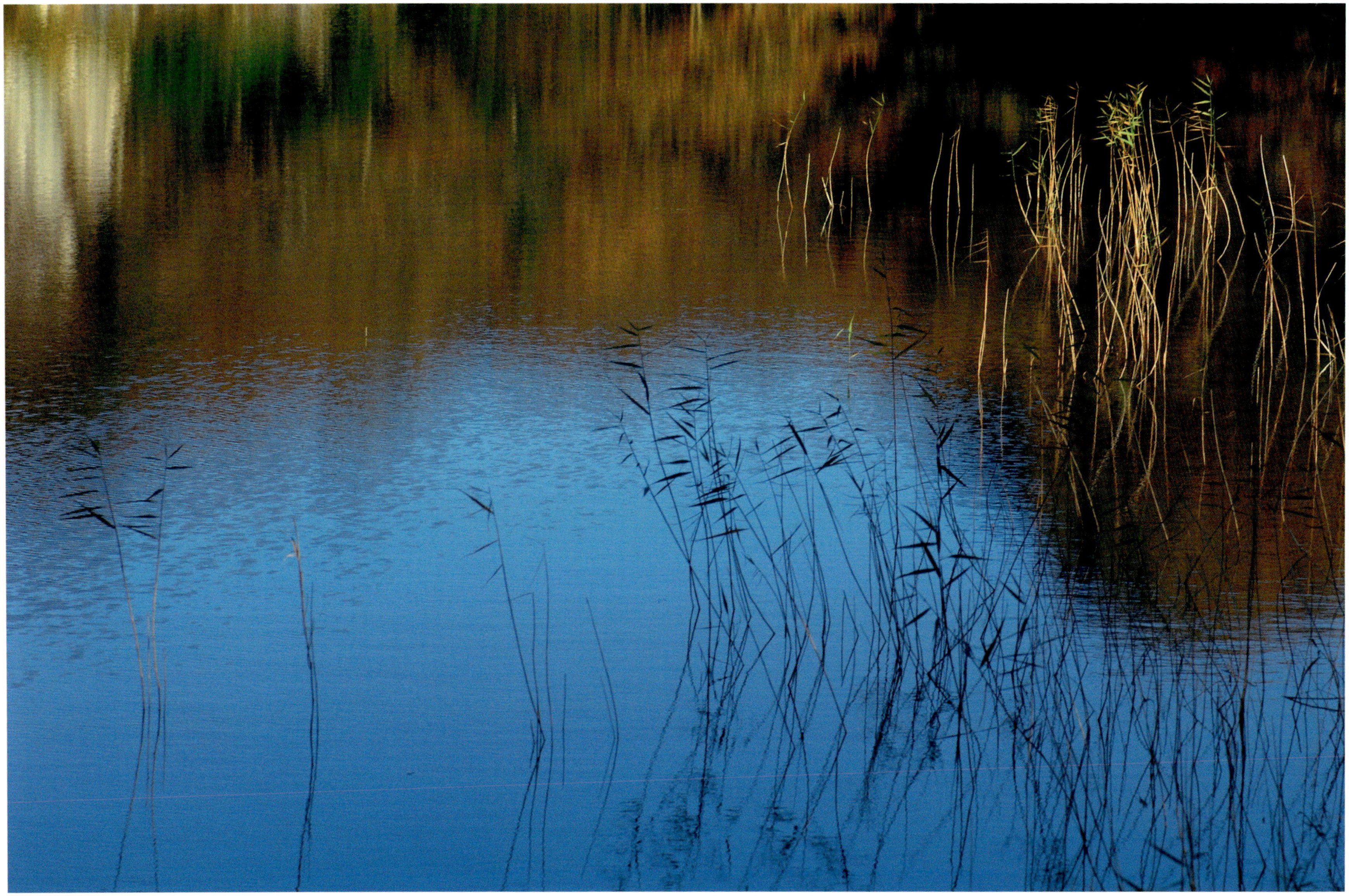

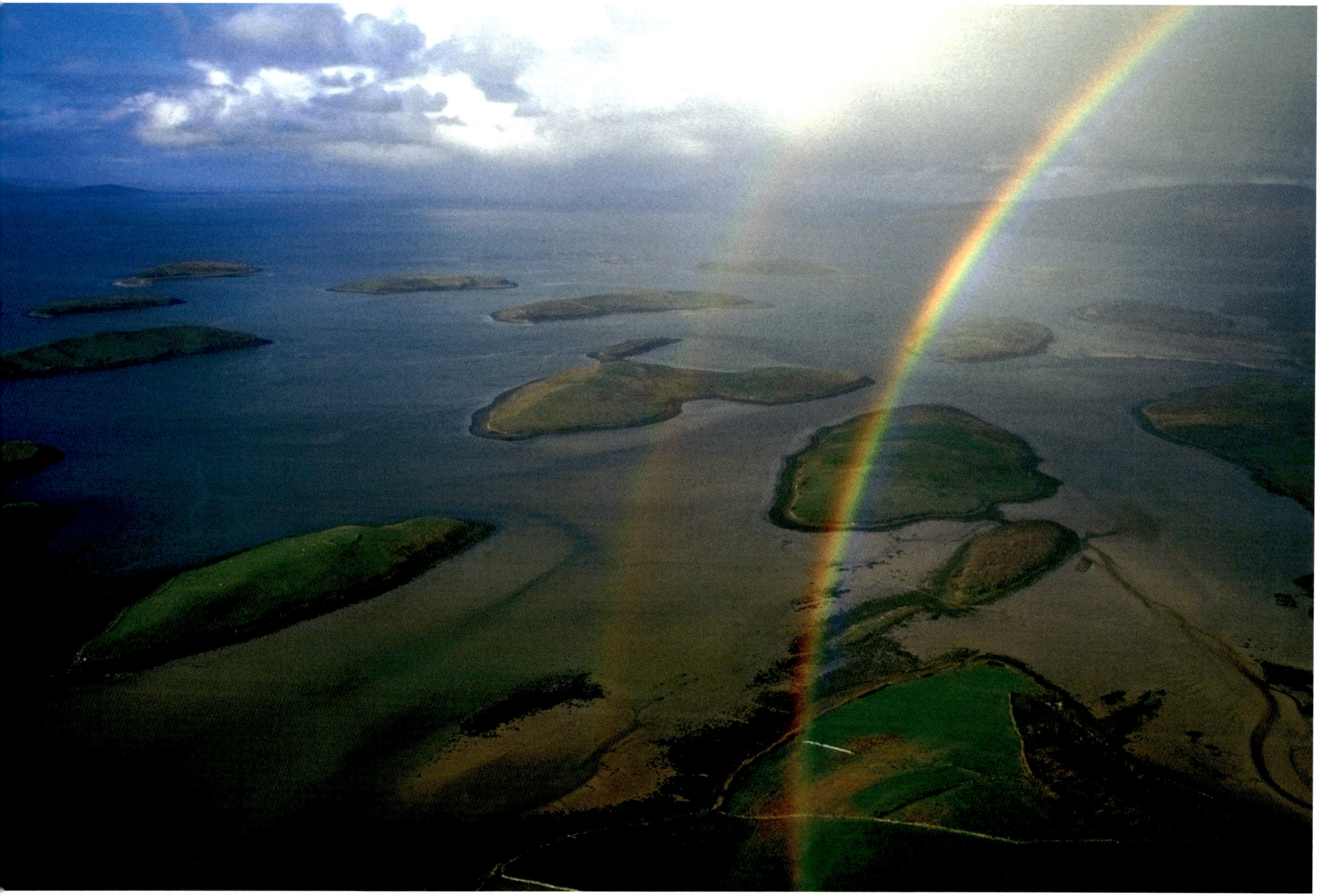

STONE SHAPED BY WATER, WATER SHAPED BY STONE

OPPOSITE Sunset in the Twelve Bens, mountains clothed with light.

BELOW Shapes of stone revealed by the flow of water.

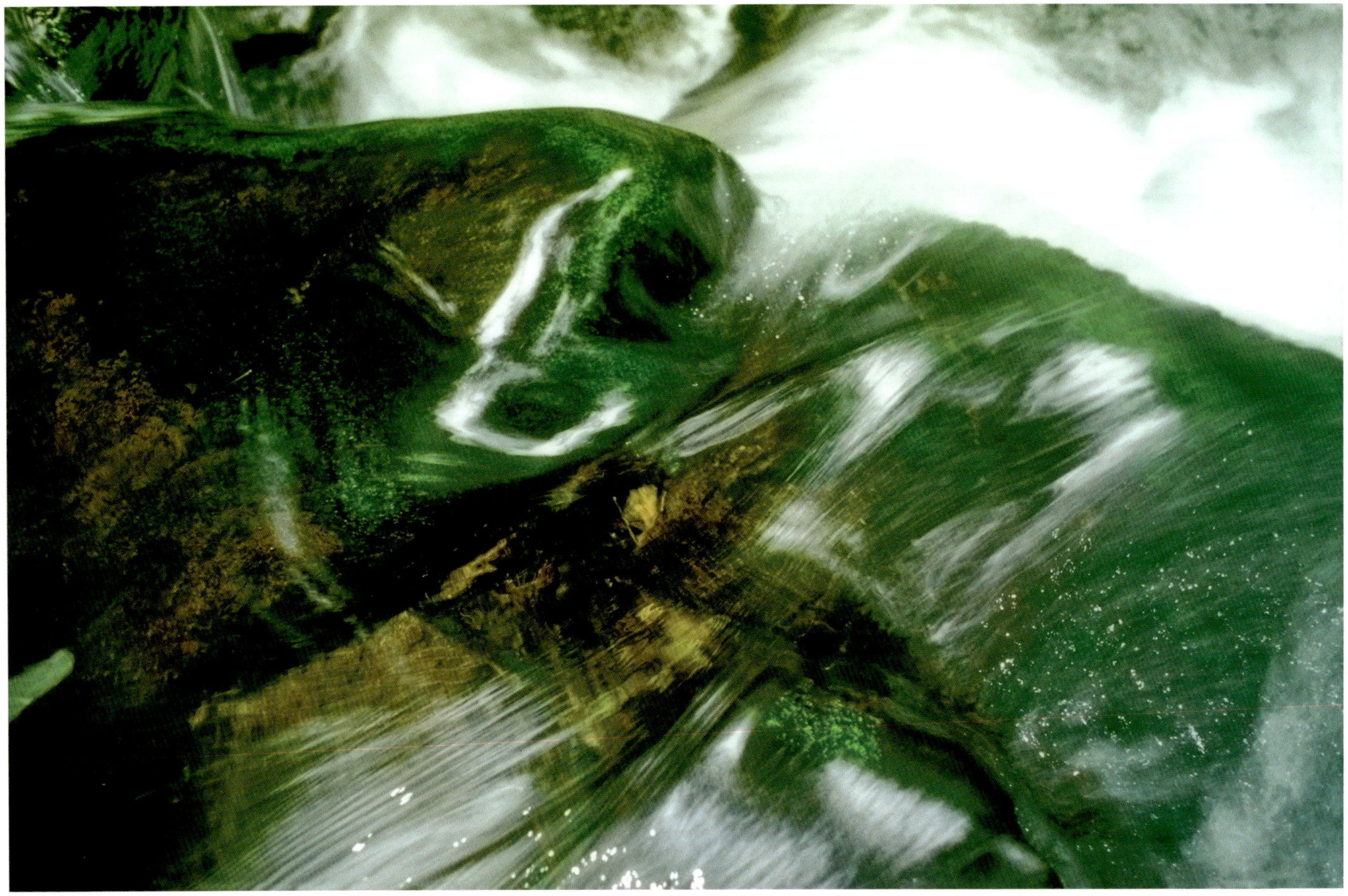

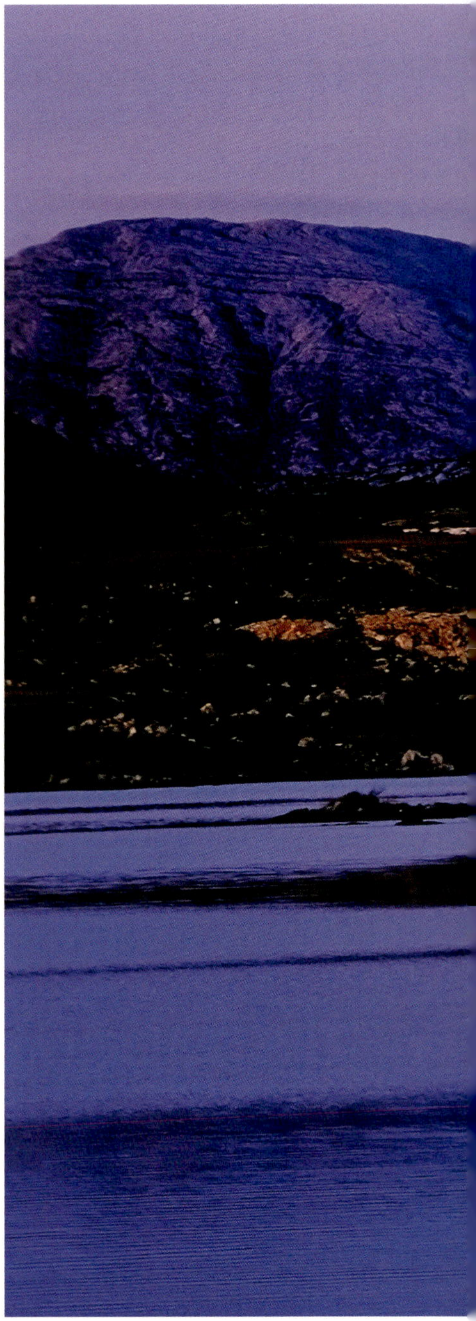

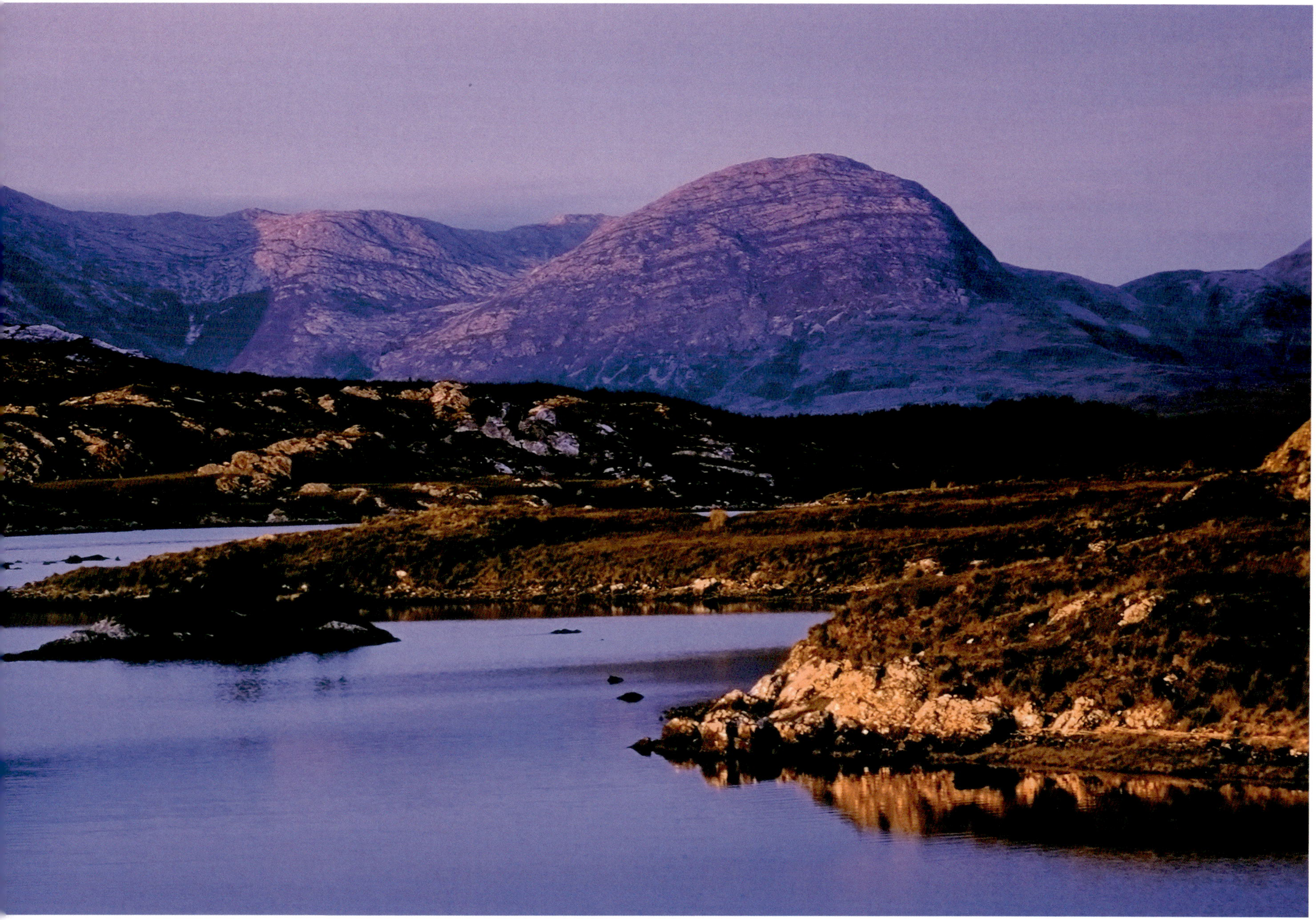

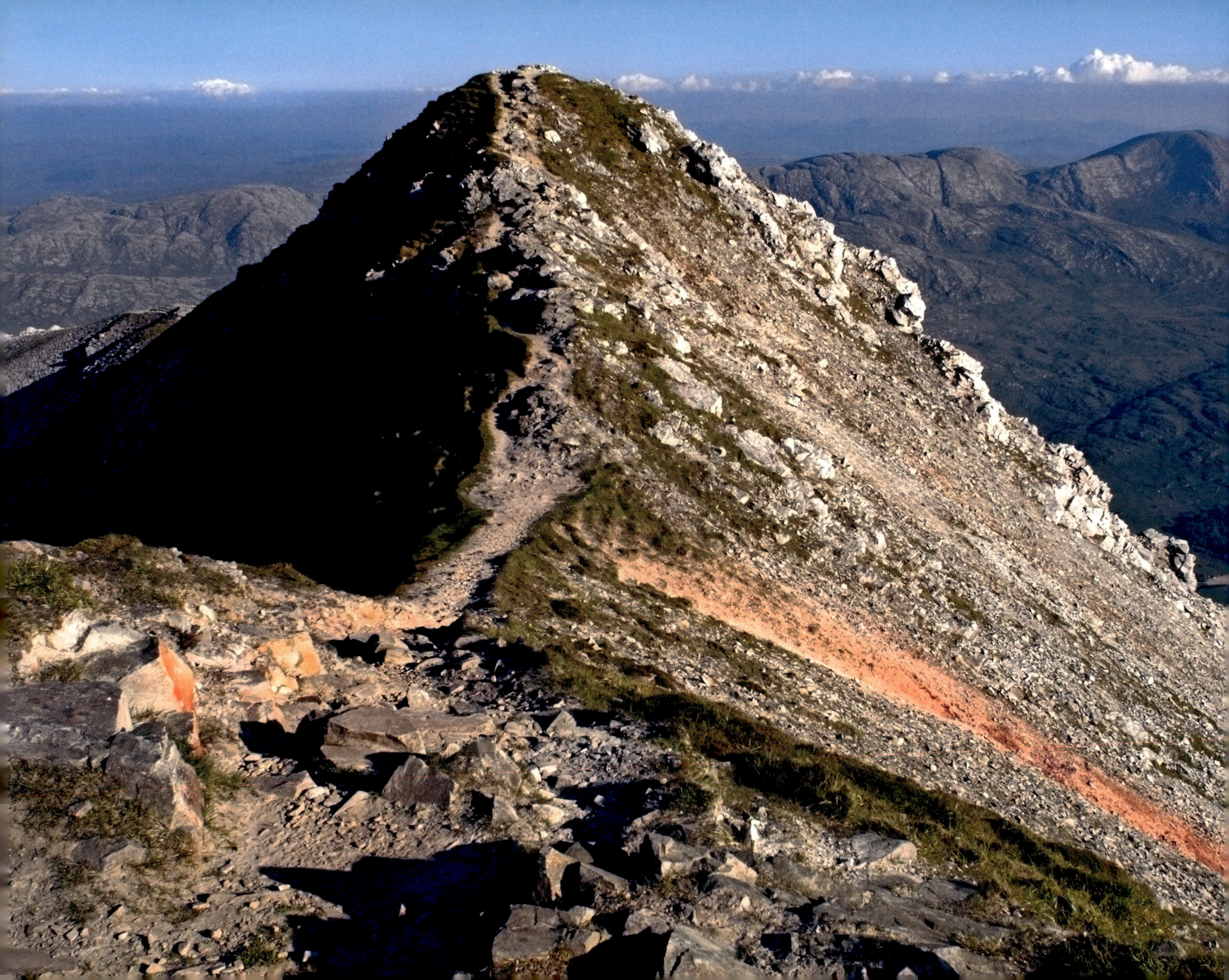

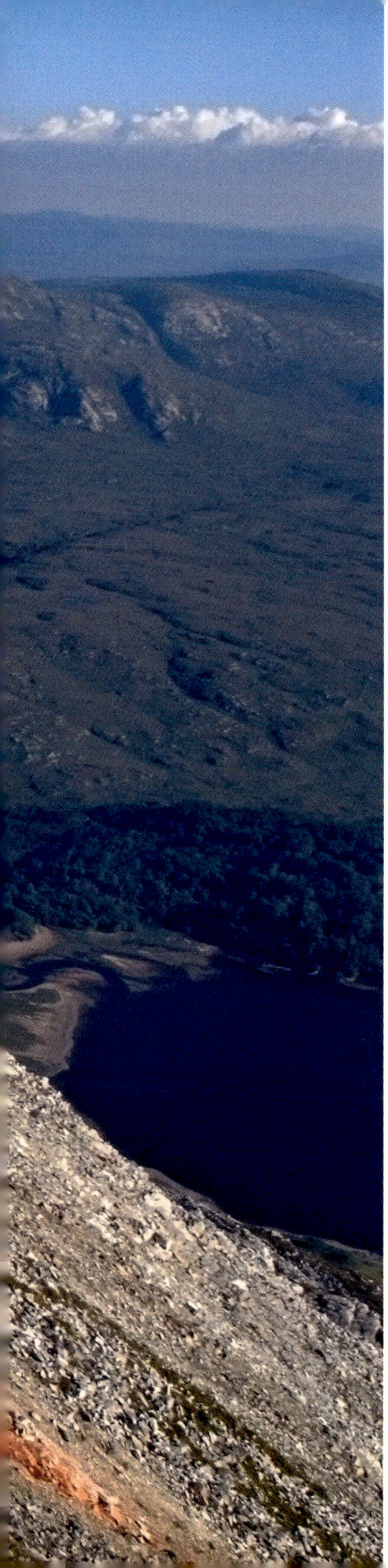

MOUNTAIN AND SEA

OPPOSITE The summit of Errigal in the late evening, Donegal.

BELOW Sea pinks stand against sunlit sea.

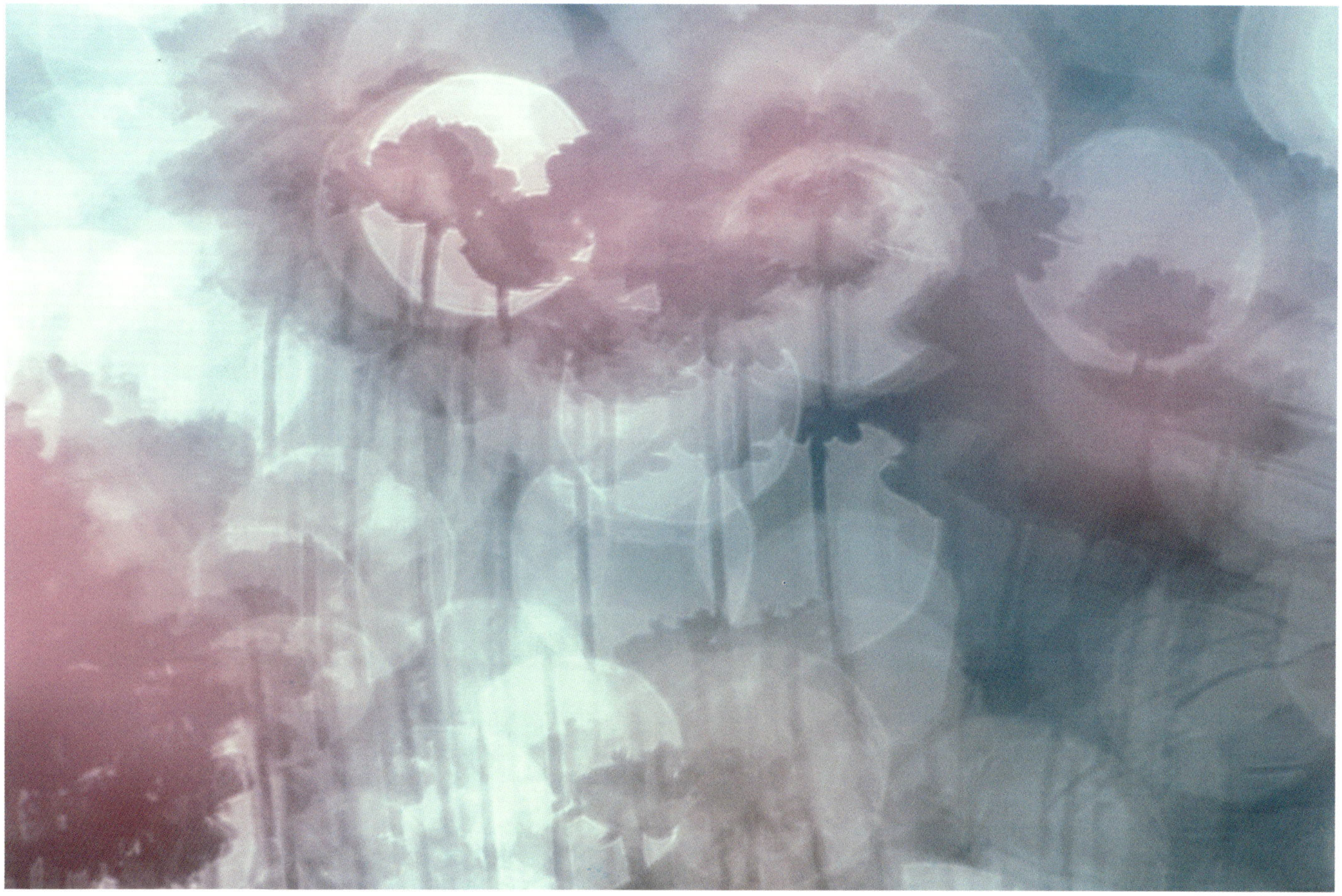

SOUL'S LONGING

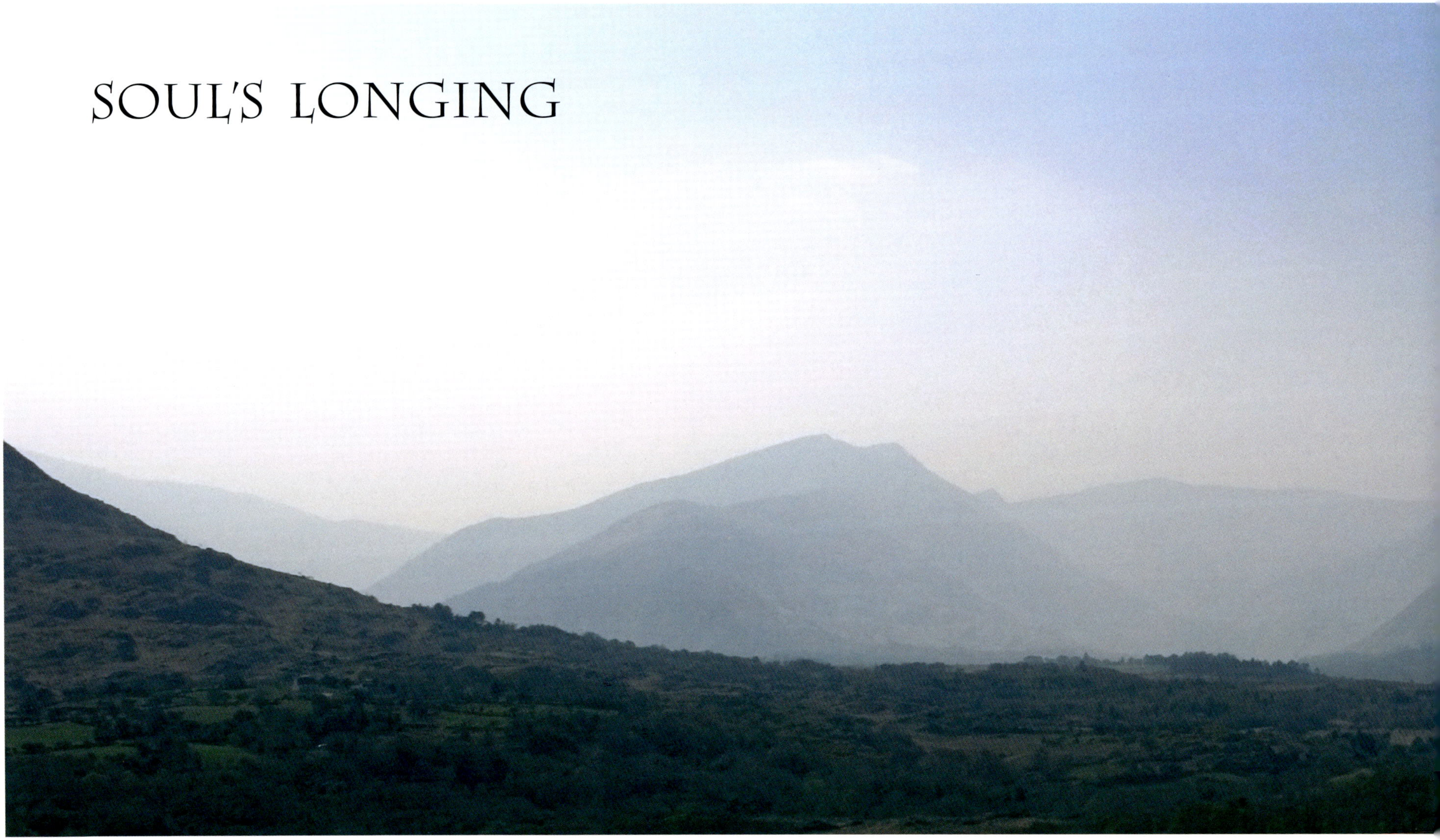

The form of our lives at this time has created a separation between the nature that lies outside ourselves, and the nature within. We have become progressively more distanced from basic realities of our existence: the day, the year, the climate. The expression, 'the environment', surroundings, underlines the truth of this split; we have come to see nature as external to ourselves, as an object of study, rather than as one of feeling. Yet at some level in each of us, there is a longing to be re-united with our own true being, the longing of the soul to be whole. In a simple way, this can be experienced by allowing ourselves to be influenced by the natural; being aligned to natural rhythms brings us back into harmony with our surroundings, and with ourselves. A respect for the ebb and flow of the day, in rising at dawn and sleeping at dark, calms and rests us; and so with the seasons, being willing to be more still in winter, more active in summer will allow our bodies the space for re-integration.

The Caha Mountains from Laragh, Beara Peninsula. *See page 160 for captions to pages 138–159, A MOUNTAIN DAY.*

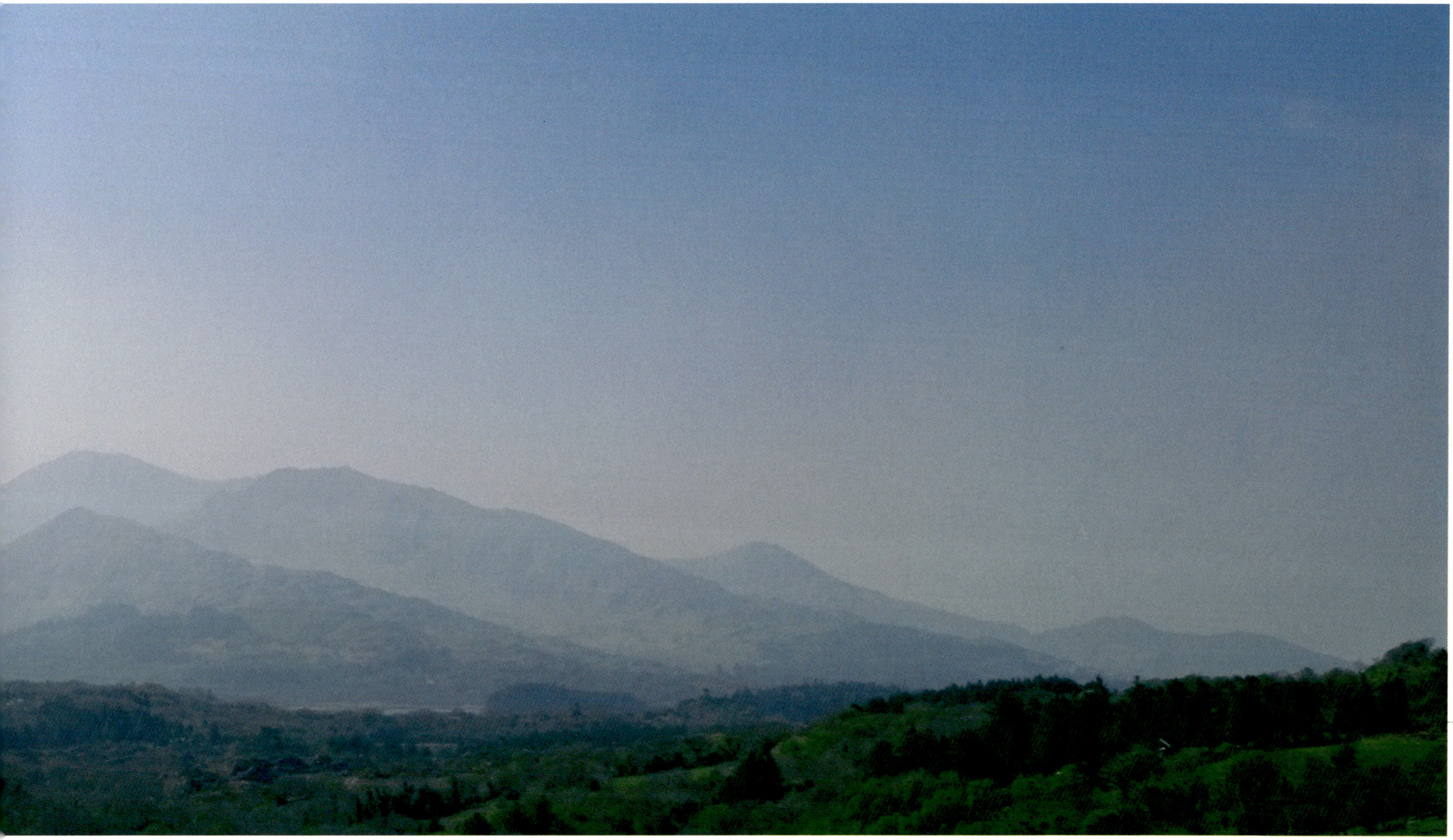

We may allow ourselves to be more exposed to the elements, to be out in rain and snow, or in the sun and wind, to experience the reality of physical life on this planet. The body begins to glow with satisfaction from having the senses fully engaged, from having the blood flowing faster, from cleansing the lungs. We grow in health when we start to reconnect with our primitive nature, which is a fundamental and basic part of our self; we fall ill when we fail to honour it. In addition to, and beyond this, we have the capacity for creative and aesthetic connection with our surroundings. Bathing our senses in beauty, whether the simple juxtaposition of physical forms to please the eye, or being drawn into metaphysical appreciation of deep truths about life, brings us into the realms of the magical, of experience which is beyond the reach of science; of knowing through feeling, of being truly aligned to ourselves. When we bring together these two aspects of our self, we can experience the possibility of being fully alive.

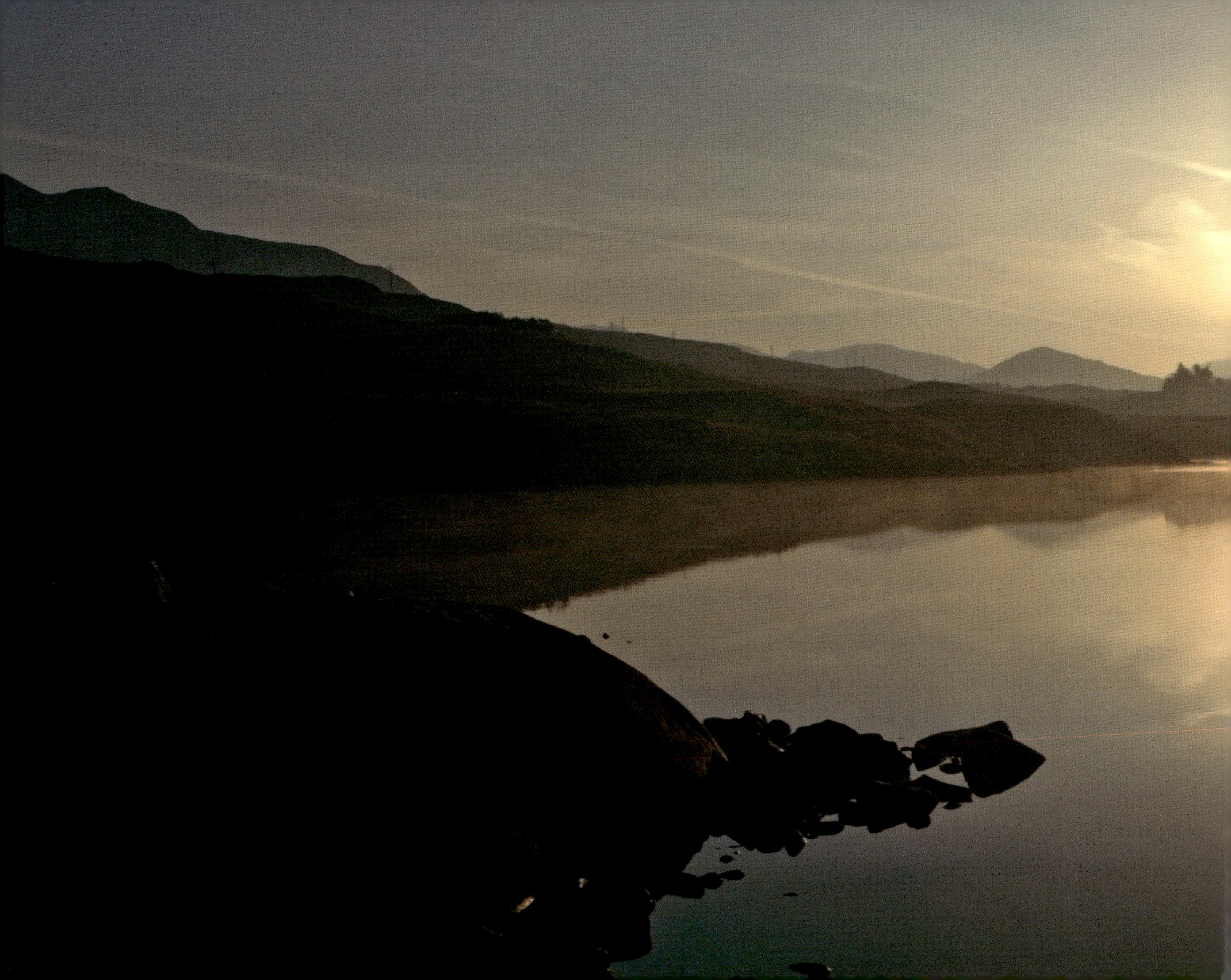

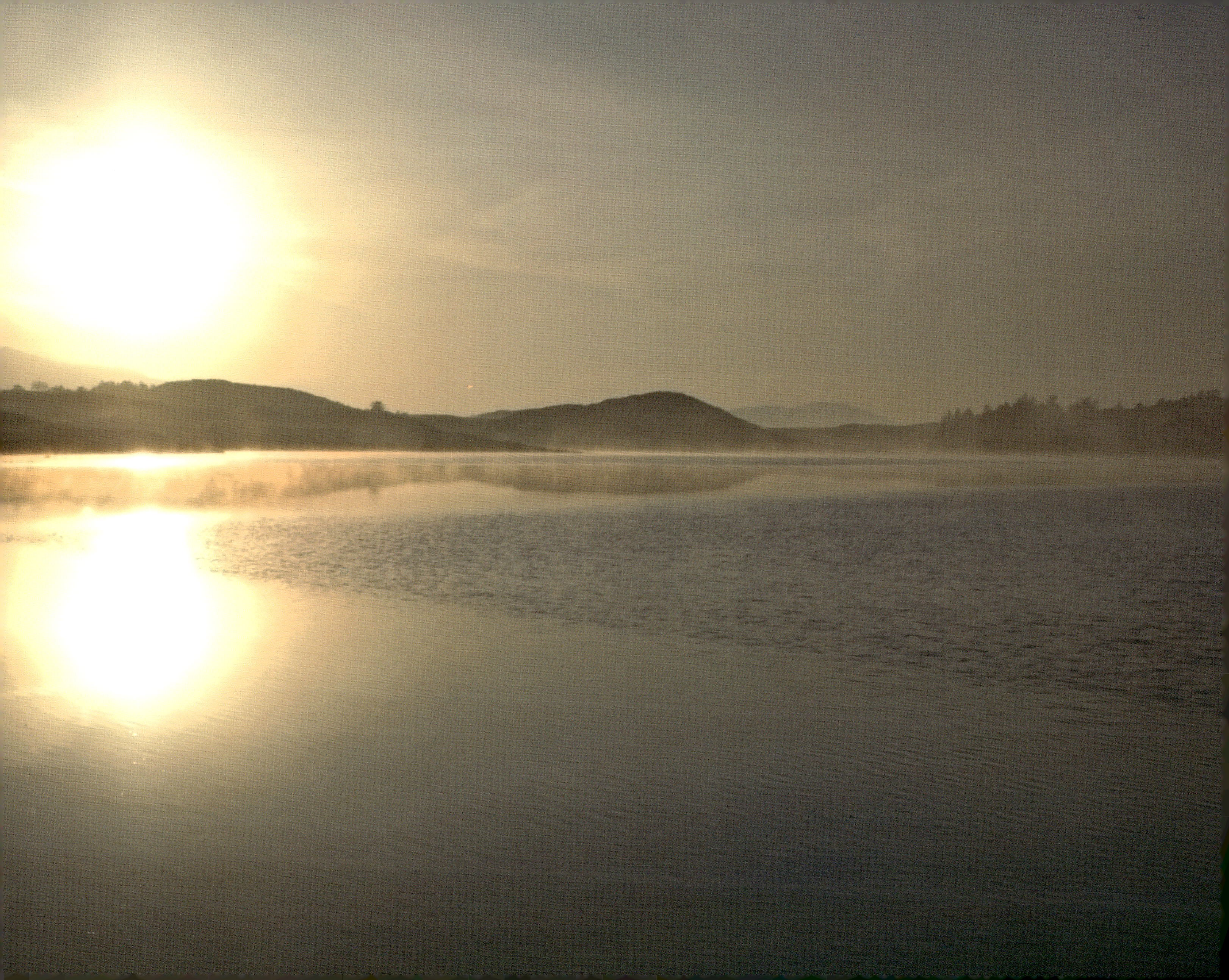

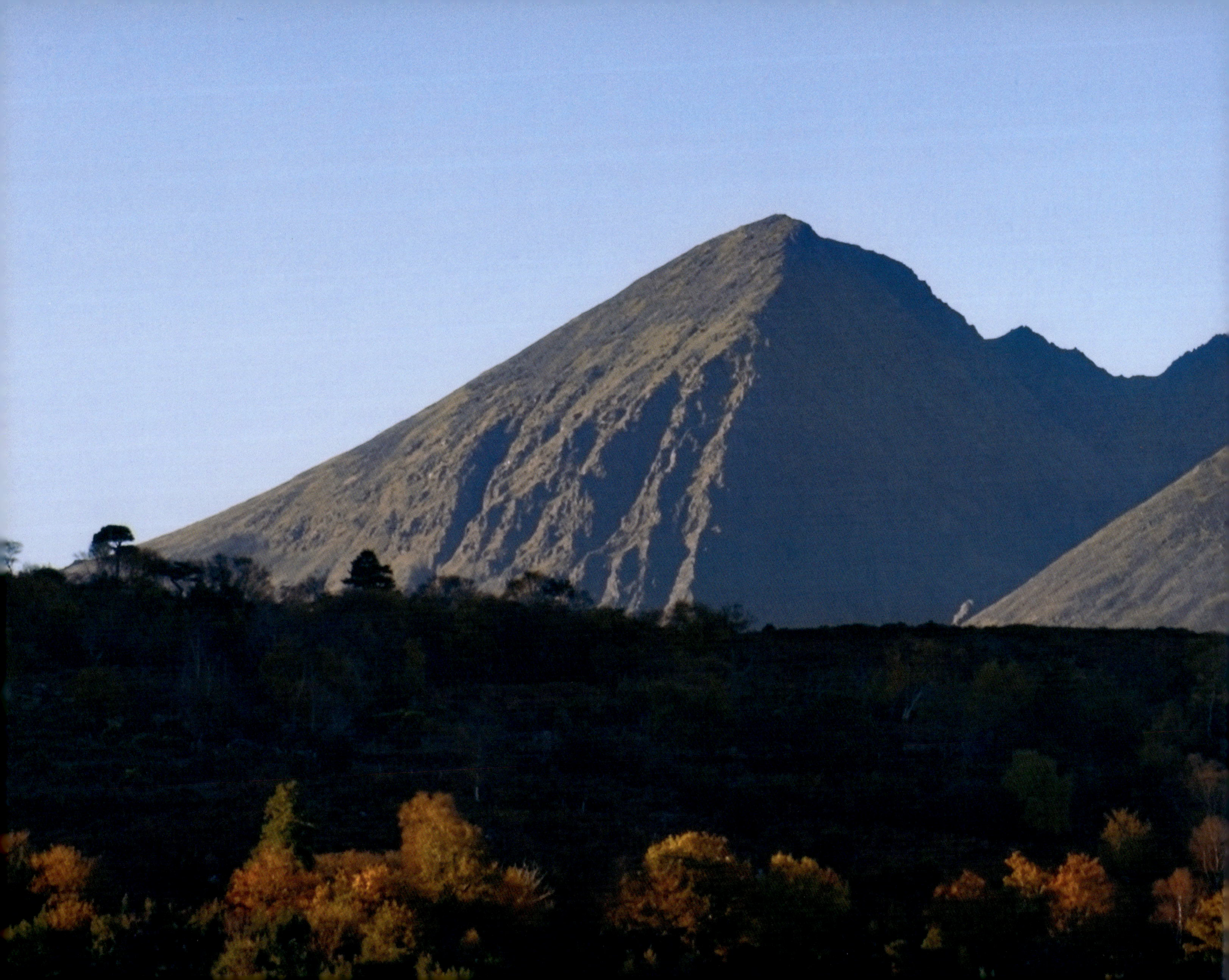

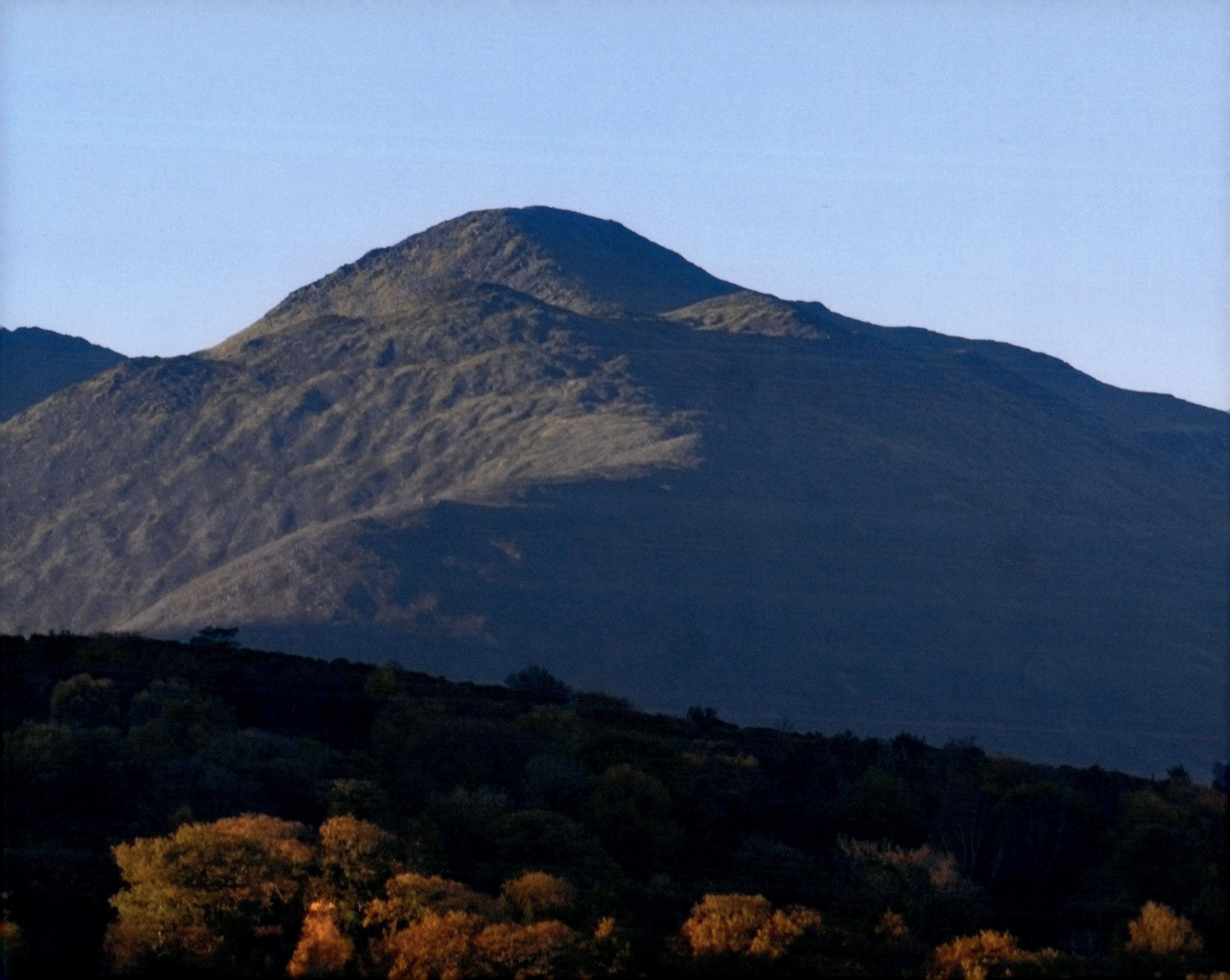

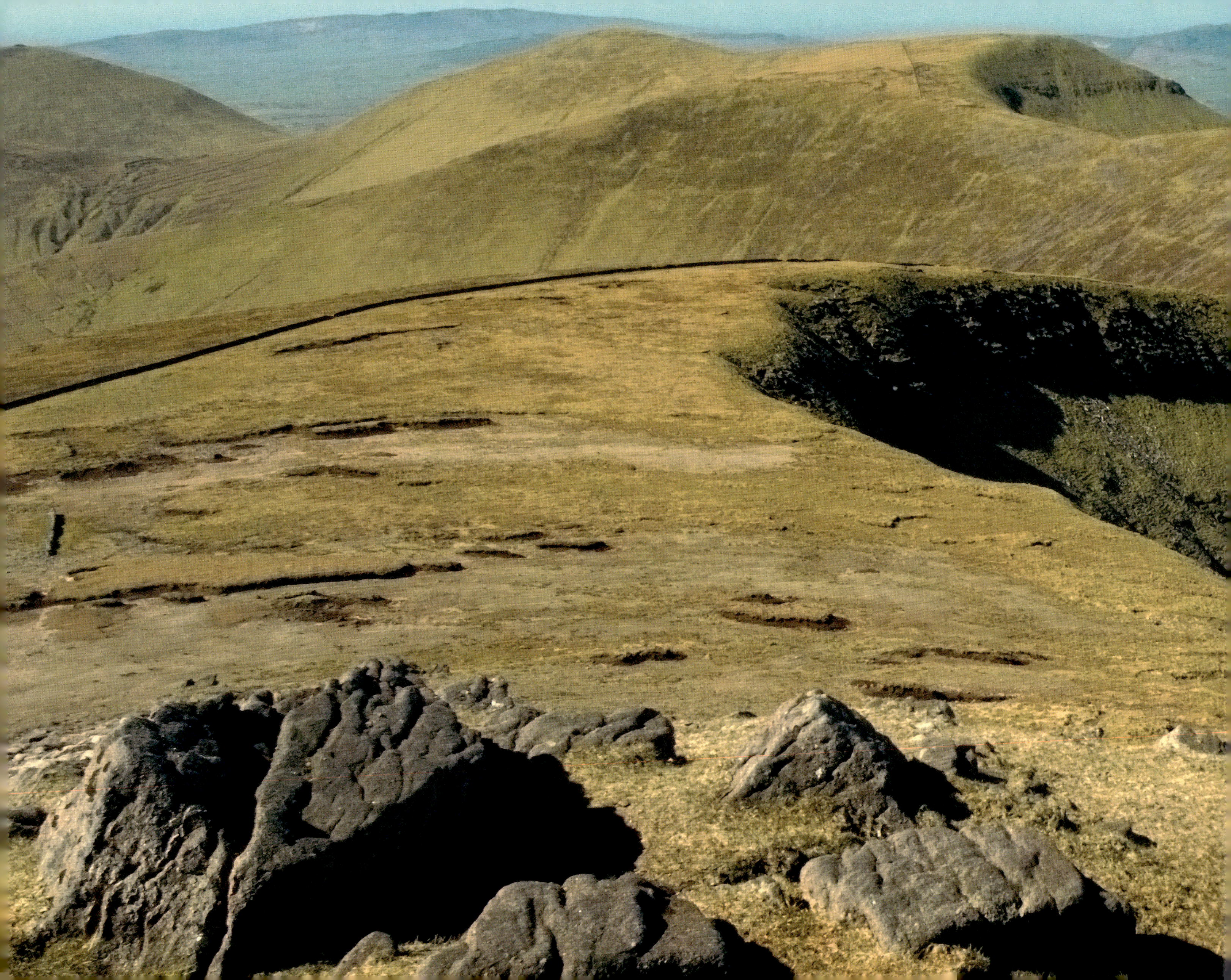

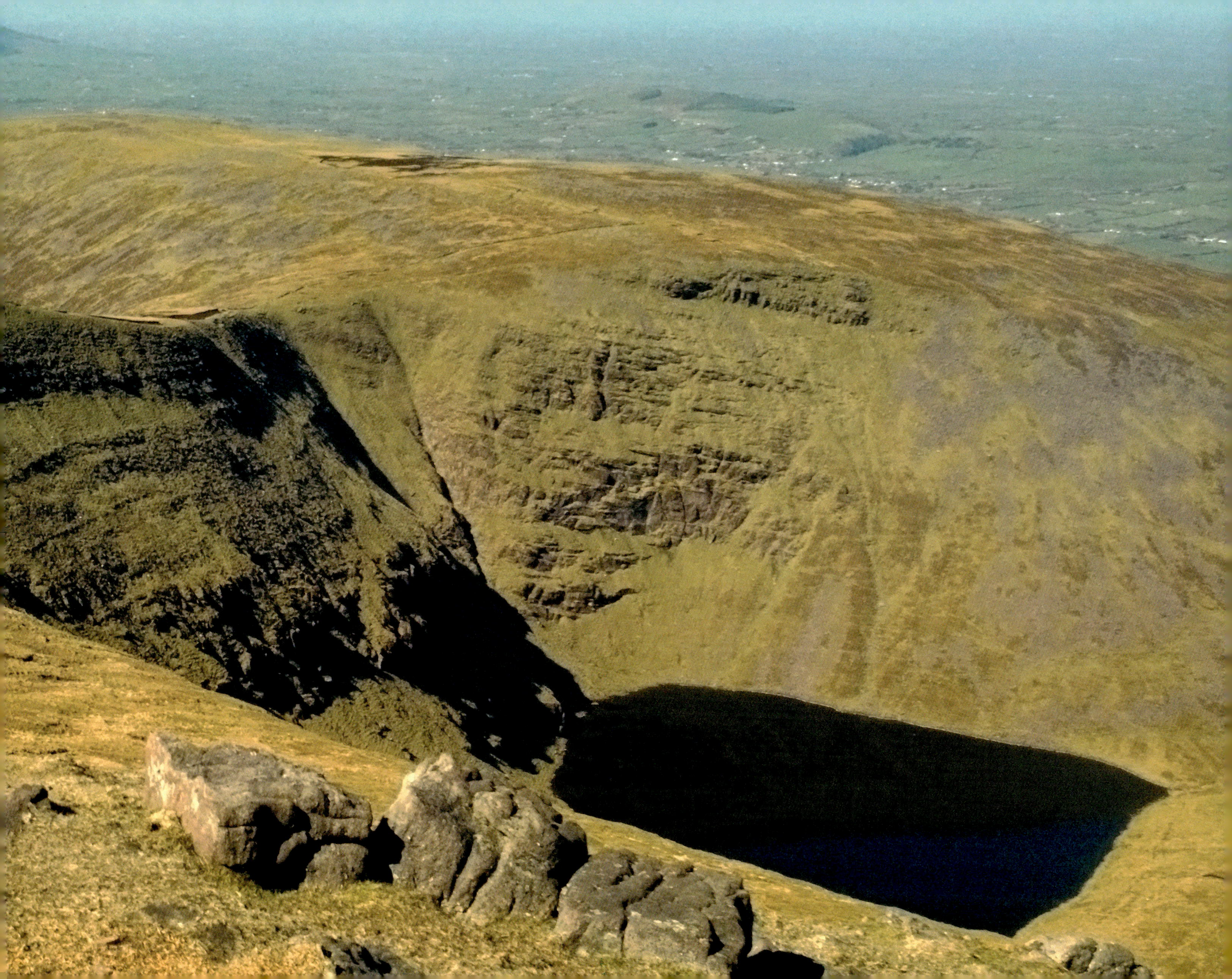

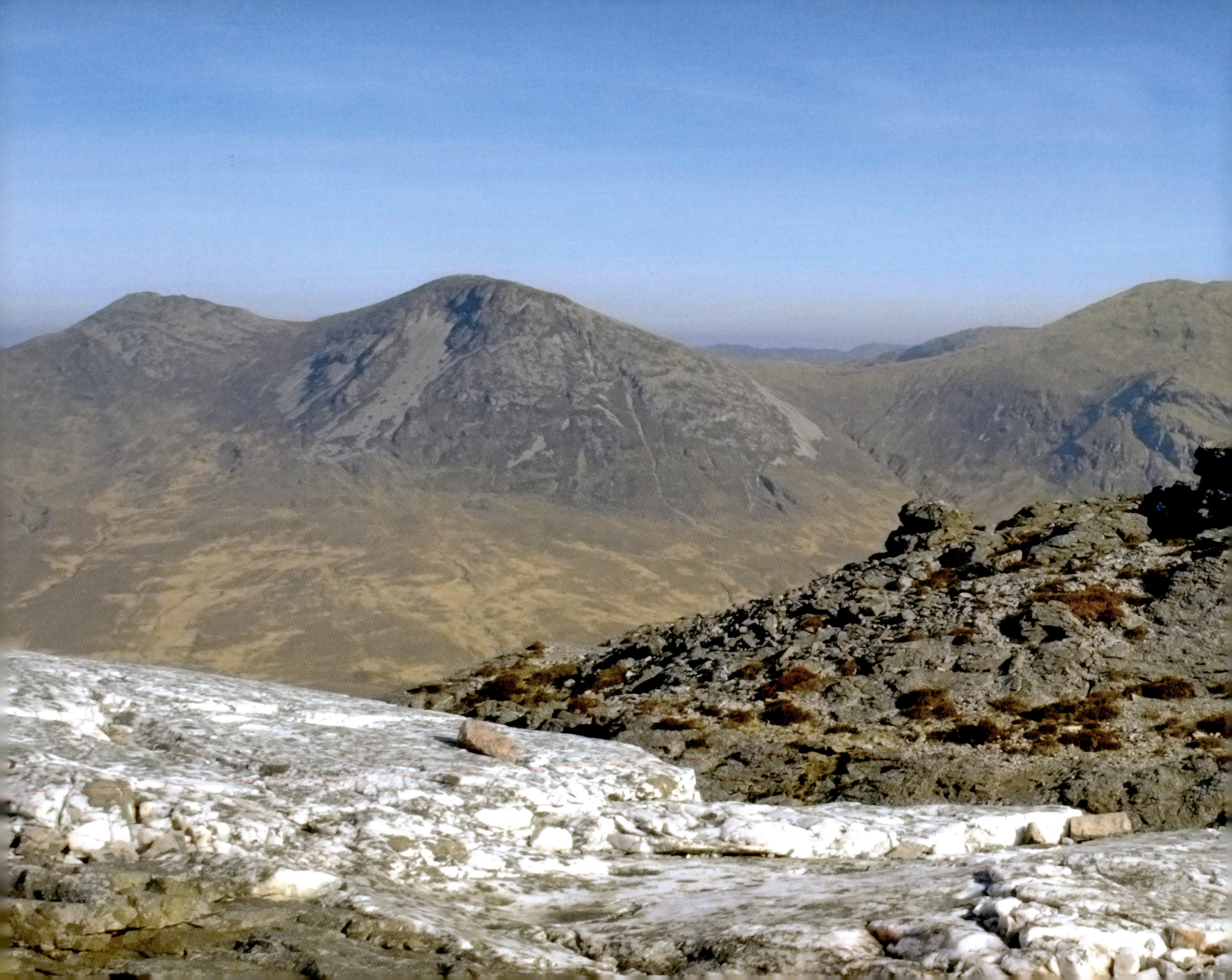

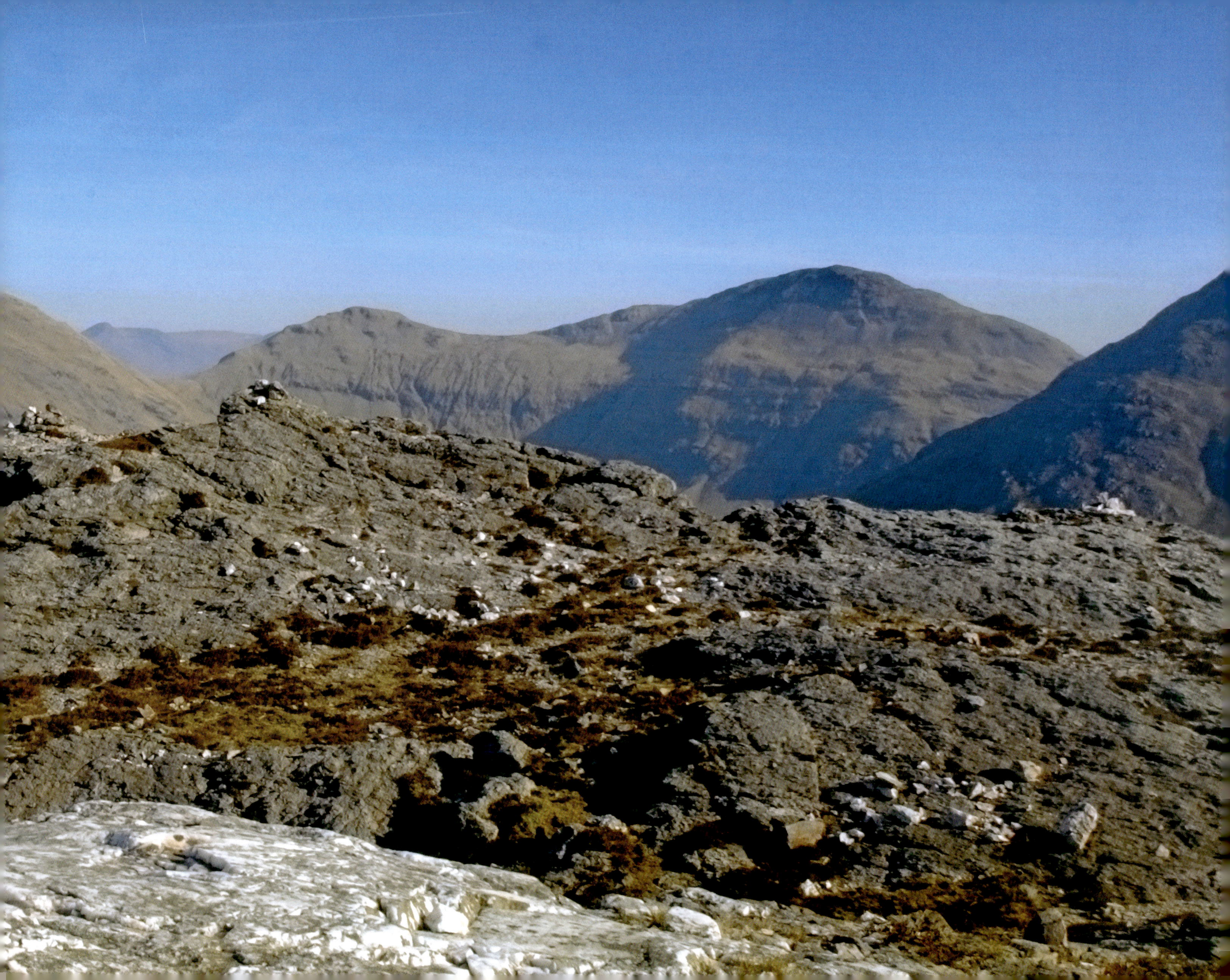

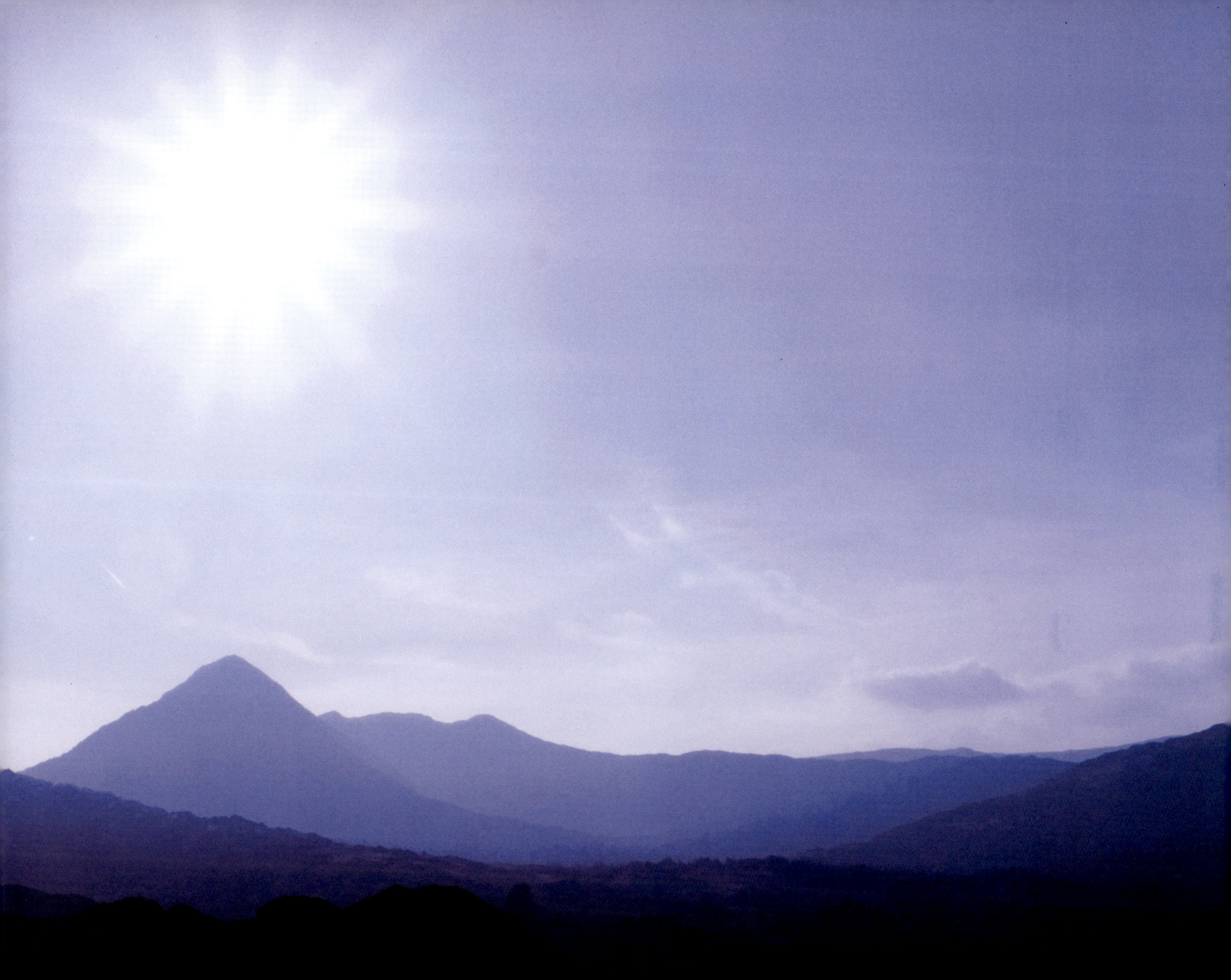

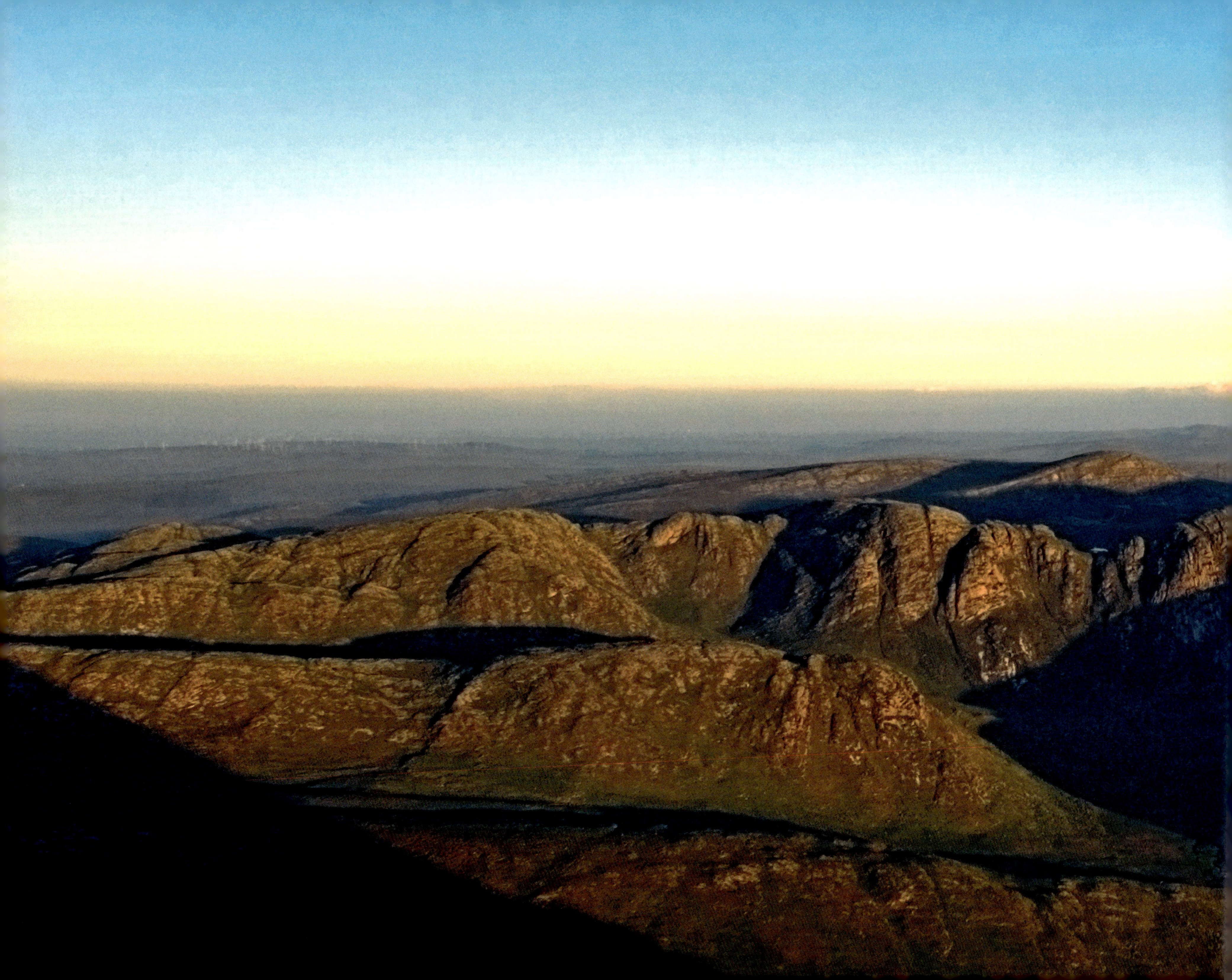

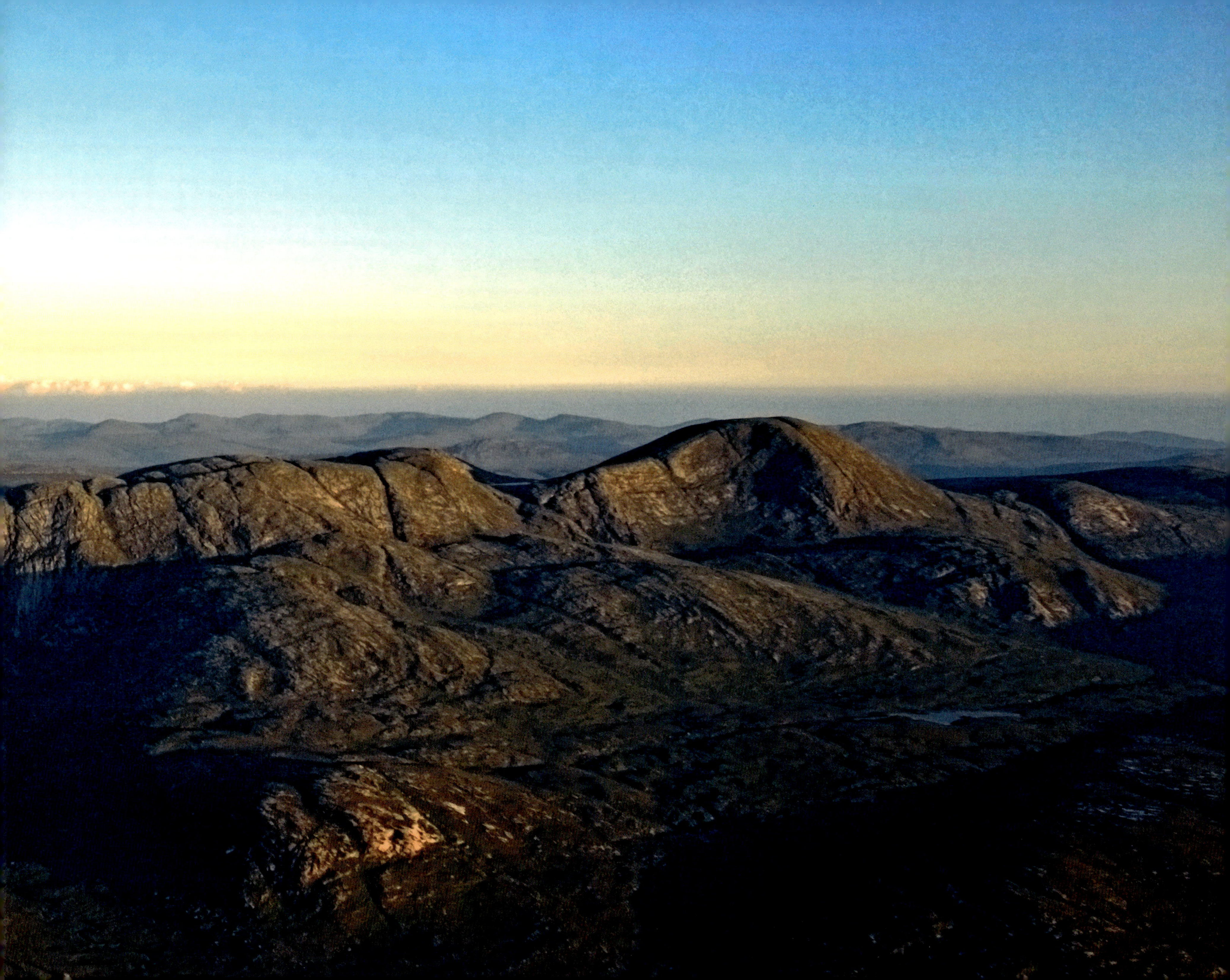

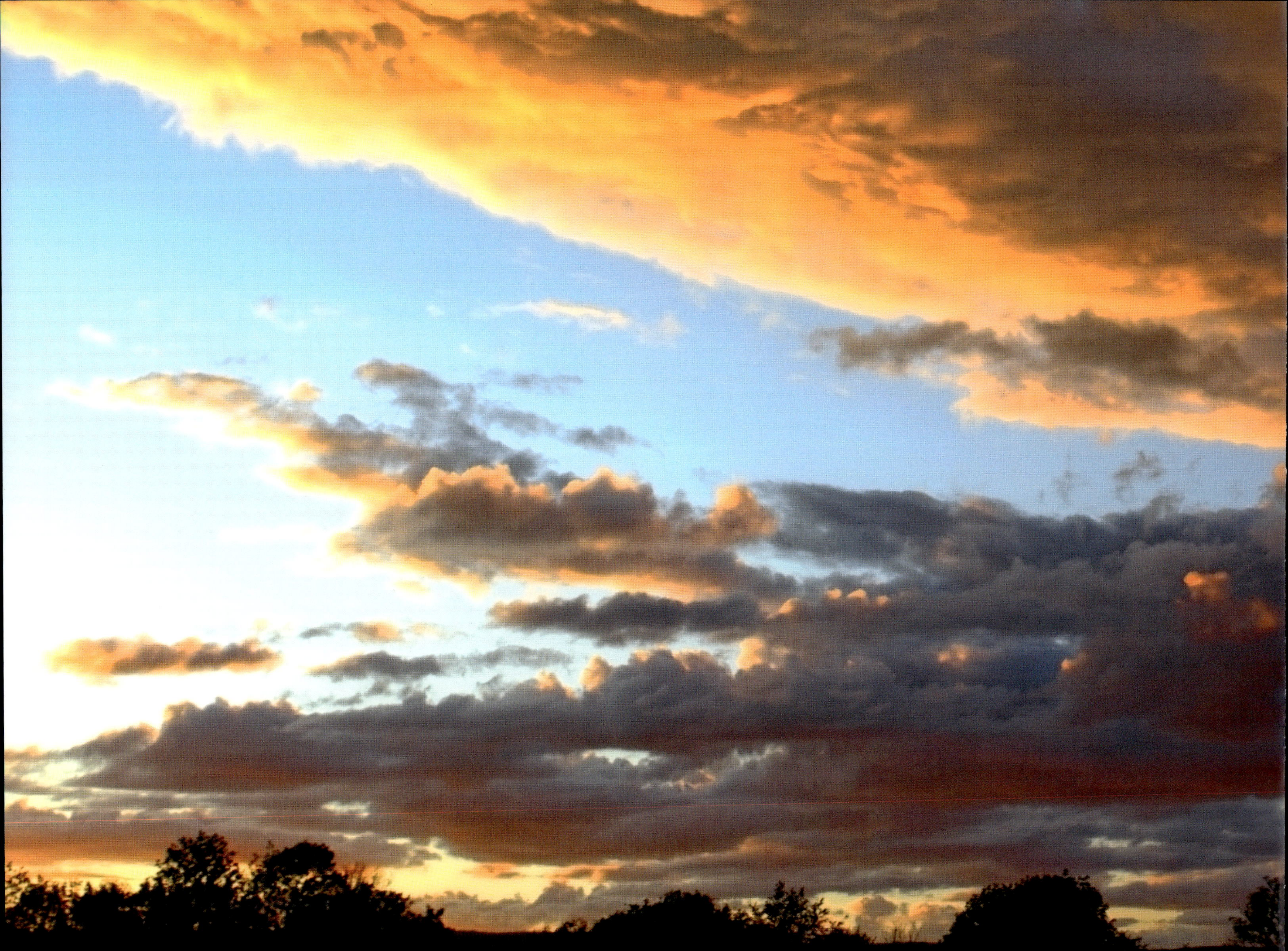

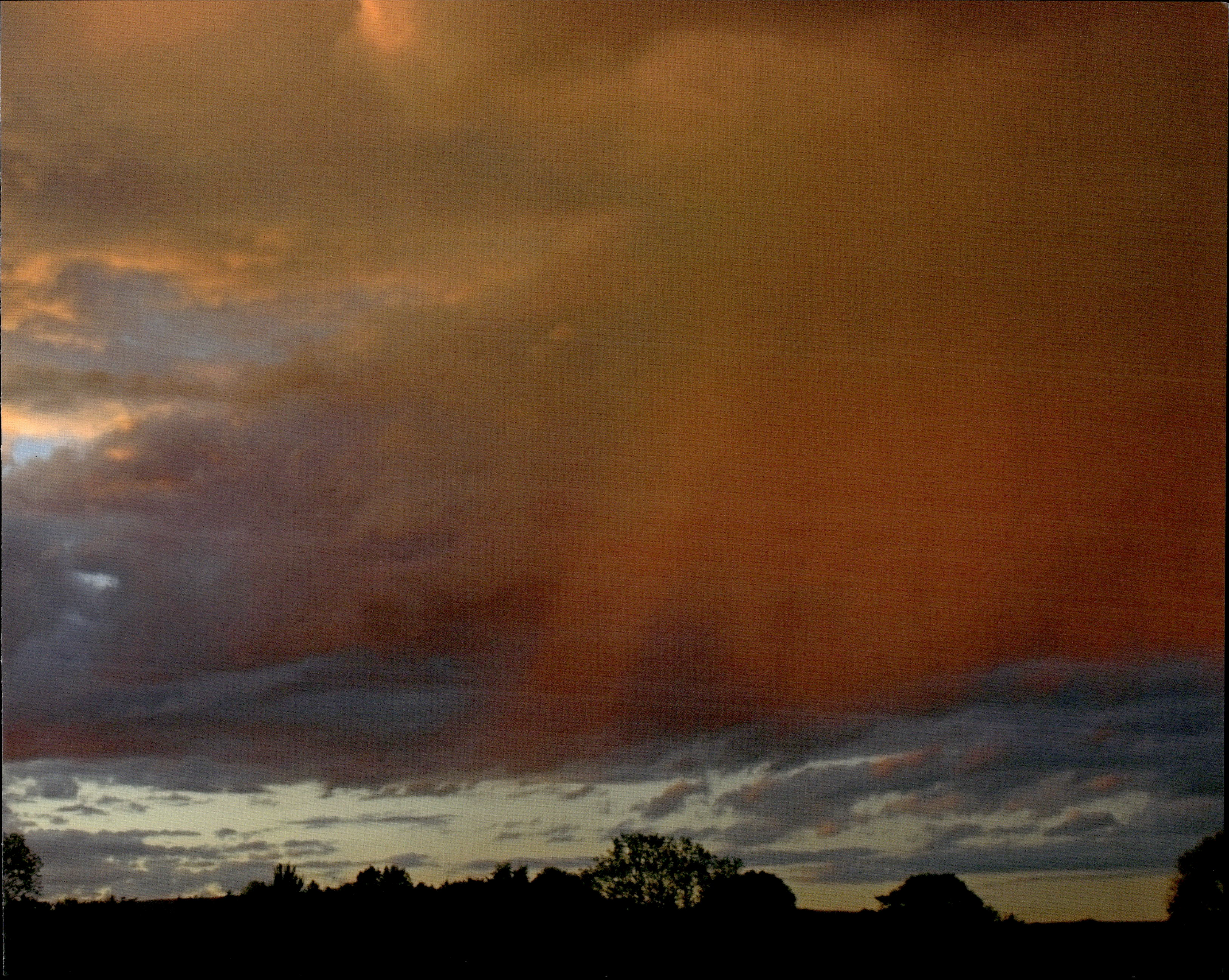

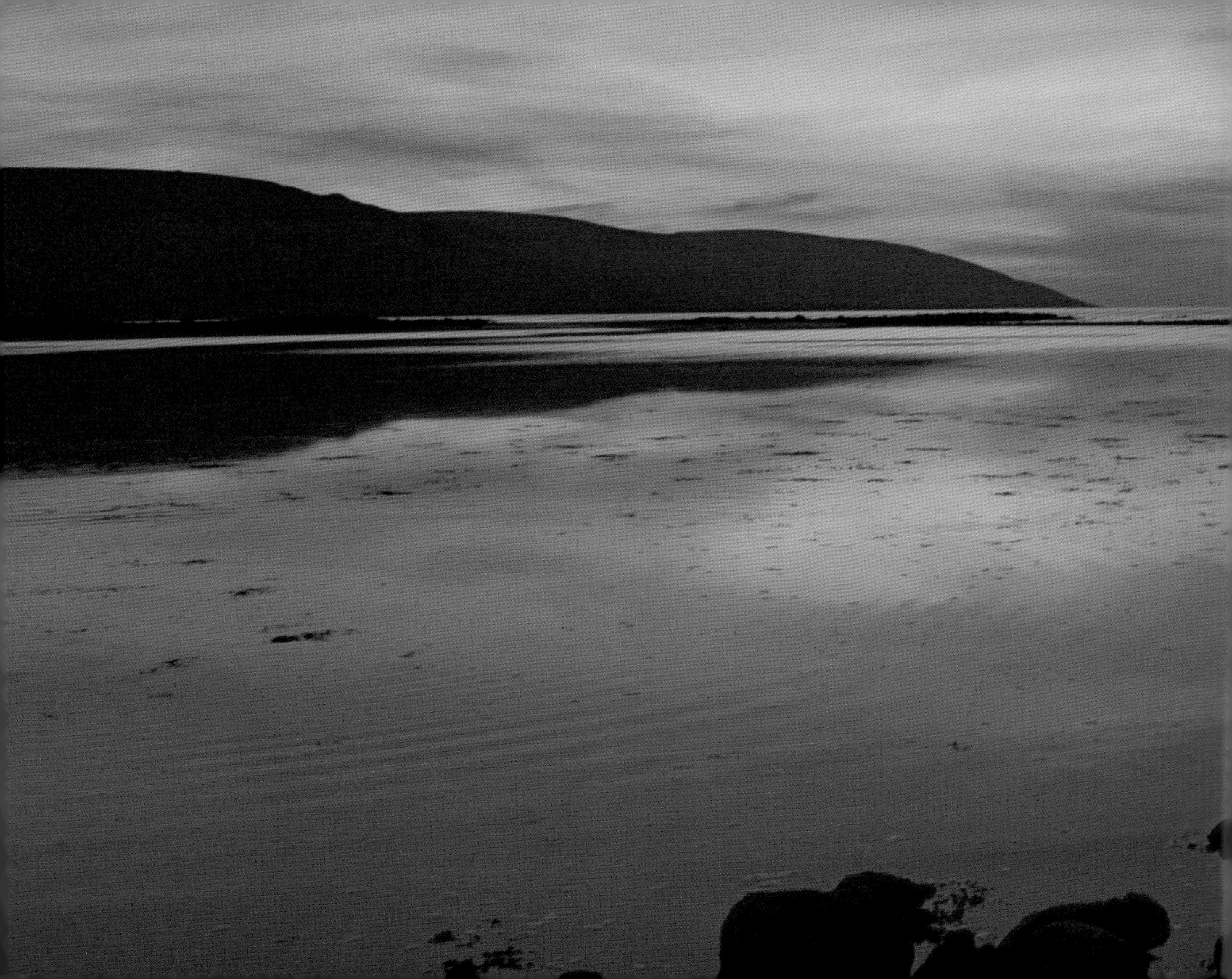

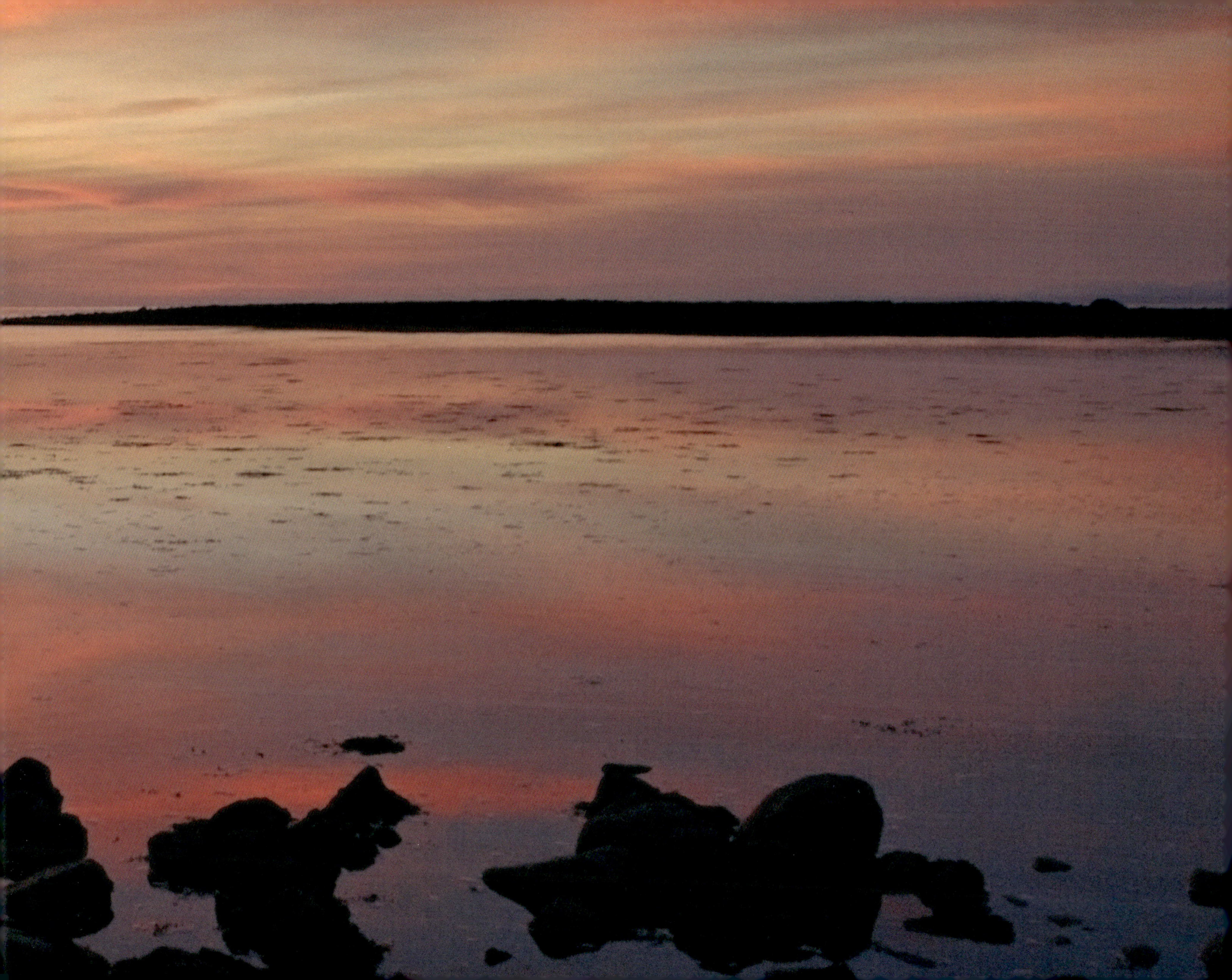

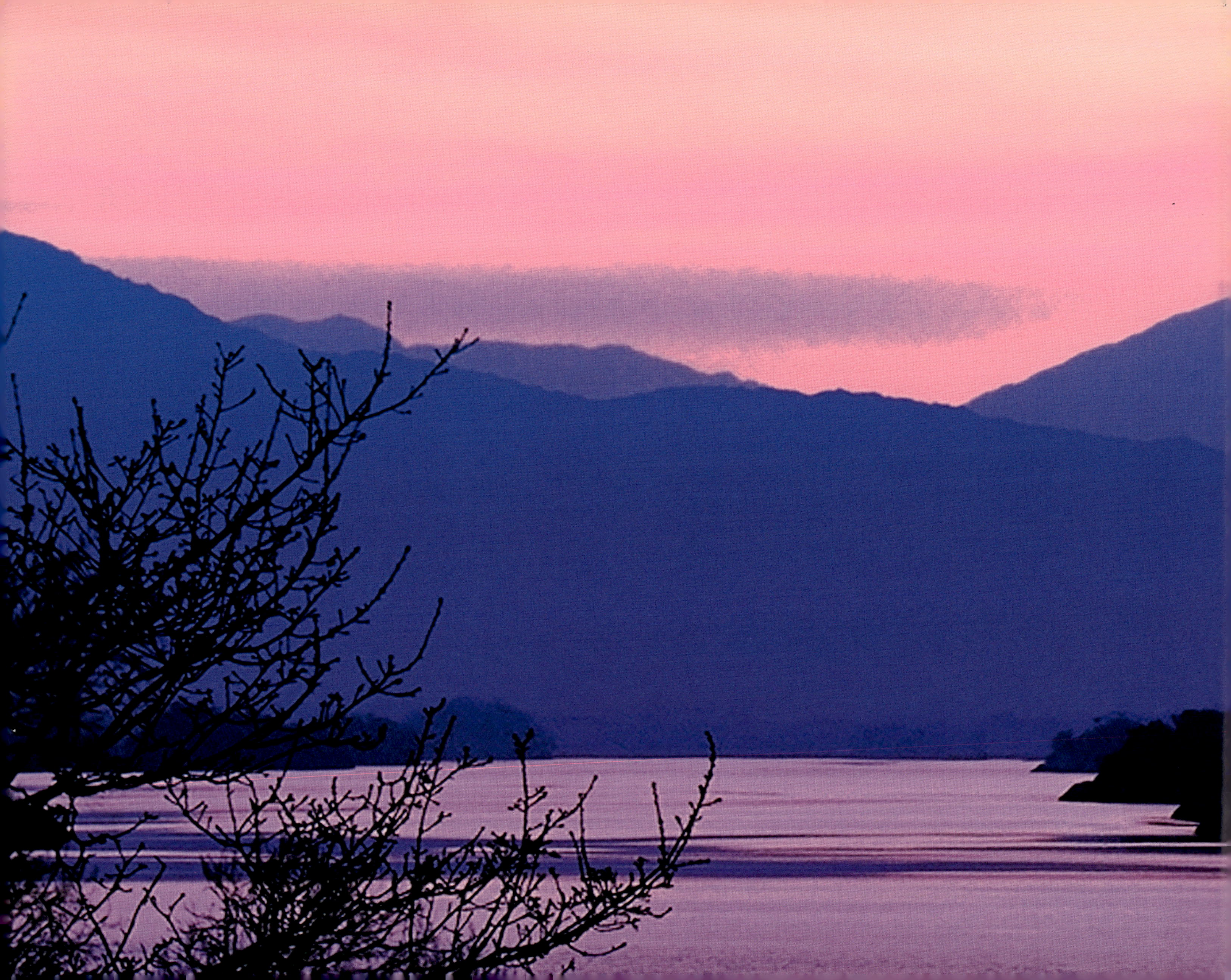

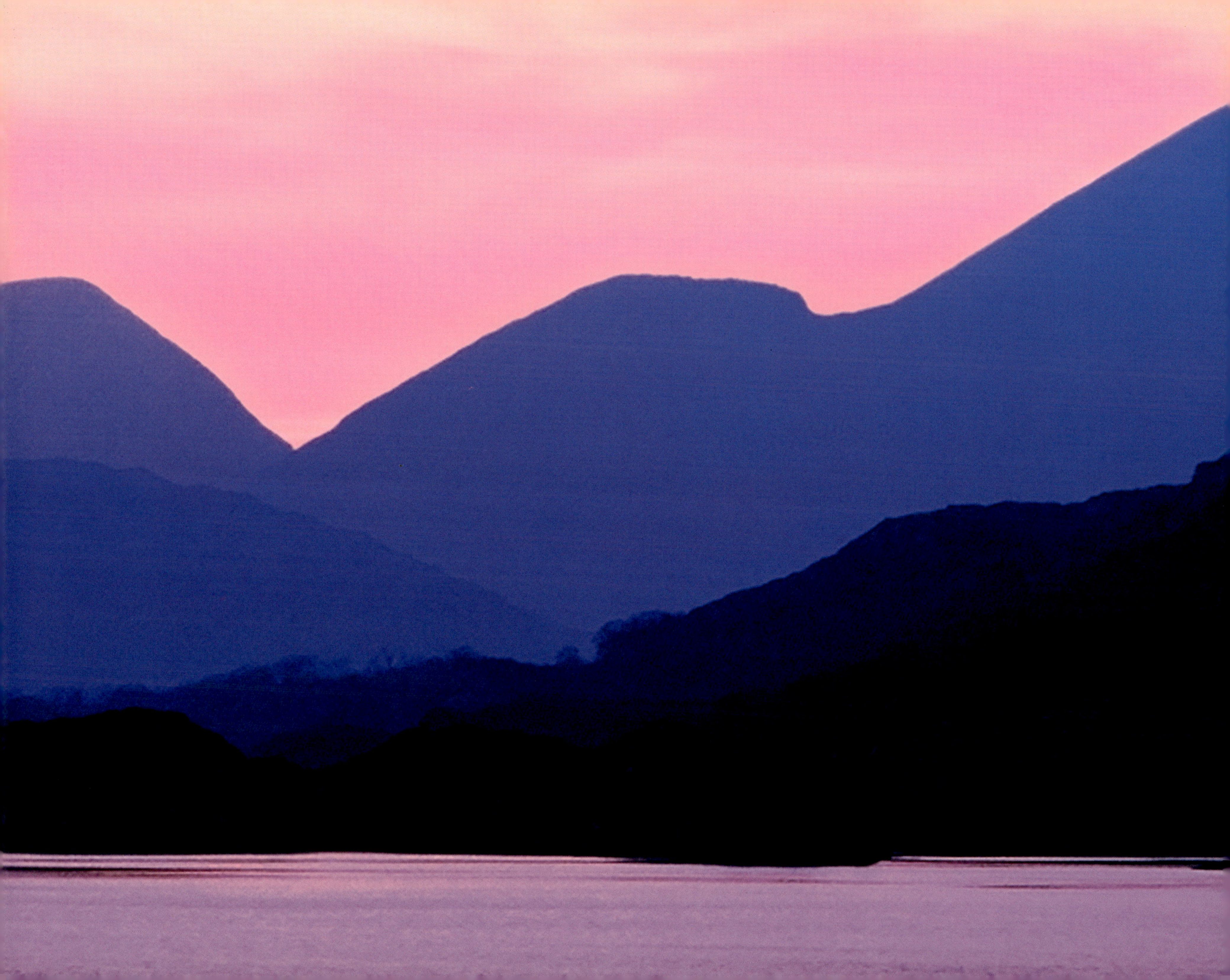

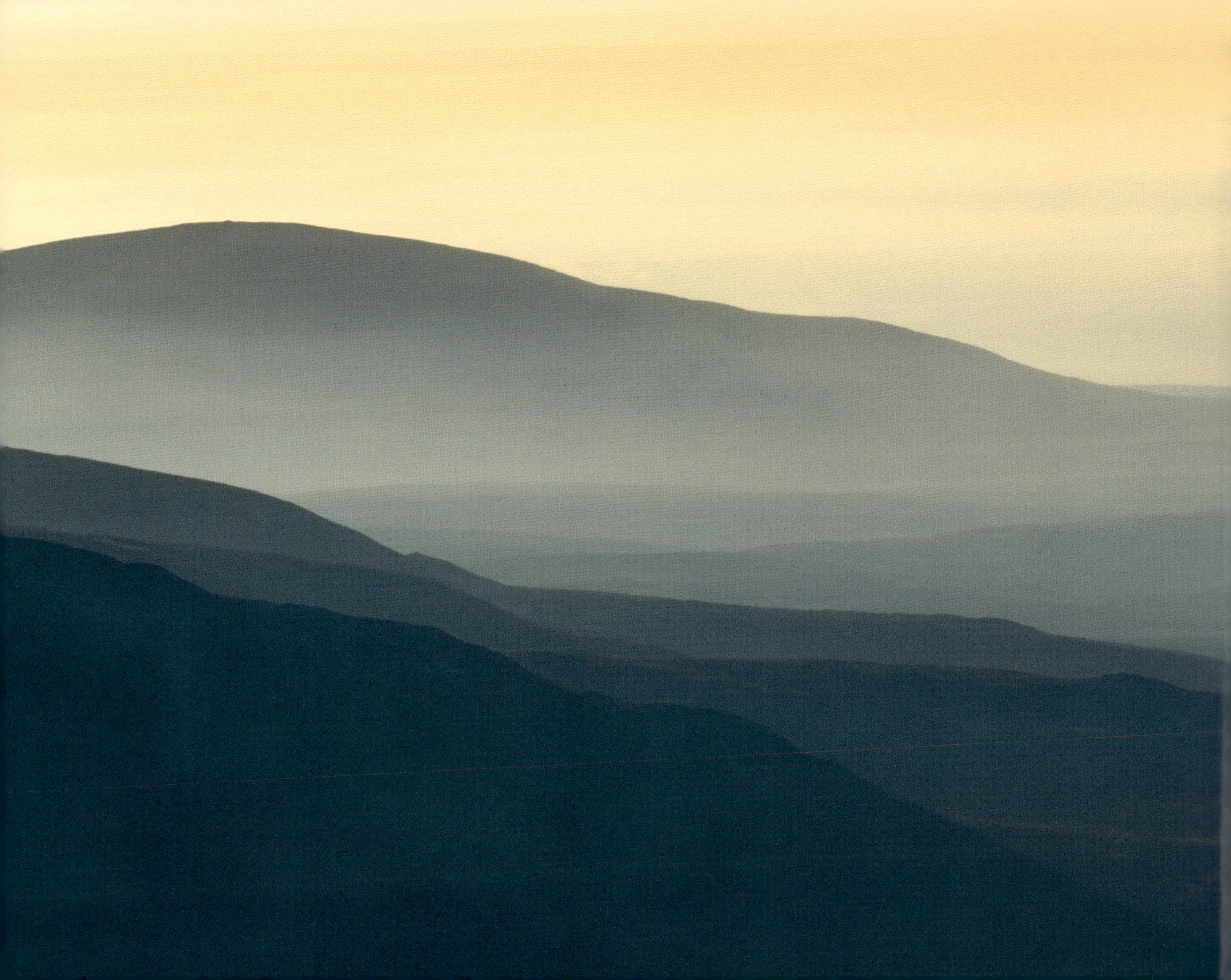

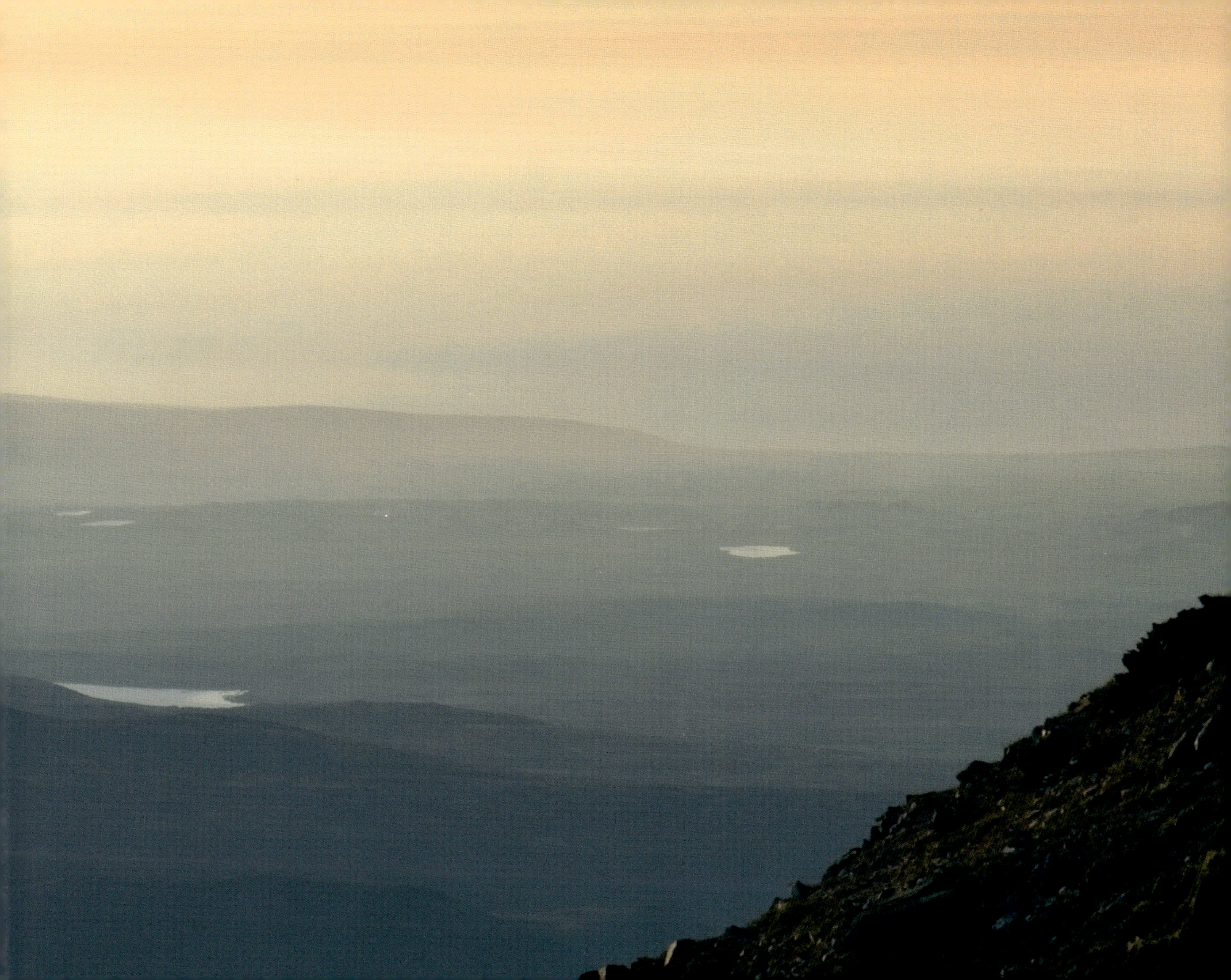

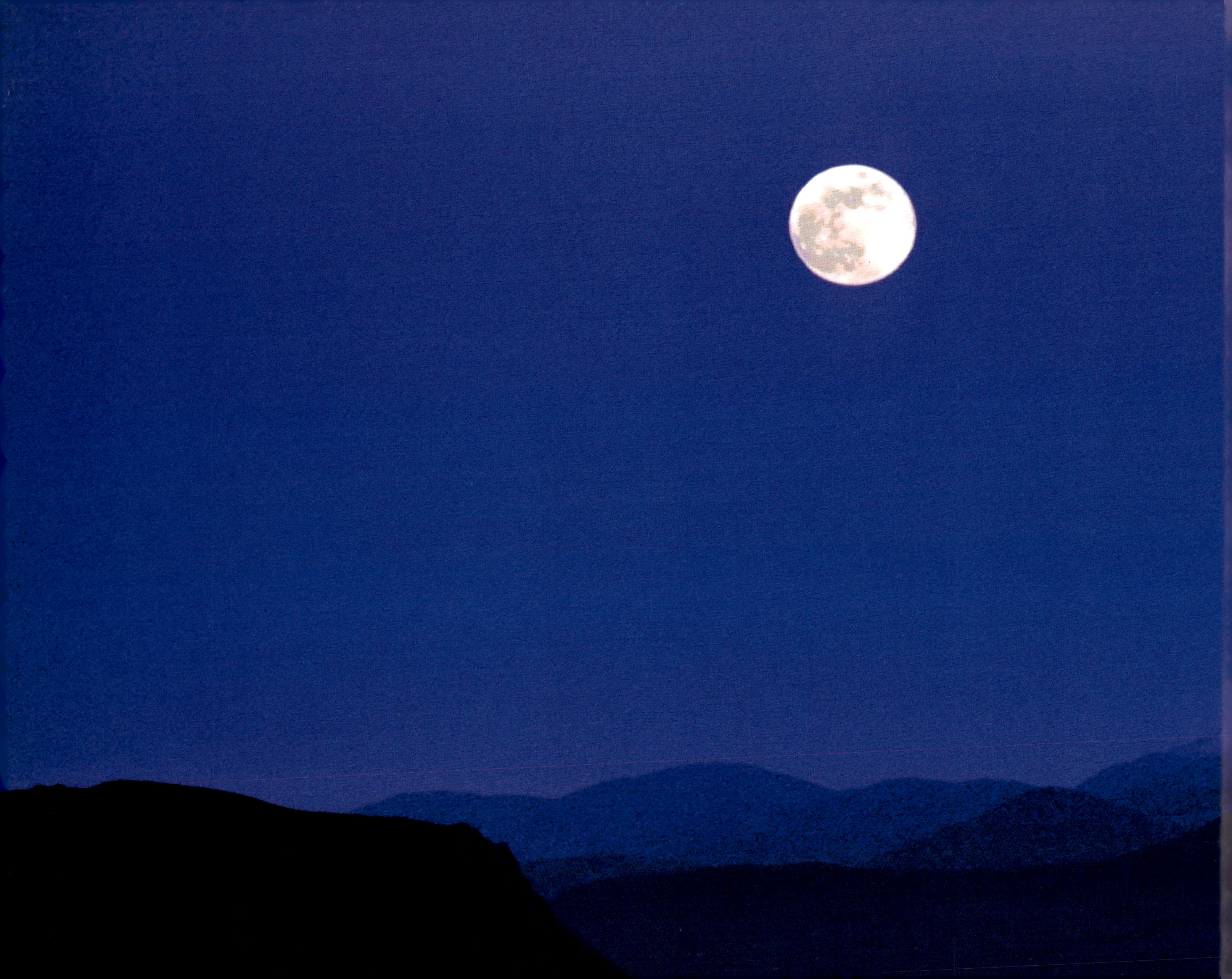

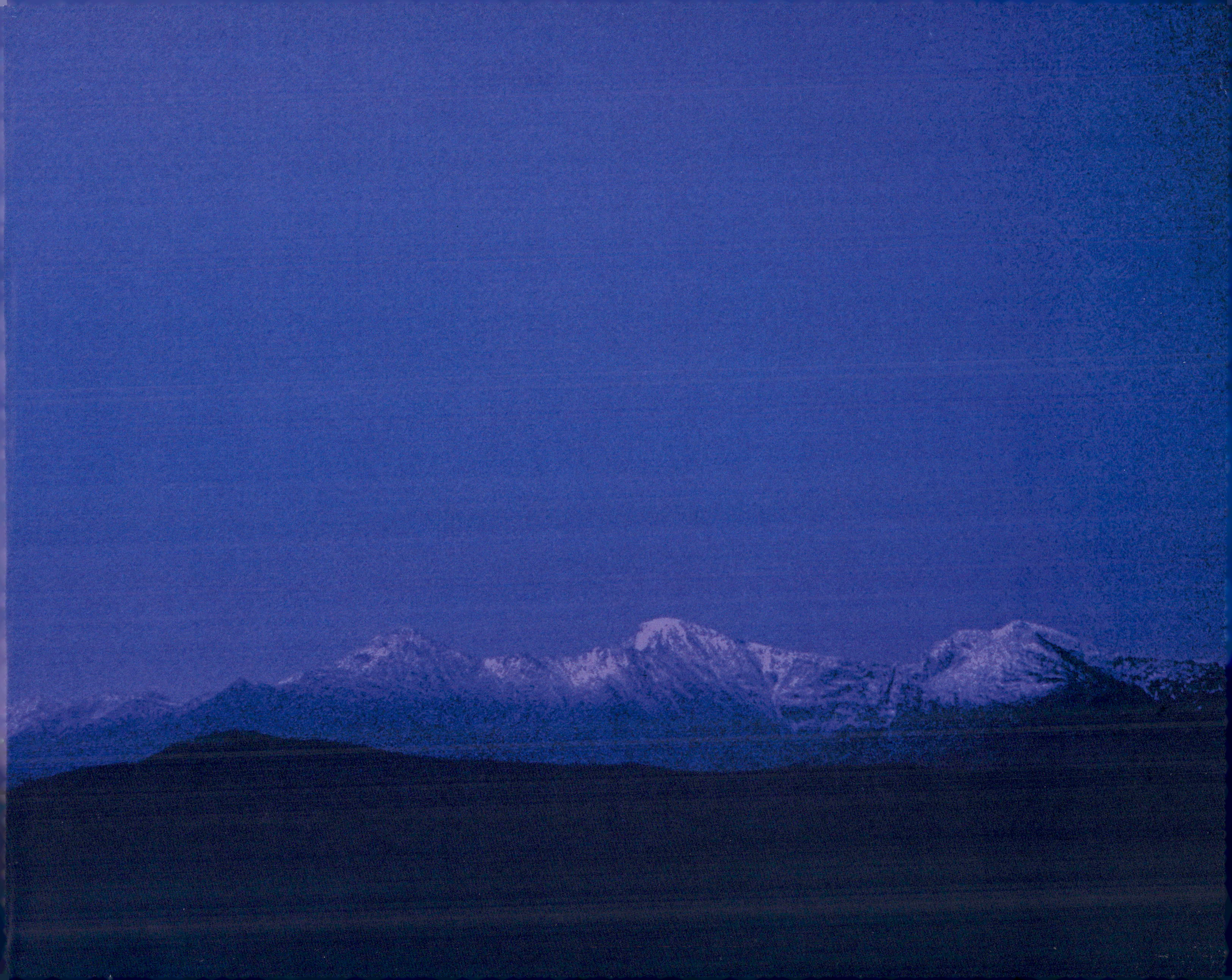

A MOUNTAIN DAY — KEY TO SOUL'S LONGING

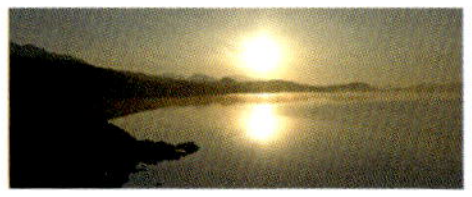	*Pages 138/139*	SUNRISE	*In the Twelve Bens, Connemara, County Galway.*
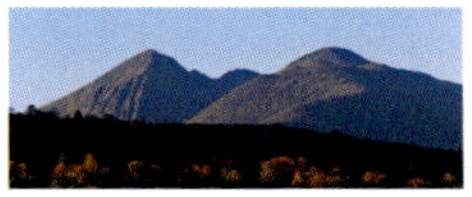	*Pages 140/141*	EARLY MORNING	*The eastern end of the Macgillycuddy's Reeks, the Gap of Dunloe, County Kerry.*
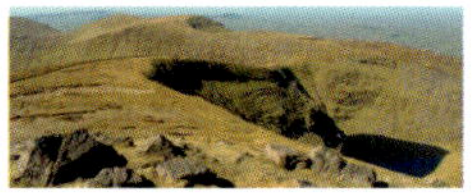	*Pages 142/143*	LATE MORNING	*The summit of Galtymore, looking to the west, County Tipperary.*
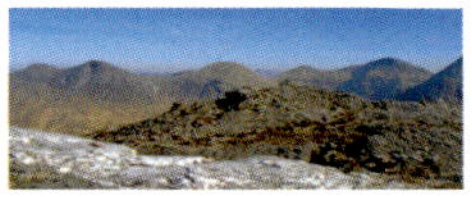	*Pages 144/145*	AFTERNOON	*In the Twelve Bens, looking north, Connemara, County Galway.*
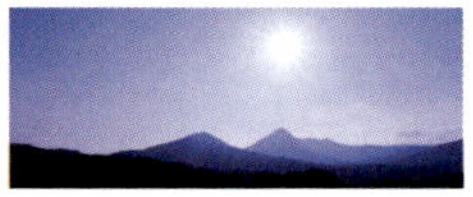	*Pages 146/147*	EARLY EVENING	*The Sugarloaf, Beara Peninsula, County Cork.*
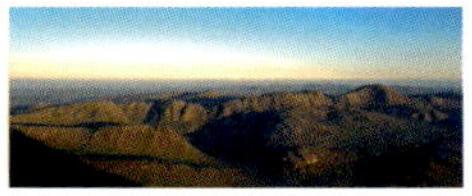	*Pages 148/149*	LATE EVENING	*Looking south to Derryveagh, Donegal.*
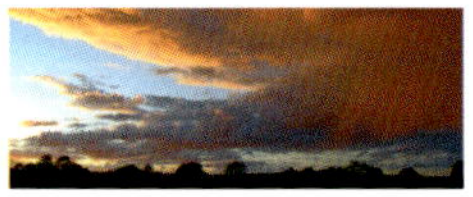	*Pages 150/151*	EARLY SUNSET	*To the west of the Wicklow Mountains, near Kildare.*
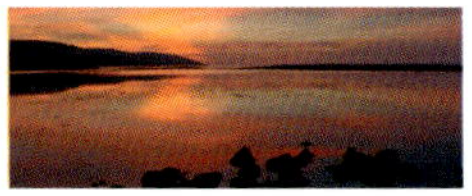	*Pages 152/153*	LATE SUNSET	*Across Galway Bay to Black Head, the Burren, County Clare.*
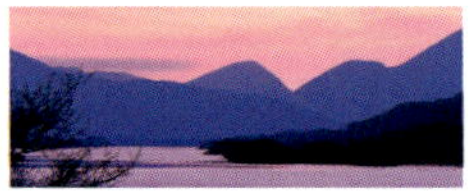	*Pages 154/155*	EARLY DUSK	*Upper Lough Leane, Broaghnabinnia, and the Macgillycuddy's Reeks, County Kerry.*
	*Pages 156/157*	LATE DUSK	*Looking west from Errigal, Donegal.*
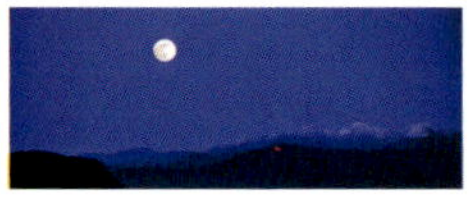	*Pages 158/159*	AFTER DARK	*Looking towards the Macgillycuddy's Reeks from the Dingle Peninsula, County Kerry.*